# Offenders, Deviants or Patients?

Aimed specifically at understanding the social context of the serious criminal offender who is deemed to be mentally abnormal, the third edition of *Offenders, Deviants or Patients?* takes into account major changes in the law, attitudes towards responsibility and liability for crime, the updating of research findings concerning mental disorders and criminality and our procedures for managing offender–patients through the criminal justice and mental healthcare systems.

Using up-to-date case examples, Herschel Prins examines the relationship between abnormality and criminal behaviour, the extent to which this relationship is used or misused in the criminal courts, and the various facilities that are currently available for the management/incarceration of offenders/patients.

Unique in its multidisciplinary approach, *Offenders, Deviants or Patients?* will be invaluable to all those who come into contact with serious offenders, as well as to those studying crime and criminal behaviour.

**Herschel Prins** has worked in the fields of criminality and mental health for some fifty years. He has served on a number of public and voluntary bodies, authored numerous books and articles and continues to teach part-time at a number of universities. This edition of his book updates the two previous editions – the first having appeared twenty-five years ago.

BY THE SAME AUTHOR

*Offenders, Deviants or Patients?*
An introduction to the study of socio-forensic problems
Tavistock, 1980

*Offenders, Deviants or Patients?*
Second Edition
Routledge, 1995

*Criminal Behaviour*
An introduction to criminology and the penal system
Second Edition
Tavistock, 1982

*Dangerous Behaviour, the Law and Mental Disorder*
Tavistock, 1986

*Bizarre Behaviours*
Boundaries of psychiatric disorder
Tavistock/Routledge, 1990

*Fire-Raising*
Its motivation and management
Routledge, 1994

*Will They Do it Again?*
Risk assessment and management in criminal justice and psychiatry
Brunner-Routledge, 1999

# Offenders, Deviants or Patients?

Third Edition

Herschel Prins

Routledge
Taylor & Francis Group

LONDON AND NEW YORK

First published 1980 by Tavistock

Second edition published 1995 by Routledge
11 New Fetter Lane, London EC4P 4EE
29 West 35th Street, New York NY 10001

Reprinted 1999

Reprinted 2001 by Brunner-Routledge
27 Church Road, Hove, East Sussex BN3 2FA
325 Chestnut Street, Suite 800, Philadelphia PA 19106

Reprinted 2004 by Brunner-Routledge
27 Church Road, Hove, East Sussex BN3 2FA
29 West 35th Street, New York NY 10001

Third edition published 2005 by Routledge
27 Church Road, Hove, East Sussex BN3 2FA

Simultaneously published in the USA and Canada by Routledge
270 Madison Avenue, New York NY 10016

*Routledge is an imprint of the Taylor & Francis Group*

Copyright © 1980, 1995, 2005 Herschel Prins

Typeset in Times by Garfield Morgan, Rhayader, Powys
Printed and bound in Great Britain by MPG Books, Bodmin, Cornwall
Paperback cover design by Richard Massing

This publication has been produced with paper manufactured to strict environmental standards and with pulp derived from sustainable forests.

*British Library Cataloguing in Publication Data*
A catalogue record for this book is available from the British Library

*Library of Congress Cataloging-in-Publication Data*
Prins, Herschel A.
    Offenders, deviants or patients? / Herschel Prins. – 3rd ed.
        p. ; cm.
    Includes bibliographical references and indexes.
    ISBN 1-58391-824-8 (Hbk : alk. paper) – ISBN 1-58391-825-6 (pbk. : alk. paper)

    [DNLM: 1. Criminal Psychology—methods—Great Britain. 2. Prisoners—psychology—Great Britain. 3. Crime—prevention & Control—Great Britain. 4. Dangerous Behavior—Great Britain. 5. Forensic Psychiatry—Great Britain. 6. Mental Disorders—rehabilitation—Great Britain. 7. Mental Health Services—organization & administration—Great Britain. WA 305 P9575o 2005] I. Title.

    HV8742.G72P74 2005
    364.3'8–dc22

                                                            2004018537

ISBN 1-58391-824-8 (Hbk)
ISBN 1-58391-825-6 (Pbk)

This book is dedicated to the staff of the Leicestershire and Rutland Forensic Mental Health Service and, in particular, the staff at the Herschel Prins Centre, Glenfield Hospital, Leicester.

Every act of authority of one man over another for which there is not an absolute necessity, is tyrannical.

Caesare Beccaria

Between the acting of a dreadful thing and the first motion, all the interim is like a phantasma or a hideous dream: the genius and mortal instruments are then in council; and the state of man like to a little kingdom suffers then the nature of an insurrection.

*Julius Caesar* Act 2 Sc.1

# Contents

# List of figures and tables

## Figures

## Tables

# List of law cases

*Bratty v. Attorney General for Northern Ireland* [1963] AC 386
*Hill v. Baxter* [1958] 1 QB 277
*HM Advocate v. Dingwall* [1867] 5 Irv 466
*K. v. United Kingdom* [1998] 40 BMLT 20
*Kay v. Butterworth* [1945] 173 LT 191
*R. [Anderson] v. Secretary of State for the Home Department* (2002) UKHL
   46 [2002] 3 WLR 1800
*R. v. Ahulwalia* [1992] *Independent Law Report*, 4 August: 7
*R. v. Birch* [1989] 11 Cr App R (S) 202 CA
*R. v. Burgess* [1991] *Independent Law Report*, 27 March: 9
*R. v. Burns* [1973] 58 Cr App R 364
*R. v. Byrne* [1960] 2 QB 396-455
*R. v. Canons Park Mental Health Review Tribunal* ex parte A. (1995)
   QB 60
*R. v. Drew* [2003] UKHL 25 *Independent Law Report*, 15 May: 18
*R. v. G. and another* (2003) UKHL 50
*R. v. Gittens* [1984] *Law Society Gazette*, 5 September
*R. v. Lipman* [1970] 1 QB 152
*R. v. Lloyd* [1967] 1 QB 175-181
*R. v. Majewski* [1977] AC 443
*R. v. Matheson* [1958] 42 Cr App R 154 1 WLR 474
*R. v. Merseyside Mental Health Review Tribunal* ex parte K. [1990] 1 All ER
   694 CA
*R. v. Podola* [1959] 3 All ER 418
*R. v. Secretary of State for the Home Department* ex parte K. [1990] 3 All
   ER 3 562 CA
*R. v. Stephenson* [1979] 3 WLR 143
*R. v. Sutcliffe, The Times* and *Guardian*, May 1981
*R. v. Turner* [1975] 2 WLR 56
*R. v. Vernege* [1982] *Crim Law Rev* December, 598-600
*Reid v. Secretary of State for Scotland* (1999) 2 WLR 28
*Ruddle v. Secretary of State for Scotland* (1999) GWD 29 1395

The law is stated as at December 2004. Proposed changes in mental health legislation are referred to at relevant places in the text.

# Acknowledgements

In the two previous editions of this book I paid tribute to a number of my teachers and colleagues who had afforded me many insights into the troubled and troublesome behaviours of those who are the subject of this third edition. In recent years, I have been much stimulated by the work of the late doctor Murray Cox (sometime visiting psychotherapist at Broadmoor High Security Hospital). Much of what I have written in Chapter 9 owes him a considerable inspirational debt. A number of Home Office officials dealt with my queries with unfailing courtesy: they include Mr P. Boshell, Head of Strategy, Parole Board; Liz Hill, Head of Public Protection, National Probation Directorate; Mr David Ireland, Criminal Law Policy Unit; and, finally, Mr Nigel Shackleford of the Mental Health Unit (who, over the years, has dealt with numerous and what must have been somewhat tedious requests on my part for information and guidance). I am grateful to the following editors and publishers for permission to reproduce parts of previously published work as indicated in the text: Sheila Bone, Director, *Northumbria Law Press*; Professor A. Good, Medical Editor, *Medicine, Science and the Law* and the *British Academy of Forensic Sciences* (which holds the copyright); Professor Malcolm MacCulloch, Editor-in-Chief, *The Journal of Forensic Psychiatry*; Professor Graham Towl, Editor; and the publishers of *The British Journal of Forensic Practice*. My thanks to Joanne Forshaw and her colleagues Claire Lipscomb and Helen Pritt at Routledge for much patience and support. However much one takes care to produce an error-free manuscript, such errors do creep in. In view of this fact, I have been singularly fortunate in having a sterling copy-editor in Helen Baxter. She has saved me many infelicities. My heartfelt thanks to my wife, Norma, for much forebearance over the years and to Mrs Janet Kirkwood, who has continued to turn "scruffy" drafts into polished texts.

# Note on case illustrations

No attempt has been made to conceal the identity of those persons whose cases have been in the public domain (for example, those who have been the subject of extensive media coverage). In all other instances, the cases derive from the author's personal experience. Every effort has been made to make the illustrations anonymous and to this end "composite" accounts have been given. Despite these necessary ethical precautions, it is maintained that the illustrations provide sufficiently authentic accounts of the issues they are intended to represent.

# Prologue

It is now a quarter of a century since the first edition of this book appeared and a decade since the second. Both editions appear, in the main, to have been well received. In the first edition (and reproduced in the second) I wrote as follows:

> The rationale for this book has emerged as a result of a general interest developed over many years concerning the understanding and treatment of offenders . . . I have come to be particularly interested in [that] borderland area that exists between mental disorder and criminal behaviour and in the relationships between the many disciplines and professionals that struggle to confront the problems inherent in these relationships. Thus, psychologists, psychiatrists, sociologists, lawyers, police scientists, social administrators, geneticists – to name but a few – have made contributions to this field.
>
> (Prins 1995: 1)

This view is even more true today when we are witnessing an apparent increase in the volume of crime, not least those crimes involving force and seriously deviant behaviour of one kind or another. The decision to produce a third edition of the work has been greatly reinforced by the views of two anonymous assessors appointed by the publishers; they considered that there was a continuing need for such a work. In addition, they made some helpful suggestions as to the content and I have been happy to include a number of these. The new edition includes reference to major changes in the law and an updating of research findings concerning mental disorders and criminality and our procedures for managing offender–patients through the criminal justice and mental healthcare systems. In addition to the range of professionals for whom the work was originally intended, the current version has also been written with an undergraduate readership in mind. This is because of the considerable expansion in undergraduate courses in criminology. In this edition, statistical material has been kept to a minimum but reference made to relevant detailed sources. When the first edition appeared in 1980 there were no substantial texts published in the UK that dealt with forensic psychiatric topics. Although the first edition never set out or claimed to be an introduction to forensic psychiatry, in the absence of any other books in the UK at that time, it seems to have been used as such. Since then, a number of excellent textbooks of forensic psychiatry have appeared, all offering (some in more detail than others) a highly professional discussion of some of the material covered in my original and present texts. In 1981 Trick and Tennent produced a useful short introductory text. In 1984 Craft and Craft edited a substantial compilation of contributions dealing with mentally abnormal offenders. In 1988 Faulk produced a very useful text aimed more specifically (but not exclusively) at psychiatric trainees. In 1990 Bluglass and Bowden and in 1993 Gunn and Taylor produced magisterial texts on the topic of forensic psychiatry. In 1994 Faulk produced a second edition of his very useful text. A further collection of very useful papers edited by Chiswick and Cope (again aimed at psychiatric trainees) appeared in 1995. The specialist field of forensic psychotherapy has been well catered for in two volumes edited by Cordess and Cox (1996) and, more briefly, by Welldon and Van Velden in 1997. The past decade has also witnessed a burgeoning of interest and publication by clinical forensic psychologists. In 1992 a slim volume was produced by Hollin; in 1993 a major work by Blackburn and in 1996 *The Handbook of Psychology for Forensic Practitioners* by Towl and Crighton. In addition, a number of other texts have appeared and these will be referred to in the chapters that follow. The present work makes no attempt to compete with any of the aforementioned works; rather it may be seen as complementary to them, being written by a non-medically qualified forensic psychiatric academic and former practitioner. As such, I have developed certain ideas that might be considered by some to be somewhat idiosyncratic and, by my severest critics, even as somewhat old fashioned. To this extent, and by way of explanation, it should be remembered that they are personal reflections forged in the light of long experience and, I hope, continuing learning. This comment should help to place my views in some kind of perspective.

During the last quarter of a century I have lectured to a range of mental health and criminal justice professionals on many of the topics addressed in the following pages. I have also taught similar material on post-graduate masters' courses at the Universities of Loughborough, Leicester and Birmingham. I have already alluded briefly to the hoped-for readership of this revised edition. To be more specific, I have in mind the increasing numbers of "law and order" professionals (sentencers, both full time and "lay"), the police, advocates, probation officers, and prison and hostel staff, forensic psychiatric clinicians and, in particular, trainee clinical and forensic psychologists, psychiatrists, mental nurses and social workers, from civil servants in those departments of state most directly involved with the subjects discussed in the book (namely the Home Office, the former Lord Chancellor's department and the Department of Health), to those who sit on adjudicating bodies (such as the Parole Board, the Home Secretary's Advisory Board on Restricted Patients (recently abolished) and the Mental Health Review Tribunal), to workers in the voluntary sector and to the trainers and mentors of all the foregoing. Finally, I hope it will also appeal to those members of the public who are frequently and understandably puzzled (and made very anxious) by the behaviour of those of their fellow citizens sometimes labelled as offenders, deviants or patients.

In this third edition I have, in the main, followed the structure of the second, but updated and amended content in the light of changes in law, practice and knowledge base. As in the second edition, I have not devoted specific chapters to female offenders, race issues or substance abuse. I have endeavoured to allude to these important topics within the general content of the book. To have devoted separate chapters to these admittedly very important aspects would have added considerably to the length of the book and I have been anxious to keep its length as much in line with the second edition as possible. For this reason, I have provided detailed references for each chapter and guidance for further reading. A few words are necessary about the choice of title for this third edition. I received a suggestion that the word *deviants* might be omitted from the title of this edition. My publishers and I have given this a good deal of thought and concluded that the inclusion of the word continues to describe the mixed and confusing place these individuals have in our lives. Some observations I made about them in the first edition are, sadly, still apposite.

They are, in the words of the late doctor Peter Scott, the "unrewarding, degenerate, not nice offender(s)" (Scott 1975: 8). We shall see, at various places in this text:

> [H]ow the system shunts them in various directions, sometimes labelling them as offenders, sometimes as patients, sometimes as deviants. The labels frequently serve to offload real responsibility and are a convenient means of rationalizing our discomfort, ambivalence and non-involvement. These shunting exercises are, of course, compounded by our reluctance to face up to issues of treatment versus punishment. They also illustrate some of the dilemmas inherent in distinguishing between normality and abnormality, sickness and sin, care and control.
> (Prins 1980: 2–3)

The labelling of, and attitudes towards, those encompassed in the title of this third edition are a representation of public and political attitudes. It is therefore relevant at this point to identify some of the more significant of these that have been present during the past decade.

## Current climate

Some of these will, of course, be picked up again in subsequent chapters. Put somewhat crudely, and at the risk of oversimplifying, the past 10 years or so have witnessed an almost morbid governmental preoccupation with, and overreaction to, the need for public protection. This concern has been reflected in a number of what might best be described as legislative themes.

First, certain changes in sentencing policy and practice introduced initially by the Criminal Justice Act 1991 (as amended by a further enactment in 1993), the Criminal Justice and Public Order Act 1994, the Crime (Sentences) Act 1997 (as amended by the Powers of Criminal Courts (Sentencing) Act 2000), the Criminal Justice and Courts Services Act 2000 and the Sex Offenders Act 1997. These and more recent enactments and proposed enactments have produced a very large number of new (mainly) community penalties; for example, combination and curfew orders, exclusion orders and drug treatment and testing orders. In brief, and taken together, the effect of these pieces of legislation, and their accompanying orders, has been to concentrate the minds of sentencers, criminal justice and mental health professionals; not only on just deserts but, as indicated earlier, on *public protection*, the latter a concern much espoused by past and present Home Secretaries. So rapid and numerous have been the various enactments and, in my view, so ill considered have been their possible overall consequences, that it has led one distinguished legal academic (who had best remain anonymous), speaking at a conference on severe personality disorder, to state that (and I paraphrase slightly) it seemed to him that legislation appeared to be written down on the back of a postcard between the Home Office and the House of Commons! The profusion of recent legislation seems to seek an uneasy and perhaps not very workable compromise between punitive and rehabilitative values, with an emphasis on the former. David Faulkner – a former high-ranking senior civil servant in the Home Office – has very cogently described this trend in terms of "exclusive" and "inclusive" views of society and human relationships. He states:

> The "exclusive" view emphasises personal freedom and individual responsibility, but is inclined to disregard the influence of situations and circumstances. It distinguishes between a deserving majority who are self-reliant, law abiding and entitled to benefit themselves without interference from others; and an undeserving, feckless, welfare dependent and often dangerous minority or underclass from whom they need to be protected . . . The contrasting "inclusive" view recognises the capacity and will of individuals to change – to improve if they are given guidance, help and encouragement; to be damaged if they are abused or humiliated.
>
> (Faulkner 1998: 165 see also Faulkner 2003)

Current and proposed legislation and practice would seem to reflect the polarization suggested by Faulkner.

Second, current mental health legislation and proposals for change have tended to focus attention on issues relating to danger to self and to others. The Mental Health (Patients in the Community) Act, 1995 is an example of this trend. In later chapters of this book I consider these issues more specifically, notably in a discussion of serious personality disorder and the assessment and management of risk. But, at this juncture, we should note a third area of concern, namely an increasing preoccupation with the introduction and maintenance of adequate supervisory procedures and, in particular, the registration of risk. Guidance and exhortation have emanated from a variety of sources – from central government (National Health Service Executive), circulars of guidance from professional bodies (such as the former Association of Chief Officers of Probation) and voluntary bodies such as the Zito Trust and the National Association for the Care and Resettlement of Offenders (NACRO). This third force for changes in practice has been prompted by the publicity and subsequent political attention given to various *causes célèbres* over the years as, for example, in the cases of Beverley Allitt, Sharon Campbell, Christopher Clunis, Jason Mitchell and others. (See Prins 1999 Chapters 4 and 5 for discussion.) These, and other cases of homicides committed by persons known to the mental health services, have been the mainspring for the proliferation of independent inquiries. The continuing need for them has been questioned in many quarters and their functions and format are likely to be placed under the general umbrella provisions of the recently established National Patient Safety Agency (NHS Confederation 2001). (See also Munro 2004.)

The individuals to be described in the various chapters in this book defy easy categorization and the clinical conditions they present do not readily or accurately conform to the legal definitions laid down in the mental health legislation. In addition, their clinical conditions may overlap in various ways; in other words they are not discrete entities and the phenomenon known as co-morbidity (a person having more than one form of mental disorder) presents additional problems. In 1993 in a NACRO Mental Health Advisory Committee Policy Paper prepared under my chairmanship, we described the mentally disordered offender population in the following terms:

> Those offenders who may be acutely or chronically mentally ill; those with neuroses, behavioural and/or personality disorders; those with learning difficulties; some who, as a function of alcohol and/or substance abuse, have a mental health problem; any who are suspected of falling into one or other of these two groups. It also includes those offenders where a degree of mental disturbance is recognised even though it may not be severe enough to bring it within the criteria laid

down by the Mental Health Act, 1983. It also applies to those offenders who, even though they do not fall easily within the definition – for example some sex offenders and some abnormally aggressive offenders, may benefit from psychological treatments.

(NACRO 1993: 4)

The individuals, and some of the problems they present and discussed in this book, fall within this fairly catholic definition; the focus of the book is primarily clinical and psychopathological. However, it is only proper to endeavour to place this approach within a broader social and philosophical context. Some of the individuals to be described later in this work present in somewhat dramatic fashion and have made the headlines. These are the cases that engage the attention of the media in their various forms. However, I wish to emphasize that there are many other less "dramatic" cases where decisions as to appropriate disposal can lead to a good deal of anxiety. This point is very well made in a useful contribution by Vaughan and Badger, who state:

> The existing literature . . . tends to concentrate on the issues raised by the most serious and dramatic cases. These are often complex and fascinating for both clinical and legal reasons . . . however [they] . . . are usually far from the everyday experience of most practitioners.
>
> (Vaughan and Badger 1995: xii)

What they say is a salutary reminder that we should avoid prurient interest in serious misdeeds; their perpetration and subsequent management, however, often provide serious food for thought, just because they *are* so "shocking". It is difficult to convey such difficulties in purely "theoretical" terms. In order to bring the problems to "life" I conclude this prologue with five illustrative examples.

### Case illustration P.1

"John" is in his fifties and comes from the West Country. Some 20 years earlier he was sent to a special (now known as secure) hospital on a hospital order (with restrictions on his discharge) under the Mental Health Act 1983, having been diagnosed as suffering from "psychopathic disorder". He had an extensive criminal record of sexual offences. The victims of his last offence had been "wooed" and "groomed" by him for some time and were all young boys. After some years in hospital, where he had received a range of "treatments" for his sexual deviancy, he was discharged into the community. He had been at liberty for about four years when he was apprehended for further offences of a similar kind; but in these latter offences he had used threats and a degree of force to secure the compliance of his victims. Those responsible for his supervision in the community (a psychiatrist and a social worker) had believed he had been doing well. However, despite his favourable presentation to them, he had been involved over many months in serious sexual misconduct. He was recalled to hospital from the community by order of the Home Secretary; he was also charged before the court with the new series of offences. Following his conviction he was again made the subject of a further hospital order. Since then he has remained in hospital; unsurprisingly, he is a model patient but affords no optimism to those entrusted with his management that he has changed his basic sexual preferences. His "psychopathic" state is regarded as virtually "untreatable" in psychiatric therapeutic terms. A critical question must be: Should he have been awarded a psychiatric disposal at this last court appearance, or would a prison sentence have been more appropriate?

## Case illustration P.2

"Florence" is in her late sixties. She has had a severe alcohol problem for many years. When in "drink" she becomes uncared for, noisy, abusive and frequently engages in minor "public" order offences. Over the years she has been the subject of police "cautions" (formal and informal), short prison sentences, probation, periods in detoxification centres and short spells in hospitals. She "floats" like some piece of flotsam on the waters of the healthcare and penal systems. No one wishes to "own" her and her condition is deteriorating slowly but steadily.

## Case illustration P.3

"Paul" is in his early fifties. He has a long record of offences of indecent exposure ("flashing"). He admits readily that he has indulged in this behaviour on many more occasions than those for which he has been prosecuted and convicted. He has received a range of penal and healthcare disposals, including numerous probation orders combined with psychiatric treatment. Despite the anxieties he feels at each court appearance and sentence, he claims he is quite unable to break what has become a compulsion. Probation officers, psychiatrists, psychologists and nurses have all been involved in various forms of therapy for his problems – to no effect. Fortunately, he is the type of exposer whose behaviour, although highly distressing to his victims, has not progressed to more serious sexual deviance, such as rape (see Chapter 6).

## Case illustration P.4

"Vincent" is a 26-year old African-Caribbean. He is considered by some psychiatrists to suffer from a form of schizophrenia that makes him highly suspicious of others and liable to engage in seriously aggressive behaviour when he feels affronted or frustrated. He lives in an area where he and his fellow African-Caribbeans complain that they feel alienated and "picked upon" more frequently by the police than their similarly-aged white contemporaries. It is considered that his schizo-phrenic illness has been deemed to play a more significant role as a determinant of his behaviour than is justified by the facts. His behaviour and its origins pose significant problems for both law and psychiatry.

### Case illustration P.5

"Pauline" is in her early forties and is serving a life sentence for her third conviction for arson with intent to endanger life. She has a record of being preoccupied with fire since childhood, has engaged in making hoax calls to the fire services and has become involved increasingly in more and more serious fire-raising behaviour. At various times she has been diagnosed as suffering from personality disorder, from depression and from schizophrenia. However, no one has considered that she easily fulfils the criteria for a conventional psychiatric diagnosis. She has spent time in both ordinary and secure psychiatric hospitals. In such establishments, she is both aggressive and disruptive; when in a state of tension she seeks to resolve it by lighting fires. The circumstances for which she received her current life sentence were that she thought her fellow residents in the aftercare hostel were "ganging up" on her. One evening, when they and the staff on duty had gone to bed, she poured a quantity of paraffin over the furniture in the communal lounge and set fire to it by means of a fuse made from rags soaked in the same substance. *She then left the premises.* Fortunately, the smoke detector in the room alerted the residents. However, several of them suffered from the effects of smoke inhalation and needed brief hospital treatment. Over the years, many approaches have been tried with "Pauline". There had been signs that she was beginning to find more acceptable ways of expressing her resentful and angry feelings and coping with the problems these created. Despite this, the doctors who gave evidence at her trial were of the unanimous opinion that her condition was untreatable within the terms of the mental health legislation. The judge, in sentencing her to life imprisonment, com-mented on her actual and potential dangerousness. He indicated that she would not be released until those responsible for her management considered it safe to do so. As we shall see subsequently, such judgments are notoriously difficult to make with total precision.

These five brief case illustrations demonstrate some of the problems involved in making firm boundary lines between normality and abnormality, "madness" and "badness". In addition, they demonstrate the problems involved in selecting the most appropriate modes of management in the interests of both the offender–patient, on the one hand, and the community, on the other. They also illustrate the problems that occur in attempting to distinguish those who have merely a nuisance value and those whose behaviour may have a more malignant quality. These and allied issues are addressed in the chapters that follow this prologue.

I begin the task by trying to demonstrate some of the difficulties that arise in attempting to determine responsibility (liability/culpability) for crime and in the manner in which this may be eroded in a variety of ways. I shall also endeavour to demonstrate the manner in which psychiatry and the law may not always operate together in harmonious fashion.

## References

Blackburn, R. (1993) *The Psychology of Criminal Conduct: Theory, Research and Practice*, Chichester: John Wiley & Sons.

Bluglass, R. and Bowden, P. (eds) (1990) *Principles and Practice of Forensic Psychiatry*, London: Churchill Livingstone.

Chiswick, D. and Cope, R. (eds) (1995) *Seminars in Practical Forensic Psychiatry*, London: Gaskell (for Royal College of Psychiatrists).

Cordess, C. and Cox, M. (eds) (1996) *Forensic Psychotherapy* (2 vols.), London: Jessica Kingsley.

Craft M. and Craft, A. (eds) (1984) *Mentally Abnormal Offenders*, London: Baillière Tindall.

Faulk, M. (1988) *Basic Forensic Psychiatry*, Oxford: Blackwell Scientific Publications.

—— (1994) *Basic Forensic Psychiatry*, 2nd ed., Oxford: Blackwell Scientific Publications.

Faulkner, D. (1998) "Building a system on evidence and principle", *Vista* 3: 164–80.

—— (2003) "The criminal justice bill: Background and prospects", *Prison Service Journal* 148: 5–8.

Gunn, J. and Taylor, P. J. (eds) (1993) *Forensic Psychiatry: Clinical, Legal and Ethical Issues*, London: Butterworth-Heinemann.

Hollin, C. R. (1989) *Psychology and Crime: An Introduction to Criminological Psychology*, London: Routledge.

—— (1992) *Criminal Behaviour: A Psychological Approach to Explanation and Prevention*, London: Falmer Press.

Munro, E. (2004) "Mental health tragedies: Investigating beyond human error", *Journal of Forensic Psychiatry and Psychology* 15: 475–93.

NACRO (1993) Mental Health Advisory Committee Policy Paper No. 1: *Community Care and Mentally Disturbed Offenders*, London: NACRO.

NHS Confederation (2001) *Briefing*, Issue No. 49, May. London.

Prins, H. (1980) *Offenders, Deviants or Patients? An Introduction to the Study of Socio-Forensic Problems*, London: Tavistock.

—— (1995) *Offenders, Deviants or Patients?*, 2nd ed., London: Routledge.

—— (1999) *Will They Do It Again? Risk Assessment and Management in Criminal Justice and Psychiatry*, London: Routledge.

Scott, P. D. (1975) *Has Psychiatry Failed in the Treatment of Offenders?* London: Institute for the Study and Treatment of Delinquency.

Towl, G. and Crighton, D. A. (1996) *The Handbook of Psychology For Forensic Practitioners*, London: Routledge.

Trick, K. L. and Tennent, G. (1981) *Forensic Psychiatry: An Introductory Text*, London: Pitman.

Vaughan, P. J. and Badger, D. (1995) *Working with the Mentally Disordered Offender in the Community*, London: Chapman & Hall.

Welldon, E. V. and Velsen, C. Van (eds) (1997) *A Practical Guide to Forensic Psychotherapy*, London: Jessica Kingsley.

## Further reading

### General

Buchanan, A. (ed.) (2002) *Care of the Mentally Disordered Offender in the Community*, Oxford: Oxford University Press. (In particular, Chapter 1 by Nikolas Rose.)

Laurance, J. (2003) *Pure Madness: How Fear Drives the Mental Health System*, London: Routledge.

Peay, J. (2002) "Mentally disordered offenders, mental health and crime", in M. Maguire, R. Morgan and R. Reiner (eds) *The Oxford Handbook of Criminology*, 3rd ed., Oxford: Oxford University Press.

Penn, D. L. and Wykes, T. (eds) (2003) Special issue on stigma, *Journal of Mental Health* 12, 3.

### Race, culture and gender issues

Allen, H. (1987) *Justice Unbalanced: Gender, Psychiatry and Judicial Decisions*, Milton Keynes: Open University Press.

Birch, H. (ed.) (1993) *Moving Targets: Women, Murder and Representation*, London: Virago Press.

Fernando, S., Ndegwa, D. and Wilson, M. (1998) *Forensic Psychiatry, Race and Culture*, London: Routledge.

Gelsthorpe, L. (2002) "Feminism and criminology", in M. Maguire, R. Morgan and R. Reiner (eds), *The Oxford Handbook of Criminology*, 3rd ed., Oxford: Oxford University Press.

Heidensohn, F. (2002) "Gender and crime", in M. Maguire, R. Morgan and R. Reiner (eds), *The Oxford Handbook of Criminology*, 3rd ed., Oxford: Oxford University Press.

Radford, J. and Russell, D. E. H. (eds) (1992) *Femicide: The Politics of Women Killing*, Buckingham: Open University Press.

# Part I

# Legal and administrative aspects

# Chapter 1

# Not in their right minds

The Law is the perfection of reason . . .
(Sir Edward Coke, *The First Part of the Institutes of the Laws of England* (1628), Bk 2, Ch. 6, p. 97)

The Law is a ass – a idiot.
(Dickens, *Oliver Twist* (1838), Ch. 51)

The two quotations, short though they are, are useful reminders of the disputes in court that frequently take place between the law, on the one hand, and psychiatry and psychology, on the other. The issues to be discussed in this chapter are complex and I have, of necessity, had to oversimplify some of them. The complexity of the subject matter is further compounded by the manner in which certain terms are used, often synonymously, by a wide range of people. Because of this, it is necessary, as a preliminary, to comment on the meaning given to such words as responsibility, capacity, culpability and liability. For people often behave like Lewis Carroll's Humpty Dumpty who, it will be remembered, said, "in rather a scornful tone", "when I use a word . . . it means just what I choose it to mean – neither more nor less" (*Through the Looking Glass*, Chapter 6). This chapter will merely provide a map, similar to those provided by motoring organizations, namely giving an outline of the main contours of a complicated terrain, but deliberately devoid of any fine detail. For the latter, the traveller must turn to the more detailed directions provided by the Ordnance Survey or similar organizations. I trust that the references to authorities cited in the chapter and the list of further reading will serve to fill these gaps. The terrain surveyed in this outline map is divided into the following areas. First, a brief consideration of some of the terms used in discussions of responsibility for crime. Second, a comparatively short historical account of the development of the concept of responsibility and allied matters. Third, a description of the manner in which the law in

England and Wales makes special provision for what can best be regarded as "erosions" of responsibility. Fourth, a brief discussion of a specific aspect of the relationship between mental disturbances and crime as a prelude to the more detailed discussion to be afforded in Chapter 3.

## Some semantic issues

A layperson is likely to use terms such as responsibility or guilt in less precise fashion than would a lawyer or student of jurisprudence. Thus the former, if asked to define the word "responsible", would probably come near to the dictionary definition: (1) "liable to be called to account (to a person or for a thing)", (2) "being *morally* accountable for one's actions; capable of rational conduct" (*Concise Oxford Dictionary*). The important point to be noted here is the emphasis I have added, because the law is not necessarily concerned with morally reprehensible conduct. In their discussion of the law relating to homosexuality and prostitution, the Wolfenden Committee made an important distinction between private and public morality. It considered that:

> Unless a deliberate attempt is made by Society, acting through the agency of the law, to equate the sphere of crime with that of sin, there must remain a realm of private morality and immorality which is, in brief and crude terms not the law's business.
> (Home Office and Scottish Home Department, 1957: 24)

The layperson may also use the word "irresponsible" to denote something more than legal lack of responsibility. For our purposes, "irresponsible" means simply lack of legal responsibility and is not used in any lay or pejorative sense.

The word "culpable" is found, not infrequently, in the literature on responsibility and related matters. For the present purposes it means blameworthiness in the criminal sense. However, if we choose to use it in this way we must acknowledge that a moral quality may creep into its usage. The word "capacity" is also sometimes used as a synonym for legal competency. Thus, in legal terms, it would seem to denote a quality existing within an individual – for example, to form an intent to act in a certain way. The word "liability" is sometimes used as being synonymous with responsibility. The *Concise Oxford Dictionary* defines "liable" as being "legally bound, or under an obligation". For my purposes, the term responsibility merely means liability to be dealt with by the criminal law and the criminal justice system.

Some years ago my friend and former colleague, the late Professor Edward Griew, drew attention to these definitional problems; he stated that responsibility is a word: "[S]o often bandied about; like an historical background it gives an air of learning to a discussion . . . it is a muddying word . . . liability is the better word as being less ambiguous" (Griew 1984: 60).

One final, but very important, point needs to be made about the term "liability". As far as the law is concerned, liability can certainly go beyond responsibility in the sense of moral culpability. For example, there are a number of offences, those of so-called "strict liability" (sometimes called "absolute liability") for which individuals may be prosecuted and punished, even though they are unaware of the existence of facts which make their conduct a criminal offence. An example of this would be the case of a shopkeeper found to have purveyed contaminated meat or other foodstuffs even though he or she did not know they were contaminated. In recent years, the House of Lords (as supreme judicial review body) has indicated that there should be some restriction in the interpretation of offences of strict liability. A seminal case was that of *Sweet v. Parsley* (1969). This concerned a young woman who was originally convicted of being concerned in the management of premises (she being the tenant of a farmhouse in Oxfordshire that she sublet to various other tenants) in which, the prosecution alleged, cannabis had been smoked. Her conviction, after appeal, was eventually overturned as a result of a ruling in the House of Lords. (For some discussion of the pros and cons of this area of concern, see Buchanan 2000: pp. 20, 21 and 97.)

### Components of legal blameworthiness

There are one or two additional terms that require clarification. An act does not make a person *legally* guilty unless his or her mind is also legally blameworthy (see also earlier comments on the difference between legal blameworthiness and moral turpitude). Lawyers denote this concept of guilt through their use of the Latin term *mens rea*. Simply put, this means having legally guilty intent or, more precisely, having the intention to commit an act that is wrong in the sense that it is *legally forbidden*. (For a full discussion see Hart 1968.) It should also be noted that there must be an act or omission; this is known in legal terms as the *actus reus*. An omission is a failure to do something; a simple example would be the failure to give precedence to persons on a pedestrian crossing. There are, of course, more complex and emotive situations in which a person may be charged with a failure to do something; such an act might amount in certain circumstances to *serious negligence*. In the past two decades there have been a number of instances where this has been an issue as, for example, in a number of multiple fatal injuries arising from disasters at sea and on land.

Such negligent acts, if they caused the death of others, *could* lead to charges of manslaughter; charges can be brought against companies and persons in managerial positions having control over the activities of their more junior staff. Prosecutions of this nature are difficult to bring and are not often successful. This is because it is very difficult to discover what is known as "a controlling mind" in the complex web of corporate organizational responsibility. As this chapter was being drafted, a prosecution was being launched against some of the companies and individuals involved in the Hatfield rail disaster. It is difficult to predict what the outcome may be (*The Independent*, 10 July 2003).

## Brief historical background

With certain exceptions (notably extreme youth or mental disturbance), men and women are to be held responsible (liable) for their acts and adjudged capable of exercising control over them. History reveals that the issue has not always been clear cut. In earlier times, it was customary for punishment to be imposed for the commission of a criminal act regardless of the mental condition of the person concerned (indeed, in England and Wales, the common law gave considerable overriding priority to the need to preserve law and order). Further back in historical time, in the Old Testament, we find examples of severe forms of punishment without mitigating features being much in evidence. However, in certain cases, if the crime appeared to be unintentional, *some* mitigation of penalty was available through the use of the "cities of refuge" for those who killed unintentionally. In addition, minors, the feeble minded and deaf mutes were often afforded special treatment under the terms of Shoteh (as described in the Jewish Talmud). In the Roman era, one can discern the beginnings of an attempt to introduce a primitive notion of diminished responsibility; and in thirteenth-century England, it seems to have been generally held that neither the child nor the madman should be held liable for crime. Henry de Bracton, author of one of the first major treatises on English law, wrote: *Furiosus non intelligit quod agit et anima et ratione caret, et non multi-mumdistas a brutis*; in other words, "an insane person is one who does not know what he is doing, is lacking in mind and reason and is not far from the brutes" (quoted in Walker 1968: 33). Although obviously benign in intent, the statement seems to have a somewhat primitive element to it, equating mental illness with the behaviour of animals. Walker (1968) and Jacobs (1971) have drawn attention to what appears to be an interesting error in another of Bracton's statements. It is worth alluding to briefly because it exemplifies some of the problems involved in tracing the evolution of legal and allied concepts. Bracton is alleged to have stated:

> Then there is what can be said about the child and the madman (furiosus), for the one is protected by the innocence of design and the other is excused by the misfortune of his *deed*.
>
> (quoted in Jacobs 1971: 25; emphasis added)

It is not altogether clear from his text why the madman is not to be held responsible. Apparently, Bracton took his text from a translation of the work of Modestinus. In its original form, this referred not to the misfortune of his deed (*infelicitas facti*) but to the misfortune of his fate (*infelicitas fati*). This would make more sense, for it would appear that in Roman law there seems to have been an assumption that an insane offender was punished sufficiently by his madness (*satis furore ipso punitur*). Complicated statements and concepts sometimes become lost or confused during translation. For example, it is highly likely that much of the controversy over some of Freud's views and findings has arisen because of difficulties in finding suitable English interpretations of terms originally conceived and described in German. Such difficulties have been very usefully illustrated by the distinguished psychiatrist and philanthropist, the late Bruno Bettelheim, as follows:

> [C]onversations with friends have disclosed that many, who, like myself, are native German speakers, and emigrated to the States in the middle of their lives, are quite dissatisfied with the way Freud's works have been rendered in English. The number of inadequacies and downright errors in the translations is enormous.
>
> (Bettelheim 1983: vii)

In the seventeenth century, the jurist Sir Edward Coke appeared to share the view of earlier authorities that the mad were punished sufficiently by their fate. In the same century, Sir Matthew Hale (in a treatise published in 1736, some 60 years after his death) tried to distinguish between the totally and the partially insane. In his view, the latter would not be exempt from criminal responsibility (see Jacobs 1971 and Clarke 1975). It seems fairly safe to assume that only very serious mental disorder ("raving lunacy") would have been recognized as giving exemption from serious crime and, in particular, homicide. However, contrary to general belief, issues relating to madness (insanity) were gradually being raised more frequently in respect of crimes less serious than homicide. Eigen states that:

> [T]he jurisprudence of insanity appears to have arisen not out of sensationalistic murders or grotesque personal assaults, but from what were rather more "garden variety" crimes.
>
> (1983: 426)

In addition, broader interpretations of what might constitute mental disorder were being admitted. For example, in the case of Arnold in 1724, the judge suggested that "if a man be deprived of reason, and, consequently of his intention, he cannot be guilty" (cited in Jacobs 1971: 27). Similar views were expressed in a famous Leicestershire case, namely that of

Laurence, fourth Earl of Ferrers. He was tried in 1760 by his fellow peers in the House of Lords for the murder of his steward, John Johnson. His history, trial and the climate of the times in which it took place have been described in lively yet scholarly fashion by a local Leicester author and solicitor, Arthur Crane (1990). A subsequent and more influential case, was that of Hadfield, who was tried for capital treason in 1800 for shooting at George III at the Drury Lane Theatre in London. Erskine, Hadfield's counsel, obtained an acquittal on the basis of the defendant having sustained serious head injuries (through sword wounds) during war service. These injuries had led Hadfield to develop delusional ideas that impelled him to believe that he had to sacrifice his life for the salvation of the world. Not wishing to be guilty of suicide and the condemnation and obloquy this would call down on his memory, he chose to commit his crime for the sole purpose of being executed for it. Hadfield's case is of interest for three reasons. First, it was *probably* the first time that brain damage (caused by a head injury) had been advanced as a relevant exculpatory factor. Second, Erskine, who was a brilliant advocate (later to become a distinguished judge), was probably more easily able to secure Hadfield's acquittal at a time when public interest in, and sympathy towards, the "mad" had been fostered by the long-standing and intermittent illness suffered by the King (a malady for which the diagnosis has always been disputed – was it a manic-depressive disorder or symptomatic of porphyria?). The third area of interest is the consequence that flowed from Hadfield's acquittal. The question that arose was where to "house" him? Despite the facilities afforded by the vagrancy laws, the common law only permitted the detention of a person such as Hadfield until he had regained his sanity. As Reznek points out, "this led to dangerous lunatics being released during 'lucid intervals'" (Reznek 1997: 18). Reznek goes on to point out that "an act of parliament hastily established . . . the existence of the special verdict "NGRI [not guilty by reason of insanity]" – allowing Hadfield to be committed indefinitely to Bethlem [Hospital] (p. 18). As we shall see shortly, the "special verdict" still exists, but is implemented fairly rarely. Not all cases were brought to such a successful conclusion as was Hadfield's. For example, a similar plea to Hadfield's entered in the case of Bellingham (who in 1812 shot the Prime Minister, Spencer-Perceval) was unsuccessful and Bellingham was condemned to death. Walker (1968) reports how a similar fate befell a contemporary of Bellingham's – an epileptic farmer named Bowler, who had killed a neighbour. However, it is the case of Daniel M'Naghten in 1843 that is of particular interest, for it was the outcome of his case and the consideration of that outcome by the senior judiciary that resulted in the formulation of a legal test of insanity. M'Naghten was a Glaswegian woodcarver who seems to have suffered from what would be described today as paranoid delusions (see Chapter 3). For example, among other delusions, he believed that the Tories were conspiring against him.

Following his arrest M'Naghten gave the following statement to the police: "The Tories in my native city have compelled me to do this. They follow and persecute me wherever I go, and have entirely destroyed my peace of mind" (Walker 1968: 91 and quoted by Reznek 1997: 19).

As a result of this particular delusion M'Naghten purchased a pair of pistols and, on 20 January 1843, mistaking the Prime Minister Sir Robert Peel's secretary (Robert Drummond) for the minister himself, shot him in the back. Drummond died some days later. In March the same year, M'Naghten went on trial. He too was represented by a very able counsel – Alexander Cockburn. Cockburn produced mental state evidence in court that suggested that M'Naghten was insane because he lacked control over his actions. He endeavoured to make out a case for a defence of partial insanity "that could lead him to commit crimes for which morally he cannot be held responsible" (Walker 1968: 94). However, the trial judge did not favour such a view and put it to the jury that if M'Naghten had been able to distinguish right from wrong they should return a guilty verdict. The jury disagreed and returned a verdict of not guilty by reason of insanity (NGRI). This verdict caused much concern and the House of Lords decided to put to a group of senior judges certain questions that arose from it. Two of the five questions put to the judges have, in combined form, come to be known as the M'Naghten Rules; in my view this is a somewhat erroneous term as they are merely a legal "test" of insanity. The "test" states, in effect that:

> [T]he jurors ought to be told in all cases that every man is to be pre-sumed sane and to possess a sufficient degree of reason to be responsible for his crimes until the contrary is proved to their satisfaction; and that to establish a defence of insanity, it must be clearly proved that, at the time of committing the act, the party accused was labouring under such a defect of reason from disease of the mind, as not to know the nature and quality of his act he was doing; or, if he did know it, that he did not know what he was doing was wrong.
>
> (quoted in Walker 1968: 100)

In essence, there are two significant parts to this statement. An accused has a defence, first, if they did not know the nature and quality of their act or, second, if they did, they did not know that it was wrong (in law). From the time they were first posited, the so-called "rules" have, understandably, been the subject of criticism. In the first place, they were framed at a time when the disciplines of psychology and psychiatry were in an embryonic state of development; a disproportionate degree of emphasis was placed on the faculties of knowing, reasoning and understanding (cognitive processes) to the exclusion of emotional and volitional factors (connative processes). (For a very helpful discussion of these issues in the Victorian era see Smith

1991 and Ward 2002.) Second, the "rules" make use of such expressions as "defect of reason", "disease of the mind", "nature and quality of his act". These terms have involved numerous debates concerning their precise legal definition and interpretation. Third, and perhaps more importantly, the criteria for "M'Naghten madness" have been so tightly drawn that its use as a defence in serious cases such as homicide has always been fraught with difficulty. Since the introduction of the Homicide Act of 1957, the Mental Health Acts of 1959 and 1983 and the total abolition of the death penalty in 1965, the number of insanity defences resulting in the "special verdict" in homicide cases has been very small (from the period 1991–2001 merely some 21 cases). It should be remembered that the insanity defence is open for use in cases other than homicide and, as we shall see when we consider the second form of the "special verdict" (unfitness to plead), it is sometimes pleaded in such cases. However, until the Criminal Procedure (Insanity and Unfitness to Plead) Act of 1991, a finding of insanity or unfitness to plead involved a fixed disposal of detention, often in a secure hospital, usually without limit of time. (See Mackay 1995 for an excellent survey of these provisions.) Lack of satisfaction with the M'Naghten "rules" led the Committee on Mentally Abnormal Offenders to suggest a number of amendments to the M'Naghten provisions and to call for the introduction of a new formulation of the special verdict, namely, not guilty on evidence of severe mental disorder (illness or impairment) (Home Office and DHSS 1975).

The Committee proposed a definition of severe mental illness that would contain one or more of the following characteristics:

(a) Lasting impairment of intellectual functions shown by failure of memory, orientation, comprehension and learning capacity.
(b) Lasting alteration of mood of such degree as to give rise to delusional appraisal of the patient's situation, his past or his future, or that of others, or to lack of any appraisal.
(c) Delusional beliefs, persecutory, jealous or grandiose.
(d) Abnormal perceptions associated with delusional misinterpretation of events.
(e) Thinking so disordered as to prevent reasonable appraisal of the patient's situation or reasonable communication with others.
           (Home Office and DHSS 1975: para 18.35 and Appendix 10)

To date, there has not been a great deal of impetus from central government or other sources to change the basic components of the insanity defence (see Buchanan 2000). However, it should perhaps be noted that the Law Commission's proposals for codification of the criminal law did include a well-considered reformulation of the insanity defence (see Law Commission 1985, 1989).

## Unfitness to plead

So far I have only considered the first form of the special verdict. In order to complete the picture in this section of the chapter we must consider the situation when an individual claims that he or she is unfit to be tried (known as "unfitness to plead" or being "under disability in relation to the trial"). By tradition, and in accordance with the principles of English justice, a court has to be satisfied that an accused person can, first, understand the charges against them, second, exercise their age-old right to challenge a juror, third, follow the evidence against them and, fourth, instruct counsel for their defence. If the accused is considered to be unable to put the foregoing into effect, he or she has customarily been held to be "unfit to plead" or, to use the term now favoured, to be "under disability in relation to the trial" ("under disability" for short). (Cases of deaf mutism may also occur rarely and, even more rarely, a person may be found to be "mute of malice". I am not considering such cases here. For a very useful discussion of the history of pleas and unfitness see Grubin 1996 and for the implications of the abolition of the right to silence as it might affect such cases see Gray et al. 2001.)

A finding of unfitness to plead occurs fairly infrequently, mainly because a person has to be seriously disabled psychiatrically in order to satisfy the relevant criteria (some 20 cases for the period 1991–2001 (Home Office 2003)). Three cases known to me professionally exemplify this aspect. The first concerned a man who was suffering from such serious psychotic delusions that, in the course of them, he killed his wife. He was still severely deluded at the time of his trial and subsequently. The second case was of a young man who was found to be so impaired in intelligence and understanding that he, too, was found unfit to plead. A third case concerned a man who, while in the grip of severe psychotic delusions, attacked a near relative. Before the Criminal Procedure (Insanity and Unfitness to Plead) Act of 1991, the only disposal available on a finding of "disability" was committal to a psychiatric hospital. This might be for a considerable period of time and the *facts* of the case might never be determined. It is possible (and in some cases even probable) that someone found to be under disability might well have had a defence to the charge if it had been put to the test in court. Momentum for change from various sources led to the 1991 Act and its more flexible provisions. These are summarized as follows:

1  Where a person is found not guilty by reason of insanity or found to be under disability (unfit to plead), a Crown or Appeal Court will no longer be bound to order detention in hospital under a restriction order within the terms, currently, of the Mental Health Act 1983 (Sections 37/41), *except in cases of murder*. (But for the legality of this see Kerrigan 2002.)

2   The following disposals are now available:
   (a) An order for admission to hospital (an "admission order"), with the option of an added restriction order.
   (b) A guardianship order under Section 37 of the Mental Health Act.
   (c) An order for supervision and treatment, placing the person under the supervision of either a probation officer or local authority social worker for a period of two years. In addition, the person will also be required to be under the care of a qualified medical practitioner. The order is similar to a community rehabilitation (formerly probation) order with a requirement for mental treatment, except that, in the event of non-compliance, there are no provisions, as in a community rehabilitation order, for a return to court or revocation of the order.
   (d) An order for absolute discharge.
   (e) There is a requirement for the medical evidence to the court to be given by two registered medical practitioners, one of whom must be currently approved under Section 12 of the Mental Health Act 1983.
   (f) Provision for a speedy trial of the facts of the case (see earlier discussion) so that the question of guilt can be determined. Such determination will be carried out by a jury separate from that empanelled to determine the defendant's state of mind. Should the jury decide that the defendant was not guilty of the alleged act or omission the court must acquit, irrespective of his or her mental state. In such a case, it is likely that the civil (i.e. non-criminal) powers of the mental health legislation would be invoked if the individual satisfied the criteria for compulsory admission to hospital.

The more flexible provisions of the 1991 Act seem to have promoted an increase in both disposals. In respect of restricted patients, the numbers for unfitness to plead cases have shown a steady increase for the period 1992–2002 (from three to 50) and for not guilty by reason of insanity cases a less marked increase from one to nine (Howard and Christopherson 2003).

### Diminished responsibility

As stated earlier in this chapter, the criteria for establishing a defence of insanity are narrowly drawn and difficult to implement. Until the introduction of the Homicide Act of 1957 the defence was used almost exclusively in cases of murder as a means of avoiding the imposition of the death penalty. The Homicide Act was introduced as a result of a minority recommendation of the Royal Commission on Capital Punishment (1953).

The purpose of the Act was to introduce a wider range of mental defences to a charge of what was then capital murder. Such a defence had been used in Scotland since the 1870s (see Buchanan 2000: 54). It was introduced in Scotland following the case of *HM Advocate v. Dingwall* (1867), in which the presiding judge referred to "murder with extenuating circumstances" (Collins and White 2003; see also Patrick 2003 and Crichton et al. 2004). In their paper, they examine the history of its development and demonstrate similar problems of interpretation in both law and psychiatry to those in England and Wales (see following). Section 2 of the Act states that:

> Where a person kills or is party to the killing of another, he shall not be convicted of murder if he was suffering from such abnormality of mind (whether arising from a condition of arrested or retarded development of mind or any inherent causes or induced by disease or injury) as substantially impaired his mental responsibility for his acts or omissions in doing or being party to the killing.

The defence is only available in cases of murder and a finding of diminished responsibility reduces a charge of murder to that of manslaughter. This permits the judge a wide degree of discretion in sentencing. Conviction on a charge of murder permits, at present, only one disposal – a mandatory sentence of life imprisonment with, if the judge so disposes, a recommendation as to the minimum length of time the convicted person should serve. Examination of Section 2 indicates the recognition of a degree of *partial* responsibility; this differs from a successful insanity defence where a finding of insanity (or for that matter unfitness to plead) acknowledges total exculpation from responsibility. The plea of diminished responsibility may be raised by the accused and, as we shall see shortly, if contested, will be decided by a jury "on the balance of probabilities". Such a test is somewhat less strict than the "beyond all reasonable doubt" burden of proof required in most criminal trials. The number of instances in which diminished responsibility has been pleaded and the number of hospital disposals in these would seem to have been diminishing in recent years. The number of Section 2 male homicide convictions for the period 1991 to 2001/2 averaged 35. The highest figure being 68 in 1992 and the lowest for which complete figures are available was 17 in 2000/01. For females, the average for the same period was nine, the highest being 14 in 1991 and the lowest for which complete figures are available was three in 2001/02. In respect of hospital disposals of such cases the average number of hospital orders with a restriction order under Section 37/41 of the MHACT, 1983 for males and females was 22 and the average number of hospital orders without restrictions was just below four (Home Office 2003: Tables 1.09 and 1.10). In an early study, Dell (1984) suggested that this might have been due to reluctance on the part of psychiatric personnel to treat those diagnosed as suffering from psychopathic disorder, either in secure conditions or ordinary psychiatric hospitals. In addition to problems of disposal, the wording of Section 2 itself has presented serious problems in court. The notion of responsibility is a difficult one to grasp. Psychiatrists have usually been willing to go somewhat beyond their remit of diagnosing mental disorder and opine as to the extent to which this may have diminished responsibility. One can question whether this latter function is properly within psychiatry's remit. Should it not be for the jury to decide? Case law has indicated that even if there is unanimous psychiatric opinion that responsibility is substantially diminished, the jury is not bound to accept that view (*R. v. Vernege*, 1982). We shall see shortly that this was certainly the case in *R. v. Sutcliffe* (1981).

Returning to the question of semantics, we may well ask ourselves what interpretation should be placed on the words "abnormality of mind"? Two aspects of this question may be discerned. First, whether or not an abnormality of mind existed and, second, whether it affected the defendant's "mental responsibility" for his or her acts. The late doctor John Hamilton, one-time Medical Director of Broadmoor Hospital, asked: "What on earth does [mental responsibility] mean? (1981: 434). And, as has already been suggested, are psychiatrists necessarily the most appropriate persons to give such opinions? The late doctor Jack Kahn, a very experienced general psychiatrist with a deep interest in matters of mental health and philosophy, once posed the dilemma for psychiatrists having to testify in court very trenchantly:

> In deviation from the normal, particularly where behaviour is concerned, there may not necessarily be a medical contribution at all. The treatment may be purely legal or social action. The aim is to bring the behaviour into conformity . . . the psychiatrist comes into the study of some human problems only by invitation, and this invitation may not be wholehearted. It is as if the psychiatrist is expected to claim authority in every problem of living, only to have that claim challenged even while his help is being sought.
>
> (Kahn 1971: 230)

It is worth noting here that Professor Thomas Szasz has for long championed the view that psychiatry should not be used overenthusiastically in matters of morality and deviance. (Szasz 1987, 1993). There would appear, then, to be a fundamental ambivalence to be overcome, even before matters of motivation and its interpretation are raised and challenged under our adversarial system of justice. Aspects of such ambivalence are well attested to in a seminal paper by Kenny (1984). He begins his contribution with an incisive discussion of the case of Hinckley, who attempted to assassinate President Reagan. He too makes some trenchant observations about the role of expert witnesses, particularly psychiatrists:

> The law should be reformed by changing statutes which force expert witnesses to testify beyond their science, by taking the provision of expert evidence out of the adversarial context, and by removing from the courts the decision whether a nascent discipline is, or is not a science.
>
> (1984: 291)

Brief reference has already been made to the notion of "abnormality of mind". In the case of Byrne – a sexual psychopath – Lord Parker, then Lord Chief Justice, described abnormality of mind and its legal implications in the following terms:

> Inability to exercise will-power to control physical acts, provided it is due to abnormality of mind from one of the causes specified [i.e. in the Homicide Act] is sufficient to entitle the accused to the benefit of the [defence]; difficulty in controlling his physical acts depending on the degree of difficulty may be. *It is for the jury to decide on the whole of the evidence* whether such inability or difficulty has, *not as a matter of scientific certainty but on the balance of probabilities* been established, and in the case of difficulty, is so great as to amount in their view to *substantial* impairment of the accused's mental responsibility for his acts.
>
> (*R. v. Byrne* 1960; emphases added)

Four further points arise from this statement. First, such a definition reinforces the much wider interpretation of mental disorder than that within the more narrow confines of the M'Naghten "rules" referred to earlier. Second, it seems to acknowledge that will power can be impaired, introducing to some extent the American concept of "irresistible impulse" – a concept not popular hitherto with English jurists. (See also Reznek 1997: 24 et seq.) Third, we can infer that the judiciary could permit the view that the mind can be answerable for behaviour. Fourth, the question of *substantial* impairment was also a matter for the jury to decide, but *how* it arose and its *causes* were questions for the doctors. As to the meaning of substantial, it has been held subsequently that "'substantial' does not mean total . . . the mental responsibility need not be totally impaired, destroyed altogether. At the other end of the scale, substantial does not mean trivial or minimal" (*R. v. Lloyd* 1967). Some of these and associated problems have been usefully analysed by Mitchell in two fairly recent papers

(Mitchell 1997a, 1997b). In order to illustrate further some of the problems referred to already, I now present four cases.

### Case illustration 1.1: Peter Sutcliffe

The case of Peter Sutcliffe attracted such notoriety and media interest that some of the key issues concerning the diminishment, or otherwise, of his "mental responsibility for his acts" have tended to be overshadowed by the horrendous nature of his crimes and the furore surrounding the circumstances of his detection or, to be more precise, his non-detection over a five-year period. The history of the latter has recently been described in detail by Michael Bilton (2003). Sutcliffe's case, and the others to be described shortly, highlight in compelling fashion many of the issues I have sought to address in this chapter thus far. A court will frequently accept a plea of diminished responsibility on the basis of agreed and uncontested psychiatric evidence: that is, the psychiatrists for the prosecution and the defence are all agreed on the diagnosis. Acceptance by the courts of pleas of diminished responsibility on *agreed* psychiatric evidence has only occurred since 1962. Between 1957 and 1962, following a High Court decision in *R. v. Matheson* (1958), the issue had to be put to a jury in all cases (Bartholomew 1983). It will be recalled that the issue of diminished responsibility is raised by the defence and its proof rests on a *balance of probabilities*. If such a plea is accepted by the judge (in a non-contested case), or by a jury (after a trial of the issue), a person who would otherwise have been liable to conviction for murder will be convicted of manslaughter, allowing the judge a wide discretion in sentencing.

As is now well known, the trial judge in Sutcliffe's case (Mr Justice Boreham refused (as was his right) to accept the agreed views of both prosecution and defence and decided to put the issue of Sutcliffe's mental responsibility for his acts to a jury. It is important to ask why this very experienced judge embarked on this particular course of action when four highly experienced senior forensic psychiatrists were all agreed on Sutcliffe's disordered mental state.

There are a number of possibilities. First, although a plea of Section 2 diminished responsibility is only available in a murder case, the judge may have been very conscious of the fact that the public might have considered it to be a somewhat contradictory and idiosyncratic state of affairs that allowed Sutcliffe to plead *guilty* to the *attempted murder* of seven women and *not guilty* to the murder of 13 (when the fact that he had actually *committed* the murders was not being disputed – merely his criminal responsibility for so doing). To the general public (but, of course, not to the legally informed) it might have seemed somewhat disturbing that such pleas were acceptable when, presumably, only good fortune saved the lives of seven of his victims. Hence, the judge might well have considered that "public interest" demanded that the issues involved be made absolutely clear.

Second, the judge would no doubt have been very conscious of the public's more general concern about the case and its notoriety. It might well have seemed to him to have been doing both the case and the public less than full justice to have disposed of it without a full and public hearing about the defendant's alleged motivation and mental state.

Third, the judge, having read the papers in the case before the actual hearing, might well have wondered at the apparent discrepancies between what Sutcliffe was alleged to have told the police in the course of their prolonged interviews with him, what he was alleged to have confided to the prison officers and what he told the psychiatrists who examined him (see Spencer 1984: 106–13 for a full discussion of some of these aspects).

Fourth, no doubt the judge would have considered the possibility of putting the case to a jury in the knowledge that, following a conviction of murder, he would not only have to pass a life sentence, but could also, by virtue of Section 1(2) of the Murder (Abolition of Death Penalty) Act 1965, add *a recommendation as to what the minimum sentence should be*. Such a possibility would not be available to him in a finding of Section 2 manslaughter. It is of interest to note here that the House of Lords has recently decided that a life sentence imposed on a mentally ill offender is not incompatible with Article 3 of the European Convention on Human Rights (*R. v. Drew* (2003) UKHL 25 in *The Independent Law Report*, 15 May 2003: 18). The judge would doubtless also be mindful that a sentence of imprisonment would also keep control over Sutcliffe's eventual release within the penal system even, as it eventually turned out, he was subsequently transferred to hospital.

For all these reasons, the judge's decision to put the whole issue to the jury seems very understandable, although the final outcome of indefinite detention in prison or hospital could have been predicted.

According to the media account of the trial we witnessed the somewhat unusual (some would say undignified) spectacle of all the psychiatric witnesses being cross-examined by the prosecution counsel – including their own, when only a few hours before all the parties in the case had been agreed on the course of action that should be taken. The manner in which the psychiatric evidence was received and commented on in the press during the trial revealed very clearly the ambivalence of society towards the intervention of psychiatry in matters of criminal behaviour referred to earlier in this chapter. This ambivalence is, of course, compounded by the fact that our adversarial system of justice does not lend itself readily to the discussion or deliberation of complex and finely drawn issues of intent and motivation. Psychiatrists, in their day-to-day practice, are accustomed to dealing with grey areas of motivation and far less with the black and white issues of fact demanded by the constraints of our justice system. Some people have suggested that the psychiatrists were "wrong-footed" in court; they were certainly subjected to a good deal of criticism, if not ridicule. On going over the various press accounts of the case, this appears to have been quite ill founded, given the constraints already referred to and the fact that journalistic accounts are inevitably highly selective. (See Prins 1983 and, in particular, the notes appended therein for references to some of the press accounts.)

Although I shall be considering the relationship between mental disorders and criminality in some detail later in the book, it is appropriate at this point to make brief comment about the relationship between some forms of schizophrenic illness and crime, since a form of schizophrenic illness was the diagnosis the psychiatrists gave to Sutcliffe's condition.

We can say that the relationship between schizophrenic illnesses and crime in general is very slight and not often *causally* related. However, the *particular* diagnosis given for Sutcliffe's disorder was *paranoid* schizophrenia. This form of schizophrenia is characterized to a large extent (but not exclusively) by delusions. There are a number of well-documented cases concerning persons who have committed homicide and other serious offences while under the influence of these, the most historic of these probably being the case of Daniel M'Naghten already referred to.

One of the most important points to remember about the paranoid disorders (and their variants) is that sufferers are likely to appear quite sane and rational in most aspects of their lives. It is only when the subject matter of their delusional beliefs is touched on that their symptoms may emerge with unexpected and frightening impact. It is not altogether surprising, therefore, that Sutcliffe was able to cover his tracks, because one can be highly paranoid, yet also be highly evasive and cunning. It is also true to say that problems encountered by the police in linking vital pieces of information only served to facilitate Sutcliffe's opportunities for evasion. As already indicated, the individual's delusional system may be so well encapsulated (highly contained) that it may not emerge until and unless the matters on which the system has fastened are explored in a detailed and systematic manner by a skilled psychiatric assessor. It is understandable, therefore, that the police and prison officers obtained one impression of Sutcliffe and the psychiatrists another; much depends on the questions one asks and the manner and skill with which one asks them.

This, of course, presents its own difficulties, for one's questioning may be determined by a particular set of preconceptions. At the time of his trial, other diagnoses of Sutcliffe's disorder appear to have been ruled out. We know that he is alleged to have once suffered a head injury. In some instances, if head injuries are serious enough to result in brain damage, they can produce delusional symptoms (as in Hadfield's case referred to earlier). Neither does a diagnosis of psychopathic disorder appear to have been entertained. Given his past history, background and apparent long-standing paranoid ideation, such a diagnosis would seem unlikely. However, an unequivocal diagnosis of paranoid schizophrenia does not seem to be altogether without its difficulties, given Sutcliffe's conflicting statements and his apparent capacity for acting with insight in order to avoid detection. Spencer suggests that:

> In his *apparent* simulation of insanity, his alleged and God-inspired delusions and the sadistic undertones of his killings, Sutcliffe falls exactly halfway between the murderers John George Haigh and Neville Heath.
>
> (1984: 112–13; emphasis added)

Spencer also suggests that a more precise defence for Sutcliffe might have been that he suffered:

[F]rom a clear-cut abnormality of mind of a strangely paranoid type. Starting in 1969, with an unexplained attack on a prostitute and enhanced in 1979 by trivial humiliation, it developed into a bizarre, homicidal hatred of women, particularly prostitutes or alleged prostitutes. It continues with a strongly sadistic overtone and possibly − perhaps probably − as the result of a low-grade schizophrenic process. Whether or not the basis was schizophrenic, there was surely substantially more than minimal or trivial diminishment of responsibility?

(1984: 113; see also Burn 1984 and Jones 1992)

The rest of the story is well known and can be recounted briefly. The jury returned a majority (10−2) verdict finding Sutcliffe guilty of murder. It is worth emphasizing here that in doing so they did not *necessarily* reject the proposition that Sutcliffe was suffering from a form of paranoid schizophrenia, only that it did *not constitute an abnormality of mind of sufficient degree to substantially impair his mental responsibility for his acts*. He was sentenced to life imprisonment, Mr Justice Boreham making a recommendation that he serve a minimum of 30 years. One year later he was refused leave to appeal. Subsequent events seem to have vindicated the views of the psychiatrists who examined him before his trial. His mental state deteriorated in prison and he was the victim of an assault by a fellow prisoner. His severity of symptoms and his vulnerability to attack presented very real problems for the prison medical authorities; eventually the Home Secretary gave authority for his transfer to a high-security hospital (Broadmoor) where he is currently detained. It is of interest to note that, even in a secure hospital setting, he has been the subject of a further serious assault by a fellow patient.

The Sutcliffe case illustrates some of the problems involved in the diminished responsibility defence, not the least of these being the area of tension that inevitably exists between psychiatry and the law. Most of these problems would be avoided if we abandoned the mandatory life sentence for murder and allowed the judiciary the same sentencing discretion as in manslaughter cases. Such a proposal has had the backing of the judiciary and those who work in the criminal justice system for many years. Sadly, the political will to agree to such a change has not been forthcoming. One can only conclude, as I did in the second edition of this book, that this is due to the establishment's overcautious approach and the apparent sacrifice of more effective and more humane disposals on the altar of political expediency.

### Case illustration 1.2: Dennis Nilsen

In 1983 very similar problems were to emerge in the almost equally notorious case of Dennis Nilsen. Nilsen admitted having sex with and killing 15 young men and subsequently dissecting, boiling and burning their bodies in order to dispose of them. He was sentenced to life imprisonment, the judge adding a minimum recommendation that he serve 25 years. The jury had convicted him of murder by a majority verdict of 10−2 on all but one of the counts against him. In the last case they reached a unanimous verdict. In arguing for a manslaughter verdict Nilsen's counsel had tried to convince the jury that "anybody guilty of such horrific acts must be out of his mind" (*The Times*, 5 November 1983). In Nilsen's case, unlike Sutcliffe's, there had been no unanimity of opinion as to Nilsen's abnormality of mind among the psychiatrists who examined him. Neither was Nilsen's alleged mental disorder as floridly psychotic or akin to a layperson's notion of "madness" as was Sutcliffe's. Nilsen was said to be suffering from a severe personality disorder manifested in part by abnormal sexual behaviour. The psychiatrists disagreed not only as to the nature of the diagnosis in his case, but also as to whether it constituted an abnormality of mind within the meaning of the Homicide Act. However, no one reading the press accounts of Nilsen's life history, the nature of his crimes and his attitudes towards his victims, could fail to agree that his behaviour was decidedly abnormal by any standards (Guardian, 5 November 1983; *The Times*, 5 November 1983). (For a detailed account of Nilsen's developmental history, life and behaviour, see Masters 1985.)

One of the key issues that emerges in Nilsen's case is similar to that in Sutcliffe's – namely the difficulty involved in fitting the inherently imprecise concepts used in psychiatry into the confining straitjacket of the law. There is an important difference between the two cases. Sutcliffe's disorder was one that might be improved (if not cured) by treatment. The more intrusive features of his delusions could be treated, and abated to some extent, by medication. In Nilsen's case, his personality disorder, even if it had constituted an abnormality of mind, was considered to be largely untreatable so that a penal as opposed to a mental health disposal may seem only marginally less helpful. However, as we shall see in Chapter 4, some severe personality disorders are capable of minimal improvement given the right approach and environment.

### Case illustration 1.3: "M.T."

In June 1984 "M.T." was jailed for life for the manslaughter of his second wife. Following a nine-day trial, he was found guilty of manslaughter, but not murder, by a unanimous jury that took only two and a half hours to reach its verdict. It was alleged in court that "M.T.", who had had a disturbed and somewhat tragic childhood, lacked maturity and showed a marked inability to control his impulses and emotions. Such a description resonates with that in the case of *R. v. Byrne* quoted earlier in this chapter.

The facts in "M.T.'s" case are, to some extent, only minimally less bizarre than those in Sutcliffe's and Nilsen's. Admittedly he had only committed one crime, but the circumstances of that single killing and the aftermath seem not only gruesome but highly pathological. According to press reports (*Guardian*, 30 June 1984) "M.T." shot his wife after she had allegedly taunted him beyond endurance concerning her sexual relations with members of both sexes. After killing her, he moved her body around the house for a week or so, occasionally talking to and kissing her corpse. He allegedly subsequently placed her body in a half-built sauna in the house. Five months later he decided to take the body to the West Country with a view to burying it. This proved unsuccessful (because of drought). He eventually left the body in some bracken overlooking a river, having cut off her head and taking it with him; it was subsequently found in the boot of his car. In "M.T.'s" case two psychiatrists testified that his responsibility was diminished and one testified against that view. It is difficult to tell whether the jury was more influenced by the opinions of the two psychiatrists who viewed him as suffering from a disorder that would substantially diminish his responsibility or whether it was his bizarre activities following the killing that led them to the view that he "must have been mad" to have behaved in such a fashion. But was his behaviour more bizarre than Nilsen's? Nilsen had sex with his victims before and after death and then lived with the results of what he had done until he could no longer dispose of their corpses safely. Samuels has some very apt words on this latter aspect:

> If a defendant just kills his victim for what appears to be a very ordinary motive such as greed or jealousy, diminished responsibility stands little chance of being established, but if the defendant has a history of mental trouble, goes in for perverted sexual practices with the victim before and after death, *mutilates the body, cuts it up* [or] sends it through the post . . . then the more horrible the killing the more likely diminished responsibility will be established, because *the further removed from normal behaviour the behaviour of the defendant, the more he appears to be mentally ill*, or so the submission runs.
>
> (1975: 199–200; emphases added)

### Case illustration 1.4: Jeffrey Dahmer

For my last example I turn to the USA. Although Jeffrey Dahmer committed his numerous murders in the USA and was dealt with by the American criminal justice system, his case has certain points in common with that of Dennis Nilsen. One of these was the attempt by his defence counsel to satisfy the court that his responsibility for his crimes was diminished by an abnormality of mind. In Dahmer's case, a defence of insanity had to be entered, because in the USA there is no exact equivalent of our Homicide Act. The relevant state statute contains reference to a lack of "substantial capacity to appreciate the wrongfulness of his conduct or conform his conduct to the requirements of the law" (Masters 1993: 227).

Dahmer's long career of killing ended, as had Sutcliffe's, by chance. He had been apprehended on another matter by two Milwaukee police patrolmen. On going to his apartment they were confronted by a gruesome collection of Polaroid pictures of dead males, severed heads and partially dismembered torsos. Later, the police were to discover even more tangible evidence – a refrigerator containing a severed head, a freezer containing two more heads and a human torso. Two skulls and a complete skeleton were found in a filing cabinet, as was a large plastic drum containing three further torsos in various stages of decomposition. Following his arrest, and for the ensuing two weeks. Dahmer confessed "that he had killed sixteen men in Milwaukee over a period of four years" (Masters 1993: 4).

To the outside world, Dahmer was a quiet, inoffensive factory worker. It is of interest to note that he had been the subject of investigation at one stage for unwelcome acts of indecency with other males in a "bath house". However, the proprietors are said not to have wished for the matter to be taken further on account of the adverse publicity it might have occasioned. It is also of some concern to note that on another occasion he had been convicted of a sexual assault and that, while waiting sentence for that offence, he had committed his fifth murder. With hindsight, it would seem that he had already given indications of his sinister preoccupation with deviant sexuality and with death. From his history it emerges that he had an overpowering need to possess and control his victims – to the point of collecting and storing their remains after death. This could well be regarded as a variant of necrophilia. (See Chapter 6 for further discussion of this topic.)

As in Nilsen's case, Dahmer's advocate sought to convince the court that a person who indulged in such compulsive behaviour must be mad rather than merely bad, but that he could in fact "retain a perfectly clear idea of what is right and good and still be compelled to do what is wrong and bad" (Masters 1993: 98). Much play was made of his long-standing sexual problems, prolonged alcohol abuse and difficulties in making social relationships with both males and females. Despite the expert evidence given on his behalf, his plea failed. The jury retired on Friday 14 February 1992 and returned earlier than anticipated with their verdicts – majority verdicts of 10–2 on five of the counts – on Saturday 15 February. He was sentenced to life imprisonment with no eligibility for parole before 70 years and was subsequently murdered in prison.

## Other "erosions" of responsibility

### Infanticide

Apart from the Homicide Act, the law makes *specific* provision for the erosion of responsibility in cases of killing in one other way. This is through the Infanticide Act 1938. This enactment (which amended an earlier Act of 1922, which, in turn, had revised much earlier legislation) was introduced in order to relieve from the death sentence for murder a woman who, under certain specific circumstances, had caused the death of her children. In such cases judges had always felt a great deal of reluctance in having to impose the death penalty (Bluglass 1990). In the context of this chapter, its creation is of interest in that it gave statutory recognition to a *specific state of mind* in a *woman* who caused, by any wilful act or omission, the death of her child *under the age of 12 months* when the balance of her mind was disturbed by reason of her not having fully recovered from the *effect of giving birth to a child or by reason of the effect of lactation (breast feeding) consequent upon that birth*. The Act was passed at a time when more emphasis was placed on what was considered to be the adverse effects of childbirth on a woman's *mental state* than would perhaps be considered as relevant today. (See also Buchanan 2000: 102.) If we examine the figures for infanticide convictions, they are very small; for the past decade, the average number of convictions every year has been about four. Almost all cases are dealt with by a community penalty such as probation (community rehabilitation) (Home Office 2003: Tables 1.09 and 1.10). There are almost always adverse social conditions or a highly complex personal situation that would more likely than not enable the case to be dealt with as a case of diminished responsibility under the provision of the Homicide Act. The complexities and anomalies are exemplified strikingly in the following case – reported in the *Guardian* newspaper:

> A woman killed her four-year old daughter shortly after the latter witnessed her mother killing her seventeen-month old baby brother by strangulation. In this case, the prosecution accepted pleas of diminished responsibility and the woman was discharged on condition she receive hospital treatment. Defending counsel said the woman had experienced a slow build-up of pressure and had suffered a depressive disorder from the birth of her son. In theory, had she killed the child within the first twelve months of his life instead of at seventeen months, she could have been charged with infanticide as well as perhaps being charged with the murder of the four-year old.
>
> (*Guardian*, 27 November 1984: 5)

This case example illustrates the somewhat outmoded and arbitrary nature of the infanticide defence. The Butler Committee put forward the view that the offence could be subsumed under the umbrella of diminished responsibility, but the Criminal Law Revision Committee favoured its retention (1980: paras 100–104: 114: 1). For a discussion of some of the implications of any change and their historical context see Lambie (2001).

### Provocation

Buchanan (2000) notes that "the defence of provocation emerged in English law in the seventeenth century" (p. 50). The Homicide Act of 1957 made "statutory provision for provocation to reduce what would otherwise be murder to manslaughter" (p. 50) thus avoiding a conviction for the former. The defence hinges on the presence or otherwise of a *sudden* loss of control and whether or not a *reasonable* person would have acted as the defendant did. Numerous difficulties have arisen in the courts' interpretations of these and have led to some contradictory decisions from the Court of Appeal (see later). It is not difficult to see that a claim of an abnormality of mind might be put forward as a reason for the defendant's response to provocation. Lord Justice Lawton held that psychiatric evidence was not necessarily admissible and in the case of *R. v. Turner* (1975) stated that:

[T]rial by psychiatrists would be likely to take the place of trial by jury and magistrates . . . psychiatry has not yet become a satisfactory substitute for the common sense of juries and magistrates on matters within their experience of life.

(quoted in Hall Williams 1980: 279)

However, in many cases the dividing line between those behaviours that can be regarded as "normal" and those that can be regarded as "abnormal" may not be quite as clear cut as Lord Justice Lawton was implying. Some support for my contention is afforded by Dell who found in her study that "in a few cases, the jury had found the defendant guilty on grounds both of diminished responsibility and provocation" (Dell 1984: 4).

More recently, other complicated legal issues have arisen; it has been held for many years that the events leading to an act carried out under circumstances of alleged provocation must be recent. In the case of *R. v. Ahulwalia* (1992) it was held by the Court of Appeal that a judge's direction to a jury:

[O]n a murder trial defining "provocation" as conduct causing a "sudden loss of self control" was in accordance with well established law and could not be faulted. If the law was wrong it was for Parliament to change it, not the courts.

However, it should be noted here that the defendant, Ahulwalia, won her appeal against a murder conviction on other grounds. A great deal of concern has also been expressed as to the apparent arbitrary fashion in which acts of provocation have been defined. For example, those who have been worried about the rights of "battered women" have been concerned that years of assaultive behaviour by husbands or partners that is patiently borne by their victims may not constitute a situation of provocation that culminates in legal retaliation or defence. The fact that it has to be a result of a *sudden* and *recent* incident of violent behaviour seems to be quite arbitrary. One has much sympathy for this view and, as stated earlier, the courts seem to reach conflicting decisions. For example, at Belfast Crown Court a woman succeeded in her plea of provocation in respect of a charge of murdering her husband. She had stabbed him to death after she had "snapped" during a drunken row. The judge is said to have told her: "I am satisfied that what caused you to snap was not just one evening's ill treatment but the accumulation of six years' abuse." He placed her on probation (*The Independent*, 2 February 1993: 5). Another case concerned a "devoted father who battered and strangled his unfaithful wife". He was said to have "snapped after years of humiliation at the hands of his wife". The judge is said to have told him: "I have never before encountered a more extreme case of *persistent* provocation [emphasis added] or degrading behaviour by a woman towards a man . . . you were goaded beyond anyone's breaking point" (*The Independent*, 6 April 1993: 3). The recent somewhat contradictory state of the law has been usefully stated and supported by a number of further case examples by Rix (2001); see also Hall (1998). Clearly, the present state of affairs can only be regarded as unsatisfactory.

### The special case of children

In English law, children below the age of 10 cannot be found guilty of an offence. Many people consider that this age is far too low and that it should be raised. Most other jurisdictions set it considerably higher, some even into the late teens. The issue was thrown into sharp relief as a result of the trial of the two 10-year old boys who abducted, and subsequently killed, the toddler James Bulger. In brief, these two boys abducted their victim from a shopping mall (where he had, for a very few but crucial moments, evaded the vigilant eye of his mother). They took him to a lonely spot two or three miles away, killed him with a horrifying degree of ferocity and then placed his body on a railway line. To add to the horror of the event, it transpired at their trial at Preston Crown Court that a number of adults might have seen the two boys with the unhappy and allegedly struggling infant, but had not felt it appropriate to intervene. Fortunately, the killing of children by other children is a rare event, but when it does occur, it produces traumatic effects for all concerned. The trial of the two boys at a Crown Court raised many concerns, not least their capacity to understand the proceedings in the austere setting of such a court. However, it is fair to say that some attempt was made to make the physical circumstances and atmosphere less intimidating. The manner of their trial received the attentions of the European Court of Human Rights, which ruled that an open trial in an adult court was intimidating for such young children. In February 2000 the former Lord Chief Justice, Lord Bingham, brought in new rules for dealing with such cases, which affects all defendants under the age of 18 facing serious criminal charges in Crown Courts in England and Wales. Lord Bingham's direction includes a ban on robes and wigs. He stated that "the trial process should not itself expose the young defendant to avoidable humiliation or distress". Other improvements should include the provision of more "user-friendly" courtroom arrangements, in which all the participants are on, or almost on, the same level. The direction further calls for young defendants to be free to sit in a place that permits easy, informal communication with their lawyers and others (paraphrased from *The Independent*, 17 February 2000). Further aspects of the case are considered in Chapter 5.

### Some other mental defences

I now consider, albeit briefly, some aspects of what can best be described as involuntary conduct and the nature of the state known as *automatism*.

*Involuntary conduct*

An act or omission is considered to be *involuntary* where it can clearly be shown to be beyond the control of the person. A frequently quoted case is that of *Hill v. Baxter* (1958) in which it was alleged that the defendant had contravened the Road Traffic Act by driving dangerously. The defendant pleaded that he had become unconscious and that he remembered nothing of the alleged incident. His plea was accepted by the magistrates on the grounds that severe loss of memory must have been caused by the sudden onset of illness that had overcome him. However, the High Court did not accept this finding, suggesting that he might just have fallen asleep. In expressing their view in this particular case, they did qualify it by stating that there might be some states of unconsciousness, or even clouded (interrupted) consciousness, such as those in a stroke or epileptic seizure, which might exclude liability in similar cases. One of the judges hearing the appeal suggested that similar exculpation from liability might have arisen if, for example, a man had been attacked by a swarm of bees and, because of their action had lost directional control of the vehicle. Hart, in his classic work (1968), had made a useful twofold distinction between those situations where the subject is conscious and where he or she is unconscious. I paraphrase it as follows:

1  *Conscious*
   (a)  Physical compulsion by another person.
   (b)  Muscular control impaired by disease, as in cases of chorea (for example Huntington's disorder).
   (c)  Reflex muscular contraction (as in the hypothetical case of the swarm of bees mentioned earlier).
2  *Unconscious*
   (a)  Natural sleep at normal time (see later discussion).
   (b)  Drunken stupor. Hart cited the example of a woman in a drunken state "overlaying" her child and thus killing it. (It could, of course, equally have been a man.)
   (c)  Sleep brought on by fatigue (as, for example, in the case of the motorist cited earlier).
   (d)  Loss of consciousness involving collapse, in certain medical conditions such as epilepsy or hypoglycaemic states.

It is likely that many of these states could lead to a successful plea for negation or serious reduction of criminal liability. Courts will always have to interpret such pleas according to individual circumstances, so that no general ruling can be found in quoted law reports or legal texts that would be appropriate in all cases. For example, if I fall asleep at the wheel of my car and cause an accident, am I to be considered to be entirely exempted from liability or will the court suggest, as it did in the well-known case of *Kay v. Butterworth* (1945), that I must have known that drowsiness was overcoming me and that, because of this, I should have stopped driving and averted an accident? (For an erudite but highly readable discussion of this topic, see Mackay 1995: Chapter 1.)

### Automatism

Automatism is a phenomenon that may occur in situations where loss of consciousness is the cause of an *involuntary* (i.e. unintentional) act. Such an act may, in certain circumstances, be held to constitute a crime. For legal purposes then, automatism means being in a state capable of action but not being conscious of that action. A well-known definition was that given in the case of *Bratty v. Attorney General for Northern Ireland* (1963): "The state of a person who, though capable of action, is not conscious of what he is doing. It means unconscious, involuntary action and is a defence because the mind does not know what is being done" (as quoted in Buchanan 2000: 97). Two types of automatism have been (somewhat arbitrarily) distinguished by the courts on various occasions – sane automatism and insane automatism. To oversimplify somewhat, it is the case currently that an insane automatism is one that is caused by some internal factor "and which has on one occasion at least manifested itself in violence" (Buchanan 2000: 98). The dividing line between sane and insane automatism is not clear cut and courts have interpreted the differences in various ways. For a finding of sane automatism there usually has to be some *external* cause such as a blow to the head, whereas an *internal* cause would consist of some form of abnormality of mind (as, for example, in a plea of diminished responsibility). A finding of insane automatism will lead to a disposal under the Criminal Procedure (Insanity and Unfitness to Plead) Act 1991. A finding of sane automatism will lead to an acquittal. Courts tend to favour restricting the automatism defence, holding that a state of automatism is not a defence if the accused is in some way to blame or is at fault for getting into that condition: for example, through getting into a state of acute intoxication. (See later discussion also.) A review of some of the recent case law reveals that it usually has been held that a person is responsible for the consequences of his decision either to do something (such as to ingest drink or other drugs) or not to stop some activity (for example, continuing to drive while beginning to feel overcome by the need for sleep).

One more obvious form of automatism is that of being in a somnambulistic state. Fenwick's monograph on the clinical aspects of automatism (1990) provides an excellent extended discussion of the relationship between somnambulism (sleep automatism) and criminal behaviour (at pp. 12–18). In particular, he offers detailed guidance for those engaged in having to try to establish a defence to a criminal charge on these grounds. He cites a number of important diagnostic and prognostic factors, such as childhood and family history, disorientation on awakening, availability of evidence from witnesses to the event, amnesia for the event, trigger factors, lack of attempts to conceal the crime, the motiveless or out of character nature of the crime and, in cases of violent crime, the possibility of a previous history of violence during a period of sleep automatism. From time to time, successful pleas in these cases are reported in the press. For example, a teenager almost killed a friend during a nightmare, but was cleared of attempted murder by a Crown Court. It was alleged that, in the course of the nightmare, he stabbed the friend with a kitchen knife and beat him with a wooden club. A psychiatrist told the court: "He committed this act during his sleep – during a night of terror." The doctor told the court that he "knew of eight or nine similar cases" (*The Independent*, 9 March 1990: 5). In this case, the defendant secured an acquittal. However, as already noted, the law seems somewhat capricious in its interpretation and implementation. For example, in the case of *R. v. Burgess* (1991) the decision was somewhat different. Here, it was held that Burgess who, while sleepwalking, acted violently without being consciously aware of what he was doing, was suffering from *a disease of the mind* and not from non-insane automatism and so could be found not guilty of the offence by reason of insanity. At his trial, Burgess had admitted attacking a sleeping female friend by hitting her on the head with a bottle and grasping her around the throat. He said that he, too, had fallen asleep and was sleepwalking. Such apparently contradictory cases are not uncommon and the law is in obvious need of clarification. (See for example Yeo 2002 for a discussion of the ambiguities in the law; although he cites Canadian cases, much of what he says can be extended to other jurisdictions such as the UK.)

## Intoxicating substances

It is not uncommon in criminal cases, particularly those involving serious violence against persons or property, for a plea to be made by the accused that their liability for their criminal acts should be diminished because of the effects of taking alcohol and/or other drugs. The law holds that being in a state of intoxication is no defence to a criminal charge; however, if the offence requires specific intent (such as that which would be required to fulfil the legal requirements for a finding of guilt on a charge of murder) the fact that the accused had been drinking might help to negate specific intent and thus might provide a defence. (See Mackay 1995 for an extended discussion of this matter.) Other crimes requiring specific intent are theft, fraud and burglary (see, for example, the cases of *R. v. Burns* (1973) and *R. v. Stephenson* (1979)). However, various legal decisions and their interpretations appear to suggest some continuing conflict of opinion on this matter. For example, in the case of *Bratty* already referred to, it was held that, in crimes such as murder, where proof of a specific intent was required, the intent *might* be negated by drunkenness and the accused might thus be convicted of a lesser offence, for example manslaughter or even unlawful wounding.

Other cases indicate just how complex the matter is. For example, in the case of *R. v. Gittens* (1984) the appellant had been tried on counts of murder of his wife and the rape and murder of his 15-year-old stepdaughter. An issue arose as to whether his admitted abnormality of mind which substantially impaired his "mental responsibility" was caused by drink or the drugs he had taken, as the prosecution contended, or whether it was due to *inherent causes coupled with the ingestion of drugs and drink* as the defence sought to establish. The jury had been directed by the trial judge to decide whether it was, on the one hand, the *drink and drugs* or, on the other, the *inherent causes* which were the main factors that caused him to act as he did. He was convicted of murder but appealed on the grounds that the jury had been misdirected, the proper question for them being whether the abnormality arising from the inherent causes substantially impaired his responsibility for his actions. His appeal was upheld and his conviction for murder substituted by a conviction for Section 2 manslaughter. Giving judgment, Lord Lane, a former Lord Chief Justice, said that it was improper *in any circumstances* to invite the jury to decide the question of diminished responsibility on the basis of "what was the substantial cause of the defendant's behaviour". The jury were to be directed, first, to disregard what they thought the effect on the defendant of the alcohol-and-drug-induced mental abnormality was, since discussion of such abnormality was *not* within Section 2(1). They were *then* to go on to consider whether the combined effect of *other matters* that *did* fall within Section 2(1) amounted to such abnormality of mind as substantially impaired his mental responsibility within the meaning of substantial as set out in *R. v. Lloyd* (1967). This being so in this case, the jury, said Lord Lane, had been misdirected.

In the case of *R. v. Lipman* (1970), the accused claimed successfully that he was under the influence of LSD (lysergic acid diethylamide) when he killed the girl he was sleeping with. Part of Lipman's defence consisted of the claim that as a result of his being in a drug-induced state he thought he was being attacked by snakes; the immediate cause of his unlucky companion's death was asphyxia caused by having part of a sheet stuffed into her mouth. However, in the later well-known case of *R. v. Majewski* (1977) the House of Lords held that, in the case of an impulsive act such as an assault, intoxication of itself would not constitute a defence. It was alleged that Majewski had been a drug addict and that he also had a personality disorder. He had been drinking heavily on the day in question and had mixed alcohol with quantities of sodium membutal and dexedrine. Having ingested what must have amounted to a highly lethal "cocktail", Majewski became involved in a fracas in a pub in the course of which he assaulted the landlord and another customer. Having been removed from the premises, he returned, brandishing a piece of broken glass (Hall Williams 1980). The case of Majewski tends to support the view that the law sees the ingestion of alcohol and other drugs as aggravating rather than mitigating factors and that voluntary intoxication is no defence. However, if an accused could show that he or she was in a state of *involuntary* intoxication, he or she may have a defence where, for example, the accused had been deliberately drugged or had had intoxicants poured into a non-intoxicating beverage without his or her knowledge. A form of defence in crimes requiring evidence of specific intent will not be likely to succeed if an accused takes alcohol against medical advice after using prescribed drugs or, for example, if he or she fails to take insulin for a diabetic condition. Mackay has drawn attention to the current problems with the present law and suggests that it is time reforms were made (Mackay 1995: 176–8).

Finally, Rix has suggested that we should make a distinction between *intoxication* and *drunkenness*. Such a clinical distinction would have interesting and potentially useful legal implications. He proposes that:

> (1) The term "alcohol intoxication" should refer to a state in which alcohol is in the body; (2) its diagnosis should be based on toxicological evidence for the presence of alcohol in body fluids or tissues; and (3) the term "drunkenness" should be used to describe behaviour displayed by people who have consumed, believe that they have consumed or want others to believe they have consumed, alcohol.
>
> (Rix 1989: 100)

## Summary and conclusion

This chapter has, inevitably, been somewhat discursive; in order to be brief I have had to take some shortcuts. Those wishing to pursue the topic in more depth will find the references and suggestions for further reading of value. The law in relation to responsibility and the various ways in which it may be eroded has followed a complex and everchanging route. For example, developments in our understanding of mental processes have affected the way in which personal responsibility for behaviour has to be viewed today, compared with 250 years ago. In addition, public attitudes to those who practise the art and science of medicine, particularly psychiatry, affect the climate of opinion in which such practitioners and judges, lawyers and others play out their roles within the arena of the courts. The ways in which responsibility may be eroded may be summarized as follows:

> *Total erosion* may be afforded by a finding of not guilty by reason of insanity and of unfitness to plead (the special verdicts).

*Partial erosion* may be afforded by a finding of diminished responsibility (but only in homicide cases) and in infanticide.

Finally, *pleas in mitigation* may be based on states of mind caused by, for example, provocation, automatism and intoxication.

In the following chapter I provide an account of the disposals available to the courts for those adjudged to be mentally disturbed in a variety of ways and the methods through which these disposals are implemented. At this point, it is important to emphasize the need to view the information presented in this book *as a whole*. The material has been divided in somewhat arbitrary fashion merely to achieve clarity of presentation.

## References

Bartholomew, A. A. (1983) *R. v. Sutcliffe*, "Letter", *Medicine, Science and the Law* 23: 222–3.

Bettelheim, B. (1983) *Freud and Man's Soul*, London, Chatto & Windus.

Bilton, M. (2003) *Wicked Beyond Belief: The Hunt for the Yorkshire Ripper*, London: HarperCollins.

Bluglass, R. (1990) "Infanticide and filicide", in R. Bluglass and P. Bowden (eds), *Principles and Practice of Forensic Psychiatry*, London: Churchill Livingstone.

Buchanan, A. (2000) *Psychiatric Aspects of Justification, Excuse and Mitigation: The Jurisprudence of Mental Abnormality in Anglo-American Criminal Law*, London: Jessica Kingsley.

Burn, G. (1984) *Somebody's Husband, Somebody's Son: The Story of Peter Sutcliffe*, London: Heinemann.

Clarke, M. J. (1975) "The impact of social science on conceptions of responsibility", *British Journal of Law and Society* 2: 32–44.

Collins, P. and White, T. (2003) "Depression, homicide and diminished responsibility: New Scottish directions", *Medicine, Science and the Law* 43: 195–202.

Crane, A. (1990) *The Kirkland Papers: 1753–1869. The Ferrers Murder and the Lives and Times of a Medical Family in Ashby-de-la-Zouch*, Ashby-de-la-Zouch, Leics: Crane Press.

Crichton, J. H. M., Darjee, R. and Chiswick, D. (2004) "Diminished responsibility in Scotland: New case law", *Journal of Forensic Psychiatry and Psychology* 15: 552–65.

Criminal Law Revision Committee (1980) *Offences Against the Person*, Cmnd 7844, London: HMSO.

Dell, S. (1984) *Murder into Manslaughter, The Diminished Responsibility Defence in Practice*, Maudsley Monograph No. 27, Oxford: Oxford University Press.

Eigen, P. J. (1983) "Historical developments in psychiatric forensic evidence: The British experience", *International Journal of Law and Psychiatry* 6: 423–9.

Fenwick, P. (1990) *Automatism, Medicine and the Law*, Psychological Medicine Monograph Supplement 17, Cambridge: Cambridge University Press.

Gray, N. S., O'Connor, C., Williams, T., Short, J. and Maculloch, M. (2001)

"Fitness to plead: Implications for case-law arising from the Criminal Justice and Public Order Act, 1994", *Journal of Forensic Psychiatry* 12: 52–62.

Griew, E. (1984) "Let's implement Butler on mental disorder and crime", in R. Rideout and B. Jowell (eds), *Current Legal Problems*, London: Sweet & Maxwell (for University College, London).

Grubin, D. (1996) *Fitness to Plead in England and Wales*, Psychology Press on behalf of the Maudsley Hospital, Monograph No. 38, London: Psychology Press.

Hall, J. (1998) "Recent legal issues in the defence of provocation", *Medicine, Science and the Law* 38: 206–10.

Hall Williams, J. E. (1980) "Legal views of psychiatric evidence", *Medicine, Science and the Law* 20: 276–82.

Hamilton, J. (1981) "Diminished responsibility" *British Journal of Psychiatry* 138: 434–6.

Hart, H. L. A. (1968) *Punishment and Responsibility: Essays in the Philosophy of Law*, Oxford: Clarendon Press.

Home Office (2003) *Statistical Bulletin: Crime in England and Wales, 2001/2002: Supplementary Volume* (C. Flood-Page and J. Taylor (eds)), January 2003, 01.03. London: Home Office.

Home Office and Department of Health and Social Security (DHSS) (1975), *Report of the Committee on Mentally Abnormal Offenders* (The Butler Committee), Cmnd 6244, London: HMSO.

Home Office and Scottish Home Department (1957) *Report of the Committee on Homosexual Offences and Prostitution* (The Wolfenden Committee), Cmnd 247, London: HMSO.

Howard, D. and Christopherson, O. (2003) *Statistics of Mentally Disordered Offenders, 2002. Statistical Bulletin*, 14/03, London: Home Office.

Jacobs, F. G. (1971) *Criminal Responsibility*, London: Weidenfeld & Nicolson.

Jones, B. (1992) *Voices from an Evil God*, London: Blake Handbooks.

Kahn, J. (1971) "Uses and abuses of child psychiatry: Problems of diagnosis and treatment of psychiatric disorder", *British Journal of Medical Psychology* 44: 291–302.

Kenny, A. (1984) "The psychiatric expert in court", *Psychological Medicine* 14: 291–302.

Kerrigan, K. (2002) "Psychiatric evidence and mandatory disposal: Article 5 compliance", *Journal of Mental Health Law* 7: 130–8.

Lambie, I. (2001) "Mothers who kill: The crime of infanticide", *International Journal of Law and Psychiatry* 24: 70–80.

Law Commission (1985) *Criminal Law: Codification of the Criminal Law: A Report to the Law Commission*, London: HMSO.

Law Commission (1989) *Criminal Law: A Criminal Code For England and Wales*, London: HMSO.

Mackay, R. (1995) *Mental Condition Defences in the Criminal Law*, Oxford: Clarendon Press.

Masters, B. (1985) *Killing for Company*, London: Jonathan Cape.

—— (1993) *The Shrine of Jeffrey Dahmer*, London: Hodder & Stoughton.

Mitchell, B. (1997a) "Diminished responsibility manslaughter", *Journal of Forensic Psychiatry* 8: 101–17.

Mitchell, B. (1997b) "Putting diminished responsibility into practice: A forensic psychiatric perspective", *Journal of Forensic Psychiatry* 8: 620–34.

Patrick, H. (2003) "Scottish Parliament acts on mental health law reform", *Journal of Mental Health Law* 9: 71–6.

Prins, H. (1983) "Diminished responsibility and the Sutcliffe case: Legal, social and psychiatric aspects", *Medicine, Science and the Law* 23: 17–24.

Reznek, L. (1997) *Evil or Ill: Justifying the Insanity Defence*, London and New York: Routledge.

Rix, J. B. (1989) "Alcohol intoxication or drunkenness: Is there a difference?", *Medicine, Science and the Law* 29: 100–6.

—— (2001) "Battered woman syndrome and the defence of provocation: Two women with something more in common", *Journal of Forensic Psychiatry* 12: 131–49.

Royal Commission on Capital Punishment (1953) *Report*, Cmnd 8932, London: HMSO.

Samuels, A. (1975) "Mental illness and criminal liability", *Medicine, Science and the Law* 15: 198–204.

Smith, R. (1991) "Legal frameworks for psychiatry", in G. E. Berrios and H. Freemen (eds), *150 Years of British Psychiatry, 1841–1991*, London: Gaskell.

Spencer, S. (1984) "Homicide, mental abnormality and offence", in M. and A. Craft (eds), *Mentally Abnormal Offenders*, London: Baillière Tindall.

Szasz, T. (1987) *Insanity, The Idea and its Consequences*, New York: John Wiley & Sons.

—— (1993) "Curing, coercing and claims making – a reply to critics", *British Journal of Psychiatry* 162: 297–800.

Walker, N. (1968) *Crime and Insanity in England* Vol. 1, Edinburgh: Edinburgh University Press.

Ward, T. (2002) "A terrible responsibility: Murder and the insanity defence in England, 1908–39, *International Journal of Law and Psychiatry* 25: 361–77.

Yeo, S. (2002) "Classifying automatism", *International Journal of Law and Psychiatry* 25: 445–58.

## Further reading

The works by Buchanan, Mackay and Reznek are recommended. In addition, for an excellent account of the practice of the law more generally see Smith, Sir John and Hogan, Brian (2002) *Criminal Law*, 10th edn., London: Butterworths. See also: McGuire, J., Mason, T. and O'Kane, A. (eds) (2000) *Behaviour, Crime and Legal Processes: A Guide for Forensic Practitioners*, Chichester: John Wiley & Sons, and Sanders, A. and Young R. (1994) *Criminal Justice*, London: Butterworths. *The Journal of Mental Health Law* and the *Criminal Law Review* will also be found helpful.

# Chapter 2

# Dealing with the consequences

A mighty maze, but not without a plan.
(Pope, *An Essay on Man*, Epistle 1)

## Introductory note

Writing this chapter has proved problematic. This is because, as I write, we are in the midst of a number of legal and administrative changes being put forward by the present government. In the first place there are major changes proposed concerning the way in which members of the judiciary are appointed, substantial modifications to the office of Lord Chancellor and the replacement of the judicial functions of the House of Lords (*The Independent*, 15 July 2003). Other proposed changes include a major revision and codification of the law relating to sex offences (see Chapter 6) and a fundamental revision of mental health legislation. As the timescale for all of these changes is at best very uncertain, I propose to describe *current* methods of dealing with mentally disordered offenders and to summarize the proposed changes as they specifically affect them. Should these changes receive the force of law through Royal Assent before this book is published, I will add an appendix or postscript summarizing them. The aim of this chapter is to provide an outline account of the main methods for dealing with mentally disordered (disturbed) offenders. First of all, I present a short historical background against which current management practices may be viewed. Then follows an account of the methods by which the mentally disturbed and disordered may be diverted from the criminal justice system. Next, we have an outline of the main mental healthcare and penal disposals available to the courts, including brief descriptions of the facilities available. And, finally, I summarize some of the government's proposals for legal and administrative changes.

## Historical context and population

### Historical context

The history of the treatment of mentally disturbed individuals who offend is closely bound up with the history of more general provision for the care of the mentally disordered. Such care and control appear to show a cyclical pattern – a kind of "flavour of the month" quality, often demonstrated more by passionate (and often irrational) conviction than by objective appraisal of need. Those of cynical disposition might well consider that such patterns have much in common with our tendency to "reinvent the wheel". The phenomenon has been ably (and humorously) described in contributions by Allderidge (1979, 1985) and by Parker. The latter has suggested that: "From early times the mentally disordered in England seem to have been afforded some protection, in principle at least, from the customary consequences of wrongdoing" (1980: 46). In a subsequent contribution she stated:

> The practice of confining the insane stretches back more that 600 years in England. The type of detained patient has varied, always including those considered to be dangerous . . . The forms of security employed have changed little over the period, perimeter security, internal locks and bars and individual restraint by both physical and chemical means have been in continuous use to a great or lesser degree in various guises up to the present day.
>
> (Parker 1985: 15)

A similar haphazard and sometimes irrational approach can be seen in the deployment of "community care" services bedevilled as they have been (and to a great extent still are) by underfunding and lack of coordination. (See for example Jewesbury and McCulloch 2002.) History teaches us that to be both "mad" and "bad" places those so designated at the bottom of the social priority pecking order; these are truly "the people nobody owns" (Prins 1993). There is another unfortunate consequence of this attitude – namely, that those who work with such "ownerless" persons may themselves sometimes feel alienated and contaminated and, as such, are as exposed to as much adverse public opinion and action as are their patients or clients. Space precludes a detailed history of the relevant legislation, but a few observations will hopefully provide a context for what is to follow. From as early as the eighteenth century, some provision existed for those who were considered to be mad and dangerous, although, as we saw in Chapter 1, this had to be extended for those found unfit to plead or not guilty by reason of insanity. However, it was not until the nineteenth century that special measures were introduced for the *public* as well as the *private* care and treatment of the mentally disordered. Such provisions were almost entirely custodial in nature and services for "criminal lunatics", as they were then called, developed separately and in piecemeal fashion as, for example, in cases such as Hadfield's described in Chapter 1. In the early twentieth century the trend to provide more specific legislation continued; for example, the Mental Deficiency Act of 1913 enabled courts to deal more effectively with "mentally defective" (handicapped) people who committed crimes, by removing them from the penal system and placing them in hospital care. Such provision, which at the time may have seemed humane, led to unfortunate consequences since, for example, it linked promiscuity with deficiency. This led to numbers of women who had given birth to illegitimate children being labelled as "moral defectives" and subjected them to long-term incarceration in a secure hospital. Minor refinements were made to the 1913 Act in the 1920s and the Criminal Justice Act of 1948 empowered courts, for the first time, to formalize the practice of placing offenders on probation with a requirement for psychiatric in- or out-patient treatment. The Homicide Act of 1957 (see Chapter 1) and the Mental Health Acts of 1959 and 1983 made a wider range of options available for the management of mentally disturbed offenders. More recent criminal justice legislation (and proposed legislation) referred to in the prologue tends to place issues of public protection to the forefront, with consequential implications for human rights issues. A succinct, but very fully referenced account of the history of provisions for mentally disordered offenders and, in particular, community provision, may be found in Laing (1999: Chapter 2; see also Prins 1999: Chapter 2). I conclude these brief contextual remarks by a short summary of certain trends during the last 30 to 40 years that have been influential in the treatment (and sometimes non-treatment) of the mentally disturbed in general and the mentally disturbed offender in particular:

1   The rundown and closure of the older mental hospitals, with re-provision by smaller acute units, resulted in much reduced overall bed capacity. With the wisdom of hindsight, one can see that such policies were perhaps premature and based on predictions about the size of future psychiatric populations and needs that were not altogether to be fulfilled. The move for rundown and closure was also fuelled by a degree of over-optimism concerning the long-term benefits of new forms of treatment.

2   A lack of emotional, professional and financial investment in community provision for a seriously disadvantaged and often unattractive group of people, the "hard to like" or "not nice, degenerate" patients so well described by Scott (1975). This reluctance to work with such individuals is exemplified with particular strength in the case of the severely personality disordered (in legal terms, the psychopathic – see Chapter 4).

3   Challenges were being made to some powerfully held assumptions about the nature and causes of mental disorders. For discussion of these earlier views, see Laing and Esterson (1970) and Szasz (1974). An excellent recent perspective may be found in Leff (2001).

4   Anxiety was being expressed about the rights of the mentally ill and an increasing concentration on civil rights issues; this concern has received recent prominence because of the proposed new mental health legislation (see later). Such concern has many laudable aspects, but brings in its wake certain iatrogenic (literally, physician-caused) consequences, not the least of these being the tendency to practise "defensive" psychiatry. This can result in a consequential denial of patients' right to treatment. A further result of this trend has been the increasing number of mentally disordered individuals in penal establishments (see later).

5   Growing concern about the degree to which black and other ethnic minority groups were being discriminated against and seriously over-represented in penal and psychiatric institutions; concern was also expressed about their untimely deaths in such establishments and in the community. See, for example, Prins et al. (1993), Liebling (1998, particularly the chapter by Jasper) and Macpherson (1999). Macpherson and his colleagues bravely pinpointed the essence of racism, emphasizing its often "hidden" nature, as follows:

> The collective failure of an organisation to provide an appropriate professional service to people because of their colour, culture or ethnic origin. It can be seen or detected in processes, attitudes and behaviour which amount to discrimination through *unwitting* prejudice, ignorance, thoughtlessness and racist stereotyping which disadvantage minority ethnic people.
>
> (Macpherson 1999: 28, 6.34; emphasis added)

6   There has been what might best be described as a reduction in the "primacy" of medicine in the treatment of the mentally disturbed. This has been evidenced by the medical profession's own acknowledgement of the importance of a team approach in the management of mentally disturbed individuals; it is also reflected in the changes being proposed in mental health legislation. Currently, the responsible medical officer (RMO) has primary and sole responsibility for patient care. If current proposals become law this will no longer be the case. Within the fields of both general and forensic psychiatry, psychologists, nurses and social workers are now developing parity with doctors in the field. However, it is true to say such developments have not been stress free; the need for a team approach was well summed up by Chiswick, a forensic psychiatrist, as long ago as 1990. He stated that:

Unfortunately, but not surprisingly, the courts and their associated institutions provide a clumsy and inappropriate vehicle for the delivery of health care . . . [this group of offenders and alleged offenders] is likely to contain people who are disadvantaged by social medical and psychiatric morbidity. They have complex treatment requirements which are unlikely to be met through the deliberations of the criminal justice system.

(1990: 755–6)

The need for multidisciplinary working will be returned to further in later chapters in this book (notably Chapters 4 and 8). At this point it is relevant to comment on the numbers of mentally disturbed offenders in penal establishments.

### Mentally disturbed offenders in the prison population

In 1998 a report published by the Office for National Statistics indicated that there were currently a disturbing number of people in prison suffering from mental illness. (Singleton et al. 1998). This, of course, was not an altogether new development, for as long ago as 1991 the Home Office and Department of Health stated that in the UK:

Although the actual number of prisoners requiring psychiatric services is not known, research has shown that the prison population has a high psychiatric morbidity . . . It is estimated that 2–3 percent of *sentenced* prisoners at any one time are likely to be suffering from a psychotic illness, and it is likely that the proportion is even higher in the remand population. Histories of alcohol and drug misuse are very common, as is neurotic illness.

(Home Office and Department of Health 1991: Annex C)

Although this extract provides an *overall* picture, some more detailed studies of penal populations may be helpful. It would appear that about one-third of the prison population requires some kind of psychiatric intervention and that, in *remand* populations, this number is likely to be higher. Numerous studies have been made of both remand and sentenced prisoners. For example, Gunn et al. (1991) examined a series of sentenced prisoners in England and Wales. They contended, by extrapolation from their sample, that: "The sentenced population included over 700 men with psychosis and [that] around 1,100 would warrant transfer to hospital for psychiatric treatment" (1991: 338) (see also Gunn 2000). Studies of *remand* prisoners tend to give even higher rates of psychiatric morbidity. More worrying is the evidence that suggests that psychiatric morbidity may be missed due to poor prison screening devices. Gavin et al. (2003) suggest that some 75 per cent of major mental illnesses in men and 66 per cent in women may be missed in this way. These authors reviewed screening processes in a local north of England prison taking male sentenced and remand prisoners. They concluded that:

> The findings in terms of numbers of new receptions screening positive for mental illness, and those in fact suffering from serious mental illnesses, were both in the range predicted from our earlier research, and in line with prevalence rates described in large scale remand prison surveys.
>
> ([see for example] Singleton et al. 1998)

Based on an admittedly small sample (616 new receptions over a 15-week period) the authors suggest that "it does not appear that large demands will be placed upon psychiatric resources if the proposed new reception health screening processes were in place, although a reorganization of the way in which services are delivered will almost certainly be required" (p. 253) (see also Duffy et al. 2003). This question of reorganization is of vital importance. As things stand at present, prisoners cannot be afforded the application of compulsory powers for treatment under current mental health legislation because prison hospitals are not deemed to be hospitals within the terms of the 1983 Mental Health Act, the only exceptions being the need for urgent treatment without consent under the common law. However, the consultation document issued with the draft Mental Health Bill does propose the possibility of compulsory treatment powers being available to prisoners who might have merited compulsory treatment in the community. There are some who consider that designating such healthcare facilities as hospitals within the meaning of the Act would solve a number of problems, particularly in relation to suicidal behaviour (see, for example, Tumim in Home Office 1990; Woolf and Tumim in Home Office 1991; also Towl et al. 2000). This may seem an attractive solution, but perhaps some caution should be espoused. If prison hospitals were to be designated as hospitals within the meaning of the Mental Health Act, 1983, it *might* mean that unless rigorous safeguards were introduced they could become the "dumping grounds" of the "not nice" patients the NHS seems reluctant to take. The most satisfactory answer would seem to reside in the "policy shift towards formal partnership between the NHS and the Prison Service for the provision of healthcare as a whole. This partnership is now set to evolve into the wholesale transfer of prison health care into the NHS over the next five years" (Kinton 2002: 305) (see also Department of Health 2002a). Additionally, the provision of "in-reach teams" in prisons by about 2006 should also help to alleviate problems caused by inappropriate detention (Kinton 2002).

Some final words of caution are necessary in concluding this section. This concerns the tendency to accept too readily that those mentally disturbed offenders detained in prison are there because if they were not, they would be in hospital. For many years the view put forward by the distinguished geneticist, the late Sir Lionel Penrose (1939), that there was an inverse relationship between prison and mental hospital populations had held considerable sway. In 1939 he published his well-known study which became known in criminological circles as "Penrose's law", namely that as the prison population rose, mental hospital populations declined and vice versa. Bowden (1993), in a critical study of this so-called "law", stated that:

> The suggestion appears to have been that there was a relatively stable mass of individuals who were in one form of environment, asylums, rather than another, prison. The two were used interchangeably. The benefit of the asylum was its effect on reducing crime.
>
> (1993: 81)

Careful examination of remand and sentenced penal populations reveals that such a state of affairs is not as clear cut as Penrose and some later writers have suggested. Further support for such criticism comes from Fowles (1993), who made a meticulous study of prison and mental hospital populations over a 25-year period. He suggested that:

> The mental hospitals have been run down but the full-blooded closure programme is still in its relatively early stages and its effects will not be felt for some time to come. Those remaining in the mental hospitals are unlikely to be of the age and sex normally associated with crime. [Moreover,] it is not possible to obtain comparable age distributions for prison populations and hospital residents.

Fowles goes on to suggest another complicating factor, namely:

> That former patients who are discharged from long-stay mental hospitals may be defined officially as living in the community but that may only mean that they are in the wards of a privately owned nursing home. The "community" means any hospital/home not owned by the NHS.
>
> (1993: 71–2)

Such criticisms of hypotheses that may have been all too readily accepted in the past indicates that the relationship between criminality and mental disturbance is much more complicated than would appear at first sight (this is examined in Chapter 3). The somewhat simplistic thinking of the kind briefly alluded to earlier has very important implications for the provision of both prison and healthcare services and the best use of resources for their maintenance.

## Diversion: keeping the mentally disturbed individual out of the criminal justice system

Even if we adopt a somewhat cautious approach to the estimates of the numbers of mentally disturbed persons held in penal establishments at various stages of their careers, and accept the caveats entered by Fowles and Bowden, we are still compelled to acknowledge that a sizeable proportion of them should not be there. Moreover, we are also forced to conclude that not only should they not be *in prison*, but, furthermore, that perhaps they *should not have entered the criminal justice system in the first place*. In Chapter 1, I demonstrated how one form of diversion from the criminal justice system operates through a finding of "unfitness to plead" (being under disability). As long ago as 1975, the Butler Committee recommended that mentally disturbed offenders might be dealt with other than through the courts:

> Where any apparent offender is clearly in need of psychiatric treatment and there is no risk to members of the public the question should always be asked whether any useful purpose would be served by prosecution . . . these remarks apply in cases of homicide or attempted homicide or grave bodily harm as in less serious cases.
>
> (Home Office and DHSS 1975: 266)

Some 15 years later the Home Office, in its now well-known circular No. 66/90 (Home Office MNP/90/1/55/8), reiterated this view as follows:

> It is government policy that, wherever possible, mentally disordered persons should receive care and treatment from the health and social services. Where there is sufficient evidence, in accordance with the principles of the *Code for Crown Prosecutors*, to show that a mentally disordered person has committed an offence, careful consideration should be given to whether prosecution is required by the public interest.
>
> (Para 2)

The circular went on to provide very detailed advice to all those agencies likely to be involved in dealing with mentally disturbed offenders (for example, the police, crown prosecution service, probation, social services, courts, health authorities, prison healthcare service). The stress on inter-agency cooperation has continued to be a central theme in mental health policy. Concern about the most appropriate action to be taken in respect of mentally disturbed offenders is, of course, not new. Two examples from history will suffice to make my point.

## Case illustration 2.1

This concerns a young man named Hwaetred, as recounted by St Guthlac (AD 674–714), who lived in so-called Dark Ages rural England:

> A young man named Hwaetred became afflicted with an evil spirit. So terrible was [his] madness that he tore his own limbs and attacked others with his teeth. When men tried to restrain him, he snatched up a double-bladed axe and killed three men. After four years of madness and with emaciated body, he was taken by his parents to several sacred shrines, but he received no help. One day, when his parents were wishing more for his death than his life, they heard of a hermit (Guthlac) on the Isle of Crowland. They took their possessed son, with limbs bound, to the hermit.
>
> (Felix, *Life of St Guthlac*, quoted in Roth and Kroll 1986: 100)

The modern recounters of this ancient story make some interesting and very relevant comments. First, they indicate that the young man's condition was seen as an illness; second, his deviance was *not* minor, for he killed three men. Third, there is no talk of revenge or attribution of criminality or of guilt; it would have been quite simple to have hunted him down and killed him, but instead attempts were made to restrain and control him within his own community. Fourth, his parents, desperate as many of the parents of the seriously mentally ill are today, seek yet further remedy in the guise of a wise man – a latter-day psychiatrist perhaps? – in the hope that a cure might be effected. One would not wish to make too much of this vignette, but it does encapsulate some of the issues raised in Roth and Kroll's account and, one wonders, how a multidisciplinary case conference today would answer the question: "What would you have done with this young man?"

## Case illustration 2.2

Some 12 hundred years later, an incident showing the other side of the coin is recorded in the *Lancet* of 14 April 1883 (pp. 648–9):

**Malice or madness?**
What is justly described as a "shocking scene in a prison" has just occurred in Dartmoor. An exceptionally "bad" young man, who was sentenced to seven years penal servitude in August, 1879, he having been no less than nine times previously convicted and flogged, was being examined in prison on Tuesday last on a charge of a violent assault on a warder, whom it seems, he nearly killed with a spade when his violence was such that with great difficulty several

warders put him in irons. The story is sickening in its brutality. What, however, must most powerfully strike the medical reader is that the narrative very closely resembles one of the old stories of a struggle with a madman in the days before the humane system of non-restraint was introduced into the asylums in this country. The question we are actuated to ask – and it is one which ought to be pressed strongly on the consideration of the Home Office – is whether this young man is not mad? He was convicted nine times before he reached the age of eighteen. Moreover, his rage is manifestly that of mania, rather than a sane being . . . Looking at the treatment – wholly unworthy of a civilised country – which Thomas Jones is undergoing in a dark cell at Dartmoor, it would be well if the enquiry necessary to reassure the public mind that a madman is not being punished when he ought to be placed under treatment could be instituted at once . . . it cannot be permitted that prison authorities should reproduce the horrors of the Spanish inquisition in one of Queen Victoria's gaols, and withal mistake a lunatic for a felon.

(Rollin 1993: 475)

### Diversion as an aspect of discretion

The practice of diversion involves the exercise of discretion at various stages of the criminal justice process; it has a long, if somewhat obscure, history. Hetherington (1989) traces its origins to the reign of Henry VIII. However, it was not until the latter part of the nineteenth century that the office of Director of Public Prosecutions was introduced. Currently, the decision to prosecute rests with the Crown Prosecution Service, which is guided by a *Code for Crown Prosecutors* within which the prosecutor has to have regard for the need for prosecution in "the public interest". A number of factors govern this latter consideration, such as likely penalty, staleness (that is, the offence was committed so long ago that its prosecution would be of questionable merit), youth, old age and infirmity, complainant's attitude and *mental illness or stress*. On this last aspect the *Code* states:

Whenever the crown prosecutor is provided with a medical report to the effect that an accused or a person under investigation is suffering from some form of psychiatric illness . . . and the strain of criminal proceedings may lead to a considerable worsening of his condition, such a report should receive anxious consideration. This is a difficult field because, in some instances, the accused may have become mentally disturbed or depressed by the mere fact that his misconduct has been discovered and the crown prosecutor may be dubious about a prognosis that criminal proceedings will adversely affect his condition to a significant extent. Where, however, the crown prosecutor is satisfied that the probable effect upon the defendant's mental health outweighs the interests of justice in that particular case, he should not hesitate to discontinue proceedings. An independent medical examination may be sought, but should generally be reserved for cases of such gravity as plainly require prosecution but for clear evidence that such a course would be likely to result in a permanent worsening of the accused's condition.

(Crown Prosecution Service nd.: 4)

A number of questions arise from this statement:

1　What variations are there in practice in making decisions whether not to prosecute, or to discontinue prosecution once it is underway within the terms of the general power to withdraw or to offer no evidence through Section 23 of the Prosecution of Offences Act 1985? In 1990a, Grounds indicated that: "There is a large gap in research knowledge in this area. Little is known about what happens to mentally disordered offenders *who do not enter criminal proceedings* and these gaps need to be filled if a complete picture is to be obtained" (emphasis added). He continued: "Such research might also indicate whether more mentally disordered offenders could, or should, be diverted away from criminal proceedings" (Grounds 1990a: 40). Since the time Grounds called for such research, some headway has been made. For example, Rowlands et al. (1996) indicated in a follow-up study that a number of individuals subjected to the diversionary process and, in particular, those with substance abuse problems were lost to the psychiatric services; and on a follow-up after one year, 17 per cent had re-offended. They called for further long-term research. Shaw et al. (2001) reported that on a two-year follow-up period one-third of those diverted to in-patient services had lost contact at 12 months; for those diverted to out-patient and community services about one-third had also lost contact. They recommend better "out-reach" assertive services.

Geelan et al. (2001) report more positive results. They suggest that: "If *appropriately* assessed in court, and *appropriate* hospital placements are arranged, successful outcome can be achieved for the majority of people diverted from custody to hospital in terms of improved mental states and a planned discharge" (p. 127; emphasis added). From examination of these and earlier studies (for example James and Hamilton 1991; Joseph 1992; Joseph and Potter 1993) it would appear that success is heavily dependent on detailed professional assessment and good communication within the system (that is, between the various professionals involved, magistrates, police, psychiatric, social and probation services; see also Exworthy and Parrott (1993, 1997). Most studies have concentrated on male offenders and reports on diversion for females are somewhat sparse. However, Parsons et al. (2001) carried out a major survey of the prevalence of mental disorder in female remand prisons and found high rates of psychiatric morbidity and that existing screening on reception (in prison) did not identify the majority of cases of mental disorder.

A formal diversionary measure was originally contained in Section 136 of the Mental Health Act 1959 and re-enacted with the same section number in the Act of 1983. This provides a constable with a power to remove to a place of safety a person, found in a place to which the public have access, who appears to be suffering from mental disorder within the meaning of the Act and appears to be in immediate need of care, protection or control. (It should be noted that the Act specifies "to which the public have access". The provision is frequently misquoted, describing it as "a public place"; the correct definition allows a much wider interpretation of the location.) The person may be detained for a maximum of 72 hours for the purposes of being examined by authorized mental health professionals. Such examination may or may not lead to admission to hospital, either informally or under the compulsory powers of the Act. The section has certain merits, but it also has some accompanying disadvantages. All too often, a police station is used as a place of safety and police stations are clearly not the best places for detaining the mentally distressed. Although the police are not always certain of their powers, research seems to indicate that they are reasonably competent at recognizing a florid psychosis when they see one. There are often delays in the arrival of the relevant professionals (for example, approved doctor and approved social worker) and communications between the parties is not always good.

Past research has indicated that the implementation of the provision afforded by Section 136 is not uniform country wide (Bean et al. 1991; NACRO 1993; more recent research is summarized in some detail by Laing 1999, notably Chapter 3). Diversion may also take place at the point of arrest. Riordan et al. (2000) showed that intervention at the point of arrest had been successful in preventing some mentally disordered individuals being "inappropriately taken into custody *and had fostered lasting and productive links between psychiatric services, the police and other agencies*" (p. 683; emphasis added). (See also Riordan et al. (2003).)

2    How much notice should be taken of an accused's view of his or her right to prosecution? Would some mentally disordered offenders *prefer* to be prosecuted in the normal way? This is of vital importance since the iatrogenic consequences of psychiatric disposal may be considerable. As we have seen, until the introduction of the Criminal Procedure (Insanity and Unfitness to Plead) Act 1991, a successful defence of insanity or unfitness to plead would involve immediate hospitalization – sometimes with a restriction order and a comparatively rare chance of the *facts* of the case being explored and determined. Hospitalization

under the Mental Health Act 1983 for offences may well result in a much longer spell of incarceration than had the defendant been dealt with by way of imprisonment.

3   Given the current state of psychiatric services (and in particular *general* psychiatric services) is it certain that a psychiatric disposal will necessarily offer the best solution? This applies with considerable force to the personality disordered and (in legal terms) to "psychopathic offenders". As already noted, hospitals and psychiatrists seem increasingly reluctant to accept such persons. Current government proposals for dealing with those showing "psychopathic disorder" and who are considered to be dangerous to others are considered in some detail in Chapter 4.

4   We have already seen how prisoners, particularly those on remand, may have varying degrees of mental disturbance that are not spotted by prison staff. For example, the depressed prisoner may be difficult to pick out in an already overcrowded remand prison; moreover, depression is an illness often unrecognized by the unwary and often contributes to suicides and suicidal gestures (see Towl et al. 2000). Some prisoners may conceal the fact that they have a serious mental health problem as, for example, in the case of the highly encapsulated delusional system of the morbidly jealous or psychotically deluded individual. Coid, in a study published in 1991, found a small number of inmates whose psychotic delusions appeared to be quite unknown to the prison staff. The modifications to prison healthcare already referred to should, one hopes, help to remedy the situation.

5   An important jurisprudential question also needs consideration. To what extent should offenders, even though mentally disturbed, be held responsible for their actions? We might exclude the floridly psychotic at the time of the offence and perhaps some of the seriously mentally impaired. How far down the line of what some have termed the "psychiatrisation" of delinquency should we go? Such a practice tends to make the prison system the dumping ground for "badness" it also enables professionals to use prisons for the projection of their own "badness" and it continues to negate rehabilitative measures within them. The *disadvantages* of non-prosecution have also been alluded to by some forensic psychiatrists. For example, Smith and Donovan suggest that:

> Excusing offending may not always be in the patient's interests. The formal legal process can be a valuable exercise in reality testing. The patient [in this instance they are writing about offences committed by psychiatric in-patients] . . . can measure his or her own perceptions of his or her own behaviour against those of society. This can be a useful preparation for life outside hospital.

The knowledge that prosecution is routine rather than exceptional, may deter further assaults and help aggressive patients to accept responsibility for their behaviour. Sometimes encouraging such patients to accept responsibility can be clinically beneficial and help to instil a sense of justice in other patients on a ward.

(Smith and Donovan 1990: 380)

They also state that non-prosecution:

[C]an reinforce the patient's belief that he or she need not control his or her behaviour. It may also leave staff feeling unsupported and there may be similar consequences if the court imposes a minimal penalty.

(1990: 381)

For example, it is possible that had Christopher Clunis's offence behaviour been dealt with by a hospital order with restrictions it would have been possible to exert more adequate control over his whereabouts and to have avoided the situation where he was able to disappear from view with, as we now know, lethal results (Ritchie et al. 1994).

Such concerns are echoed beyond our immediate shores. In a paper on the issue of determining criminal responsibility in France, Lloyd and Bénézech state:

The main problem . . . was how to determine the exact amount of free will each individual had at the time of the criminal offence. It was relatively easy to assess the absence of criminal responsibility in cases of severe mental disorder or handicap; intermediate mental states, however, present considerable difficulties in assessment, as did the measuring of constraints on the free will of normal men and women.

(Lloyd and Bénézech 1991: 282)

6   In deciding on diversion or discontinuance, how much consideration should be given to the views of victims? This is a delicate and difficult matter with considerable ethical implications. It needs to be seen against the climate of increasing attempts to allow victims more "say" in what should happen to offenders and the establishment of opportunities for some offenders and victims to enter into "dialogue". It is an aspect of "restorative" justice in which offenders witness at first hand the damage they have caused (*The Independent*, 23 July 2003: 9). In the past, such schemes have been limited to younger offenders, but they are now to be extended to adults. Such participation has much to commend it, but the role of victims and the extent to which they actually participate in

criminal justice and forensic psychiatric decision-making processes requires very careful consideration. There is a fine dividing line between what may be quite appropriate involvement and undue influence being exerted by those who have been the victims, or who are a victim's family members. It should be remembered that our long-established system of law making and the delivery of justice have their roots in the avoidance of possible personal vengeance.

7    Can we identify more clearly those aspects of law and practice that tend to militate against the effective use of diversion? There is anecdotal evidence to suggest that agencies tend to disclaim responsibility (notably financial) for the individual. For example, the sad saga of patchy development of medium and low-secure accommodation attests to the importance of trying to ensure that funds are "ring-fenced" (Department of Health and Home Office 1992). At the individual (case) level, would not the notion of funds travelling with the patient/offender offset a great deal of "buck passing"? At a more personal level, professionals are often reluctant to see a problem from a colleague's point of view. This is not necessarily deliberate obfuscation or intransigence on their part, but is a product of differences in role perceptions among professionals trained in different ways. Far more needs to be done to address relationship problems of this kind and forensic psychiatric or criminology centres could play a significant role in this (see Riordan et al. 2003). In the midst of inter-professional squabbles the offender/patient suffers and the more inadequate of them continue to play their "stage army" parts in the criminal justice and health care arenas; parts so well described by Rollin as long ago as 1969. The homeless ethnic minority groups, particularly African-Caribbean populations, fare particularly badly in this respect. The mentally handicapped are another sad illustration – a truly vulnerable group whom nobody really wishes to own. They may find themselves with increasing frequency back within the criminal justice system – a phenomenon that the Mental Deficiency Act 1913 was designed specifically to prevent.

In an excellent review of 10 years' published and unpublished contributions on diversion, James concluded that:

> Court diversion can be highly effective in the identification and acceleration into a hospital of mentally disordered offenders . . . However, most court diversion services are currently inadequately planned, organized or resourced and are therefore of limited effect . . . a central strategy is required, and properly designed and adequately supported court services should be incorporated into, and understood to be a core part of mainstream psychiatric provision.
>
> (James 1999: 507)

He goes on to suggest that: "without such action, the future of court diversion lies in doubt". Two further specific problems can be identified; a reluctance on the part of courts to grant bail in some suitable cases (see Hucklesby 1997) and a problem in obtaining reports from increasingly busy general psychiatrists. Vaughan et al. (2003) suggest that more use could be made of a wider range of mental health professionals in the penal and community systems for obtaining information that would assist the courts in making mental health disposals. They state:

> By using existing court diversion schemes prison mental health teams . . . [and other professionals] . . . it is hoped that this will result in more timely and reliable flow of psychiatric information . . . the mentally disordered defendant should benefit from a better informed bench when they are considering his/her disposal.
>
> (Vaughan et al. 2003: 255)

In summary, diversionary practice may be set out somewhat crudely in the following five stages:

*Stage 1*    Informal diversion by the police.
*Stage 2*    Formal implementation of Section 136 of the Mental Health Act 1983.
*Stage 3*    Referral for psychiatric examination before court hearing and discontinuance of prosecution at any stage thereafter.
*Stage 4*    Disposal through mental health services at court or after sentence. (See later discussion under other healthcare disposals.)
*Stage 5*    Disposal through these services at a later stage in sentence – for example, transfer under the Mental Health Act from prison to hospital.
*Note*: These stages have been set out in a somewhat oversimplified fashion; they may, of course, overlap.

The effectiveness of diversion will be limited if we do not take into account the following factors:

(a) Placing current interest and activity concerning diversionary activities within their historical context.
(b) Recognizing that collaboration, cooperation and effective teamwork are much harder to achieve than has been thought to be the case hitherto.
(c) Recognizing that these fundamental difficulties may make their appearance in disguised form through the guise of financial constraints and limitations.

(d) Recognizing the possibility that for some offenders, diversion to the healthcare system in its under-funded and under-resourced state may be a less satisfactory option than entry into the criminal justice system.

(e) Recognizing that, despite some current useful research, we still lack adequate information about the effectiveness of diversionary activity and about what happens *long term* to those diverted.

(f) Recognizing that it is all too easy to assume that offenders wish to be diverted and that, for some, diversion may reduce their sense of personal responsibility to adverse effect.

(g) Recognizing that diversion may deflect attention from the lack of medical and psychiatric facilities within penal establishments.

## Other healthcare disposals

In order to keep the material in this section within reasonable limits, I provide merely an outline account of facilities. Readers wishing to obtain more detailed information will find it in the works cited and in the works listed for further reading at the end of the chapter.

The *legal basis and structure* of mental health services in England and Wales have undergone considerable changes in recent years and are described in considerable detail by Eldergill (2002). Those readers wishing to examine international comparative provisions will find the *International Journal of Offender Therapy and Comparative Criminology*. The *International Journal of Law and Psychiatry* and the *International Journal of Forensic Mental Health* very useful sources of information.

I have confined my description, almost exclusively, to provisions for adult offenders and offender–patients. However, there is continuing concern about the circumstances of young people (children and young people under 16) who have committed homicide and other grave crimes and who are held in a variety of institutions. Such young people will often have to cross the boundaries between psychiatric, social and penal care. *Public* concern is not difficult to register; witness the fact that it is alleged that some 200,000 people signed a petition to ensure that the Home Secretary "imprisoned for life" the two young killers of James Bulger. Happily, good sense and humanity prevailed and the two young men concerned were released under conditions of anonymity, but not without further public outcry. A person convicted of murder, who was less than 18 at the time of the offence was committed, will be ordered to be detained during Her Majesty's Pleasure (Section 53(1) Children and Young Person's Act 1933). To all intents and purposes, this is similar to a life sentence, except that the offender may be detained "in such place and under such conditions as the Secretary of State may direct". The places chosen for such detention will vary according to the age and the mental condition of the offender and his or her circumstances, all of which may change over time. Thus, a youthful offender so detained may commence his or her sentence in a local authority residential establishment, a healthcare establishment or in a secure hospital, young offenders' institution or, if detained for long enough, may be transferred to an adult prison. Such would have been the outcome for the killers of James Bulger had they not been released before this became a distinct probability. Poeple who are under *17* and convicted of crimes other than murder, for which a sentence of life imprisonment may be passed on an adult, may be sentenced to detention for life under Section 53 of the 1933 Act (as amended by the Criminal Justice Act 1961, the Criminal Justice Act 1991 and the Criminal Justice and Public Order Act 1994). The effect of the 1994 Act was to extend the age range to those aged *10* or over, for the same range of offences as applied before to those aged *14* and under *18* (NACRO 1996: 1). Such a sentence has virtually the same effect as one of detention during Her Majesty's Pleasure. The oversight of the care and control of children and young people subject to the sentences just outlined rests jointly with the Home Office and the Department of Health, the latter being the central government department having overall responsibility for the care and control given by local authorities and others to all children and young people.

The backgrounds and conditions under which Section 53 offenders are detained have been examined very fully by Boswell (1996). Her study revealed a number of serious problems concerning their care and containment. These included: lack of adequate help in assisting these young people to understand the reasons for their behaviour (although it has to be said that in the case of the killers of James Bulger, this issue seems to have been addressed); disruption to their education caused by their being moved from childcare to penal provision as they grew older (see earlier); and a lack of adequate training in social skills. Boswell also found a very high degree of child physical and sexual abuse in their backgrounds. Sadly, the care of such disturbed children and young people has been found wanting in other institutions in recent times as, for example, in certain care homes in Leicestershire (Kirkwood Report: Leicestershire County Council 1993) and Sir Stephen Tumim's inquiries into prison suicides by young people (Home Office 1990). The problem seems to be a perennial one (Prins 1991).

The material that now follows is divided into three sections. The first is concerned with enquiries into mental state and allied matters; the second deals with hospital provision; and the third covers penal provision.

### Enquiries into mental state and allied matters

In Chapter 1, reference was made to the state of mind of those accused of offences such as homicide and other grave crimes. I now consider, briefly, the procedures available for causing inquiry to be made into the mental state of such persons. In the case of those charged with murder, reports are prepared *automatically* by the Prison Health Care Service. The practice seems to have arisen mainly because of the importance attached in the past to the need to secure detailed psychiatric evidence in cases where the death penalty could still be imposed and because of the seriousness with which all accusations of murder were (and still are) treated. The statutory requirements for the provision of mental condition reports are laid down in the Criminal Justice Act 1991, Section 4(3) as follows:

> Before passing a custodial sentence other than one fixed by law [i.e. murder] on an offender who is, or appears to be mentally disordered, a court should consider:
>
> (a) any information before it which relates to his mental condition [whether given in a medical report, or a pre-sentence report or otherwise]; and
> (b) the likely effect of such a sentence on that condition and on any treatment that may be available for it.

Note that pre-sentence reports are normally provided by the National Probation Service; in days gone by they were known as *probation* or *social enquiry reports*. Reports into an accused's mental and physical state may also be prepared at the instigation of the Director of Public Prosecutions (DPP) or by the accused's legal advisers. In almost all cases of alleged murder, the reports will be prepared in custody but, in certain exceptional cases, an accused may be granted bail on condition that he remain in a psychiatric hospital for reports to be prepared. In cases of grave crimes, where the accused's mental condition may give rise to doubts as to diagnosis or the case is problematic in other ways, the investigations should also include thorough physical, neurological and biochemical investigations.

As indicated earlier, psychiatric reports will be prepared in cases of alleged murder and in other cases where the motivation for the offence may seem unclear. Certain sexual offences and cases of arson (see Chapters 6 and 7) would fall into this category, as would cases involving less serious crimes which seem to have occurred "out of the blue" or in repetitive fashion and in front of witnesses. It is difficult to obtain precise figures for the number of psychiatric reports prepared in any one year, but one can estimate that they are provided in about 2–4 per cent of all cases coming before the courts.

### Remands to hospital

Currently, Section 35(1) of the Mental Health Act 1983 empowers magistrates' and Crown Courts to order the remand of an accused person to *hospital* for the preparation of a report into his or her mental condition.

This provides an alternative to remanding an accused in custody in situations where it would not be practicable to obtain the report on bail (for example, if the accused decided to breach a *bail* requirement that he or she should reside in hospital for examination, the hospital would be unable to prevent that person from leaving; the *remand to hospital* under Section 35 gives the hospital the power to *detain* the accused). This power to remand to hospital applies also to any person *awaiting trial* by the Crown Court for any offence punishable by imprisonment or any person who has been convicted but not yet sentenced (but excludes persons charged with murder). The power may be exercised only if an appropriately authorized medical practitioner (see later) reports orally or in writing that there is reason to believe that the accused is suffering from mental illness, psychopathic disorder, severe mental impairment or mental impairment. In the first instance, a remand may be for up to 28 days; after this initial period, the accused may be remanded for periods of up to 28 days for a maximum of 12 weeks. It should be noted that the criteria for *remands to hospital* are more limited than those that obtain *for remands on bail*. In the case of remands to hospital the court has to be satisfied that the accused is suffering from one or other of the four forms of mental disorder described in the act and for which a hospital order may be made (see later). In a review of Section 35, Bartlett and Sandland outline a number of problems that beset the provision "both in terms of resources and frameworks and in terms of the legislative detail" (Bartlett and Sandland 2000: 169). Readers should consult their work for a detailed account of their criticisms. The use of Section 35 is not very frequent; in 1996–7, 267 admissions were made; as Bartlett and Sandland report, this figure "was lower than for any previous year in the decade" (p. 167).

*Remands for treatment*

Section 36 of the Mental Health Act 1983 empowers the Crown Court to remand an accused person to hospital for treatment (other than a person charged with murder). The court must be satisfied on the written or oral evidence of *two* medical practitioners authorised under Section 12 of the Act that the accused is suffering from *mental illness* or *severe mental impairment* of a nature or degree that makes it appropriate for him or her to be detained in hospital for medical treatment. In the first instance, the remands may be for up to 28 days. The remand may be renewed at 28-day intervals for a period of up to 12 weeks. The court is also empowered to terminate the remand for treatment at any time, for example, in the event of the accused recovering or in the event of the court hearing that no effective treatment is possible. It should be noted that the powers under Section 36 are only exercisable in respect of those suffering from *mental illness* and *severe mental impairment*, not those suffering from *mental impairment* or *psychopathic disorder*. As Bartlett and Sandland suggest, this is presumably because "persons suffering from these [latter] conditions would be of problematic treatability" (p. 167). The section appears to be used quite rarely – on average some 30–40 admissions per year (Bartlett and Sandland 2000: 167).

### Interim hospital orders

In addition to their powers under Sections 37 and 41 of the Act (see later) courts are empowered under Section 38 to make an interim hospital order. As with the preceding provisions, the court has to be satisfied on duly approved medical evidence that this is the most appropriate course of action and that an accused is suffering from one of the four categories of mental disorder defined in the Act. The provision is likely to be of use in those cases where the court wishes to make some evaluation of an accused's likely response to treatment without irrevocable commitment on either side. Such an order may be made in the first instance for a period of up to 12 weeks; it may be renewed for periods of up to 28 days to a maximum total period of 12 months (Crime (Sentences) Act 1997, Section 49(1)). The court may also terminate an interim hospital order after considering written or oral evidence of the responsible medical officer (RMO) at the hospital, if it makes a full hospital order (see later), or if it decides to deal with the offender in some alternative fashion. Some 56 such orders are made annually.

### Hospital orders

Section 37 of the Act enables courts to make hospital or guardianship orders. (The latter are not considered here, as their use is very infrequent in both civil and criminal commitments, and their demise is likely under the proposed new mental health legislation.) In order to make a hospital order the court must be satisfied as to the following:

(a) That, having regard to all the circumstances, including the nature of the offence, antecedents of the offender, and the unsuitability of other methods of disposal, a hospital order is the most suitable method of dealing with the case.
(b) The accused has been *convicted of an offence* punishable with imprisonment (other than murder). In the magistrates' court an order may be made without proceeding to conviction provided the court is satisfied that the defendant committed the act or made the omission charged, and that the person is suffering from mental illness or severe mental impairment.
(c) That the offender is suffering from one or other of the four disorders defined in the Act and it is of a nature or degree so that *it is appropriate*

*for the offender to be detained in hospital for medical treatment*, and in the case of *mental impairment* or *psychopathic disorder* that the medical treatment *is likely to alleviate or prevent a deterioration in the patient's condition*. Reports are required by two doctors, one of whom must be approved for the purpose under Section 12(2) of the Act. It should be stressed that the condition *must* be one that merits compulsory detention in hospital and is *not* one that could be treated by other means, for example by a requirement for mental treatment under a community rehabilitation order (formerly known as a probation order).

Some 600–700 such orders are made annually by the courts (Bartlett and Sandford 2000). A hospital order lasts initially for six months, is renewable for a further six months and is then renewable at annual intervals. A patient so detained may be discharged by the RMO at any time and the patient or his or her nearest relative may also make application to the Mental Health Review Tribunal (MHRT) at regular intervals. In the draft Mental Health Bill it is proposed to abolish the right of application by the nearest relative. Under Section 117 of the Act, aftercare must now be provided for those who cease to be detained under Section 37 and who leave hospital. The implementation of such aftercare is now made more specific by the provision of detailed guidance in recent years for care programming and management (see, for example, Eldergill 2002).

### Restriction orders

Section 41 of the Act enables a Crown Court (but *not* a magistrates' court) to make a restriction order. The criteria for making such an order are as follows:

1   That, following conviction, it appears to the court, having regard to
    (a)  the nature of the offence
    (b)  the offender's antecedents
    (c)  the risk of his or her committing further offences if discharged, that a restriction order is necessary *for the protection of the public from serious harm.*
2   That at least one of the doctors authorised under Section 12(2) of the Act whose written evidence is before the court has also given that evidence orally.

The criterion I have italicized did not appear in the 1959 Mental Health Act and was inserted in the 1983 Act to ensure that only those offender–patients who were considered likely to constitute a serious risk to the public would be subjected to the serious restrictions on liberty that follow the making of such an order (see later).

Serious harm to the public is not defined in the Act. However, in recent years, the Court of Appeal has, through a number of its decisions, provided guidance as to the nature and quality of serious harm. In particular, in the case of *R. v. Birch* (1989), it was decided that "the court is required to assess not the seriousness of the *risk* that the defendant will re-offend, but the risk that if he does so the public will suffer serious harm . . . the potential harm must be *serious*, and a high possibility of a recurrence of minor offences will no longer be sufficient" (quoted in Jones 2001: 222; emphasis added). During the past decade there has been an increase in the number of restriction orders made – on average some 200 plus; most of them have been made in respect of offenders with a diagnosis of mental illness rather than of psychopathic disorder or mental impairment (Bartlett and Sandford 2000: 186).

In theory, a restriction order may be made for a specific period or without limit of time; the latter is now the preferred course of action since it permits more flexibility in the difficult task of assessment and prognosis. The effects of a restriction order are considerable in respect of the "liberty of the subject":

1   The offender–patient cannot be given leave of absence from the hospital (as they can be under non-restricted orders), be transferred elsewhere, or be discharged by the RMO without the consent of the Home Secretary.
2   The Home Secretary may remove the restrictions if he considers they are no longer needed to protect the public from serious harm. Should the order continue in force without the restriction clause, it has the same effect as an order made under Section 37 of the Act.
3   The Home Secretary may, at any time, discharge the offender–patient absolutely or subject to conditions. In considering those restricted cases (a) which are considered to be particularly problematic, (b) which are considered to be in need of special care in assessment, and (c) where there may be thought to be a fear of possible future risk to the public, the Home Secretary would seek the advice of his Advisory Board on Restricted Patients (formerly known as the Aarvold Board but recently abolished). (See later for further details of the Board's one-time constitution and functions.)

Under Section 73 of the Act the Mental Health Review Tribunal (MHRT) may exercise its own powers concerning restricted patients in the following manner:

1   The tribunal *must* order the patient's *absolute* discharge if it is satisfied that:

(a) an offender–patient is not now suffering from one of the forms of mental disorder specified in the Act that makes it appropriate for him or her to be detained in hospital for medical treatment

(b) *or* it is not necessary for the health and safety of the offender–patient or for the protection of other persons that he or she should receive such treatment

(c) *and* it is not appropriate for the offender–patient to remain liable to be recalled to hospital for further treatment.

However, in the important cases of *R. v. Merseyside Mental Health Review Tribunal* ex parte K. (1990) and *R. v. Secretary of State for the Home Department* et parte K. (1990), it was held that a tribunal which was satisfied that the restricted patient was not suffering from a mental or psychopathic disorder was nevertheless entitled to order the conditional discharge of the patient and was not, as had hitherto held to be the case, obliged to order his or her absolute discharge. The court appeared to have in mind the possibility of a need for a residual power to recall the patient in the event of a relapse at some future date.

2    A conditionally discharged offender–patient may be recalled to hospital by the Home Secretary at any time during the duration of the restriction order, but the patient has to be referred to a Mental Health Review Tribunal for a prompt hearing into the recall, the reasons for it and any representations the offender–patient may wish to make. It has also been held by the Court of Appeal (*R. v. Secretary of State for the Home Department* ex parte K., 1990) that the Home Secretary does not have to rely on medical evidence in order to recall a restricted patient to hospital, even if medical opinion was of the view that the patient was not suffering from mental disorder. This wide discretion was held to lie entirely in the hands of the Home Secretary and the public interest would, if necessary, take precedence. However, this view was subsequently challenged by the offender–patient who took his case to the European Court of Human Rights. The court held that "in the absence of an emergency, there had been a breach of Article 5(1) in recalling 'K.' without up-to-date medical evidence to demonstrate that he was suffering from a true mental disorder" (*K. v. United Kingdom*, 1998). In citing this case, Jones (2001) indicates that "the recall of conditionally discharged patients should conform with this judgement" (p. 234). An order for conditional discharge may contain a range of requirements held to be conducive to the welfare of the offender–patient and, more importantly, for the protection of the public. (For a helpful analysis of the management of restricted offender–patients in the community, see Street 1998.)

Under the 1959 Act, tribunals could only *advise* the Home Secretary on the discharge of restricted patients. As can be seen, they now have the power themselves to order the patient's discharge. In order to exercise these wider powers, tribunals must be chaired by a senior legal practitioner approved by the Lord Chancellor, such as a circuit judge or person of equivalent status. (See later discussion of functions of MHRTs.)

### Hospital and limitation directions

Section 46 of the Crime (Sentences) Act 1997 introduced a new disposal that is to be found in Sections 45A and 45B of the 1983 Mental Health Act; it is known in the vernacular as a "hybrid order". A hospital direction is defined in the 1983 Act as "a direction that, instead of being removed to and detained in a prison, the offender may be removed to and detained in such hospital as may be specified in the direction". The court may also add a "limitation direction", which, to all intents and purposes, is similar to the effect of a restriction order made under Section 41 of the Act. The disposal is only available to a Crown Court. Its purpose is to ensure that should a psychopathically disordered offender not respond to hospital treatment he or she may be transferred to prison. Currently the provision applies *only* to those diagnosed as psychopathically disordered, but the proposed new mental health legislation will permit its use for other categories of mental disorder. (For further descriptions, see Bartlett and Sandland 2000: 189–94 and Jones 2001: 240–45.) Current practice suggests that such orders are not highly favoured by the courts and are made very infrequently. Detailed criticisms of the use of such orders have come from the legal, criminological and forensic psychiatric quarters. For examples of the former, see Laing (1997) and Walker (1996) and for the latter, see Darjee et al. (2000, 2002) and Eastman (1996).

### Transfer of prisoners found to be mentally disordered

Sections 47–52 of the Mental Health Act 1983 enable the Home Secretary to order the transfer of sentenced or unconvicted prisoners from prison to hospital if they are found to be suffering from mental disorder as defined in the Act (see for example the case of Peter Sutcliffe described in Chapter 1). Under the provisions of Section 47, an order in respect of a *sentenced* prisoner *may* be made without restrictions, but it will be much more likely to be made with restrictions under the provisions of Section 49. Bartlett and Sandland report that in the period 1997–98 "of 247 orders made under Section 47 only 31 were unrestricted" (2000: 196). If the Home Secretary is notified by the RMO or a Mental Health Review Tribunal that such a person no longer needs treatment for mental disorder, he has two possibilities open to him:

1    If the offender–patient has become eligible for parole or has earned statutory remission, he can order his or her discharge.
2    Alternatively, he can order that the patient be remitted to prison to serve the remainder of his or her sentence. (For examples of the effects of such transfer on sentenced prisoners, see Grounds 1990b, 1991.)

### "Psychiatric probation orders"

The heading has been placed in quotation marks because although they are commonly known as "psychiatric probation orders" their correct title under recent legislation should be "psychiatric community rehabilitation orders". The provision has been available under statute since the Criminal Justice Act of 1948 and is now provided under more recent criminal justice legislation. The Criminal Justice Act 1991 permits this form of treatment provided:

1    A hospital, or other establishment, will receive him or her and is willing to provide treatment.
2    The court has before it the oral or written evidence of one doctor (approved under Section 12(2) of the Mental Health Act 1983) indicating that the offender's condition requires, and may be susceptible to, treatment (but is not such as to warrant his or her detention in pursuance of a hospital order). Such an order may be made for a period of up to 3 years and may be on an in- or out-patient basis.

As far as a hospital or other institution is concerned, the offender–patient has informal status and there is no power to detain him or her compulsorily (as there is under the provisions of the Mental Health Act). Should the offender–patient leave, the probation officer may, of course, take action for breach of requirement of the order. However, it is not open to the court to sanction proceedings for a breach of the order if, for example, the offender–patient refuses a physical form of treatment such as electro-convulsive therapy (ECT). Such orders are of use in cases of milder forms of mental illness and where it is considered there is no indication of potential serious harm to the offender and/or the public. The limited research that has been carried out into this form of treatment indicates that it is useful in circumstances where there is good cooperation between the psychiatric and probation services. However, the use of such orders is not frequent and has in fact been declining in recent years (Home Office 1997). (For recent accounts see Clark et al. 2002 and Richardson et al. 2003; see also Stone 2003.)

The arrangements for the disposal of mentally disturbed offenders are set out in Figure 2.1.

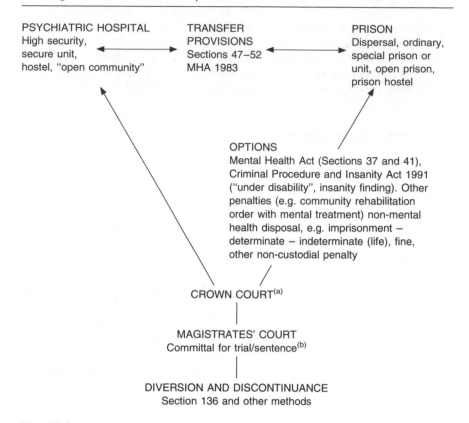

PSYCHIATRIC HOSPITAL
High security,
secure unit,
hostel, "open community"

TRANSFER
PROVISIONS
Sections 47–52
MHA 1983

PRISON
Dispersal, ordinary,
special prison or
unit, open prison,
prison hostel

OPTIONS
Mental Health Act (Sections 37 and 41),
Criminal Procedure and Insanity Act 1991
("under disability", insanity finding). Other
penalties (e.g. community rehabilitation
order with mental treatment) non-mental
health disposal, e.g. imprisonment –
determinate – indeterminate (life), fine,
other non-custodial penalty

CROWN COURT[a]

MAGISTRATES' COURT
Committal for trial/sentence[b]

DIVERSION AND DISCONTINUANCE
Section 136 and other methods

Notes: (a) Powers available to the Crown Court are also exercisable on appeal by the Court of Appeal. (b) Magistrates may also commit to the Crown Court with a view to a hospital order being made *with restrictions*.

Figure 2.1   Disposal of mentally disordered and disturbed offenders through the criminal justice, mental health and penal systems

## Hospital provision: Secure and semi-secure accommodation

A number of mentally disordered and disturbed offenders will be detained in ordinary psychiatric hospitals. Those who have committed grave crimes, and who are considered to be an immediate danger to the public if at large may, as we shall see shortly, be detained in a high-security (formerly known as a "special") hospital. In the latter stages of their rehabilitation towards the community, such offender–patients may be transferred to an ordinary psychiatric hospital or, more likely, to a medium and subsequently perhaps to a low-security unit. Until fairly recently, due to the absence of these less secure units and a reluctance on the part of ordinary psychiatric hospitals to take offender–patients, some of them might remain in conditions of high security for far longer than their condition or the safety of the public warranted. The situation is not quite so serious today, but sadly there are still some instances of lengthy delays in transfer. The Glancy (Department of Health and Social Security (1974)) and Butler Committees (Home Office and Department of Health and Social Security (1974)) both stressed the need for the setting up of medium secure units and the need for "ear-marked" funds to be made available for the purpose. In the event, such funds were used by health authorities for other purposes and it took a considerable time to "free up" the necessary funding.

Over the years there have been a number of problems in developing the *range* of units required to meet the varied problems presented by offender–patients. First, in the past, the secure units tended to be seen as an answer to the problem of the management of the difficult or disruptive patient detained in *ordinary* psychiatric hospitals. (It is important to note here that about one-third of offender–patients detained in one or other of the three high-security hospitals – to be described shortly – are not offenders, but have been transferred to high security accommodation because of their severely disruptive or violent behaviour.) To some extent, the situation has been eased in recent years by the establishment of special units catering for such patients who demonstrate what is known as "challenging behaviour". Second, in the past, secure units have tended to be seen as "mini-high-security" hospitals. Third, most of the medium secure units were designed to take offender–patients for a maximum of two years. A number of such patients have longer term needs for some form of secure accommodation. To meet this need, a small number of low-security units have been (and are being) set up. They are seen largely as a final "staging post" before final return to rehabilitation in the open community. Fourth, medium secure units are likely to cater on their admission wards for some quite acutely mentally ill patients. For some patients who are considered suitable for transfer from a high-security hospital, the presence of such ill patients is likely to have an unfortunate impact on them on arrival at a unit. This is because, over the years, they are likely to have reached a degree of emotional and mental stability and achieved freedom from acute psychotic symptoms. To suddenly find themselves placed in such a setting can be a very traumatic experience. Sometimes, such a placement has led to a break-down in a secure hospital patient's phased rehabilitation. Over the past 20 years or so there have been a number of studies describing the characteristics of treatment regimes for offender–patients located in conditions of medium security. The selection of references that follows may help readers who wish to research this aspect further; many of the papers provide details of other relevant literature. (See for example James et al. 1997.) Murray (1996) surveyed the use of beds in NHS medium secure units in England. Trends in admissions to one regional secure unit over a 15-year period have been described by Brown et al. (2001). Demographic and other characteristics of first admission patients in a similar unit have been described by Ricketts et al. (2001) and the needs of rural areas have been described by Jones et al. (2002). Watson (1998) has described the factors that influenced the design of regional secure units (see also Greenhalgh et al. 1996). Moss (1998) has provided a book-length account of the development and practice of medium secure provision by the private sector; more recently Castro et al. (2002) have published a small-scale follow-up study of such patients. Follow-up studies of patients in the public sector have been made by Quinn and Ward (2000).

## High-security (formerly special) hospitals

Under the provisions of Section 4 of the National Health Service and Community Care Act 1990, the Secretary of State for Social Services is required to provide and maintain such institutions as are necessary for persons subject to detention under the mental health legislation who, in his opinion, require treatment in conditions of special security because of their "dangerous, violent or criminal propensities". However, as already noted, about one-third of all such detained patients are *not* offenders, but are detained because of their difficult, disruptive or violent behaviour in ordinary psychiatric or mental handicap hospitals. There are three (formerly four) high-security hospitals in England (Broadmoor, Rampton and Ashworth (formerly Moss Side and Park Lane)) but none in Wales or Northern Ireland. The State Hospital at Carstairs in Scotland is the equivalent of an English high-security hospital and the Central Hospital at Dundrum in Dublin performs some of the functions of its English counterparts. Because Northern Ireland has no high-security hospital it sends a few of its more dangerous offender–patients to Carstairs or, more frequently, to Ashworth. The former "special hospitals" have had a long and, from time to time, somewhat chequered history. Formerly administered directly by the Department of Health, then by a specially created health authority – the Special Hospitals Service Authority (SHSA) – they have now been merged with general NHS provision, the aim being to bring these establishments alongside more general psychiatric practice and to reduce the isolation that seems to have plagued them over the years. A short account now follows of the three hospitals in question. They have about 1,300 patients, divided pretty much in equal numbers between them (Fennell and Yeates 2002).

### BROADMOOR

This is the oldest of the hospitals having been established in 1863, in Berkshire. Once beset by severe overcrowding, some relief was afforded by the building of Park Lane (now Ashworth) Hospital. However, the provision for female patients has been the subject of continued criticism in recent years and, at one time, its handling of ethnic minority (particularly African-Caribbean) patients left a good deal to be desired (see Prins et al. 1993). However, it appears that ethnic issues have recently begun to be addressed in a more sympathetic and constructive manner.

### RAMPTON HOSPITAL

Rampton, in North Nottinghamshire, was established in 1914 and in its earlier days tended to specialize in the management of mentally impaired offender–patients. It now has a more mixed population and there has been recent concentration on work with the severely personality disordered, notably those considered to be dangerous. This is evidenced by the "establishment" of a pilot special unit for the treatment of such patients. Overcrowding was once a serious problem and the hospital was the subject of an intensive inquiry into allegations of ill treatment of patients. However, in the last decade or so, the hospital has moved out of its "backwater" status (DHSS 1980: iii) and been revitalized by the appointment of an energetic review board and of more forward-looking staff at all levels.

### ASHWORTH COMPLEX

The complex, located at Maghull, Liverpool, consists of the former Moss Side (established 1933) and Park Lane (established 1974) Hospitals. At one time, Moss Side took mainly mentally impaired patients, but following integration with Park Lane, it now takes all three categories (mentally ill, mentally impaired and psychopathic) although there is some degree of specialization, notably in the management of the psychopathic (see later).

As already indicated, the high-security hospitals have come in for a good deal of criticism in the past, a lot of it justified. However, even their severest critics acknowledge that such institutions have to undertake a tremendously difficult task in attempting to combine containment, clinical treatment and rehabilitation in a climate of opinion that does not give high priority to the care of the "mad and the bad". There have been abuses, as witnessed in the damning report of Sir Louis Blom-Cooper's inquiry into conditions at Ashworth (Department of Health 1992), and the more recent inquiry into managerial and other deficiencies at the personality disorder unit at the same hospital (Fallon et al. 1999). The authors of the latest report described the establishment as "a scandalous and corrupt hospital". One result of the Fallon inquiry was increased concern over security. Sir Richard Tilt – former Director of the English Prison Service – was commissioned to carry out an inquiry (Tilt et al. 2000).

The review team made numerous recommendations, which included increasing physical perimeter security, increasing security measures within the hospital and increasing staff levels in the security service departments. The report has recently been criticised by two senior forensic psychiatrists – Tim Exworthy and Professor John Gunn (Exworthy and Gunn 2003). In brief, they regret the report's overemphasis on physical means of security and the extent to which these could be damaging to "relational" aspects of the hospital's environment. Tilt, in a reply to these criticisms, takes a different view, stating: "I believe firmly, as did all the members of my team, that the key to running successful treatment-orientated high security hospitals lies in ensuring that the public, patients and staff feel safe about their operation" (Tilt 2003: 548).

There have been recent calls for the high security hospitals to be closed down and replaced by smaller units. Wisdom suggests that the expertise that *does* reside in the secure hospitals needs to be maintained and not dissipated. Tidmarsh (1998), a very experienced former senior consultant at Broadmoor, indicates that patients at the hospital would prefer its current good facilities over and above proximity to relatives and friends. He puts the position very clearly:

> To decant these patients into worse facilities would be inhumane. To provide the equivalent safety in half a dozen mini Special Hospitals would be extremely expensive. If they were built on green field sites they would suffer from all the problems of isolation that have beset the existing Special Hospitals . . . It would seem therefore both humane and politically expedient to give up this idea, to lift the planning blight from the existing Special Hospitals and to provide them with the strong leadership they need to escape from the more unfortunate aspects of their recent history.
>
> (Tidmarsh 1998: 508)

Without being overoptimistic about their future, it is reasonable to suggest that the high-security hospitals are likely to embrace better times. Being part of the NHS general psychiatric provision should go some way to offset their former "splendid isolation" – an isolation that served to foster complacency in the past. Better trained and motivated staff are coming forward and the sometimes less than helpful attitudes of the Prison Officers' Association has been dissipated to a major extent. The fact that the two pilot centres for the management of dangerous personality disordered patients are located in Rampton and Broadmoor also augurs well for the future. Major research projects are being undertaken and some of these are described briefly but helpfully by Kaye and Franey (1998).

### Maximum secure accommodation in Scotland and Ireland

The State Hospital at Carstairs (established in 1944) has its functions defined in the Mental Health (Scotland) Act of 1984 – its "clientele" is, to all intents and purposes, the same as those in the high-security hospitals south of the border. It normally houses some 200 or so offender–patients, the majority suffering from psychotic illness. As already indicated, it very occasionally receives patients from Northern Ireland.

### Eire

The Central Hospital at Dundrum has a predominantly male population of some 100 or so offender–patients, about half of whom are said to suffer from schizophrenic illness. A large percentage of these patients are the subjects of transfer from prison.

## Penal provision

### Prison psychiatric services

Brief reference has already been made to prison psychiatric care. This section provides some further detail. Acts of 1774 and 1779 required prisons to appoint a physician and an organized full-time medical service began with the establishment of the Prison Commission in 1887. Such appointments can be seen as the forerunners of a range of other professional appointments that were subsequently to swell the ranks of prison staffs, for example chaplains, psychologists, specialist nursing officers, probation officers (formerly prison welfare officers), education personnel and works and occupations staff. The history of mental health services in prisons reveals that there were a number of early attempts to describe and classify mentally disordered offenders received in prison. Perhaps one of the most significant was the report authored by East and de Hubert (1939), which, to some extent, paved the way for the foundation of Grendon Underwood psychiatric prison in 1962 (see later). It is possibly not widely known that, over the years, prison medical staff have had general oversight of the total care of *both prisoners and prison staff and also a concern with environmental health matters*. As indicated earlier in this chapter, such work is now becoming an NHS responsibility and the post of prison medical officer will be phased out in due course. Sadly, there are still a number of mentally disordered offenders who should be in hospital (although the numbers of "transfer directions" under the Mental Health Act have increased modestly in recent years), and an even greater number who, while not fulfilling the strict criteria for transfer under the mental health legislation, would benefit from psychiatric oversight and management. In a recent paper, Dr John Reed, former Chief Medical Inspector, HM Inspectorate of Prisons, expressed his concern over the continuing delays in transferring mentally disturbed prisoners to NHS hospitals. However, he is cautious about extending treatment for non-consenting patients in prison beyond emergencies, as advocated by some (see, for example, Earthrowl et al. 2003; Wilson and Forrester 2002), on the grounds that prisons currently do not have adequate medical resources to carry out such treatments safely.

A substantial work describing and analyzing the work of Grendon is that by Genders and Player (1995). Prisoners' views concerning Grendon have recently been very thoughtfully described by Wilson and McCabe (2002). A more anecdotal account has been written by Smartt (2002). There are a number of other therapeutically orientated units within the prison system (examples being at HMP Wakefield and Wormwood Scrubs and the Young Offenders' Institution at Feltham). A "second Grendon" was opened at HMP Dovegate, Staffordshire, in 1991. An interesting feature of this establishment is that it was procured under private contract (see Genders 2003). Three further developments should be noted by way of concluding this section. First, the report entitled *The Future Organisation of Prison Health Care* published in 1999 set out the policy of prison healthcare being provided by a partnership with the NHS based on the principle of equivalence (Home Office 1999). Second, the development of prison "mental health in-reach services", which is now in a process of rapid development. And, in 2001 the Department of Health, HM Prison Service and the National Assembly for Wales published an important document setting out a strategy for the development and modernizing of mental health services in prisons (Department of Health, HM Prison Service, National Assembly for Wales 2001). Finally, it should be noted that the full transfer of responsibility for prison healthcare will be fully implemented over a 5-year period.

### Supervision in the community

At some point in their careers, attempts will be made to relocate offenders and offender–patients into the community. Those dealt with through the penal system, even though they may have mental health problems, will be dealt with through release on parole or life licence. Those who have been dealt with under the terms of a hospital order with restrictions will be released on what is known as a "conditional discharge". Supervision of those dealt with through the penal system will be undertaken by a probation officer and, if there are mental health problems, supervision may also include psychiatric intervention. Those released through the mental health system will be supervised by either a probation officer or a local authority social worker. At one time, the supervision of restricted patients was almost always undertaken by the probation service; today, supervision is more likely to be undertaken by a local authority social worker. Individual circumstances will govern the choice. If the offender–patient was previously well known to the probation service, then it will most likely be the probation service that will be asked to supervise. If additional community resources are required, such as a hostel or daycare facility, then social services will be most likely to be chosen. In addition to social supervision, almost without exception, the offender–patient will also be under the care and supervision of a named psychiatrist and perhaps a community psychiatric nurse. In both penal and healthcare orders for release there will be specific requirements, such as place of residence, notification of change of address etc. and any other requirements that are deemed to be in the interests of the offender/offender–patient and, most importantly, the safety of the public.

Issues relating to public safety and the assessment and management of risk are extremely important and are dealt with in detail in Chapter 8. In restricted cases, it is essential that there is open and constructive liaison between the social supervisor and the psychiatrist. Clear procedures for this should be established between the parties involved – offender–patient – social supervisor – psychiatrist and community nurse. The Home Office issues guidelines on best practice and these are updated from time to time. Not infrequently, decisions have to be made at a time of crisis. For example, an offender–patient's behaviour may have deteriorated to the extent that recall to hospital may need to be considered or, in the case of a parolee or life licensee, recall to prison. The worker carrying responsibility for the case (and by definition they will almost always be complex and difficult) should have easy access to their line management for support and advice. Access for further advice from the relevant department of the Home Office (mental health unit or parole unit) is essential. Cases in which advice would need to be sought would include those where there appears to be an actual or potential risk to the public, where contact with the offender/offender–patient has been lost, where there has been a substantial breach of the discharge conditions or where the individual's behaviour suggests a need for recall for further in-patient treatment or where the offender/offender–patient has been charged with, or convicted of, a further offence. An offender–patient who is recalled to hospital by order of the Home Secretary has to have his or her case referred to a Mental Health Review Tribunal within one month of his or her recall. (See earlier discussion of the evidence required for such recall.) In deciding whether or not to issue a warrant for recall the Home Secretary will treat each case on its merits. If an offender–patient has been hospitalized in the past for very serious violence or homicide, comparatively minor irregularities of conduct or failure to cooperate within the terms of the conditional discharge *might* well be sufficient to merit the consideration of recall. Similar considerations apply in relation to offenders released on parole or life licence. If all goes well, the conditions of a life licence, such as the requirement to live in a specific place, to report to a probation officer, to receive visits or not to take specific employments, may be cancelled – but customarily not before some four or five years have elapsed; the life licence itself remains in force for life. In the case of conditionally discharged restricted patients, the requirements for supervision, or the order for conditional discharge itself, may be lifted by the Home Secretary or by Mental Health Review Tribunal. Currently, there are several hundred life-sentence prisoners being supervised by the probation service and a similar number of conditionally discharged restricted patients by local authority social workers, probation officers and psychiatrists (and community mental health staff in some cases).

## National decision-making and advisory bodies

Brief reference has been made to the mechanism of parole, to the Mental Health Review tribunal and to the Home Secretary's one-time Advisory Board on Restricted Patients. Each of these is now considered in a little more detail.

### Parole Board

The arrangements for release on parole and life licence were initiated in the Criminal Justice Act of 1967 and have been amended from time to time. The Act of 1967 established the Board as an independent body, appointed by the Home Secretary, to offer him or her advice and to take decisions on his or her behalf on the early release of determinate or life-sentence prisoners. More recent enactments have increased the categories of prisoners who are made subject to parole supervision. Over the years its independence has been further marked by the Board's establishment as an executive non-departmental public body from 1 July 1996.

The work of the Board has been accompanied by a considerable increase in the size of its membership. Under the terms of the 1967 Act the Board was required to include among its members the following categories of people:

- a person who holds, or has held, judicial office
- a psychiatrist
- a person who has experience of the supervision or aftercare of discharged prisoners (usually a chief or assistant chief probation officer)
- a person who has made a study of the causes of crime and the treatment of offenders (usually an academic criminologist).

The Board currently includes a number of members of each of these categories and, in addition, it includes "independent" members who are qualified by a range of varied experiences to make significant contributions to the Board's work. Membership of the Board for the year 2001–2002 consisted of a full-time chairman, three full-time members, and about 100 part-time members.

The functions of the Board are set out in the latest annual report of the Board for 2001–2002 (Parole Board 2002) as follows:

- Considers, under the Criminal Justice Act 1991, the early release of determinate sentenced prisoners serving four years or more. By the Parole Board (Transfer of Functions) Order 1998, the Board has delegated authority to decide applications from prisoners serving less than 15 years; for those serving 15 years or more it makes a recommendation to the Secretary of State.
- Considers, under Part II of the Crimes (Sentences) Act 1997, the release of mandatory life sentenced prisoners and makes recommendations to the Secretary of State.[a]
- Has authority, under the Crime (Sentences) Act 1997, to direct the release of discretionary life-sentenced prisoners, those given life sentences under Section 2 of the 1997 Act (now Section 109 of the Powers of Criminal Courts (Sentencing) Act 2000) and persons detained during Her Majesty's Pleasure.[b]
- Makes, under the Criminal Justice Act 1991 (in the case of determinate-sentenced prisoners) or the Crime (Sentences) Act 1997 (in the case of life-sentenced prisoners), recommendations to the Secretary of State on the revocation of licences of prisoners who have breached their licence conditions and considers representations by prisoners who have been recalled to prison.
(Annual Report of the Parole Board and Accounts 2001–2: 2002: 22)

*Notes*: (a) Mandatory life sentences are those given to those convicted of murder. (b) Discretionary life sentences are those given to those convicted of certain grave crimes such as manslaughter, rape, arson, etc.

A recent judgement by the European Court of Human Rights, in the case of Stafford in May 2002, has changed the procedures by which mandatory life-sentence cases are dealt with. Hitherto, such cases were considered by the Board "on paper"; such cases must now be dealt with by an oral hearing (as is the case for other life-sentence cases). The final decision in such post-tariff cases will henceforth rest with the Board and not with the Home Secretary. This ruling will greatly increase the Board's workload[1]

(Parole Board 2003). The then Chairman of the Board, David Hatch, in his foreword to the Annual Report, provided clear recognition of this increase in the Board's functions and the consequent workload:

> These workload changes are immense and tinkering at the edges clearly will not deliver what is required of us, change will have to be fundamental. As oral hearings accelerate, it is becoming ever clearer that the Board is moving from being an Executive Body to a full-blooded Tribunal. This, together with the increasing influence of the European Court of Human Rights, raises serious questions . . .
>
> (Annual Report of the Parole Board 2001–2: 2002: 6)

The Chairman's reference to the European Court of Human Rights reflects the gradual erosion of the powers of the Home Secretary as a result of that body's judgements in matters of sentencing and subsequent release. This erosion has been gathering momentum over the past decade, a momentum most of us would applaud.

### Mental Health Review Tribunal (MHRT)

Mental Health Review Tribunals were introduced by the Mental Health Act 1959. They were intended to serve as a replacement for the role of the lay magistracy under previous lunacy legislation in safeguarding the rights of patients subject to detention; they also replaced some of the functions of the old Board of Control to which a patient could make representations against detention in hospital. The role and scope of the Tribunals were extended under the Mental Health Act 1983; the Act gave greater opportunities for appeal against detention and for the automatic review of patients' cases at regular intervals if they had not applied themselves. The MHRT is a *judicial* body and has considerable statutory powers that are independent of any government agency such as the Home Office.

Currently, the main purpose of an MHRT is to review the cases of compulsorily detained patients and, if the relevant criteria are satisfied, to direct their discharge. This task involves examination of complex and often conflicting elements giving rise to concern for the liberty of the patient (or offender–patient), on the one hand and, as with the Parole Board, the protection of the public, on the other. The functions of the MHRT are likely to change considerably if the government's current proposals receive statutory authority (these proposed changes are dealt with later in this chapter). There are MHRTs for each health authority region. MHRT panels consist of three members; a legal member (who presides), a medical member (almost always a psychiatrist of considerable experience) and a so-called "lay" member, who is neither a lawyer nor a doctor. As indicated earlier, panels hearing "restricted" cases must be presided over by a circuit judge or lawyer of equivalent standing. All three Tribunal members have equal status, an equal role in the decision-making process and in drafting the reasons for the final decision. Hearings are almost always in private but, in certain circumstances, a patient may request a public hearing. These days patients are almost always legally represented. In particularly difficult or possibly contentious cases, other interested parties, such as the Home Office, may be legally represented, usually by counsel. Tribunals have not been without their critics. Peay made an extensive critical study of Tribunal decision making (Peay 1989).

Two inquiries into homicides committed by former offender–patients made serious criticisms of the system. In the first of these, the case of Andrew Robinson, details of his original offence were inadequate so that the Tribunal had to make decisions on imperfect evidence. At one Tribunal, the patient had refused to be examined by the medical member (a requirement under Tribunal rules). Despite this, the Tribunal went ahead, determined the case and gave the patient an absolute discharge. The inquiry team acknowledged that at the various Tribunal hearings the members were often having to act on the information before them and that this information was often seriously inadequate (Blom-Cooper et al. 1995).

In the second case, that of Jason Mitchell, the inquiry team made further criticisms of Tribunal practice. The first of these concerned the making of a deferred conditional discharge that contained requirements beyond the Tribunal's legal remit. Blom-Cooper and his colleagues (1996) made a number of recommendations: (a) clinical psychologists should be added to the list of "lay" members who can be appointed to MHRTs; (b) MHRTs should have available more detailed information about an offender–patients index offence (this has subsequently been remedied, to some extent, by the Home Office); (c) in restricted cases (as was Mitchell's), the medical member of the Tribunal should preferably be a forensic psychiatrist; (d) MHRT members should be afforded follow-up; in those cases where an offender–patient had re-offended in serious fashion after discharge, a confidential retrospective review should be held (see Brunning 1996). (For those readers wishing to learn more about Tribunals, their functions and the issues arising from them, Eldergill's magisterial work is a mine of information (Eldergill 1997).)

The MHRT is not to be confused with the Mental Health Act Commission. The latter was established by the Mental Health Act 1983 to oversee the welfare and interests of detained patients. Some of its functions are to deal with complaints and to appoint "second opinion" doctors who are required to intervene in certain circumstances when compulsory treatment is being proposed. It is required to present a report on its work to parliament every two years. The Commission has no power to order the release of detained patients. As with the MHRT, if government proposals receive the force of law in due course, its functions will virtually disappear and be taken over by a new body. (See the concluding section of this chapter.)

### Home Secretary's Advisory Board on Restricted Patients

Following the conviction and sentence of the late Francis Graham Young for murder by poisoning, the Home Secretary, acting on the recommendation of the inquiry into Young's case (Home Office and DHSS 1973), established a non-statutory advisory committee (known then as the Aarvold Board) to advise him in those restricted cases: (a) that were considered to be particularly problematic; (b) that were considered to need special care in assessment; and (c) where there was thought to be a fear of possible future risk to the public. This committee, known as the Home Secretary's Advisory Board on Restricted Patients, merely proffered advice to the Home Secretary. In recent times, it dealt with very few cases and its workload decreased considerably, to the extent that the Board was abolished in September 2003. This currently leaves the MHRT as the sole body in cases where the Home Secretary has not approved the offender–patient's conditional discharge himself. Membership of the Committee was small; it included a legal chairperson, two psychiatrists, a director of social services, a chief probation officer and two other members who were considered to have wide experience of the criminal justice system.

## Proposals for legislative and administrative changes

### Background to the legislative proposals

The 1983 Mental Health Act was hailed as a much needed reform of previous mental health legislation, notably the Mental Health Act of 1959. However, over the next few years, various deficiencies in the 1983 Act became apparent. Some of these concerned problems of interpretation of the Act and, in particular, the legal requirements in respect of offender–patients. Under the Act of 1959, very few cases went to judicial review on points of law and practice; under the 1983 Act, a very large number of cases have been reviewed by this means. One thing that emerged from these various deliberations and decisions was the highly complex nature of the 1983 Act. These facts, coupled with excessive anxiety about the behaviour of a number of mentally disturbed individuals in the community, for example, the activities of people such as Michael Fagin, who gained entry to the Queen's bedroom, and Ben Silcock who managed to get into the lion's enclosure at London Zoo, all helped to provoke a need for change; a change that was further promoted by a small number of homicides committed by patients or ex-patients of the mental health services. Such events led central government to the view that "community care" was failing; this gave further impetus to an already acknowledged need for reform. There is also little doubt that media "hype" added to these concerns. The proposals for reform have followed a lengthy and complicated route and it is possible to refer to them only in outline here. Those wishing to pursue them should consult the works quoted.

In November 1999 the government published a consultation document (Department of Health 1999a) based in part on the advice of an expert committee chaired by Professor Genevra Richardson. Professor Richardson's Committee (Department of Health 1999b) was given a narrow and highly prescribed remit by the Department of Health; in the event, a number of their very sensible proposals did not appear in the consultation document. (For summaries of the main proposals in the White Paper see Prins 2001a, 2001b. The second of these papers, "Offenders, deviants or patients", reflects the ambiguity and uncertainty that surround "high-risk" patients and offender–patients as evidenced in the White Paper.) These reviews were then followed by further government publications, entitled (somewhat confusingly) *Reforming the Mental Health Act* (Department of Health 2000). There are three parts to this documentation: *Part I* sets out the new legal framework; *Part II* deals with the "high-risk patients"; and *Part III* consists of a summary of the consultation responses to the earlier government proposals.

Following these publications, the government published in 2002 its draft Mental Health Bill (Department of Health 2002a), which was accompanied by explanatory notes (2002b) and a consultation document (2002c). With the publication of what would seem to most observers to be a "deluge" of consultation material, one must conjecture that the government had in mind that many of the far reaching changes they proposed would not be favourably received. This proved to be the case and criticisms of the proposals have come from every conceivable quarter in the mental health field. Most of the criticisms have centred around the proposed all embracing definition of mental disorder and the possibilities of abrogation of individual human rights for those adjudged to be severely personality disordered and dangerous. Despite the expectations of many that the Bill would be debated in parliament in the 2003 session, this was not the case and the Bill did not, in fact, appear in the Queen's Speech in November 2002. However, in June 2004 the Secretary of State for Health indicated that the draft Bill would be introduced in time for the Queen's Speech in November (*The Independent*, 16 June 2004: 2). Indeed, the second draft Bill has now been presented and referred to in a cross-party committee of MPs and peers for consideration, because of its "complex nature" (*The Independent*, 9 September 2004: 5). Expression of the almost unanimous criticisms and opposition to the proposals may be found in Bindman et al. (2003),

Grounds (2001), Moncrieff (2003), Peay (2000) and Sugarman (2002). (For an excellent review of recent Scottish proposals, see also Darjee (2003).)

## Summary of main proposals

### General psychiatric provision

This is a redefinition of mental disorder, namely: "Mental disorder means any disability or disorder of mind or brain which results in impairment or disturbance of mental functioning; and 'mentally disordered' is to be read accordingly." It should be noted here that the specific exclusion of sexual deviation and alcohol dependence, which appears in the 1983 Act, is not mentioned. The 1983 Act (Section 1(3)) prohibits detention "by reason only of promiscuity or other immoral conduct, sexual deviance, or dependence on alcohol or drugs".

The Mental Health *Review* Tribunal will disappear and be replaced by a Mental Health Tribunal; this new body will authorize both admission and discharge, a significant departure from previous practice that may well have human rights implications. The Mental Health Act Commission will be replaced by a new body – a "Commission for Mental Health". This new body will not carry out the inspectorial functions of the Mental Health Act Commission, but will, it appears, exercise a monitoring function over diverse aspects of the care of patients as, for example, the quality of staff training, appointments to the new Tribunals, advocacy arrangements etc. Under the proposed legislation, it will be possible to make non-resident orders for compulsory assessment and treatment in the community. The power to make guardianship orders under existing legislation is to be abolished. This would seem to indicate that the future emphasis will be on medical treatment rather than on "care" as is inherent in the concept of guardianship. However, guardianship under both the 1959 and 1983 Acts has not been widely used.

### Specific proposals relating to offenders

*Part III* of the draft Bill clarifies the conditions under which a person may be remanded for reports to be provided on bail and in custody; such reports in future will be known as mental health reports. The Bill provides for a "care plan" for those being dealt with by remand or committal to hospital. Powers of Crown and Appeal Courts to make restriction orders remain much the same, but the power to make a hospital and limitation direction is by implication no longer restricted to persons suffering from "psychopathic" disorder as this category of disorder is no longer separately defined. Hospital orders are replaced by the term "mental health orders".

*Note*: It should be emphasized that these summaries give only the briefest details of the proposals in the draft Bill. Those requiring elaboration should consult the draft Bill (Department of Health 2002) and, in particular, the explanatory notes (Department of Health 2002). I deal with the controversial proposals for dealing with those demonstrating severe personality disorder and considered to be dangerous in Chapter 4.

## Conclusion

This chapter has covered a wide range of topics concerning the legal and administrative arrangements for dealing with mentally disturbed and disordered offenders. It is important to reiterate that law and practice are currently in a state of flux. In the chapters that follow, the emphasis is on clinical aspects of treatment and management.

## Note

1    In the case of *Stafford v. United Kingdom* (2002) 35 EHRR 1121, the European Court of Human Rights held that prisoners serving mandatory life sentences for murder, once the minimum period required for the penal aspect of the sentence had been served, should have their cases reviewed and decided by a quasi-judicial body and *not* by the Home Secretary. In November 2002 the House of Lords decided in the case of Anderson (*R. [Anderson] v. Secretary of State for the Home Department* (2002) UKHL 46 [2002] 3 WLR 1800) that the manner in which the sentence was determined should be in open court and dealt with as part of the sentencing process. The Home Secretary has not taken kindly to these erosions of his powers and at the time of writing (autumn 2003) has put forward proposals in the Criminal Justice Bill currently being debated in parliament to establish sentencing guidelines for certain classes of killers. Whole-life sentences would be passed on multiple murderers, murders that showed premeditation, sexual or sadistic murders, terrorist murders and murderers previously convicted of murder. Other forms of murder would attract a starting point of 30 years (for example, murder of a police or prison officer, murders involving firearms etc.). It is not clear how the finer distinctions will be made between these different forms of murderous activity. In addition, the Home Secretary proposes to establish a new body to deal with sentencing guidelines; membership would include representatives from the police, prison and probation services and victims of crimes. (*Source: Penal Policy File*, No. 91: *Howard Journal* (2003) 42: 394–5.)

## References

Allderidge, P. (1979) "Hospitals, madhouses and asylums: Cycles in the care of the insane", *British Journal of Psychiatry* 134: 321–4.

—— (1985) "Bedlam: Fact or phantasy", in W. F. Bynum, R. Porter and M. Shepherd (eds), *The Anatomy of Madness: Essays in the History of Psychiatry*, Vol. 2: *Institutions and Society*, London: Tavistock.

Bartlett, P. and Sandland, R. (2000) *Mental Health Law: Policy and Practice*, London: Blackstone Press.

Bean, P., Bingley, W., Bynoe, I., Rassaby, E. and Rogers, A. (1991) *Out of Harm's Way*, London: MIND.

Bindman, J., Maingay, S. and Szmukler, G. (2003) "The Human Rights Act and mental health legislation", *British Journal of Psychiatry* 182: 91–4.

Blom-Cooper, L., QC, Hally, H. and Murphy, E. (1995) *The Falling Shadow: One Patient's Mental Health Care, 1978–1993*, London: Duckworth.

Blom-Cooper, L., QC, Grounds, A., Parker, A. and Taylor, M. (1996) *The Case of Jason Mitchell: Report of the Independent Panel of Inquiry*, London: Duckworth.

Boswell, G. (1996) *Young and Dangerous: The Backgrounds and Careers of Section 53 Offenders*, Aldershot: Avebury Publishing.

Bowden, P. (1993) "New directions for service provision" in W. Watson and A. Grounds (eds), *The Mentally Disordered Offender in an Era of Community Care*, Cambridge: Cambridge University Press.

Brown, C. S. H., Lloyd, K. R. and Donovan, M. (2001) "Trends in admissions to a regional secure unit (1983–1997)", *Medicine, Science and the Law* 41: 35–40.

Brunning, J. (1996) "The case of Jason Mitchell: Report of the independent panel of inquiry", *Mental Health Review Tribunal's Members' News-sheet* 17, 5–7.

Castro, M., Cockerton, T. and Birke, S. (2002) "From discharge to follow-up: A small-scale study of medium secure provision in the private sector", *British Journal of Forensic Practice* 4: 31–9.

Chiswick, D. (1990) "Applied criminology", *Current Opinion in Psychiatry* 3: 754–7.

Clark, T., Kenny-Herbert, J., Baker, J. and Humphreys, M. (2002) "Psychiatric probation orders: Failed provision or future panacea", *Medicine, Science and the Law* 42: 58–63.

Coid, J. (1991) "Psychiatric profiles of difficult disruptive prisoners", in K. Bottomley and W. Hay (eds), *Special Units for Difficult Prisoners*, Hull: Centre for Criminology and Criminal Justice, University of Hull.

Crown Prosecution Service (n.d.) *Code for Crown Prosecutors*, London: Crown Prosecution Service.

Darjee, R. (2003) "The reports of the Millan and Maclean Committees: New proposals for mental health legislation for high-risk offenders in Scotland", *Journal of Forensic Psychiatry* 14: 7–25.

Darjee, R., Crichton, J. and Thomson, L. (2000) "Crime and Punishment (Scotland) Act, 1997: A survey of psychiatrists' views concerning the Scottish 'hybrid order'", *Journal of Forensic Psychiatry* 11: 608–20.

—— (2002) "Crime and Punishment (Scotland) Act, 1997: A survey of sentencers' views concerning the Scottish 'hybrid order'", *Medicine, Science and the Law* 42: 76–86.

Department of Health (1992) *Report of the Committee of Inquiry into Complaints About Ashworth Hospital*, Vols. 1 and 2 (Chairman, Sir Louis Blom-Cooper, QC), Cmnd 2028-I and II, London: HMSO.

—— (1999a) *Reform of the Mental Health Act, 1983: Proposals for Consultation*, CM 4480, London: TSO.

—— (1999b) *Report of the Expert Committee: Review of the Mental Health Act, 1983 (Richardson Report)*, London: TSO.

—— (2000) *Reforming the Mental Health Act: Part I, The New Legal Framework, Part II, High-Risk Patients, Part III, Summary of Consultation Responses*, CM 5016-I, CM 5016-II, London, TSO.

Department of Health (2002) "Prison Health Transferred to Department of Health", *Department of Health Press Release* 64N/02, 24 September (quoted in Kinton 2002).

—— (2002a) *Draft Mental Health Bill*, CM 5538-I, London: TSO.

—— (2002b) *Draft Mental Health Bill – Explanatory Notes*, CM 5538-II, London: TSO.

—— (2002c) *Consultation Document*, CM 5538-III.

Department of Health, HM Prison Service, National Assembly for Wales (2001) *Changing the Outlook: A Strategy For the Development and Modernising of Mental Health Services in Prisons*, London: Department of Health

Department of Health and Home Office (1992) *Review of Health and Social Services for Mentally Disordered Offenders and Others Requiring Similar Services* (Chairman, Dr John Reed, CB) *Final Summary Report*, Cmnd 2088, London: HMSO.

Department of Health and Social Security (DHSS) (1974) *Revised Report of the Working Party on Security in NHS Psychiatric Hospitals (Glancy Report)*, London: DHSS.

—— (1980) *Report of the Review of Rampton Hospital (Boynton Report)*, Cmnd 8073, London: HMSO.

Duffy, D., Lenihan, S. and Kennedy, H. (2003) "Screening prisoners for mental disorders", *Psychiatric Bulletin* 27: 241–2.

Earthrowl, M., O'Grady, J. and Birmingham, L. (2003) "Providing treatment to prisoners with mental disorders", *British Journal of Psychiatry* 182: 299–302.

East, W. N. and de Hubert, W. H. B. (1939) *Psychological Treatment of Crime*, London: HMSO.

Eastman, N. (1996) "Hybrid orders: An analysis of their likely effects on sentencing practice and on forensic psychiatric practice and services", *Journal of Forensic Psychiatry* 7: 481–94.

Eldergill, A. (1997) *Mental Health Review Tribunals: Law and Practice*, London: Sweet & Maxwell.

—— (2002) "The legal structure of mental health services", *Journal of Mental Health Law* 7: 139–68.

Exworthy, T. and Gunn, J. (2003) "Taking another tilt at high-secure hospitals", *British Journal of Psychiatry* 182: 469–71.

Exworthy, T. and Parrott, J. (1993) "Evaluation of a diversion scheme from custody at magistrates' courts", *Journal of Forensic Psychiatry* 4: 497–505.

—— (1997) "Comparative evaluation of a diversion from custody scheme", *Journal of Forensic Psychiatry* 8: 406–16.

Fallon, P., QC, Bluglass, R., Edwards, B. and Daniels, G. (1999) *Report of the Committee of Inquiry into the Personality Disorder Unit, Ashworth Special Hospital* (2 Vols. and executive summary), CM 4194(I) and (II), London: TSO.

Fennell, P. and Yeates, V. (2002) "To serve which master? – criminal justice policy, community care and the mentally disordered offender", in A. Buchanan (ed.), *Care of the Mentally Disordered Offender in the Community*, Oxford: Oxford University Press.

Fowles, A. J. (1993) "The mentally disordered offender in an era of community care", in W. Watson and A. Grounds (eds), *The Mentally Disordered Offender in an Era of Community Care*, Cambridge: Cambridge University Press.

Gavin, N., Parsons, S. and Grubin, D. (2003) "Reception screening and mental health needs assessment in a male remand prison", *Psychiatric Bulletin* 27: 251–3.

Geelan, S. D., Campbell, M. J. and Bartlett, A. (2001) "What happens afterwards? A follow-up study of those diverted from custody to hospital in the first 2.5 years of a metropolitan diversion scheme", *Medicine, Science and the Law* 41: 122–8.

Genders, E. (2003) "Privatisation and innovation – rhetoric and reality: The development of a therapeutic community prison", *Howard Journal of Criminal Justice* 42: 137–57.

Genders, E. and Player, E. (1995) *Grendon: A Study of a Therapeutic Prison*, Oxford: Clarendon Press.

Greenhalgh, N. M., Wylie, K., Rix, K. J. B. and Tamlyn, D. (1996) "Pilot mental health assessment and diversion scheme in an English metropolitan petty sessional division", *Medicine, Science and the Law* 36: 52–8.

Grounds, A. T. (1990a) "Transfers of sentenced prisoners to hospital", *Criminal Law Review* June: 544–51.

Grounds, A. T. (1990b) "The transfer of sentenced prisoners to hospital 1960–1963: A study of one special hospital", *British Journal of Criminology* 31: 54–71.

Grounds, A. T. (1991) "The mentally disordered offender in the criminal process: Some research and policy questions", in K. Herbst and J. Gunn (eds), *The Mentally Disordered Offender*, London: Butterworth-Heinemann (in association with the Mental Health Foundation).

Grounds. A. T. (2001) "Reforming the Mental Health Act", *British Journal of Psychiatry* 179: 387–9.

Gunn, J. (2000) "A millennium monster is born", *Criminal Behaviour and Mental Health* 10: 73–6.

Gunn, J., Maden, A. and Swinton, M. (1991) *Mentally Disordered Prisoners*, London: Home Office.

Hetherington, T. (1989) *Prosecution in the Public Interest*, London: Waterlow.

Home Office (1990) *Report of a Review into Suicides and Self-Harm in Prison Service Establishments in England and Wales* (*Report by Judge Tumim to the Home Secretary*), Cmnd 1383, London: HMSO.

—— (1991) *Prison Disturbances, 1990, Report of an Inquiry by The Rt Hon Lord Justice Woolf* (Pts 1 and 2) *and His Honour Judge Stephen Tumim* (Pt 1), London: HMSO.

—— (1997) *Probation Statistics, England and Wales*, London: Government Statistical Service.

Home Office and Department of Health (1991) *Review of Health and Social Services for Mentally Disordered Offenders and Others Requiring Similar Services: Steering Committee* (Chairman, Dr John Reed, CB). *Report of the Services Advisory Groups with Glossary*, London: HMSO.

Home Office and Department of Health and Social Security (DHSS) (1973) *Report of the Review of Procedures for the Discharge and Supervision of Psychiatric Patients Subject to Special Restrictions (Aarvold Report)*, Cmnd 5191, London: HMSO.

—— (1974) *Interim Report on the Committee on Mentally Abnormal Offenders* (*Butler Committee*), Cmnd 5698, London: HMSO.

—— (1975) *Report of the Committee on Mentally Abnormal Offenders (Butler Committee)*, Cmnd 6244, London: HMSO.

Hucklesby. A. (1997) "Court culture: An explanation of variations in the use of bail by magistrates' courts", *Howard Journal of Criminal Justice* 36: 129–45.

James, D. (1999) "Court diversion at 10 years: Can it work, does it work and has it a future?", *Journal of Forensic Psychiatry* 10: 507–24.

James, D. V. and Hamilton, L. W. (1991) "The Clerkenwell scheme – assessing efficacy and cost of a psychiatric liaison service to a magistrates' court", *British Medical Journal* 303: 282–5.

James, D., Cripps, J., Gilluley, P. and Harlow, P. (1997) "A court-focused model of forensic psychiatry provision to Central London: Abolishing remands to prison", *Journal of Forensic Psychiatry* 8: 390–405.

Jewesbury, I. and McCulloch, A. (2002) "Public policy and mentally disordered offenders in the UK", in A. Buchanan (ed.), *Care of the Mentally Disordered Offender in the Community*, Oxford: Oxford University Press.

Jones, C., Jones, B. and Ward, S. (2002) "Mentally disordered offenders: The need for a diversion service in a rural area", *British Journal of Forensic Practice* 4: 19–23.

Jones, R. (2001) *Mental Health Act Manual*, 7th ed., London: Sweet & Maxwell.

Joseph, P. (1992) *Psychiatric Assessment at the Magistrates' Courts*, London: Home Office and Department of Health.

Joseph, P. and Potter, M. (1993) I "Diversion from custody" – psychiatric assessment at the magistrates' court" and II "Effect on hospital and prison resources", *British Journal of Psychiatry* 162: 325–30 and 330–4.

Kaye, C. and Franey, S. (1998) "Research and development", in C. Kaye and A. Franey (eds), *Managing High Security (Forensic Focus 9)*, London: Jessica Kingsley.

Kinton, M. (2002) "Should we allow compulsory mental health treatment in prisons?", *Journal of Mental Health Law* 8: 304–7.

Laing, J. (1997) "The likely impact of mandatory and minimum sentences on the disposal of mentally disordered offenders", *Journal of Forensic Psychiatry* 8: 504–8.

—— (1999) *Care or Custody? Mentally Disordered Offenders in the Criminal Justice System*, Oxford: Oxford University Press.

Laing, R. D. and Esterson, A. (1970) *Sanity, Madness and the Family: Families of Schizophrenics*, Harmondsworth: Penguin.

Leff, J. (2001) *The Unbalanced Mind*, London: Weidenfeld & Nicolson.

Leicestershire County Council (1993) *The Leicestershire Inquiry, 1992: Report of an Inquiry Into Aspects of the Management of Children's Homes in Leicestershire between 1973 and 1986* (Chairman, Andrew Kirkwood, QC), Leicester: Leicestershire County Council.

Liebling, A. (1998) *Deaths of Offenders: The Hidden Side of Justice*, Winchester: Waterside Press (on behalf of the Institute for the Study and Treatment of Delinquency).

Lloyd, M. G. and Bénézech, M. (1991) "Criminal responsibility in the French judicial system", *Journal of Forensic Psychiatry* 2: 281–94.

Macpherson, Sir W. (1999) *The Stephen Lawrence Inquiry*, Vols. 1 and 2, CM 4262 I and II, London: TSO.

Moncrieff, J. (2003) "The politics of a new Mental Health Act", *British Journal of Psychiatry* 183: 8–9.

Moss, K. R. (1998) *Medium Secure Psychiatric Provision in the Private Sector*, Aldershot: Ashgate Publishing.

Murray, K. (1996) "The use of beds in NHS medium secure units in England", *Journal of Forensic Psychiatry* 7: 504–24.

NACRO (1993) *Mental Health Advisory Committee (Policy Paper No.1): Community Care and Mentally Disordered Offenders*, London: NACRO.

—— (1996) *Youth Crime Section: Briefing Paper, September*, London: NACRO.

Parker, E. (1980) "Mentally disordered offenders and their protection from punitive sanction", *International Journal of Law and Psychiatry* 3: 461–9.

—— (1985) "The development of secure provision", in L. Gostin (ed.), *Secure Provision: A Review of Special Services For the Mentally Ill and Mentally Handicapped in England and Wales*, London: Tavistock.

Parole Board (2002) *Annual Report*, London: TSO.

—— (2003) *Business Plan, 2003–2004*, London: TSO.

Parsons, S., Walker, L. and Grubin, D. (2001) "Prevalence of mental disorder in female remand prisons", *Journal of Forensic Psychiatry* 12: 194–202.

Peay, J. (1989) *Tribunals on Trial: A Study in Decision Making Under the Mental Health Act, 1983*, Oxford: Clarendon Press.

—— (2000) "Reform of the Mental Health Act, 1983: Squandering a lost opportunity", *Journal of Mental Health Law* 3: 5–15.

Penrose, Sir L. (1939) "Mental disease and crime: Outline for a study of European statistics", *British Journal of Medical Psychology* 18: 1–15.

Prins, H. (1991) "The avoidance of scandal: A perennial problem", *Medicine, Science and the Law* 31: 277–9.

—— (1993) "The people nobody owns", in W. Watson and A. Grounds (eds), *The Mentally Disordered Offender in an Era of Community Care*, Cambridge: Cambridge University Press.

—— (1999) *Will They Do it Again? Risk Assessment and Management in Criminal Justice and Psychiatry*, London: Routledge.

—— (2001a) "Whither mental health legislation [locking up the disturbed and the deviant], *Medicine, Science and the Law* 41: 241–9.

—— (2001b) "Offenders, deviants or patients – comments on Part Two of the White Paper", *Journal of Mental Health Law* 5: 21–6.

Prins, H., Backer-Holst, T., Francis, E. and Keitch, I. (1993) *Report of the Committee of Inquiry into the Death in Broadmoor Hospital of Orville Blackwood and a Review of the Deaths of Two Other Afro-Caribbean Patients: Big, Black and Dangerous?* London: Special Hospitals Service Authority (SHSA).

Quinn, P. and Ward, M. (2000) "What happens to special hospital patients admitted to maximum security?", *Medicine, Science and the Law* 40: 345–9.

Reed, J. (2003) "Mental health care in prisons", *British Journal of Psychiatry* 182: 287–8.

Richardson, T., Kenny-Herbert, J., Baker, J. and Humphreys, M. (2002) "Probation orders with a condition of psychiatric treatment: A descriptive study", *Medicine, Science and the Law* 43: 80–4.

Ricketts, D., Carnell, H., Davies, S., Kaul, A. and Duggan, C. (2001) "First admissions to a regional secure unit over a 16-year period: Changes in demographic and service characteristics", *Journal of Forensic Psychiatry* 12: 78–89.

Riordan, S., Wix, S., Haque, M. S. and Humphreys, M. (2003) "Multiple contacts with diversion at the point of arrest", *Medicine, Science and the Law* 43: 105–10.

Riordan, S., Wix, S., Kenny-Herbert, J. and Humphreys, M. (2000) "Diversion at the point of arrest: Mentally disordered people and contact with the police", *Journal of Forensic Psychiatry* 11: 683–90.

Ritchie, J., Dick, D. and Lingham, R. (1994) *Report of the Committee of Inquiry Into the Care and Treatment of Christopher Clunis*, London: HMSO.

Rollin, H. (1969) *The Mentally Abnormal Offender and the Law*, Oxford: Pergamon.

—— (1993) "A hundred years ago: Malice or madness?" *British Journal of Psychiatry* 162: 575.

Roth, M. and Kroll, J. (1986) *The Reality of Mental Illness*, Cambridge: Cambridge University Press.

Rowlands, R., Inch, H., Rodger, W. and Soliman, A. (1996) "Diverted to where? What happens to diverted mentally disordered offenders?", *Journal of Forensic Psychiatry* 7: 284–96.

Scott, P. D. (1975) *Has Psychiatry Failed in the Treatment of Offenders?* London: Institute for the Study and Treatment of Delinquency.

Shaw, J., Tomenson, B., Creed, F. and Perry, A. (2001) "Loss of contact with psychiatric services in people diverted from the criminal justice system", *Journal of Forensic Psychiatry* 12: 203–10.

Singleton, N., Meltzer, H., Gatward, R., Coid, J. and Deasy, D. (1998) *Psychiatric Morbidity among Prisoners in England and Wales*, London: Office of National Statistics.

Smartt, U. (2001) *Grendon Tales: Stories From a Therapeutic Community*, Winchester: Waterside Press.

Smith, J. and Donovan, M. (1990) "The prosecution of psychiatric in-patients", *Journal of Forensic Psychiatry* 1: 379–83.

Stone, N. (2003) *A Companion Guide to Mentally Disordered Offenders*, 2nd ed., Crayford, Kent: Shaw and Sons.

Street, R. (1998) *The Restricted Hospital Order: From Court to the Community: Home Office Research Study 186*, London: Home Office Research and Statistics Directorate.

Sugarman, P. (2002) "Detaining dangerous people with mental disorders", *British Medical Journal* 325: 659.

Szasz, T. (1974) *The Myth of Mental Illness*, New York: Harper & Row.

Tidmarsh, D. (1998) "Asylums or crude cauldrons of containment? The future of the special hospitals", *Journal of Forensic Psychiatry* 9: 505–8.

Tilt, R. (2003) Letter, *British Journal of Psychiatry* 182: 548.

Tilt, R., Perry, N. and Martin, C. (2000) *Report of the Review of Security at the High Security Hospitals*, London: Department of Health.

Towl, G., Snow, L. and McHugh, M. (eds) (2000) *Suicides in Prisons*, Leicester: British Psychological Society Books.

Vaughan, P., Austen, C., le Feuvre, M., O'Grady, J. and Swyer, B. (2003) "Psychiatric support to magistrates' courts", *Medicine, Science and the Law* 43: 255–9.

Walker, N. (1996) "Hybrid orders", *Journal of Forensic Psychiatry* 7: 469–72.

Watson, W. (1998) "Designed to care: The clinician-led development of England's regional secure units", *Journal of Forensic Psychiatry* 9: 519–31.

Wilson, D. and McCabe, S. (2002) "How HMP Grendon works in the words of those undergoing therapy", *Howard Journal of Criminal Justice* 41: 279–91.

Wilson, S. and Forrester, A. (2002) "Too little, too late? The treatment of mentally incapacitated prisoners", *Journal of Forensic Psychiatry* 13: 1–8.

## Further reading

### Mental health law etc.

Bartlett, R. and Sandland, R. (2000) *Mental Health Law: Policy and Practice*, London: Blackstone Press (offers a critical appraisal).

Department of Health and Welsh Office (1999) *Mental Health Act, 1983: Code of Practice*, London: TSO (guide to best practice in the mental healthcare and management of detained patients and certain others).

Stone, N. (2000) *A Companion Guide to Sentencing. Part One.* Ilkley: Owen Wells.

### Diversion

James, A. (1994) *The NACRO Diversion Initiative for Mentally Disturbed Offenders: An Account and an Evaluation.* London: Home Office, NACRO and Mental Health Foundation.

—— (1996) *Life on the Edge: Diversion and the Mentally Disordered Offender*, Vol. 1: *Policy Report*, London: Mental Health Foundation.

### Female offender–patients

Allen, H. (1987) *Justice Unbalanced: Gender, Psychiatry and Judicial Decisions*, Milton Keynes: Open University Press.

Kesteven, S. (2002) *Women who Challenge: Women Offenders and Mental Health Issues*, London: NACRO.

### High security

Black, D. A. (2003) *Broadmoor Interacts: Criminal Insanity Revisited*, Chichester: Barry Rose Publishers (clinical aspects of the work of Broadmoor Hospital for the years 1959–1983 written by its one-time head psychologist).

Winchester, S. (1999) *The Surgeon of Crowthorne*, Harmondsworth: Penguin (fascinating biographical account of a Broadmoor patient who made a significant contribution to the work on the first version of the Oxford English Dictionary).

# Part II

# Clinical aspects

# Chapter 3

# Minds diseased

It is the very error of the moon;
She comes more near the earth than she was wont,
And makes men mad.

*(Othello* Act 5 Sc. 2)

O! Let me not be mad, not mad, sweet heaven;
Keep me in temper; I would not be mad!

*(King Lear* Act 1 Sc. 5)

Canst thou not minister to a mind diseased?

*(Macbeth* Act 5 Sc. 3)

## Introduction

Our three opening epigraphs are intended to provide the focus and indicate the content of this chapter. The first is a reminder of the many myths that surround "madness"; the second suggests the fear of "madness"; the third is indicative of our efforts to replace madness with sanity in offenders and offender–patients. The myths and fear surrounding "madness" (particularly if "madness" is linked to "badness") accounts for the problems involved in establishing various forms of community provision – notably units and hostels. In a study carried out by Holden et al. into the use of public consultation exercises in relation to establishing secure mental health facilities (Holden et al. 2001), the authors found that health trusts "tended to underestimate the depth of public feeling and this fostered residents' suspicions and hostility". To offset these problems, the authors suggest that their findings "highlight the need for trusts to be open with all interested parties as early as possible. The maintenance of an on-going dialogue with local residents, politicians, media, service-user groups, community health councils and statutory bodies is essential" (Holden et al. 2001: 513). In a thought-provoking paper highly relevant to this problem, Pilgrim and Rogers critically examine the extent to which politicians (in particular) "remain concerned about the special threat which psychiatric patients allegedly pose to public safety". They note "three contextualising factors: public prejudice; the widening remit of deviance control by psychiatry during the twentieth century; and inconsistent societal sanctions about dangerousness (Pilgrim and Rogers 2003: 7). In providing a degree of support for this view Walsh et al. (2003) found that in a study of some 700 patients with established psychotic disorders, those with psychosis were found to be "at considerable risk of violent victimisation in the community" (p. 233). This is a helpful countervailing view to the political and public notion of the dangers posed by the mentally ill. In preceding chapters, I made reference to certain forms of mental disturbance and their possible relationship to criminal behaviour. Such reference was in very general terms; in this chapter, I consider aspects of mental disturbance and its relationship to criminality in more detail. The term "mental disturbance" is used here, as in preceding chapters, to include mental disorder as currently defined in the Mental Health Act 1983 in England and Wales; (although, as indicated in Chapter 2, a new definition is being proposed, which, in effect, will be more all embracing). As I write this chapter (November 2003) the anticipated Mental Health Bill is yet not in the Queen's Speech; the minister promises further consultation (*The Independent*, 27 November). Currently, the definition includes mental illness (not further defined), mental impairment, severe mental impairment, psychopathic disorder and any other disorder or disability of mind. I have chosen to use the term "mental disturbance" because it enables us to consider a wide range of other disorders and abnormalities, some of which would not necessarily satisfy the criteria for compulsory admission under the Mental Health Act. Admittedly, "mental disturbance" is a somewhat vague term and, as we have seen, it has certainly led to difficulties for the courts in attempting to determine what constitutes such an abnormality within the meaning of the Homicide Act 1957. The term is used in this chapter merely to encompass a range of disordered mental states, but its imperfections are recognized. (For a more detailed definition see NACRO 1993: 4.) As I hope to demonstrate, it is reasonably easy to define mental illnesses, especially those with clear-cut aetiology (cause); it is harder to define, with a degree of acceptable precision, such conditions as mental handicap (learning disability), particularly in its milder presentations, and conditions such as personality (psychopathic) disorder. However, what we do know with some degree of certainty, is that mental disturbance is likely to be present in all cultures (although it may present in a variety of ways) and at all levels of society, including political and other influential figures. This possibility can have frightening possibilities as Freeman has so ably demonstrated (see, for example, Freeman 1991).

## "Moving the goalposts"

At the outset we are faced with the difficult task of trying to establish any clear causal connections, or even associations, between mental disturbance and criminality. This is because we are trying to make connections between very complex and different phenomena; and these phenomena are the subject of much continuing debate concerning both definition and substance. It is as if the "goalposts" for the "game" were constantly being shifted. Let us take the case of mental illness as an example of this phenomenon. There are those who seek to suggest that some forms of mental illness do not even exist. A well-known proponent of this view was Professor Szasz who, in many of his books and papers, suggested that persons are often diagnosed as mentally ill on the grounds that they have problems in living and that these problems may affront society. Society then turns to psychiatrists to remove them from public view and conscience (see, for example, Szasz 1987). The foregoing is a somewhat bald and simplistic view of Szasz's work and he has written substantial rebuttals of his critics (see, for example, Szasz 1993). His arguments do have a kernel of truth in that he alerts us to the manner in which psychiatry may be abused. They also have a certain attractive seductiveness, but they also contain a quality of rhetoric that has been criticized by both psychiatrists and non-psychiatrists (see, for example, Roth and Kroll 1986; Sedgwick 1982). In the 1960s there existed a popular view that much mental illness had its origins in "conspiracies" and "mixed messages" within families. This view is exemplified in the work of the late doctor Ronald Laing, and his colleagues (see, for example, Laing and Esterson 1964). At the other end of the spectrum we have the more biologically orientated view that found expression in some of the earlier textbooks of psychiatry. Professor John Gunn once put the position into perspective very ably when he stated:

> Somewhere in the confusion there is a biological reality of mental disorder . . . this reality is a complex mixture of diverse conditions, some organic, some functional, some inherited, some learned, some acquired, some curable, others unremitting.
>
> (1977a: 317)

This complex picture is also compounded by the fact that the prevalence and presentation of mental disturbances appear to change over time. Some investigators such as Hare (1983) and Scull (1984) have concluded, albeit very tentatively, that the schizophrenic illnesses as we know them today possibly did not exist on any large scale in earlier times. However, anecdotal and clinical evidence would suggest that such assertions need to be viewed with a degree of caution (see Bark 1985; Eastman 1993; Gunn 1993). It is worth mentioning here that, in earlier times, there may well have been individuals presenting with psychiatric signs and symptoms in whom, these days, we would recognize a physical or organic origin. In the Middle Ages, for example, malnourishment produced a pellagric (nutritional deficiency) state with its psychological and psychiatric consequences. The use of bad/ adulterated flour probably produced ergot poisoning, which, in turn, could produce signs and symptoms of mental illness. It has been suggested that episodes of the so-called "dancing mania" seen in post-mediaeval Italy and surrounding countries were probably due to such a cause (Camporesi 1989). Lead was commonly used in making cooking utensils and in water pipes; this could produce lead poisoning, which, in turn, might produce confused and disturbed behaviour. Some people afflicted by a state of "possession" probably may have suffered from similar organic causes. (For discussion of such states see Enoch and Ball 2001: Chapter 11 and Prins 1990: Chapter 3). Occupations have also been shown to have their hazards. Very few of my students can recall why Lewis Carroll described the "Hatter", at the famous tea party in *Alice in Wonderland*, as "mad"; he did so because people who worked in the hat-making industry were exposed to mercury and mercurial poisoning can produce signs and symptoms of mental disturbance. It has also been suggested that Isaac Newton's well-known episodes of withdrawal from public life and activity may have been due to the effect of the mercuric substances with which he experimented (see Gleick 2003; Klawans 1990). During the past few years, much concern has been expressed about the effects of lead emissions on children's behaviour and there is a school of thought that maintains that poor-quality diet (particularly if it contains amounts of junk foods and excess additives) may produce hyperactivity and anti-social behaviour in some children. However, clear evidence of this, in either the USA or Britain, is not yet available. It is difficult to provide precise figures for the numbers of people suffering from mental disorders. In the government publication, *Modernising Mental Health Services* (Department of Health 1998), it is suggested that depression in one form or another "will affect nearly half of all women and a quarter of all men in the UK before the age of 70". They quote from a major survey published in 1995 which showed that "one in six adults aged 16–64 had suffered from some type of mental health problem in the week prior to being interviewed, the most common being 'neurotic' conditions like anxiety and depression; and a very small proportion of the population – less than 1 per cent – had a more severe and complex psychotic mental illness, such as schizophrenia" (1.2–1.4). Such statistics can only provide a very rough indicator of the mental health of a nation. This is because there are likely to be not inconsiderable numbers of individuals suffering from a degree of mental disturbance/distress who do not present for treatment at either their general practitioner (the most likely first port of call) or at a hospital (unless acutely mentally unwell, suicidal etc). What we *do* know is that the cost of mental disorders, both in terms of distress to the sufferers and their families and others close to them, is considerable. These predicaments are well described by Jeremy Laurance, health editor of *The Independent*, in his recent book on the mental health system (Laurance 2003). Much of it is "hidden" from view and the figures we have represent only the tip of the iceberg. (Perhaps it is worth noting here that the same is true for the "hidden" nature of much criminal activity; the "iceberg" phenomenon is equally important in this respect.)

When we come to consider criminal behaviour we are faced with problems similar to those outlined already. At its simplest, crime is merely that form of behaviour defined by society as illegal and punishable by the criminal law. At various time in our history, acts once judged as criminal have been redefined or even removed from the statute books – as, for example, in the case of attempted suicide and adult (or now near-adult) male consenting homosexual acts committed in private. *New* offences are also created, particularly in time of war or civil commotion. Moreover, our increasingly complex technological society has required the introduction of a wide range of laws and regulations governing many aspects of our conduct. Since much criminal behaviour is somewhat arbitrarily defined, and there are arguments about the existence and definitions of mental disturbances, it is hardly surprising that we find difficulty in trying to establish the connections between these two somewhat ill-defined and complex behaviours. Be this as it may, there are occasions when some mental disturbances do seem to be closely associated with criminal conduct and aspects of this connection are now considered in some detail.

Mental disturbances (disorders) have been classified in a variety of ways. The two most widely acknowledged classification systems – particularly for purposes of cross-cultural research – are the *Diagnostic and Statistical Manual of Mental Disorders*, published by the American Psychiatric Association (2000) and the *ICD-10-International Classification of Mental and Behavioural Disorders*, published by the World Health Organization (WHO 1992). These substantial texts cover every aspect of diagnosis and classification. Readers should also consult one or other of the standard textbooks of psychiatry, a good recent example being the very detailed two-volume 2,000-page work, *The New Oxford Textbook of Psychiatry* (Gelder et al. 2000). Table 3.1 provides a much simplified classification of mental disorders followed by some explanatory comment.

## Some common misnomers

It is not uncommon for some of the specialist terms used in psychiatry to fall into common use or be used in a pejorative fashion. My sometime colleague on the Mental Health Review Tribunal (MHRT), Doctor John Grimshaw, used to make this clear in our induction courses for new MHRT members (Grimshaw, unpublished course lecture notes 1997). For example, demented

*Table 3.1*    Outline classification of mental disorders (disturbances)

| | |
|---|---|
| *Functional psychoses* | Affective disorders<br>Schizophrenic illnesses |
| *Neuroses (psychoneuroses, neurotic reactions)* | Mild depression<br>Anxiety states<br>Hysteria (hysterical reactions)<br>Obsessive compulsive states |
| *Mental disturbance as a result of infection, disease, metabolic and similar disturbance, trauma* | Includes the epilepsies[a] |
| *Mental disturbance due to the ageing process* | Includes the dementias |
| *Abnormalities of personality (e.g. psychopathic disorders; some sexual deviations)* | Includes unusual psychiatric syndromes – "eponymous conditions" (see Table 3.2 and text[c]) |
| *Substance abuse (alcohol, other drugs, solvents)* | |
| *Mental impairment (learning disability); also known as mental handicap, retardation[b]* | Includes chromosomal abnormalities |

Notes: (a) Strictly the epilepsies are not mental disorders as such but are mainly the province of neurology. They are included here because they can produce psychiatric and psychological sequelae (consequences). (b) This condition has been known throughout its history by many different names. Fortunately, some of the older more pejorative terms (such as feeble mindedness, idiocy, deficiency, amentia, oligophrenia) are now no longer used. However, prejudice (as with mental illnesses) remains. (c) The somewhat simple and arbitrary nature of this classification is acknowledged. It is also very important to recognize that disorders may overlap – a condition known technically as *co-morbidity*. (For example, someone showing symptoms of psychopathic disorder may also suffer from a depressive illness.) In this 3rd edition I have included more detailed reference to certain unusual conditions, often called "eponymous" (see Table 3.2).

does not mean agitated, hysterical does not mean excited and noisy, manic does not mean rushing around (although, as we shall see, people in a manic state may act somewhat frenetically); schizophrenia does not mean split personality as in Stevenson's story of Dr Jekyll and Mr Hyde; rather, it refers to a gradual "splintering" or disintegration of the personality. Neurotic does not mean over-fussy or overanxious; and depression in the clinical sense, means being decidedly unwell and not just "pissed off" or "miserable". Barbara Vine, in her novel *Gallowglass*, provides a wonderful distinction between the two phenomena (Vine, 1990: 14–15).

## Functional psychoses

This term is used to describe a group of severe mental disorders for which, as yet, no evidence of underlying organic brain disorder has been conclusively demonstrated. However, there is some evidence to suggest that in time a biological basis for these disorders may be found. The two illnesses subsumed under this heading are (1) the *affective disorders* (*manic-depressive illness*) and (2) the *schizophrenic illnesses*. I consider first the affective disorders. In doing so I must emphasize once again that *only the barest outline* is provided of this and the following disorders. Specialist texts should be consulted for detail concerning their aetiology and management.

## Affective disorders

The underlying characteristic of an affective disorder is a basic disturbance of mood (hence the term affective, meaning relating to affect or mood). In cases of *mild* depressive disorder (see later), the disturbance of mood may be sufficiently slight for it to be almost unnoticeable to those quite close to the person – to such an extent that its onset may be unnoticed. As noted in Chapter 2, this may account for the occasional failure of prison staffs to "spot" depression in a newly remanded prisoner. In *severe* depressive disorder, the mood disturbance is much more pronounced; a useful *aide-mémoire* is that the main characteristics are those of "loss" (of energy, of libido [sexual drive], weight, appetite, interest in oneself and one's environment). Such features may be so pronounced that the person concerned may be quite unable to perform normal daily routines and functions.

Accompanying characteristics may include varying degrees of tension, severe feelings of guilt, lack of concentration, disturbances in sleep patterns and preoccupation with what the sufferer believes to be disturbed bodily functions (such as bowel or bladder functions). For example, loss of appetite may lead to constipation, which, in turn, may lead to acute abdominal discomfort; the depressed person may then come to believe that some kind of cancerous tumour is eating away at their bowels – maybe as a punishment for some imagined "sin". Some forms of depressive disorder are also characterized by agitation, restlessness and irritability; such presentations, being somewhat atypical of depression, can lead to possible misdiagnoses. In very severe states of depression, the degree of retardation of function may be such that suicidal action will be precluded. However, as recovery takes place, such thoughts may become prominent and the person may have enough psychic and physical energy to put them into action. It is therefore of the utmost importance that such patients and their families are counselled as to the risks involved in premature discharge from hospital. This is demonstrated in the following case illustration.

## Case illustration 3.1

A male patient, aged 45, had developed many of the signs of serious depression over the preceding few months (abnormally high level of anxiety, disturbed sleep pattern, loss of appetite resulting in weight loss and consequent preoccupation with bowel functions, believing he might have a tumour). He took an overdose of sleeping tablets (prescribed by his GP for his insomnia), was admitted to a local hospital and subsequently transferred to a psychiatric unit. Having received some treatment for his depression he felt better; his brother persuaded him to take his discharge (against medical advice). Two days later, he went out alone for a walk, threw himself under a train and was decapitated.

At the other end of the spectrum is the condition known as *mania* or *hypomania* (the latter condition being the more common and is just below "full-flight" mania). The condition is the very opposite of depressive illness. Here, activities are speeded up in gross and frenetic fashion, grandiose ideas are developed and the person becomes uncontrollably excitable, overactive, socially (and sexually) disinhibited and is totally lacking in insight. Attempts by family, friends and professionals to interfere with what the sufferer believes to be his or her lawful activities may result in serious injury to themselves. This total lack of insight normally demands admission to hospital under compulsory powers. Given treatment (usually drugs such as lithium carbonate) the condition can be remedied, the mood quietens down and a degree of insight regained.

There is no overall consensus as to the classification and aetiology of affective disorders. Some authorities take the view that two types may be discerned – *endogenous* (that is, where no clear precipitating factors can be seen) and *exogenous* (or *reactive*); in the latter, some stressful life event is thought to have precipitated the illness. When states of depression alternate with episodes of manic illness, the term *manic-depressive psychosis* is sometimes used. Some authorities refer to the depressive phase of this particular illness as "bipolar" depression, using the term "unipolar" depression for those cases in which manic illness is not present. Bipolar depressive states need careful monitoring, since someone may suffer a severe depressive state following a manic episode; in such cases, suicide is always a risk.

Classification, even if somewhat crude, is of importance from the point of view of treatment. Generally speaking, endogenous depression, if proving intractable, responds best to moderate applications of ECT (electro-convulsive therapy) and exogenous depression seems to respond best to medication supplemented by psychotherapy of some kind. However, I should stress that the modes of treatment I have outlined briefly, and the indicators for them, are not necessarily as clear cut as I have suggested.

### Severe depressive disorder and crime

From time to time, we find cases in which a person charged with a grave offence such as homicide is found to be suffering from severe depressive disorder at the time of the offence. West, in his study of cases of *Murder Followed by Suicide*, suggested that sufferers from psychotic depression may:

[B]ecome so convinced of the helplessness of their misery that death becomes a happy escape. Sometimes, before committing suicide, they first kill their children and other members of the family . . . Under the delusion of a future without hope and the inevitability of catastrophe overtaking their nearest and dearest as well as themselves, they decide to kill in order to spare their loved ones suffering.

(West 1965: 6)

Schipkowensky has also stressed the extent to which the "patient feels his personality is without value (delusion of inferiority). His life is without sense, it is only [one of] everlasting suffering, and he feels he 'deserves' to be punished for his imaginary crimes" (1969: 64–5).

### Case illustration 3.2

*The Independent*, 16 February 2002 (p. 3) reports the case of a young mother who was found dead at the foot of a cliff in Scotland. It was said that she was suffering from post-natal depression. She was believed to have thrown her two children over the cliff and then killed herself. The police reported that the mother and her children had "plunged about 100 feet to a ledge on the side of [a] hill". It was reported that she had a history of mental health problems.

### Case illustration 3.3

I recall the case of a young man under my supervision many years ago during my work as a probation officer. He had become severely depressed and became so convinced that the world was a terrible place in which to live that he attempted to kill his mother, his sister and then himself. Only swift medical intervention saved all their lives. Following a court appearance, he was made the subject of hospital care; he responded well to treatment and made a good recovery.

Trying to estimate the extent and duration of a depressive illness and its relevance to serious offences such as homicide is very difficult. Gunn et al. put the position very clearly:

It is very difficult to establish *unless several helpful informants are available* whether a depressed murderer is depressed because he has been imprisoned for life, depressed because of the conditions in which he has been imprisoned, depressed by the enormity of his crime, or whether he committed murder because he was depressed in the first place.

(1978: 35; emphasis added)

The comment by Gunn et al. emphasizes the importance of the avail-ability of a full social history of the offender and the circumstances in which the crime was committed.

Finally, in this brief discussion of depression and crime, a comment by Higgins is very significant:

> Depression may result in serious violence, tension and pre-occupation building up over a protracted period and an assault committed in a state of grave psychological turmoil. The act itself might then act as a catharsis, the individual not afterwards appearing depressed nor complaining of depression *and the diagnosis then being missed.*

> (1990: 348; emphasis added)

### Hypomanic disorder and crime

I have already alluded to some of the main features of this disorder. From time to time, persons suffering from manic disorder of varying degrees of severity may come to the attention of the courts because of their out-rageous, insightless and potentially dangerous behaviour. The following two case examples illustrate the nature of the condition; in the second example, the outcome was such that a court appearance was avoided.

### Case illustration 3.4

This case concerns a car salesman in his twenties. He initially impressed his employer as a bright, energetic and very enthusiastic worker. However, it was not long before his ideas and activities took a grandiose and highly unrealistic turn. For example, he sent dramatic and exaggerated letters daily to a wide range of motor manufacturers. His behaviour began to deteriorate rapidly, he lost weight through not eating (he "never had time") and he rarely slept. One night, in a fit of rage directed towards his "unsympathetic" employer, he returned to the car show-rooms, smashed the windows and did extensive damage to several very expensive cars. He appeared in court, was remanded for psychiatric reports and was even-tually hospitalized under the Mental Health Act.

### Case illustration 3.5

A young woman became increasingly convinced that members of the cabinet were her close friends and would assist her in her grandiose schemes for the develop-ment of a quite unrealistic business enterprise. When her calls to Downing Street were not reciprocated, she became increasingly angry and threatened with physical violence those she saw as obstructing her. She was quite without insight, did not believe she was ill and because of her threats to others she was hospitalized, but not before some consideration was given to prosecuting her for threatening behaviour.

Following treatment by medication, her mood became slightly less high, although she remained very irritable, somewhat disinhibited and showed little insight. It was envisaged that she would need to remain in hospital for some time until her mood stabilized and her potentially dangerous preoccupations diminished.

The characteristics of this type of patient are worth reemphasizing, since they justify the "mental illness" label very clearly. They consider themselves to be omnipotent and become convinced that their wildest ideas are, in fact, entirely practical. Because there is no impairment of memory, they are capable of giving persuasive rationalized arguments and explanations for support of their actions. It is important to stress that such persons are very difficult to treat without the use of compulsory powers, since they fiercely resist the idea that anything is wrong with them. However, although lacking insight, they can appear deceptively lucid and rational; it is this that makes their behaviour a very real risk to others. As already noted, they can be not only hostile, but also physically aggressive to those they consider are obstructing them in their plans and activities. Persons in full-flight hypomanic states can be some of the most *potentially* dangerous people suffering from a definable mental illness. (See also Higgins 1990.)

### Schizophrenic illnesses

At one time, it was customary to speak of schizophrenia in the singular; to some extent, this is still the case, but increasingly, the recognition that there are a variety of "illnesses" within this term has led some to prefer the use of the word in the plural or the use of the descriptive term the *schizophrenias*.

Controversy exists concerning both the causes and classification of these disorders. Currently, it is safe to suggest that environmental and social factors play a significant part in the onset and duration of the illnesses, but there are certainly likely to be neuro-biochemical factors that may determine the onset and course of the illness in the first instance. In other words, a person may have an "in-built" predisposition to develop the disorder which may be enhanced or precipitated by environmental stresses (see Murray et al. 2002).

The most important single characteristic feature of schizophrenic illness is the disintegration and, in some cases, apparent destruction of the personality. In the schizophrenic illnesses, we are dealing with what can best be regarded as a "splintering" of the mind – the personality shatters and disintegrates into a mass of poorly operating components rather than a near division into two parts – as lay interpretations of the word would imply (see earlier discussion). In particular, there is likely to be a degree of incongruity between thoughts and emotions. The main signs and symptoms of the illnesses fall under the following broad headings, although they will not necessarily be present in every case. As we shall see, some of them are of considerable forensic importance:

1   *Disorders of thinking.* Delusions are common; for example, a person may believe that his or her thoughts are being stolen by others.

2   *Disorders of emotion.* These may range from excessive anxiety and perplexity and a flattening of mood (sometimes interrupted by severe outbursts of rage), on the one hand, to complete incongruity of affect (emotion), on the other: for example, giggling at something non-sufferers would consider sad.

3   *Disorders of volition.* The key characteristic here is likely to be apathy and a consequent withdrawal from social intercourse. The individual may behave in a very negative fashion – a presentation known technically as *negativism.*

4   *Psychomotor symptoms.* Periods of complete lack of emotion or a stuporose state may be interspersed with outbursts of sudden and unpredictable violence.

5   *Hallucinations.* In the schizophrenias, these are mostly (but not exclusively) of an auditory nature. They may consist of voices that tell the sufferer to do certain things or, alternatively, the person may state that his or her thoughts can be heard and controlled by others. Occasionally, the individual may believe that people are interfering with them: for example, if this supposed interference is sexual, it may result in an unprovoked assault on an innocent stranger.

Over the years, psychiatrists and others (with varying degrees of agreement) have tended to classify the schizophrenic illnesses in the following fashion. I have simplified the classification but not, I hope, to the point of oversimplification. However, in practical terms, the following divisions listed are usually more complicated and not so clear cut; readers should be aware of this. For example, I have not made reference to those illnesses on the "borderland" of schizophrenia such as the so-called "schizo-affective disorders" where, as the term implies, the sufferer may demonstrate signs and symptoms of both a schizophrenic and an affective (depressive) disorder. It is also very important to recognize that some of the signs and symptoms of schizophrenic illness can be present in other disorders, including certain organic conditions and alcohol- or drug-induced psychoses. Such "co-morbidity" has important implications when we come to consider forensic psychiatric aspects of the schizophrenias:

1   *Simple schizophrenia.* In these cases, the onset appears to be fairly gradual, occurs in early adult life and is so insidious that the initial signs and symptoms may not be recognized by those near to the sufferer. Social behaviour is impoverished and the emotions appear to be "blunted" or shallow. The course of the illness and its lengthy duration may gradually "wear away" the personality, involving a schizophrenic "process" of steady deterioration.

2   *Hebephrenic schizophrenia* (from the Greek for "youthful"). The onset, which occurs most frequently in late teenage or early adult life, is often quite florid and dramatic and accompanied by delusions and halluci- nations. The individual may deteriorate fairly rapidly and require urgent treatment.

3   *Catatonic schizophrenia.* This condition is seen much more rarely today than in the past; this is due, in part, to the early use of certain drugs that seem helpful in this condition. The key characteristics are withdrawal from social intercourse accompanied by muteness, the latter sometimes interspersed with occasional episodes of unprovoked violence. In some cases, the limbs may be rigid and board-like. In others, they take on a curious characteristic known as *flexibilitas cerea* (waxy flexibility) in which the limbs are placed and then left in the most contorted positions almost indefinitely. Attempts to return them to normal merely result in the patient returning them to their original position. The violent outbursts shown by such patients are fortunately rare; these, and the violence exhibited in cases of acute hypomania, probably account for the small number of incidents of *serious* violence committed by psy- chiatric patients.

4   *Paranoid schizophrenia and paranoid states.* In these cases, the keynotes are irrational over-suspiciousness and ideas of self-reference. Such persons may be convinced that people are continually talking about them, for example accusing them of sexual indiscretions or persecuting them in other ways. As I shall demonstrate shortly, such ideas are quite irrational and are highly impervious to reasoned explanation and discussion.

### Schizophrenic illnesses, violence and dangerous obsessions

This is an emotive topic and rational discussion is not helped by the manner in which the media tend to "hype up" individual cases and, in the process, lead the public to extrapolate from these singular and rare events to those suffering from schizophrenic illnesses more generally. However, it has to be acknowledged that research over the last decade has indicated that, given certain conditions, there does seem to be an association between some forms of schizophrenia (notably the paranoid varieties) and violence. Indi- cations of such evidence may be found in contributions by Hodgins (1992), Hodgins and Gunnar-Janson (2002), Hodgins and Muller-Isberner (2001), Link et al. (1992), Link and Steuve (1994), Lindqvist and Allebeck (1990), McNeil et al. (1988), Monahan (1992, 2002), Monahan et al. (2001), Swanson et al. (1990), Taylor (1995) and Wesseley et al. (1994). Two more recent contributions that add to the evidence are Moran et al. (2003) and Walsh et al. (2002) (see later).

Notorious cases tend to "hit the headlines", Sutcliffe, referred to in Chapter 1, being a case in point. Many years earlier, a man called John Ley – a former Australian senior law officer – was convicted of conspiring to murder a man he deludedly believed to have seduced his wife. Ley was sentenced to death but, after sentence, was found to be suffering from a paranoid illness; he was sent to Broadmoor where he subsequently died. In more recent times, Ian Ball was ordered to be detained in a (special) high-security hospital as a result of an elaborate and skilful (yet highly delusional) plan to kidnap Princess Anne in the Mall in London. And, of course, there have been cases in the USA of murderous attacks on political figures by individuals allegedly suffering from some form of schizophrenic illness.

It is important to stress that people suffering from this type of disorder may begin to demonstrate "oddnesses" of behaviour *for some time before the disorder emerges in an acute or very obvious form.* Intervention at this stage may, in some cases, help to prevent a tragedy (see, for example, Hodgins and Muller-Isberner 2004). Some of the research studies just mentioned suggest that certain factors may help to contribute to violence in some schizophrenic patients. It is very important to consider these factors in order to give the lie to the popular media conception that all schizophrenic patients are potentially violent. (In point of fact, they are more likely to harm or suffer harm to themselves than others (Walsh et al. 2003).) These would appear to be as follows:

(a) Active delusions seem to be powerful factors where the patient perceives some threat, where there is a lessening of mechanisms of self-control and dominance of the patient's mind by perceived forces that seem to be beyond his or her control. These phenomena are sometimes described in the literature as "perceived threat and control override (TCO) . . . TCO involves the belief that (1) others are controlling one's thoughts by either stealing thoughts or inserting them directly into one's mind; and (2) others are plotting against one, following one and wanting to hurt one physically" (Bjorkly and Havik 2003). However, Monahan (2002) suggests the espousal of a degree of caution in respect of delusions: in the very large-scale MacArthur study of the relationship between psychotic illness (notably schizophrenia) and violence, he and his colleagues found that:

> [T]he presence of delusions [did] not predict higher rates of violence among recently discharged psychiatric patients . . . In particular, the much discussed findings of a relationship between threat/control override delusions and violence were not confirmed . . . on the other hand, non-delusional suspiciousness – perhaps involving a tendency towards misperception of others' behaviour as

indicating hostile intent – does appear to be linked with subsequent violence, and may account for the findings of previous studies.

(Monahan et al. 2002: 68–9)

(b) When the disorder is associated with the ingestion of drugs or other forms of substance abuse. For example, Wheatley (1998) studied a sample of schizophrenic patients detained under the Mental Health Act in a medium secure unit. His results confirmed a high degree of co-morbidity of alcohol and substance abuse and schizophrenia in detained and forensic patients (see also Marshall 1998). Similarly, in a large-scale American survey involving patients in the community, Steadman et al. (1998) found the incidence of violence was substantially elevated by the abuse of drugs and alcohol.

(c) The impact of co-morbid personality disorder on violent behaviour in psychosis has been emphasized by Moran et al. (2003). They examined a sample of 670 patients with established psychotic illness. When screened for the presence of co-morbid personality disorder, they found 28 per cent exhibited the disorder and these patients "were significantly more likely to behave violently over the two-year trial period [involved in the study]" (p. 129). The importance of co-morbidity and dual diagnosis is also emphasized in a comprehensive review by Crichton. He concluded that "the more *specific* that studies have been in comparing particular diagnosis and symptom cluster with *specific* criminal behaviour, the more useful they have been in establishing causality. An emerging theme is the importance of dual diagnosis, particularly substance misuse and psychosis and violent crime" (Crichton 1999: 659; emphasis added).

(d) Concurrent social problems such as homelessness tend to contribute to the likelihood of violence.

### Paranoid disorder and "dangerous obsessions"

In this section I include some lesser known psychiatric conditions that do not fit easily into more conventional psychiatric classification, standing as they do on the "boundaries of psychiatry" (see Prins 1990: Chapter 2) (see Table 3.2).

For additional references to many of these conditions found in the table, see Bhugra and Munro (1997), Enoch and Ball (2001), Franzini and Grossberg (1995), Friedmann and Faguet (1982) and Prins (1990).

As already noted, one of the key characteristics of those suffering from one or other of the forms of paranoid illness is their systematized delusional beliefs (and sometimes hallucinatory experiences). These may take the form of irrational and unshakeable beliefs that they are being persecuted by

*Table 3.2*   Some unusual psychiatric conditions[a]

| | |
|---|---|
| Othello syndrome[b] | The patient (usually male) harbours the delusional belief that his spouse or partner is unfaithful |
| Capgras syndrome | A rare disorder, in which the sufferer believes that a closely related relative has been replaced by a double |
| Frégoli's syndrome | In which a false identification of persons connected with the individual occurs in strangers |
| De Clérambault's syndrome | The patient believes that someone not known to them personally (and usually of some fame) is in love with them |
| Cotard's syndrome | Sufferer has delusions of nihilism and poverty |
| Ekbohm's syndrome | Patient has delusions of infestation by insects, maggots, etc. |
| Munchausen's syndrome and Munchausen by Proxy | The individual seeks attention by repeated attempts to gain hospital admission for non-existent medical conditions. Munchausen by proxy is similar, but a child is the focus of the "false illness" in order for the parent to gain attention; the harm to the child often being caused by the parent (usually the mother). The preferred, more recently introduced, term is fabricated and induced illness (FII) |
| Gilles de la Tourette's syndrome | Seen in childhood and adolescence; main features are uncontrollable tics and suggestive, and sometimes obscene, utterances by the patient |
| Folie à deux, Folie à trois, Folie à plusieurs | A condition in which beliefs of delusional intensity are transmitted from the patient to significant others in their close environment |
| Couvade syndrome[c] | A husband exhibits the features of pregnancy as being experienced by his wife or partner |
| Koro (Shook Yang) genital retraction syndrome | A belief that the penis is shrinking |

*Notes*: (a) Some of these conditions are termed "eponymous" in recognition of the fact they were first described by a particular individual. Such appellations are not peculiar to psychiatry. There are many such titles in general medicine; for example, Grave's disease, being a form of goitre; Huntington's disorder (formerly known as Huntington's chorea), a degenerative hereditary terminal disorder of the nervous system; Bright's disease, a disease of the kidneys; Chron's disease, a chronic form of bowel disorder. (b) Syndrome means, in general terms, the signs and symptoms of a disease or combination of behavioural characteristics. (c) Both Couvade and Koro are best described as "culture-bound syndromes"; other examples are "amok" and "possession" states.

others or that they have a need to be the persecutor (as we saw in Sutcliffe's case). It is important to emphasize here that such systems of belief are not necessarily peculiar to those suffering from a schizophrenic disorder; they may be part of an affective illness or be associated with chronic alcohol abuse or, in some cases, organic disorder. Two points of cardinal importance need emphasizing here. First, such sufferers may begin to develop certain oddnesses of behaviour for some time *before the disorder emerges in an acute or very obvious form*; sensitive observation and possible intervention *may*, in some cases, help to prevent a tragedy. However, it has to be acknowledged that this may be very difficult on both clinical and ethical grounds (see Chapter 8). Second, persons developing paranoid beliefs may do so in an encapsulated (contained) form; thus, a seriously paranoid person may appear perfectly sane and in command of him or herself in all other respects. The illness may be so well encapsulated that an unwary or unskilled observer can be easily misled. It is only when the matters the delusional system has fastened onto are broached that the severity of the disorder may be revealed.

The sinister and potentially highly dangerous nature of these forms of disorder are clearly delineated in a condition known variously as "morbid jealousy", "sexual jealousy", "delusions of infidelity" etc. This disorder will now be used as an example of these particular disorders of thinking and behaviour. Dealing with the phenomena in this way can be used to illustrate by way of extrapolation similar kinds of behaviours in which obsessional preoccupations can become highly dangerous. For this reason, I shall also include a brief discussion of the fairly recently described preoccupation with the phenomenon of "stalking", although, of course, not all stalkers suffer from mental disorder in the medical sense. As indicated earlier, some of these conditions are given a variety of titles. It might be more helpful to abandon these discrete categories and consider the totality of these phenomena within a framework of "dangerous obsessions", irrespective of the focus of the unwanted attentions. In suggesting this, I am conscious that I am dealing here with a highly selected range of dangerous obsessions; others are, of course, equally dangerous, particularly when they are motivated by overwhelming desires for control and subjugation, as in some forms of serious personality (psychopathic) disorder. Many years ago, Lagach (1947) made the important observation that love involved two elements: a desire to dedicate and give oneself to the beloved – *amour oblatif* – and the desire to possess and subjugate, which he called *amour captatif*. He considered that those who fell into the second category were especially prone to jealousy. Jealousy is, of course, a universal phenomenon that varies in intensity from the so-called "normal" to the intensely pathological. A very useful discussion of the "generality" of jealousy may be found in Pines (1998) and clinical management of the condition is discussed in a comprehensive account by White and Mullen (1989). Jealousy has been described in a variety of ways in the world's great literature. There are examples in *The Decameron* and in the work of Tolstoy; and, of course, one of the best descriptions of its potential lethality and intractability is graphically described by Shakespeare. Emilia, wife to Iago and maid to Desdemona, puts it in these terms:

But jealous souls will not be answer'd so;
They are not ever jealous for the cause,
But jealous for they are jealous; 't is a monster
Begot upon itself, born on itself.

(*Othello* Act 3 Sc. 4)

And the condition is further depicted by Shakespeare in *The Winter's Tale*, where the irrationally jealous Leontes says:

were my wife's liver
Infected as her life, she would not live
The running of one glass.

(Act 1 Sc. 2)

In my view, the characterization of Leontes gives a more powerful exemplification of delusional jealousy than the description of Othello – to the extent that I have suggested elsewhere that we might describe the condition as the *Leontes* rather than the *Othello* syndrome (Prins 1996). In more modern times, the crime writer Patricia Cornwell has an apt observation on the nature of dangerous obsessive love:

Attraction turns to obsession, love becomes pathological. When he loves, he has to possess because he feels so insecure and unworthy, is so easily threatened. When his secret love is not returned, he becomes increasingly obsessed. He becomes so fixated his ability to react and function becomes limited.

(Cornwell 1995: 221)

She also makes a further compelling and disturbing observation: "Murder never emerges full blown from a vacuum. Nothing evil ever does" (p. 312).

The boundary between "normal" and "abnormal" in this field is difficult to delineate with precision. Mullen (1981), who has made very significant contributions to the study of pathological love, states: "In our culture, jealousy is now regarded not just as problematic or undesirable, but increasingly as unhealthy, as a symptom of immaturity, possessiveness, neurosis and insecurity" (Mullen 1981: 593).

And in similar fashion, Higgins, a very experienced forensic psychiatrist, also believes that "the boundary between normal and morbid jealousy is indistinct":

Jealousy, or a tendency to be jealous, can be a normal relative transient response in an otherwise well adjusted individual to frank infidelity; one feature in an individual with a paranoid personality disorder . . . or a frankly delusional idea arising suddenly and unexpectedly either as a single delusional idea or one of a number of related ideas in a typical psychosis.

(Higgins 1995: 79)

There is no universal agreement as to the causes of "encapsulated" delusional jealousy. However, a number of explanations have been offered. For example, the person suffering from the delusion may themselves have behaved promiscuously in the past and have harboured an expectation that the spouse or partner will behave in similar fashion. Other explanations have embraced the possibility of impotence in the sufferer with consequent projection of feeling a failure on to the spouse or partner. Freudian and neo-Freudian explanations stress the possibility of repressed homosexuality resulting in fantasies about the male consort of a spouse or partner. Pines suggests the importance of a "triggering event". She states that: "Although jealousy occurs in different forms and in varying degrees of intensity, it always results from an interaction between a certain predisposition and a particular triggering event" (1998: 27). She considers that predispositions to jealousy vary widely between individuals. For someone with a high predisposition, a triggering event can be as minor as a partner's glance at an attractive stranger passing by. For most people, however, the trigger for intense jealousy is a much more serious event, such as the discovery of an illicit affair. For others, the trigger can be imagined (as reported by R. Dobson in *The Independent*, 3 September 1998: 14).

The following three case illustrations demonstrate the irrational nature of such sufferers' beliefs.

### Case illustration 3.6

This is a case described by the nineteenth-century physician Clouston and presented in the first edition of Enoch and Trethowan's classic work *Uncommon Psychiatric Syndromes* (1979: 47):

I now have in an asylum, two quite rational-looking men, whose chief delusion is that their wives, both women of undoubted character, have been unfaithful to them. Keep them off the subject and they are rational. But on that subject they are utterly delusional and insane.

### Case illustration 3.7

The following case, drawn from my own experience, supports the irrationality of belief so graphically described by Clouston. This concerned a man in his sixties, detained in hospital without limit of time (Sections 37/41, Mental Health Act 1983) with a diagnosis of mental illness. He had been convicted of the attempted murder of his wife and had a history of infidelity during the marriage. There was a family history of mental illness. The index (original) offence consisted of an attempt to stab his wife to death and a serious assault on his daughter, who had tried to intervene to protect her. He gave a history of prolonged, but quite unfounded, suspicions of his wife's infidelity. He arranged to have her followed, interrogated her persistently as to her whereabouts (which were always quite innocent) and searched her personal belongings for proof of her alleged unfaithfulness. He even inspected her underclothing for signs of seminal staining in order to confirm his delusional beliefs. He also believed that neighbours and others were colluding with his wife to aid her in her alleged unfaithfulness. As is so often the case, he was regarded as a model patient, well liked by staff and other patients and, to the unwary and uninformed observer, presented himself as completely rational and reasonable. It was only when asked about his wife that his delusional ideas about her expressed themselves with ominous intensity.

Although he had been detained in hospital for some years and his delusional ideas were not so intrusive as they were on admission, they were still easily evoked. The likelihood of his release was remote. His wife had been urged to sever her connections with him entirely and make a new life her herself. However, as is sometimes the case, she was reluctant to do so, hoping that her husband's attitude would change. The wife's attitude is of considerable importance. This is because, in such cases, the irrational beliefs held by the sufferer are not easily amenable to treatment; the wife is likely, therefore, to be at considerable risk whenever the offender or offender–patient is released. Some cynical professionals, when asked what the best treatment is, have been known to respond by saying "geographical", meaning that the woman would be strongly advised to move home and change her name; it seems that the woman in such an instance is doubly victimized. Supervision of these and similar cases requires the utmost vigilance and a capacity to spot subtle changes in both mood and circumstances. It is well known that sufferers from delusional jealousy and similar delusional states have what the late doctor Murray Cox used to describe as "unfinished business" to complete. Even if, sadly, the first victim dies as a result of the delusionally held beliefs, surrogate victims may be sought out and be similarly at risk. Careful questioning of the pathologically jealous individual is essential. Mullen (1996: 240) puts it as follows:

> The clinician attempting to treat a patient or client in whom jealousy features must keep constantly in mind the possibility of an escalation of conflict producing resort to violence. Careful and repeated questioning of the jealous individual and their partner is advisable, and, wherever possible, informants outside the relationship should be consulted.

### Case illustration 3.8

The third example demonstrates the manifestation of the disorder in a less severe form and is somewhat unusual in that it is described by the sufferer. It demonstrates the possibility of improvement (in a less severe case) and was provided by Christine Aziz (1987) some years ago in a national newspaper. Her jealousy, which developed in relation to her partner:

> [C]ame unannounced one warm autumn day; a tight pain in the stomach, sweating and nausea. Still cocooned in the intense early days of love, I discovered Simon (her partner) had slept with someone else and, even more hurtful, had denied it. Jealousy had come to stay. The occasional twinge was bearable, but this torment was the surgeon's knife without the anaesthetic. It came unannounced and for hours; the evil turned me into a stranger to those who knew and loved me.

### Case illustration 3.9

A near-psychotic state of jealousy was recently depicted in the BBC's adaptation of Trollope's novel, *He Knew He was Right* (April–May 2004). In the television presentation, Louis develops an unshakeable delusional belief that his wife has been having an affair with a member of parliament – a man who, it must be said, has an alleged reputation as a "womanizer". He eventually dies in a severely weakened and highly distressed state.

In Christine Aziz's case, she was happily able to realize to some degree, that her behaviour was irrational; she was eventually helped through behavioural psychotherapy to deal with it and find some peace of mind.

### Erotomania

The notion of pathological (obsessive) possessiveness may assist us in linking pathological jealousy, on the one hand, and erotomania, on the other. It will also act as a useful springboard for a discussion of "stalking". Erotomania (*psychose passionelle*) is a condition in which the sufferer believes with passionate and irrational conviction that a person, who is usually older and socially quite unattainable (such as an important public figure), is in love with them. The condition is also sometimes described eponymously as de Clérambault's Syndrome (see Table 3.2). Taylor et al. (1983) suggest five criteria for making the diagnosis in the female:

1   Presence of the delusion that the woman is loved by a specific man.
2   That the woman has previously had very little or no contact with this man.
3   The man is unattainable in some way.
4   That the man nevertheless watches over, protects or follows the woman.
5   That the woman should remain chaste.

Some of these criteria could, of course, be applied if the sufferer were male. Taylor and her colleagues found that medication helped their patients to feel more relaxed, but that this did not lead necessarily to an early resolution of their amorous beliefs. As with delusional jealousy, the condition can be a potentially dangerous one, since sufferers may seek to attack those who reject their "advances" and those whom they consider to be their rivals for the attentions of those they obsessively love. Some of these activities are characteristic of the behaviour of certain so-called "stalkers" and we consider these next.

### "Unwelcome attentions" – stalking

Each era seems to produce its own shibboleths, be they adult sexual behaviour (and abuse), child abuse, including child sexual abuse of various kinds (for example, ritual satanic abuse), so-called "serial killing" (see Chapter 5) and, more recently, errant medical practitioners, internet pornography and violence in the work place (see also Chapter 5). To this last, we must now add the behaviour known popularly as "stalking". As Melloy (1998) aptly states: "Stalking is an old behaviour, but a new crime. Shakespeare captured certain aspects of it in the obsessive and murderous thoughts of Othello." He goes on to remind his readers that "Louisa May Alcott, wrote a novel about stalking in 1866, *A Long Fatal Love Chase*, which remained undiscovered and unpublished for over a century" (p. xix). There is a growing recent literature on the topic and in what follows I have been highly selective; readers will find the books referred to helpful in filling in the gaps in my presentation. In England, we have been somewhat slower than other countries to introduce legislation to deal with the problem; for example, the North Americas have had anti-stalking (harassment) legislation for some time. The Protection from Harassment Act of 1997 came into being because of a growing concern about the phenomenon fostered by the publication of a number of cases of well-known people who had been the subject of what can perhaps best be described as "unwelcome attentions". Section 1(1) of the 1997 Act states that a person must not pursue a course of conduct: (a) which amounts to harassment of another and (b) which he knows, or ought to know, amounts to harassment of another. The Act does not provide a specific definition of harassment and the courts tend to rely on the subjective experiences of victims.

The Act creates two "levels" of the offending behaviour. The first is to be found in Section 2 of the Act and may be dealt with summarily (i.e. by a magistrates' court) and is currently punishable by a maximum sentence of six months' imprisonment. The second, and more serious form of the offence, is that of causing fear of violence (Section 4) and is punishable on indictment by a maximum penalty of five years' imprisonment imposable by a Crown Court. (See Finch (2002) for a detailed critical discussion of the Act.)

Harris (2000) carried out a study into the effectiveness of the legislation. She found that: "The most common reason given for harassment was that the complainant had ended an intimate relationship with the suspect. Victims were often unaware of the existence of the legislation and that [they] had often endured the unwanted behaviour for a significant time before reporting it." Overall, the conviction rate in those cases ending in a court hearing was 84 per cent; a conditional discharge was the most frequent disposal. Something over half of the convictions were accompanied by a "restraining order"; this is an option available to the courts under the Act as a means of endeavouring to prevent a repetition of the harassment. A study by Petch (2002) adds weight to Harris's findings into the effectiveness of the Act. He concluded that: "The Act would be more effective if it was used by police, prosecutors and the courts more consistently. A programme of widespread dissemination of the provisions within the Act is now called for" (p. 19). Legal and psychological aspects have also been reviewed by McGuire and Wraith (2000). The extent to which the "public" have a clear perception of what constitutes "stalking" has been explored in an interesting paper by Sheridan and Davies (2001).

Readers may be surprised to know how widespread the problem is. In a study conducted by Budd and Mattinson (2000), as part of the regular updating of the *British Crime Survey*, it was estimated that in defining stalking as "an experience of persistent and unwanted attention" 2.9 per cent of adults aged between 16 and 59 had been stalked in the year of the survey. This, they state, equates to 900,000 victims. An estimated 770,000 victims had been distressed or upset by the experience and 550,000 victims had been subjected to violence, threatened with violence or had been fearful that violence would be used. Risks of these unwanted attentions were particularly high for young women between 16 and 19. About one-third of the incidents were carried out by someone who was in an intimate relationship with the victim, a further third involved an acquaintance of the victim and only one-third of incidents involved strangers. The victims' most common experiences were "being forced to talk to the offender, silent phone calls, being physically intimidated and being followed". A quarter of male victims and one-fifth of the women said the perpetrator had used physical force: "Seven in ten victims said they had changed their life-style as a result of the experience. Women were more likely to have done so than men." Other research carried out into the perceptions of stalking on the part of both men and women tends to add weight to these findings (see Sheridan et al. 2000; Sheridan et al. 2001; Sheridan et al. 2002; see also Groves et al. 2004).

There have been numerous attempts to classify stalkers by their motives and behaviour. Kemphuis and Emmelkamp (2000) conducted an extensive review of these aspects. In particular, they noted the work of Harmon et al. (1995), Mullen et al. (1999), Wright et al. (1996) and Zona et al. (1993). The authors of the review suggest that "most authors agree on the importance of the relationship between stalking in the context of some sort of prior relationship and stalking where there has not been a real relationship at all" (p. 207). They quote the classification by Zona et al. (1993): "(a) the 'classic' erotomanic stalker who is usually a woman with the delusional belief that an older man of higher social class or social esteem is in love with her (see entry under de Clérambault in Figure 3.2; (b) the love-obsessional stalker, who is typically a psychotic stalker targeting famous people or total strangers; and, most common, (c) the simple obsessional stalker, who stalks after a 'real' relationship has gone sour leaving him with intense resentment following perceived abuse or rejection" (p. 207).

They also quote Mullen et al. (1999), who have made highly significant contributions to this topic. They present a slightly different classification under five headings: "(a) the rejected stalker, who has had a relationship with the victim and who is often characterized by a mixture of revenge and desire for reconciliation; (b) the stalker seeking intimacy, which includes individuals with erotomanic delusions; (c) the incompetent stalker – usually intellectually limited and socially incompetent individuals; (d) the resentful stalker, who seeks to frighten and distress the victim; and finally (e) the predatory stalker, who is preparing a sexual attack." It is not difficult to see that the individuals illustrated in both these classifications can prove to be potentially highly dangerous. For this reason Kemphuis and Emmelkamp suggest that: "There is a clear need to derive a consensus on a typology of stalkers, with associated diagnostic criteria. At present there is no evidence that one proposed typology is superior to another. The typology eventually agreed upon should have clear implications for treatment" (p. 207). Before leaving this subject, we should note that abuse of internet facilities has added another dimension in the form of what has been described as "cyberstalking". An interesting and worrying example of this phenomenon has recently been provided by Bocij and McFarlane (2003) and Bocij et al. (2003). Finally, a word of explanation is needed for dealing with the phenomenon of stalking in this chapter. Readers will be quick to discern that in many respects it is a crime of violence and could, quite legitimately, have found a place in Chapter 5. My reason for including it here is that it is so often characterized by highly delusional beliefs; however, I acknowledge that the decision to include it here is somewhat arbitrary.

## More minor offences

Those suffering from schizophrenic illnesses sometimes commit more minor offences. What forms do these take? In some cases, where the illness is of insidious onset, there is often an accompanying decline in social competence; in which case the sufferer may well succumb to temptations (sometimes prompted by others) that they may well have resisted had they been in good mental health. Those suffering from so-called "simple schizophrenia" may demonstrate a steady diminution of social functioning accompanied by withdrawal from society. Such sufferers may come to the attention of the authorities through offences such as begging, breach of the peace (insulting words and behaviour) or acts of vandalism (criminal damage). They often form part of the sad "stage army" described so aptly by Rollin nearly 40 years ago (Rollin 1969), shunted as they are between hospital, prison and community and referred to in Chapter 2.

## Summary

Although, as I have indicated, the contribution of schizophrenic and associated illnesses to criminality is very low, they may be of considerable importance in *particular cases*, notably when a degree of co-morbidity exists and any delusions experienced are of a persecutory nature. For those who may have professional involvement with the individual concerned (for example, probation officers and other social workers, penal institution and other residential staffs, the police, general practitioners etc.) it is as well to be aware of the significance of even slight changes in behaviour, but also, more importantly, to be aware of *atypical* behaviour. These may give clues (along with other evidence) to the possibility of an underlying schizophrenic illness. (See, for example, Gunn and Taylor 1993: Chapter 8.)

## Neuroses (psycho-neuroses, neurotic reactions) and crime

The terms "neuroses" and "psycho-neuroses" (which, for the most part, are used synonymously, psycho-neuroses being the older term) when used correctly (and not pejoratively – see earlier discussion) describe a wide range of conditions that are characterized by certain specific mental and physical signs and symptoms. It is erroneous to think that the neuroses are less disabling than psychotic conditions. Although the signs and symptoms in neurosis may not be so florid, the effects of some neurotic conditions can be severely disabling, as in obsessive-compulsive states where sufferers are compelled to undertake ritual activities that gravely affect their lives. As with the classifications of mental disturbances more generally, there is no absolute consensus as to classification, but for our purposes the following should suffice:

1   mild depression
2   anxiety states
3   hysterical states
4   obsessive-compulsive states.

In this chapter I concentrate on mild depression, anxiety and hysterical conditions and even this concentration will inevitably be somewhat superficial. Those readers wishing to obtain comprehensive accounts of them should consult the two-volume *New Oxford Textbook of Psychiatry*, edited by Gelder et al. (2000). It is also as well to remember that any classification is not discrete; that is, the conditions and their signs and symptoms frequently overlap. We also need to remember an important distinction between (a) common neurotic traits (seen in most of us!); (b) more serious neurotic traits or reactions; and (c) fully developed neurotic illness. The notion of a continuum here (as with more serious mental illnesses such as the psychoses) is a useful one.

## Mild depression

Instances of mild depression may not always be immediately recognized. This is because the behaviour of the sufferer may depart only slightly from the "norm". However, many of the signs and symptoms of serious (psychotic) depression referred to earlier may be present but in less severe form. The following is an example.

## Case illustration 3.10

A married woman of 60, of previously impeccable character, for no apparent reason (she had plenty of money with her) stole a tin of beans from a supermarket. The offence seemed quite out of character and when she appeared in court she was remanded for a psychiatric examination. This subsequently showed that she had suffered for a considerable time from mild depression. One of the effects of her depression was to leave her confused. She was made the subject of a community rehabilitation order (probation order) with a requirement for out-patient treatment.

In a study carried out many years ago, Woddis (1964) cited several cases in which stealing occurred against a background of depressive illness. Most of his examples were of middle-aged or late middle-aged women. However, he also cited the unusual case of a young man of 21 charged with the persistent theft of motor vehicles. He had a history of recurrent mild depressive attacks that seemed to be clearly associated time-wise with his thefts. Abreactive (drug) treatment helped him to reveal, while under its influence, that his offences had started at the time his father had been burned to death in a lorry accident. The young man had intense feelings of guilt that he had not reached his father in time to rescue him. When these matters were brought more clearly into consciousness and clarified, the stealing stopped. From time to time, I have come across cases of young men and women who have claimed that they have embarked on a series of crime because they felt "low" or "fed up" – as though the offending behaviour would supply a "buzz" or a "lift" for their low spirits. This element of needing a "high" will be referred to again in relation to the seriously personality disordered in the next chapter. Occasionally, the past and recent histories of these young men and women have revealed a number of depressive elements, but it would have been difficult to have applied the clinical label "neurotically depressed" to many of them. Such examples illustrate the need for very careful history taking so that the relevance of depressive factors may be assessed as accurately as possible.

### Anxiety states and crime

True anxiety states are characterized by a morbid or pervasive fear or dread. They may occur as a single symptom or in conjunction with other psychiatric disturbances, such as depressive illness. Often, such anxiety can be said to be associated with some specific environmental situation or stress, as in the phenomenon of post-traumatic stress disorder (PTSD). This disorder has been the subject of much litigation following war service and natural or man-made disasters of one kind or another. In other cases, it is said to be "free floating", a nameless and non-specific dread. Symptoms can include palpitations, giddiness, nausea, irregular respiration, feelings of suffocation, excessive sweating, dry mouth and loss of appetite. Anxiety states in "pure culture" rarely account for criminal acts, but morbidly anxious individuals may feel so driven by their anxieties that they may commit an impulsive offence. Such rare offences also seem to occur in individuals where the anxiety is accompanied by, or associated with, an obsessive and perfectionist personality. The following case is an example of such phenomena.

### Case illustration 3.11

A young man in his early twenties made a serious and unprovoked attack on an innocent passer-by in the street. As he put it: "I just exploded. I don't know why; the tension I had been feeling lately become unbearable." Subsequent psychotherapy over a long period revealed a very vulnerable personality accompanied by a lack of self-esteem and a compulsive need to work in order to keep unnamed anxieties at bay. Later, as psychotherapy continued, it became apparent that many of his problems were associated with his relationship with his father, which bordered on hatred. The innocent bystander just *happened* to look like his father and, therefore, the assault was in many respects no mere accident. (I refer to this phenomenon of "innocent stranger" assault again in Chapter 8).

Finally, I should emphasize that anxiety has been discussed here in a very specific and narrow sense. I am not referring to situations in which an offender or alleged offender is apparently almost pathologically anxious in the context of his or her present predicament (for example, facing a court hearing or being detained in prison). The comments by Gunn et al. (1978), quoted earlier in relation to depression, are equally relevant in this connection.

## Hysterical and associated states and crime

The clinical condition of hysteria has a long history and can be defined very loosely as the existence of mental or physical symptoms for the sake of some advantage (for example, compensation or attention of some kind), although the sufferer is not completely aware of the motive. As we saw earlier, the term is often used quite incorrectly by layfolk. It is not to be taken to mean "having hysterics" or acting histrionically (highly dramatically), although both these characteristics may be demonstrated by hysterics in certain situations. It needs also to be distinguished from *hysterical personality*. Hysterical symptoms may be classified in a somewhat oversimplified fashion as follows:

1   Those associated with the senses, for example deafness or blindness.
2   Those associated with motor symptoms, for example paralysis, spasms or tremors (somatization disorder/Briquet's syndrome).
3   Those where mental symptoms present, such as memory loss (which may sometimes be associated with a fugue or wandering state), pseudodementia, Ganser syndrome (see later), stupor, hysterical phobias. These may also present as anxiety and depressive states in which the person may react in difficult or unpleasant situations with symptoms of these latter disturbances of mind. The keynotes in all these disorders are symptoms of *conversion* or *dissociation* (sometimes known nowadays as dissociative states). Conversion symptoms may occur, for example, in hysterical states in the form of fits which may be superficially similar to those produced in epilepsy (see later). Dissociation arises when the individual has a conflict that produces anxiety as described, for example, in Breuer and Freud's (1936) early work on hysteria, but the latter is overcome by some manifestation of physical or mental illness, which submerges the real anxiety. Because of the processes at work, one not infrequently notices in hysterical individuals that the emotions that should accompany events, or memories of them, are often inappropriate; thus an account of an incident given by an hysteric, which one would expect to produce sadness, may be given with a bland smile on the face.

From a forensic psychiatric point of view, it will be fairly obvious that a number of these conditions are of considerable importance – of these, hysterical amnesia, fugues and the Ganser syndrome are the most significant and are now considered in more detail. Amnesias due to *organic* disorders or disease are dealt with in the section concerned with these states but again, as with other mental conditions, there are degrees of overlap. In some instances, it is difficult, if not impossible, to distinguish a genuine hysterical illness from simulation or malingering. The following are pointers to possible differences:

1   In malingering, the motivation is more or less at a conscious level. The symptoms are usually of sudden onset and have some connection with a situation the malingerer is keen to avoid; see Enoch (1990) and Heinze (2003) for the uses of psychological testing. See also Pollock (1996) and Resnick (1994).
2   The malingerer's "symptoms" are usually overacted and exaggerated, as was the case with Haigh, the so-called "acid bath murderer", who feigned insanity to avoid conviction and sentence for murder (for details see Prins 1990: Chapter 5). It is possible for even highly skilled professional workers to be misled occasionally; some chronic mental hospital patients or clinic attenders can become adept at picking up and simulating a range of psychiatric signs and symptoms.
3   The signs may be present only when the malingerer is being observed. This is very important from a forensic psychiatric point of view, as a true picture of the supposed malingerer may emerge only after fairly lengthy and close observation. Generally speaking, it is highly unusual for skilled observers to be fooled but, very occasionally, it can happen as the following case illustrates:

### Case illustration 3.12

A man was sentenced to be detained in hospital under the Mental Health Act, having been convicted of a series of sexual assaults on males. The doctors who examined him had always shared *some* doubts about the nature of his illness. Over time, it emerged that he had feigned illness. He was discharged from hospital, arrested following discharge, prosecuted and sentenced for perverting the course of justice; the prison sentence passed was of a length commensurate with what he would have received had he been given a penal disposal in the first instance. (For an interesting account of malingered psychosis see Broughton and Chesterman (2001).)

4   Symptoms may be sometimes made to order. For example, if the examiner of the suspected malingerer suggests a certain symptom of illness being feigned is absent in the individual's presentation, the malingerer will sometimes try to produce it.
5   When feigning illness, many of the usual signs and symptoms associated with the illness may be missing.

There are two other conditions allied to malingering that must be mentioned as they are also of forensic psychiatric interest. The first is *pseudo-dementia* and the second is the *Ganser syndrome*. Pseudo-dementia, as the name implies, is closely akin to malingering or simulation of insanity. An individual of normal intelligence may say, for example, that $4 + 4 = 9$, or will incorrectly give, or strangely twist, the most simple facts. In these cases, the examiner will usually have the impression that the person knows the right answers. However, differential diagnosis is sometimes very difficult, because pseudo-dementia may coexist alongside a genuine organic defect or illness.

The Ganser syndrome is, in many ways, very like pseudo-dementia and takes its name from the physician S. J. M. Ganser, who first described the condition in a lecture given in 1897, calling it "A Peculiar Hysterical State". Ganser stated that:

> The most obvious sign they present consists of their inability to answer correctly the simplest questions which are asked of them, even though by many of their answers they indicate they have grasped, in large part, the sense of the question, and in their answers they betray at once a baffling ignorance and a surprising lack of knowledge which they most assuredly once possessed, or still possess.
>
> (translated in Schorer 1965: 123)

Another phenomenon that should be mentioned here is so-called "hysterical amnesia". From time to time, offenders may claim an amnesic episode for their crime or the events leading up to it. A classic example was that of Gunther Podola, tried and convicted in 1959 for killing a police officer (*R. v. Podola* [1959] 3 All ER 418). There appears to be a consensus that the difference between a genuine and feigned amnesia attack is more likely to be one of degree than of kind. Both conditions may exist in the same person and be serving a common purpose, namely loss of memory for an alleged crime. Power, a former very experienced prison medical officer, suggests (1977) that the following pointers may help to elicit whether an amnesia is genuine:

1 An amnesic episode of sudden onset and ending may be suggestive of a feigned loss of memory.
2 The crime itself may give clues. Motiveless crime may be committed in an impulsive fashion, without any premeditation or attempt to conceal it; it may be committed with unnecessary violence and in the presence of witnesses.
3 Careful comparisons of the accounts given by police and by the defendant may provide helpful evidence of inconsistencies.

4    Have there been past amnesic episodes? If so, the current episode may
     be more likely to be a genuine one. This is also true, of course, in
     determining the relevance of past episodes of somnambulism in cases
     where somnambulism is being used as a defence against responsibility
     for crime (see Chapter 2). In an interesting and somewhat provocative
     paper Stone (1992) suggests that it is often unproductive to try to
     determine with any degree of exactness whether an amnesia is organic
     or psychogenic. He also notes that *victims*, especially of violent crime
     "can suffer from memory loss similar to that seen in . . . perpetrators"
     (p. 342). He goes on to state that: "It is perhaps in this direction that
     the way forward lies in understanding the causes of psychogenic
     amnesia without the hindrance of having to decide whether the amnesia
     is genuine or not, a task that is fruitless" (p. 342). For discussion of
     amnesia more generally, see Lishman (1997), Porter et al. (2001) and
     Whitty and Zangwill (1977).

Before passing onto "organic" factors, it is important to mention two
hysterical-type phenomena that have assumed an increasing degree of
interest in recent years. The first concerns the controversial phenomenon
of so-called "multiple personality disorder". The currently accepted criteria
are: (1) the existence within the person of two or more distinct personalities, each with its own relatively enduring pattern of perceiving, relating
to and thinking about the environment and self; and (2) at least two of
these personalities or personality states taking full control of the person's
behaviour. The presentation is likely to be characterized by the coexistence
of relatively consistent, but alternate separate, sometimes very numerous,
identities with recurring episodes of distortion of memory and frank
amnesia. Recent studies have suggested that this strange disorder may not
be as uncommon as was once thought to be the case. However, an alternative (and quite convincing) view is that the medical attention such people
receive merely serves to facilitate the expression of the symptomology and
adds to its proliferation (see Enoch and Ball 2001: Chapter 6; James 1998;
James and Schramm 1998; Keyes 1995; Merskey 1992; Prins 1990: Chapter
2; Wilson 1993).
     The second concerns the phenomenon known as Munchausen's syndrome
and Munchausen's syndrome by Proxy or fabricated and induced illness.
As we noted earlier in this chapter, in the first form of the disorder the
person complains of, and receives, extensive treatment for various somatic
complaints, travelling from one hospital to the next (sometimes they are
described as "hospital hoboes" or "hospital addicts"). The term itself
(Munchausen syndrome) is something of a misnomer. First, because the
famous eighteenth-century nobleman from whom the name of the condition
is derived may have been a great fabricator and wanderer, but he was *not*
addicted to hospitals. Second, the term is considered by some to be too

narrow for what is believed to be a wide range of personality disorders. In an interesting paper, Hardie and Reed (1998) suggest that conditions such as fantastic lying (*pseudologia fantastica*) and factitious disorder (Munchausen-type syndrome) and what they call impostership, could usefully be subsumed under a new heading of "deception syndrome"; and Gibbon (1998) has described Munchausen's syndrome presenting as an acute sexual assault. In a subsidiary condition, Munchausen's syndrome by Proxy (fabricated and induced illness), a mother or significant other may inflict a variety of injuries on her child, requiring hospital treatment. In such cases, there appears to be a pattern of attention-seeking behaviour and the derivation of vicarious satisfaction from the attention given to the child. In recent times, the methods used by those professionals to detect this particular syndrome have been considered to be questionable and improperly intrusive (see Prins 1990: Chapter 2; Tantam and Whittaker 1993).

## Mental disturbance (disorder) as a result of "organic" and allied conditions

For the sake of simplicity I propose to consider all of these conditions under the broad, but somewhat unscientific, rubric of "organic" disorders. The reason for including them is that, although some of them figure but rarely in criminal activity, it is their very rarity that makes them important. This is because professionals without a medical training or orientation are often, understandably, somewhat ill informed about physical (organic) conditions that may play an important part in a person's behaviour or misbehaviour. This applies with particular force to those in the social work and counselling professions, where an understanding of human behaviour is frequently based on an emphasis on psychological, social and emotional influences. The importance of what might be described as "brain behaviour" in determining responsibility for crime, in an age in which we now have sophisticated devices for measuring such activity (such as a variety of brain-scanning techniques) has been described by Buchanan (1994) (see also Howard 2002).

### Infections

These include meningitis, encephalitis and a number of viral infections. It is not uncommon for marked changes in behaviour to occur after an infective illness such as encephalitis, particularly in children; these changes may sometimes be accompanied by the development of aggressive and anti-social tendencies. It is also worth noting here that in older or elderly persons infections of the urinary tract (UTIs) may produce confusion and disorientation and unless a urine analysis is undertaken, the signs and symptoms may be mistaken for a stroke or other cerebral disorder.

### Huntington's disorder (formerly known as Huntington's chorea)

This is a comparatively rare, directly transmitted, hereditary condition. The onset of the disorder (which is terminal) is most likely to occur in the middle years of life and is characterized by a progressive deterioration of physical, mental and emotional functioning, including the choreiform (jerky) movements characteristic of the disorder. Sufferers from the condition may sometimes behave unpredictably and anti-socially, although such instances are not common. Because of the hereditary transmission of the disorder and its terminal nature, relatives need adequate counselling and support.

### General paresis

This is a form of neurosyphilis and is also known as *dementia paralytica* or general paralysis of the insane (GPI). The disorder develops as a result of a primary syphilitic infection and attacks the central nervous system (CNS). Symptoms may appear many years after the original infective incident. Individuals suffering from the disorder may begin to behave unpredictably and irritably. Such signs may be accompanied by euphoria and grandiosity; and indeed the presenting signs and symptoms may be mistaken for a hypomanic attack (see earlier discussion). Any acts of "outrageous" behaviour in a person of previous good character on the part of a person so afflicted should alert professionals to the possibility of the disorder being present. Today, neurosyphilis is not seen with any degree of frequency (whereas in the nineteenth and early twentieth centuries it was fairly widespread). Its disappearance is due largely to early diagnosis and the use of antibiotics.

### Alcoholic poisoning and crime

The prolonged and regular ingestion of alcohol may bring about serious brain damage with consequent behaviour changes. It may lead to disorders of consciousness, known as "twilight states". One such phenomenon is sometimes described as *mania à potu* in which the afflicted individual may react in an extreme manner to even very small amounts of alcohol; such states may result in violent outbursts. Both chronic alcoholism and alcoholic psychosis are characterized by impairment of memory. Such impairment often results in the person trying to fill in gaps in their accounts of events by use of their imagination – a phenomenon known technically as confabulation. It is seen in conditions such as Korsakoff's syndrome. This particular condition also presents with nutritional deficiency and abnormalities in the peripheral nerve endings. Alcohol acts as a cerebral depressant (although people often mistakenly regard it as an effective euphoriant). The Porter in *Macbeth* describes it well in relation to sexual matters, as follows:

> Lechery, sir, it provokes, and unprovokes: it provokes the desire, but it takes away the performance. Therefore, much drink may be said to be an equivocator with lechery; it makes him, and it mars him; it sets him on, and it takes him off . . . makes him stand to, and not stand to.
>
> (Act 2 Sc. 3)

In other words, it may be mistakenly believed to improve sexual performance, whereas, in fact, it results most commonly in failed erection and incapacity. In its more severe manifestations it has earned the appellation "brewer's droop". It is important to recognize that alcohol may act as a significant disinhibitor and that its effects on individuals who may already have brain damage from other causes may be considerable and catastrophic.

### Other toxic substances

Earlier in this chapter, reference was made to the effects on behaviour of such substances as contaminated flour, mercury etc. In addition, chemicals used in industrial processes where there is inadequate fume extraction may affect behaviour and produce states of confusion; these may lead to aggressive outbursts. Such instances are, of course, rare, but because of their comparative rarity their importance may be overlooked by the unwary.

### Metabolic, other disturbances and crime

Low blood sugar (*hypoglycaemia*) may occur in certain predisposed individuals who have gone without food for a prolonged period. Judgement may become impaired, they may show extreme irritability coupled with a degree of confusion and in such a state they may come into conflict with the criminal justice system. Such states are important in cases such as diabetes or, more particularly, unrecognized diabetes. Prompt action may be necessary before coma (or even death) intervenes. Those with untreated excess thyroid levels (*thyrotoxicosis*) may become irritable, aggressive and occasionally anti-social. In recent years, a good deal of interest has been focused on the relevance of the menstrual cycle to criminality, particularly violent criminality. Dalton (1982) had been involved in a small number of homicide cases where pleas have been put forward that pre-menstrual syndrome

(PMS) constitutes an abnormality of mind within the meaning of the Homicide Act 1957. However, such pleas do not appear to have become widespread (D'Orban 1983).

### Brain trauma, tumour, brain diseases and crime

It is important to emphasize that, from time to time, cases of brain trauma or tumour are missed – sometimes with tragic consequences. An injury to the brain (however caused) is quite likely to produce a degree of concussion that may sometimes be prolonged. Such injuries may give rise to mental retardation (learning disability) or to forms of epilepsy (see later discussion of both these phenomena). Such persons may be amnesic, but such amnesia will differ from the amnesia described earlier. Following recovery of consciousness, there may be noisy delirium – a condition *not* observed in hysterical or malingered amnesia. Organically, amnesic individuals may sometimes appear to be normal initially and only gradually, following careful examination, does it emerge that they have been behaving "automatically" (see Fenwick 1990, 1993). In contrast, in cases of hysterical amnesia, memory may return spontaneously within 24 hours or so. Organically amnesic persons are likely to want to do their best to remember events and may appear to be annoyed by their defective memory. In contrast, hysterical amnesics may show a complete inability to recall any events before a specific time. In addition, hysterically amnesic individuals, unlike those showing organic amnesia, may have perfect command of their speech and be well in control of their other faculties (see Williams 1979). The following case illustrates some of the tragic forensic consequences of brain damage.

### Case illustration 3.13

> This concerned a former miner, aged 36, whose personality changed after suffering severe head injuries in a pit accident. Following essential brain surgery, he suffered hallucinations and became aggressive towards his family. During one of these episodes, he threw burning coals around the living room, setting fire to the house. He was charged with arson, convicted and made the subject of a probation order with a requirement that he undertake medical treatment.
>
> (*Leicester Mercury*, 29 September 1984: 11)

Occasionally, the dementing processes of advancing old age (of which *Alzheimer's disease* is the most well-known example) may be associated with behaviour that is not only out of character, but also may be highly impulsive, disinhibited and aggressive. Any such behaviour occurring "out of the blue" in late mid-life that seems odd, out of character and carried out (perhaps repeatedly) in the presence of witnesses, should alert police, prosecuting and probation authorities to the possibility of a dementing process or to the presence of a malignancy of some kind. In respect of the latter, tests are now available that enable even quite small brain tumours to be diagnosed. In addition, clinical and forensic psychologists have developed a range of tests that can determine the presence and extent of a dementing process (see Miller 1992; Miller 1999). In a recent timely contribution, Yorston (1999) reminds us that research into the elderly is sparse and, as he states:

> With an ageing population and ever-dwindling continuing care resources, the elderly are going to come into conflict with the law more often. If justice and humanitarian principles are to be upheld, the need for specialist assessment and management of elderly offenders is likely to increase.
>
> (Yorston 1999: 193) (see also Curtice et al. 2003)

Perhaps we should also note here that increasing attention is being paid to the elderly as *victims* of aggression and violence (see Brogden 2001; Brogden and Nijhar 2000).

### Epilepsies, associated disorders and crime

The epilepsies in their various presentations are not, strictly speaking, psychiatric illnesses, but neurological disorders manifested primarily by an excessive or abnormal discharge of electrical activity in the brain. Many thousands of people will have an epileptic attack of one kind or another at some stage in their lives; even for those who have major attacks, it is usually possible to lead a perfectly normal life with the aid of medication. There are many forms of epilepsy and they have been reviewed extensively in the standard textbooks, such as that by Lishman in the various editions of his book *Organic Psychiatry* (1997). Some forms of epilepsy may be caused by head injury or brain damage, others are of unknown origin (*idiopathic*). There are several types of epileptic phenomena: *grand mal* (major convulsions); *petit mal* (often so minor as to be non-discernible to the onlooker); *temporal lobe epilepsy* (sometimes characterized by sudden unexpected alterations of mood and behaviour and, therefore, of particular forensic psychiatric interest); *Jacksonian epilepsy* (an eponymously named form of the disorder named after Hughlings Jackson (himself a sufferer) who first identified it). This is a localized cerebral convulsion following traumatic brain damage; partial seizures and more generalized convulsive seizures. Fenwick, in a number of papers, has described in some detail the relationship between epileptic seizures and diminishment of responsibility for crime (see, for example, Fenwick 1993). Gunn (1977b, 1978) carried out a number of classic and important surveys into the relationship between epilepsy and crime more generally (particularly violent crime). He found that more epileptic males were taken into custody than would have been expected by chance – a ratio of some 7–8:1,000. This is considerably higher than the proportion of epileptics found in the general population. About one-third of Gunn's cases were found to be suffering from temporal lobe epilepsy and temporal lobe cases were found to have a higher previous conviction rate. However, it was the group suffering from idiopathic epilepsy that had received disproportionately more convictions for violence than any other group.

Gunn cautions us not to place too much emphasis on the relationship between epilepsy and crime. In doing so, he makes three very important points. First, the epilepsy itself may generate social and psychological problems, which in turn can lead to anti-social reactions. Second, harmful social factors, such as overcrowding, parental neglect and allied problems, may lead to a higher than average degree of both epilepsy and anti-social behaviour. Third, environmental factors such as those just described may lead to behavioural disturbances that not only lead to brushes with the law, but may also aggravate accident and illness proneness. Such disturbances in themselves may produce an excess prevalence of epileptic phenomena. In this respect, it is of interest to note a study by Fearnley and Zaatar (2001) in which they explored the presence in a family history of epilepsy in prisoners detained in HM Prison Liverpool. The indications were "that prisoners have a high prevalence of family history of epilepsy". The study also showed that "prisoners who report such a history have significantly more psychological problems than those prisoners without such a family history" (p. 305). Although it has been stated that there is no very strong *proof* of a general relationship between epilepsy and crime (particularly violent crime), it may well be very important in the individual case (see Delgado-Escueta et al. 1981). For this reason, expert assessment is very important as is careful community monitoring. This is particularly the case if the person is on medication. Not only does this need to be taken regularly, but horrendous results may occur if such medication is taken with alcohol (even in small amounts) or with illicit drugs. It is also important to note that repetitive fits over prolonged periods may result in further brain damage.

There is a further collection of signs and symptoms akin to epileptic phenomena, described as episodic dyscontrol syndrome; sometimes also described as "intermittent explosive disorder" or "limbic" rage. Lucas (1994), in a very comprehensive review of the literature on the condition, cites some 15 or so alternative labels that have been used over the years. The features, found in a very small group of individuals who, in the absence of demonstrable epilepsy, brain damage or psychotic illness, may show explosively violent behaviour without any clearly discernible stimuli, so that the explosive reaction seems out of all proportion to minimal provocation. Lewis and Carpenter (1999), in a paper discussing the legal implications of the condition, suggest that:

> Episodic dyscontrol is relatively easy to diagnose and responds very well to drug therapy, eliminating any unwanted (by the sufferer as well as society) existing violent behaviour and any possible future "criminal" behaviour. Recognition of the condition may result in justice being metered out for genuine, remorseful sufferers, differentiated from people who *choose* violence (for whatever reason) or at least have the capacity to choose violence.
>
> (Lewis and Carpenter 1999: 21)

They go on to suggest that individuals engaging in this form of behaviour should be able to claim partial exculpation of criminal responsibility by an extension of the existing law as framed under the Homicide Act 1957. However, Lucas, in his extensive review of the topic, is less sanguine about the diagnosis, suggesting that:

> Despite its 25 year survival, episodic dyscontrol may represent [an] impracticable or obsolete idea . . . and as such may be destined for the compost heap of history . . . The fate of psychiatric concepts, however, is not determined by merit alone and episodic dyscontrol may yet prove another tenacious perennial, which to change metaphors, will long survive its obituaries.
>
> (Lucas 1994: 401)

The debate will doubtless continue.

## Mental impairment (learning disability), chromosomal abnormalities and crime

### Mental impairment

As indicated earlier, various descriptive terms have been used for what we now term learning disability. It is important to emphasize at this point that laypeople sometimes confuse mental *illness* with *mental impairment* (the term I shall use henceforth); the two conditions are entirely separate, but they can coexist in some individuals. In general and oversimplified terms, it can be said that the mentally *ill* person starts life with normal intelligence but, for a variety of reasons (as described earlier in this chapter), becomes ill and deviates from the so-called "norm". The mentally *impaired* person never had the endowment of normal intelligence or lost it in infancy or in early life. This point is demonstrated clearly in the use of the now obsolete descriptive term for the condition, *amentia*, or *oligophrenia*, which mean lack or absence of mind. It must be stressed that mental impairment is a *relative* concept. It used to be assumed, quite incorrectly, that the degree of impairment could be assessed purely in terms of intellectual capacity as measured by IQ tests. Although these are still of some importance, it is imperative to have regard for the social functioning of the individual, in particular family and social supports or lack of them.

### Causal factors

There are a very large number of known possible causes for mental impairment. Some of the most familiar are as follows:

1   Infection in the parent, notably *rubella* (German measles) contracted in early pregnancy.
2   Illness in infancy or early childhood, for example, meningitis or encephalitis (as already discussed).
3   Brain damage to the infant before, during or after birth. This may occur as a result of prematurity or as a result of *anoxia* (lack of oxygen) due to various causes. Brain damage (mild or severe) after birth may occur as a result of physical child abuse or neglect by parents or others.
4   Chromosomal abnormalities, of which the best known is Down's syndrome, named after Dr Langdon Down who first described it as a specific condition. In the past it was known as Mongolism – a wholly inappropriate label (see later discussion).
5   Other "inborn" causes, for example, the disorder known as *phenylketonuria*, a condition in which some children are unable to cope with the phenyaliline content of normal diets; failure to observe a correct dietary regime will result in severe mental impairment.
6   Exacerbation of an existing mild impairment (from whatever cause) by lack of social and intellectual stimulation, poor nutrition and poor ante- and post-natal care.
7   Exposure to certain illicit drugs in pregnancy; or exposure to certain therapeutic drugs and vaccines used in infancy.
8   Exposure to radiation.

### Mental impairment and crime

Cases of mild or moderate mental impairment are the most likely conditions to come to the attention of the criminal justice system. In any event, as Day points out: "The contribution of the mentally handicapped to the criminal statistics is small." He goes on to suggest that:

> Although the prevalence of offending in the mentally handicapped appears to have remained unchanged over the years, increase is to be anticipated in the coming years as implementation of Care in the Community policies expose more mentally handicapped people to greater temptations and opportunities for offending and the "hidden offences" which occur regularly in institutions become more visible.
>
> (Day 1993: 116; see also Day 1997; Reid 1990)

The following is a summary of the ways in which the mentally impaired are likely to come to the attention of the criminal justice system:

1   The degree of impairment may be severe enough to prevent the individual from understanding that his or her act was legally wrong. In such cases, issues of responsibility will arise and decisions will have to be made as to whether or not to prosecute the alleged offender. (See Chapter 1.)
2   The moderately impaired individual may be more easily caught in a criminal act.
3   Such offenders may be used very easily by others in delinquent escapades and find themselves acting as accomplices – sometimes unwittingly, sometimes not.
4   An individual's mental impairment may be associated with a disorder that may make him or her particularly unpredictable, aggressive and impulsive.
5   Some mentally impaired offenders have problems in making understood their often harmless intentions. Thus, a friendly overture by them may be misinterpreted by an uninformed or unsympathetic recipient as an attempted assault. The initial overture may be rebuffed therefore. This may lead to surprise and anger on the part of the mentally impaired individual and he or she may then retaliate with aggression.
6   A moderately mentally impaired individual may be provoked quite readily into an uncharacteristic act of violence.
7   The attitude to legitimate expressions of sexuality in some of the mentally impaired may be naive, primitive, unrestrained and lacking in social skills. Such deficits may account for the number of sexual offences that appear to be found in the backgrounds of detained mentally impaired patients in the high security hospitals (see Day 1997; Green et al. 2003).
8   Mentally impaired persons may be especially vulnerable to changes in their social environments that would not have the same impact on their more well-endowed peers. A moderately mentally impaired person may

manage perfectly well as long as he or she has the support of parents, other relatives or friends. Should this be interrupted by death, or for any other reasons, such persons may then indulge in delinquent acts as a means of trying to relieve the stresses of their situation. The following case examples will help to demonstrate the vulnerability of the mentally impaired to changes in circumstances and other pressures (see Kearns 2001). (See also special (2001) issue of *British Journal of Forensic Practice* 3, 1 and special (2003) section of *Legal and Criminological Psychology* 8, 2: 219–66.)

### Case illustration 3.14

A man of 26 was charged with causing grievous bodily harm to a young woman by hitting her over the head with an iron bar. She was entirely unknown to him and although he denied the offence vehemently, he was convicted by the Crown Court on the clearest possible evidence. As a child he had suffered brain damage, which had resulted in a mild degree of mental impairment, accompanied by the kind of impulsive, aggressive and unpredictable behaviour referred to at point 4 in the preceding list. He had been before the courts on a number of occasions and had eventually been sent to a hospital for the mentally handicapped. He was discharged some years later to the care of his mother. Subsequent to his discharge, he committed the offence just described and was placed on probation. His response was poor. He was impulsive and erratic and regressed to very childish behaviour when under stress. The family background was problematic: the parents had divorced (acrimoniously) when the offender was quite small; a brother suffered from a disabling form of epilepsy; and other members of the family showed decidedly eccentric lifestyles. (Such a family would no doubt today be called "dysfunctional".) Shortly after the probation period expired, he committed a particularly vicious and unprovoked assault on a small girl and was sentenced to a long term of imprisonment.

### Case illustration 3.15

This case illustrates some of the problems identified under point 6 in the foregoing list. For many years, a mildly mentally impaired man in his forties had worked well under friendly, but firm supervision. His work situation changed, with the result that his new employers felt he was being lazy and did not have much sympathy for his disabilities. In addition, his new workmates teased and picked on him. One day, one of them taunted him about his lack of success with the opposite sex. Goaded beyond endurance, the defendant stabbed his tormentor with a pitchfork in his chest, causing quite serious internal injuries. When the case came to the Crown Court, evidence was given as to his mental condition, his social situation and the manner in which he had been provoked. The court made a hospital order under the Mental Health Act.

*Suggestibility*

From the foregoing comments it will be seen that the mentally impaired individual may be especially vulnerable to pressures from others. When this takes the form of alleged pressure to commit crimes they may not have committed, the situation can become very serious indeed. Unfortunately, there have been a number of cases in which impressionable and suggestible individuals (some of them formally assessed as mentally impaired) have been the victims of miscarriages of justice. For example, three young men were alleged to have been responsible for the murder of a man named Maxwell Confait. All three were deemed to be vulnerable because of varying degrees of handicap. The same applied to the late Steven Kisko, also accused, convicted of and sentenced for murder. In his case, the Court of Appeal ruled that "special care needs to be taken where the defendant suffers from a 'significant degree of mental handicap' if the only evidence against him is his confession" (Kellam 1993: 361). Kellam goes on to make the important point that: "There seems no reason to think that the court meant to limit (handicap) to lack of mental capacity alone" (p. 362). The Police and Criminal Evidence Act 1984, and subsequent codes of practice, introduced certain safeguards in respect of police interrogations, most notably the availability of an "appropriate adult", when vulnerable persons are being interviewed (Nemitz and Bean 2001; Pearse and Gudjonsson 1996). In this context, vulnerability would be held to include both the mentally ill and the mentally impaired and those thought for other reasons to be especially suggestible (Norfolk 2001; Pearse and Gudjonsson 1997). Better formal training for "appropriate adults" and police interrogators is gradually being introduced and clinical and forensic psychologists have made impressive contributions to this work (see, for example, Gudjonsson 1992; McBrien et al. 2003; Shepherd 1993).

## Chromosomal abnormalities and crime

In the early 1960s a considerable degree of interest was aroused by the finding that a number of men detained in high-security hospitals and prisons carried an extra Y chromosome (XYY).[1] Such men were often found to be taller than average, came from essentially *non-delinquent backgrounds* and occasionally had records of violence. Subsequent research has proved inconclusive concerning the prevalence of such abnormalities, not only in penal and similar populations, but also in the community at large. Although the leads offered have potential for further and interesting development, there appears to be no strong evidence to suggest a causal link between specific genetic defects or abnormalities and crime, particularly violent crime. In a review of a number of studies in this area, Day (1993: 113) concluded that: "The personal variables of tallness, intelligence and educational grade and the social variables of parental and family background bore closer relations to the possibility of conviction than genotypic abnormalities."

## A concluding cautionary note

This chapter has had to encompass, in brief form, a wide range of complex material. Because of this, it would be all too easy for the reader to conclude that we are on sure ground in describing and delineating mental disturbances and disorders. The truth is that there are still vast grey areas in this field and much more work is needed before we can be at all certain as to aetiology and the best methods of treatment. Despite this, much valuable work has been, and is being, done, notably in the field of brain biochemistry and its allied disciplines. Trying to equate mental disturbances with criminal behaviour is therefore quite hazardous, especially when we remember that crime itself is not a "static" phenomenon. It is also very important to recall that both gender and race play a very important part in any study of the relationship between mental disturbances and crime. Despite much research, we are still not sure why certain ethnic minority groups (notably African-Caribbeans) seem overrepresented in penal and psychiatric populations (Prins et al. 1993).

Women, when they offend, tend to receive proportionately more psychiatric disposals than men. Fewer women seem to be assessed as "psychopathic"; they seem more likely to be described as having hysterical characteristics. Is this because the latter labels are regarded as more clinically correct or because a male-dominated society and criminal justice system tend to label women in this way? Some researchers (for example, Allen 1987) have suggested that the apparent discrepancies in sentencing are less than obvious. Allen's central thesis is that such divergences cannot be explained entirely by differences in the mental makeup of male and female offenders and that such divergences may occur regardless of their psychiatric symptomatology. She makes the often forgotten point that: "The importance of the current imbalance lies not so much in the excess of psychiatry in relation to female offenders as its deficiency in relation to males" (Allen 1987: xii). Some of the behaviours only touched on in this chapter are now given more detailed treatment in those that follow; we begin with the vexed topic of severe personality (psychopathic) disorders.

## Note

1   A brief word of explanation concerning normal chromosome distribution may be helpful to those new to this field. Normal human cells contain 46 chromosomes; these are arranged in 23 pairs of different shapes and sizes. They may be seen and classified under high-power microscopy once they have been suitably prepared for examination. Different chromosomes contain different genes. One pair of chromosomes called X and Y determine sex. In the female, these consist

of a matched pair, XX, and in the male an unmatched pair, XY. This normal patterning may sometimes become altered (*translocated*) in a variety of ways, resulting in an extra X or extra Y chromosome or some other variant.

# References

Allen, H. (1987) *Justice Unbalanced: Gender. Psychiatry and Judicial Decisions*, Milton Keynes: Open University Press.

American Psychiatric Association (APA) (2000) *Diagnostic and Statistical Manual of Mental Disorders*, 4th ed., text revision DSMIV-TR, Washington, DC: APA.

Aziz, C. (1987) "Prey to the green-eyed monster", *The Independent*, 10 November: 15.

Bark, N. M. (1985) "Did Shakespeare know schizophrenia? The case of poor mad Tom in King Lear", *British Journal of Psychiatry* 146: 346–8.

Bhugra, D. and Munro, A. (1997) *Troublesome Disguises: Undiagnosed Psychiatric Syndromes*, Oxford: Blackwell.

Bjorkly, S. and Havik, O. E. (2003) "TCO symptoms as markers of violence in a sample of seventy violent psychiatric in-patients", *International Journal of Forensic Mental Health* 2: 87–97.

Bocij, P. and McFarlane, L. (2003) "Seven fallacies about cyberstalking", *Prison Service Journal* 149: 37–42.

Bocij, P., Bocij, H. and McFarlane, L. (2003) "Cyberstalking: A case study of serial harassment in the UK", *British Journal of Forensic Practice* 5: 25–32.

Breuer, J. and Freud, S. (1936) *Studies in Hysteria*, New York: Putnam.

Brogden, M. (2001) *Geronticide: Killing the Elderly*, London, Jessica Kingsley.

Brogden M. and Nijhar, P. (2000) *Crime, Abuse and the Elderly*, Cullompton, Devon: Willan Publishing.

Broughton, N. and Chesterman, P. (2001) "Malingered psychosis", *Journal of Forensic Psychiatry* 12: 407–22.

Buchanan, A. (1994) "Brain, mind and behaviour revisited", *Journal of Forensic Psychiatry* 5: 232–6.

Budd, T. and Mattinson, J. (2000) *Stalking: Findings From the British Crime Survey*, Home Office Research, Development and Statistics Directorate, No. 129, London: Home Office.

Camporesi, P. (1989) *Bread of Dreams: Food and Fantasy in Early Modern Europe*, Cambridge: Polity Press.

Cornwell, P. (1995) *Body of Evidence*, London: Warner Books.

Crichton, J. M. (1999) "Mental disorder and crime: Coincidence, correlation and cause", *Journal of Forensic Psychiatry* 10: 659–77.

Curtice, M., Parker, J., Wismayer, F. S. and Tomison, A. (2003) "The elderly offender: An 11-year survey of referrals to a regional forensic-psychiatric service, *Journal of Forensic Psychiatry* 14: 253–65.

Dalton, K. (1982) "Legal implication of PMS", *World Medicine* 17: 93–4.

Day, K. (1993) "Crime and mental retardation", in K. Howells and C. R. Hollin (eds), *Clinical Approaches to the Mentally Disordered Offender*, Chichester: John Wiley & Sons.

—— (1997) "Sex offenders with learning disabilities", in S. G. Read (ed), *Psychiatry in Learning Disability*, London: Saunders.

Delgado-Escueta, A. V., Mattson, R. H. and King, L. (1981) "The nature of aggression during epileptic seizures", *New England Journal of Medicine* 305: 711–16.

Department of Health (1998) *Modernising Mental Health Services. Section I,* December, London: DoH.

D'Orban, P. T. (1983) "Medico-legal aspects of the pre-menstrual syndrome", *British Journal of Hospital Medicine* 30: 404–9.

Eastman, N. L. G. (1993) "Forensic psychiatric services in Britain: A current review", *International Journal of Law and Psychiatry* 16: 1–26.

Enoch, D. (1990) "Hysteria, malingering, pseudologia fantastica, Ganser syndrome, prison psychosis, and Munchausen's syndrome", in R. Bluglass and P. Bowden (eds), *Principles and Practice of Forensic Psychiatry*, London: Churchill Livingstone.

Enoch, D. and Ball, H. (2001) *Uncommon Psychiatric Syndromes*, 4th ed., London: Arnold.

Enoch, D. and Trethowan, W. (1979) *Uncommon Psychiatric Syndromes*, 2nd ed., London: Butterworth-Heinemann.

Fearnley, D. and Zaatar, A. (2001) "A cross-sectional study which measures the prevalence and characteristics of prisoners who present with a family history of epilepsy", *Medicine, Science and the Law* 41: 305–8.

Fenwick, P. (1990) *Automatism, Medicine and the Law* (Psychological Medicine Monograph, Supplement No. 17), Cambridge: Cambridge University Press.

—— (1993) "Brain, mind and behaviour: Some medico-legal aspects", *British Journal of Psychiatry* 163: 565–73.

Finch, E. (2002) "Stalking: A violent crime or a crime of violence", *Howard Journal* 41: 422–33.

Franzini, L. R. and Grossberg, J. M. (1995) *Eccentric and Bizarre Behaviours*, Chichester: John Wiley & Sons.

Freeman, H. (1991) "The human brain and political behaviour", *British Journal of Psychiatry* 159: 19–32.

Friedmann, C. T. H. and Faguet, R. A. (eds) (1982) *Extraordinary Disorders of Human Behaviour*, New York and London: Plenum Press.

Gelder, M. G., Lopez-Ibor, J. J. Jr and Andreasen, N. C. (eds) (2000) *New Oxford Text-Book of Psychiatry* (2 Vols.), Oxford: Oxford University Press.

Gibbon, K. (1998) "Munchausen's syndrome presenting as an acute sexual assault", *Medicine, Science and the Law* 38: 202–5.

Gleick, J. (2003) *Isaac Newton*, London: Fourth Estate.

Green, G., Gray, N. S. and Willan, P. (2003) "Management of sexually inappropriate behaviours in men with learning disabilities", *Journal of Forensic Psychiatry* 13: 85–110.

Groves, R. M., Salfati, C. G. and Elliot, D. (2004) "The influence of prior offender/victim relationship on offender stalking behaviour", *Journal of Investigative Psychology and Offender Profiling* 1: 153–67.

Gudjonsson, G. (1992) *The Psychology of Interrogations, Confessions and Testimony*, Chichester: John Wiley & Sons.

Gunn, J. (1977a) "Criminal behaviour and mental disorders", *British Journal of Psychiatry* 130: 317–29.

—— (1977b) *Epileptics in Prison*, London: Academic Press.

Gunn, J. (1978) "Epileptic homicide: A case report", *British Journal of Psychiatry* 132: 510–13.

—— (1993) "Epidemiology and forensic psychiatry", *Criminal Behaviour and Mental Health* 3: 180–93.

Gunn, J. and Taylor, P. J. (eds) (1993) *Forensic Psychiatry: Clinical, Legal and Ethical Issues*, London: Butterworth-Heinemann.

Gunn, J., Robertson, G., Dell, S. and Way, C. (1978) *Psychiatric Aspects of Imprisonment*, London: Academic Press.

Hardie, T. J. and Reed, A. (1998) "Pseudolgia fantastica, factitious disorder and impostership – a deception syndrome", *Medicine, Science and the Law* 38: 198–201.

Hare, E. (1983) "Was insanity on the increase?", *British Journal of Psychiatry* 142: 439–55.

Harmon, R., Rosner, R. and Owens, H. (1995) "Obsessive harassment and eroto-mania in a criminal court population", *Journal of Forensic Sciences* 40: 188–96.

Harris, J. (2000) *The Protection from Harassment Act, 1997 – An Evaluation of its Effectiveness*, Home Office Research, Development and Statistics Directorate, No. 130, London: Home Office.

Heinze, M. C. (2003) "Developing sensitivity to distortion: Utility of psychological tests in differentiating malingering and psychopathology in criminal defendants", *Journal of Forensic Psychiatry* 14: 151–77.

Higgins, J. (1990) "Affective disorders" in R. Bluglass and P. Bowden (eds), *Principles and Practice of Forensic Psychiatry*, London: Churchill Livingstone.

—— (1995) "Crime and mental disorder II: Forensic aspects of psychiatric disorder", in D. Chiswick and R. Cope (eds), *Seminars in Practical Forensic Psychiatry*, London: Gaskell.

Hodgins, S. (1992) "Mental disorder, intellectual deficiency and crime", *Archives of General Psychiatry* 49: 476–83.

Hodgins, S. and Gunnar-Janson, C. (2002) *Criminality and Violence among the Mentally Disordered: The Stockholm Metropolitan Project*, Cambridge: Cambridge University Press.

Hodgins, S. and Muller-Isberner, R. (2001) *Violence, Crime and Mentally Disordered Offenders: Concepts and Methods for Effective Treatment and Prevention*, Chichester: John Wiley & Sons.

—— (2004) "Preventing crime by people with schizophrenic disorders", *British Journal of Psychiatry* 185: 245–50.

Holden, C., Lacey, A. and Monach, J. (2001) "Establishing secure mental health facilities: The outcome of public consultation exercises", *Journal of Mental Health* 10: 513–24.

Howard, R. C. (2002) "Brainwaves, dangerousness and deviant desires", *Journal of Forensic Psychiatry* 13: 367–84.

James, D. (1998) "Multiple personality disorder in the courts: A review of the North American experience", *Journal of Forensic Psychiatry* 9: 339–61.

James, D. and Schramm, M. (1998) "Multiple personality disorder presenting to the English courts: A case study", *Journal of Forensic Psychiatry* 9: 615–28.

Kearns, A. (2001) "Forensic services and people with learning disabilities in the shadow of the Reed Report", *Journal of Forensic Psychiatry* 12: 8–12.

Kellam, A. M. P. (1993) "False confessions: A note on the McKenzie judgement", *Psychiatric Bulletin* 17: 361–2.

Kemphuis, J. H. and Emmelkamp, P. M. G. (2000) "Stalking: A contemporary challenge for forensic and clinical psychiatry", *British Journal of Psychiatry* 176: 206–9.

Keyes, D. (1995) *The Minds of Billy Milligan*, Harmondsworth: Penguin.

Klawans, H. L. (1990) *Newton's Madness and Further Tales of Clinical Neurology*, London: Bodley Head.

Lagach, E. D. (1947) *La Jalousie Amoureuse*, Paris: Presses Universitaires de France.

Laing, R. and Esterson, A. (1964) *Sanity, Madness and the Family*, London: Tavistock.

Laurance, J. (2003) *Pure Madness: How Fear Drives the Mental Health System*, London: Routledge.

Lewis, O. and Carpenter, S. (1999) "Episodic dyscontrol and the English criminal law", *Journal of Mental Health Law* 1: 13–22.

Lindqvist, P. and Allebeck, P. (1990) "Schizophrenia and crime: A longitudinal follow-up of 644 schizophrenics in Stockholm", *British Journal of Psychiatry* 157: 345–50.

Link, B. J. and Steuve, A. (1994) "Psychotic symptoms and violent/illegal behaviour of mental patients compared to community controls", in J. Monahan and H. J. Steadman (eds), *Violence and Mental Disorder: Developments in Risk Assessment*, Chicago and London: Chicago University Press.

Link, B. J., Andrews, H. and Cullen, F. T. (1992) "The violent and illegal behaviour of mental patients reconsidered", *American Sociological Review* 57: 275–92.

Lishman, W. A. (1997) *Organic Psychiatry*, 3rd ed., Oxford: Blackwell.

Lucas, P. (1994) "Episodic dyscontrol: A look back at anger", *Journal of Forensic Psychiatry* 5: 371–407.

Marshall, J. (1998) "Dual diagnosis: Co-morbidity of severe mental illness and substance misuse", *Journal of Forensic Psychiatry* 9: 9–15.

McBrien, J., Hodgetts, A. and Gregory, J. (2003) "Offending and risky behaviour in community services for people with intellectual disabilities in one local authority", *Journal of Forensic Psychiatry* 14: 280–97.

McGuire, B. and Wraith, A. (2000) "Legal and psychological aspects of stalking: A review", *Journal of Forensic Psychiatry* 11: 316–27.

McNeil, D. E., Binder, R. and Greenfield, T. (1988) "Predictions of violence in civilly committed acute psychiatric patients", *American Journal of Psychiatry*, 145: 965–70.

Melloy, J. R. (ed.) (1998) *The Psychology of Stalking: Clinical and Forensic Perspectives*, San Diego and London: Academic Press.

Merskey, H. (1992) "The manufacture of personalities: The production of personality disorder", *British Journal of Psychiatry* 160: 327–40.

Miller, E. (1999) "The neuropsychology of offending", *Psychology, Crime and Law* 5: 297–318.

Miller, L. (1992) "Neuropsychology, personality and substance abuse in a head injury case: Clinical and forensic issues", *International Journal of Law and Psychiatry* 15: 303–16.

Monahan, J. (1992) "Mental disorder and violent behaviour: Perceptions and evidence", *American Psychologist* 74: 511–21.

Monahan, J. (2002) "The McArthur studies of violence risk", *Criminal Behaviour and Mental Health, Supplement: Festschrift to John Gunn* 12: S67–S72.

Monahan, J., Steadman, H. J., Silver, E., Applebaum, P. S., Robbins, P., Clark, P., Mulvey, E. P., Roth, L. H., Grisso, T. and Banks, S. (2001) *Rethinking Risk Assessment: The McArthur Study of Mental Disorder and Violence*, Oxford: Oxford University Press.

Moran, P., Walsh, E., Tyrer, P., Burns, F., Creed, F. and Fahy, T. (2003) "Impact of combined personality disorder and violence in psychoses: Report from the UK 700 trial", *British Journal of Psychiatry* 182: 129–34.

Mullen, P. (1981) "Jealousy: The pathology of passion", *British Journal of Psychiatry* 158: 593–601.

—— (1996) "Jealousy and the emergence of violent and intimidatory behaviours", *Criminal Behaviour and Mental Health* 6: 194–205.

Mullen, P. E., Pathé, M. and Purcell, R. (1999) "Study of stalkers", *American Journal of Psychiatry* 156: 1244–9.

—— (2000) *Stalkers and their Victims*, Cambridge: Cambridge University Press.

Murray, R., Walsh, E. and Arseneault, L. (2002) "Some possible answers to questions about schizophrenia that have concerned John Gunn", *Criminal Behaviour and Mental Health, Festschrift to John Gunn, Supplement* 12: S4–S9.

NACRO (National Association for the Care and Resettlement of Offenders) (1993) *Community Care and Mentally Disordered Offenders (Policy Paper No.1)*, Mental Health Advisory Committee (Chairman, H. Prins), London: NACRO.

Nemitz, T. and Bean, P. (2001) "Protecting the rights of the mentally disordered in police stations: The use of the appropriate adult in England and Wales", *International Journal of Law and Psychiatry* 24: 595–605.

Norfolk, G. (2001) "Fit to be interviewed by the police: An aid to assessment", *Medicine, Science and the Law* 41: 5–12.

Pearse, J. and Gudjonsson, G. (1996) "How appropriate are appropriate adults?, *Journal of Forensic Psychiatry* 7: 570–80.

—— (1997) "Police interviewing and legal representation: A field study", *Journal of Forensic Psychiatry* 8: 200–8.

Petch, E. (2002) "Anti-stalking laws and the Protection from Harassment Act, 1997", *Journal of Forensic Psychiatry* 13: 19–34.

Pilgrim, D. and Rogers, A. (2003) "Mental disorder and violence: An empirical picture in context", *Journal of Mental Health* 12: 7–18.

Pines, A. M. (1998) *Romantic Jealousy: Causes, Symptoms, Cures*, London: Routledge.

Pollock, P. H. (1996) "A cautionary note on the determination of malingering", *Psychology, Crime and Law* 3: 97–110.

Porter, S., Birt, A. R., Yuille, J. C. and Hervé, H. F. (2001) "Memory for murder: A psychological perspective on dissociative amnesia in legal contexts", *International Journal of Law and Psychiatry* 24: 23–42.

Power, D. J. (1977) "Memory, identification and crime", *Medicine, Science and the Law* 17: 132–9.

Prins, H. (1990) *Bizarre Behaviours: Boundaries of Psychiatric Disorder*, London: Routledge.

Prins, H. (1996) "Othello, Leontes or what you will: A comment on Crichton", *Journal of Forensic Psychiatry* 7: 630–3.

Prins, H., Backer-Holst, T., Francis, E. and Keitch, I. (1993) *Report of the Committee of Inquiry into the Death of Orville Blackwood and a Review of the Deaths of Two Other Afro-Caribbean Patients: "Big, Black and Dangerous?"*, London: Special Hospitals Service Authority (SHSA).

Reid, A. (1990) "Mental retardation and crime", in R. Bluglass and P. Bowden (eds), *Principles and Practice of Forensic Psychiatry*, London: Churchill Livingstone.

Resnick, P. (1994) "Malingering", *Journal of Forensic Psychiatry* 5: 1–4.

Rollin, H. (1969) *The Mentally Abnormal Offender and the Law*, Oxford: Pergamon.

Roth, M. and Kroll, J. (1986) *The Reality of Mental Illness*, Cambridge: Cambridge University Press.

Schipkowensky, N. (1969) "Cyclophrenia and murder", in A. V. S. Ruck and R. Porter (eds), *The Mentally Abnormal Offender*, London: J. and A. Churchill.

Schorer, C. E. (1965) "The Ganser syndrome", *British Journal of Criminology* 5: 120–31.

Scull, A. (1984) "Was insanity on the increase? A reply to Edward Hare", *British Journal of Psychiatry* 144: 432–6.

Sedgwick, P. (1982) *Psycho-politics*, London: Pluto Press.

Shepherd, E. (ed.) (1993) *Aspects of Police Interviewing* (Division of Legal and Criminological Psychology, Monograph, No. 18), Leicester: British Psychological Society.

Sheridan, L. and Davies, G. M. (2001) "What is stalking? The match between legislation and public perceptions", *Legal and Criminological Psychology* 6: 3–17.

Sheridan, L., Davies, G. and Boon, J. (2001) "The course and nature of stalking: A victim perspective", *Howard Journal* 40: 215–34.

Sheridan, L., Gillett, R. and Davies, G. (2000) "Stalking: Seeing the victim's perspective", *Psychology, Crime and Law* 6: 267–80.

—— (2002) "Perceptions and prevalence of stalking in a male sample", *Psychology, Crime and Law* 8: 289–310.

Steadman, H., Mulvey, E. P., Monahan, J., Robbins, P. C., Applebaum, P. S., Grisso, T., Roth, L. H. and Silver E. (1998) "Violence by people discharged from acute psychiatric-in-patient facilities and by others in the same neighbourhoods", *Archives of General Psychiatry* 55: 393–401.

Stone, J. H. (1992) "Memory disorders in offenders and victims", *Criminal Behaviour and Mental Health* 2: 342–56.

Swanson, J. W., Holtzer, C. E., Ganju, V. K. and Juno, R. T. (1990) "Violence and psychiatric disorder in the community: Evidence from the epidemiologic catchment area surveys", *Hospital and Community Psychiatry* 41: 761–70.

Szasz, T. (1987) *Insanity: The Idea and its Consequences*, New York: John Wiley & Sons.

—— (1993) "Curing, coercing and claims-making: A reply to critics", *British Journal of Psychiatry* 162: 797–800.

Tantam, D. and Whittaker, J. (1993) "Self wounding and personality disorders", in P. Tyrer and G. Stein (eds), *Personality Disorder Reviewed*, London: Gaskell.

Taylor, P. J. (1995) "Motives for offending among violent and psychotic men", *British Journal of Psychiatry* 147: 491–8.

Taylor, P. J., Mahendra, B. and Gunn, J. (1983) "Erotomania in males", *Psychological Medicine* 13: 645–50.

Vine, B. (aka Ruth Rendell) (1990) *Gallowglass*, London: Viking.

Walsh, E., Buchanan, A. and Fahy, T. (2002) "Violence and schizophrenia – examining the evidence", *British Journal of Psychiatry* 180: 490–5.

Walsh, E., Moran, P., Scott, C., McKenzie, K., Burns, T., Creed, R., Tyrer, P., Murray, R. M. and Fahy, T. (2003) "Prevalence of violent victimisation in severe mental illness", *British Journal of Psychiatry* 183: 233–8.

Wesseley, S. C., Castle, D., Douglas, A. J. and Taylor, P. J. (1994) "The criminal careers of incident cases of schizophrenia", *Psychological Medicine* 24: 483–502.

West, D. J. (1965) *Murder Followed by Suicide*, London: Macmillan.

Wheatley, M. (1998) "The prevalence and use of substance abuse in detained schizophrenic patients", *Journal of Forensic Psychiatry* 9: 114–30.

White, G. L. and Mullen, P. E. (1989) *Jealousy: Theory, Research and Clinical Strategies*, New York and London: Guilford Press.

Whitty, C. W. M. and Zangwill, O. L. (eds) (1977) *Amnesia: Clinical, Psychological and Legal Aspects*, London: Butterworth.

Williams, M. (1979) *Brain Damage, Behaviour and the Mind*, Chichester: John Wiley & Sons.

Wilson, S. (1993) "Multiple personality personality", in P. Tyrer and G. Stein (eds), *Personality Disorder Reviewed*, London: Gaskell.

Woddis, G. M. (1964) "Clinical psychiatry and crime", *British Journal of Criminology* 4: 443–60.

World Health Organization (1992) *Classification of Mental and Behavioural Disorders: Clinical Descriptions and Diagnostic Guidelines*, Geneva: WHO.

Wright, J. A., Burgess, A. J., Burgess, A. W. et al. (1996) "A typology of stalking", *Journal of Interpersonal Violence* 11: 487–502.

Yorston, G. (1999) "Aged and dangerous: Old age forensic psychiatry", *British Journal of Psychiatry* 174: 193–5.

Zona, M. A., Sharma, K. K. and Lane, J. C. (1993) "A comparative study of erotomania and obsessive subjects in a female sample", *Journal of Forensic Sciences* 38: 894–903.

# Further reading

## Brain mechanisms

Pinker, S. (1999) *How the Mind Works*, London: Penguin (stimulating and sometimes provocative discussion of mind-body-society relationships).

## Learning disability

See Section 10 in *Vol. 2* of *The New Oxford Textbook of Psychiatry* (2001), particularly subsections 10.5.1 and 10.5.2 by Tonge, B. J. and Dolsen, A.

# Chapter 4

# "But someone has to deal with them"*

And thus I clothe my naked villany . . .
And seem a saint when most I play the devil.

(Richard III Act 1 Sc. 3)

A devil, a born devil, on whose nature
Nurture can never stick; on whom my pains
Humanely taken, all, all lost, quite lost.

(The Tempest Act 4 Sc.1)

## Introductory note

In this chapter, I shall consider a group of individuals who do not fit easily within current delineations of mental disorders and who evoke emotive responses from professionals and laypersons alike. It is also important to indicate at the outset that the definition of *psychopathic disorder* within current mental health legislation does not necessarily equate with the definitions and descriptions of many aspects of the disorder within clinical texts – as, for example, in *The Diagnostic and Statistical Manual of Mental Disorders*, DSM IV(R), (APA 1994) or in the *International Classification of Diseases* (ICD 10) (WHO 1992). Given these discrepancies, it is difficult to be precise as to the condition one is about to describe. At the risk of being criticized, but for the sake of simplification, I shall use the term "psychopathic disorder" to encompass serious anti-social personality disorder (APA 1994), dissocial personality disorder (WHO 1992) and, perhaps somewhat more controversially, the newly "coined" disorder known as "dangerous severe personality disorder". (For a penetrating discussion of

---

* Some of the material in this chapter is from my (2002) paper "Psychopathic disorder – concept or chimera", which appeared in the *Journal of Mental Health Law* 8: 247–61, reproduced with permission from Northumbria Law Press.

the genesis of this last, see Gunn 2000.) The two opening epigraphs point to several of the key problems in dealing with the concept of psychopathic disorder. The quotation from *Richard III* suggests the manner in which the so-called psychopath is able to "mask" his persistent criminality behind a façade of charm and normality; to such an extent that Cleckley called his seminal work on the disorder *The Mask of Sanity* (Cleckley 1976). The second quotation illustrates the long-standing but not very helpful nature versus nurture debate and the psychopath's resistance to punishment or treatment (see later).

## Nature of personality

More generally, not only are there difficulties in defining personality with any degree of accuracy, but it is a word used in common parlance to cover a variety of attributes and behaviours. Trethowan and Sims suggest that:

> Personality may be either considered subjectively, i.e. in terms of what the [person] believes and describes about himself as an individual, or, objectively in terms of what an observer notices about his more consistent patterns of behaviour . . .
> Personality will include such things as mood state, attitudes and opinions and all these must be measured against how people comport themselves in their social environments. If we describe a person as having a "normal" personality, we use the word in a statistical sense indicating that various personality traits are present in a broadly normal extent, neither to gross excess nor extreme deficiency. Abnormal personality, is, therefore, a variation upon an accepted yet broadly conceived, range of personality.
>
> (1983: 225)

When we come to consider what Trethowan and Sims describe as the extremes of personality the two definitions of personality disorder as given in the DSMIV and ICD 10 amplify these. The *DSMIV* defines them as:

> An enduring pattern of inner experience and behaviour that deviates markedly from the expectations of the individual's culture, is pervasive and inflexible, has an onset in adolescence or early childhood, is stable over time, and leads to distress or impairment.
>
> (as quoted in NIMHE 2003: 9)

The ICD 10 defines personality disorder in the following terms:

> A severe disturbance in the characterological condition and behavioural tendencies of the individual, usually involving several areas of

the personality, and nearly always associated with considerable personal and social disruption.

(op. cit.) (see also Tyrer et al. 2003)

Both these definitions indicate that personality disorders may present in a variety of forms. The ICD 10 definition comes nearer to indicating the seriously deviant (and delinquent) end of the spectrum ("considerable personal and social disruption"). It is this aspect that is given expression in the current Mental Health Act's definition of psychopathic disorder:

A persistent disorder or disability of mind (whether or not including significant impairment of intelligence) which results in abnormally aggressive or seriously irresponsible conduct on the part of the person concerned.

(Mental Health Act 1983: Section 1(2))

The modern concept of personality disorder seems to represent two interlocking notions. The first suggests that it is present when *any* abnormality or personality causes problems *either* to the person himself or herself *or* to others. The second, and the one with which we are more specifically concerned in this chapter, carries a more pejorative connotation; it implies unacceptable, anti-social behaviour coupled with a notion of dislike for the person showing such behaviour and a rejection of them (see later discussion). Sometimes, the word "psychopath" is used for this purpose. Such usage has led to many difficulties for academics, lawyers, sentencers, psychiatrists and other healthcare and criminal justice professionals (see, for example, Gayford and Jungalwalla 1986). The following scenario gives some indication of the scale of the problems involved in definition and management.

Over 25 years ago I made the following observations in a paper that appeared in the *Prison Service Journal* (Prins 1977):

Imagine if you can, a top-level conference has been called to discuss the meaning of that much used and abused word *psychopathy*. You are privileged to be an observer at these discussions at which are present psychiatrists, psychologists, sociologists, lawyers, sentencers, theologians, philosophers, staff of penal establishments and special hospitals, social workers and probation officers. You have high expectations that some total wisdom will come from this well-informed and experienced group of people and that a definition will emerge that will pass the closest scrutiny of all concerned. After all, *this* is a gathering of *experts*. Alas, your expectations would have a quality of fantasy about them, for in reality you would find as many definitions as experts present. Let me just present one or two examples of this statement. There would be little agreement among psychiatrists; for some continental psychiatrists, the term would be used to cover a very wide range of mental disorders, including those we might describe as neuroses in this country; for some psychiatrists (for example, from the United States), the term might include minor disorders of personality and for others, the term might be synonymous with what we would describe as recidivism. The lawyers in the group would disagree also. Some might well accept the definition in the Mental Health Act, 1959 . . . [as it then was] . . . which describes psychopathy as a "persistent disorder or disability of mind (whether or not including subnormality of intelligence) which results in abnormally aggressive behaviour or seriously irresponsible conduct on the part of the patient and requires or is susceptible to medical treatment . . ." However, they would immediately begin to ask questions about the legal implications of the words "disability of mind" and "irresponsible conduct". At this stage, the philosophers would no doubt chip in and also ask searching questions about the same terms. Later on in the discussion, a theologian might start asking awkward questions about the differences between "sickness" and "sin" and "good" and "evil". The representative from the field of sociology in the group might usefully remind us that psychopaths lack what they describe as a capacity for role-taking, i.e. seeing yourself in an appropriate role in relation to others in their roles in [their] environment. And so the discussion would go on and on. Don't assume that it has ever been different. For one hundred and fifty years the arguments have raged over definition, classification and management.

(Prins 1977: 8–9)

Readers of this book might well ask: "Have things changed much since you wrote that?" To which I would be forced to answer: "Not that much." Today, such a group might well be somewhat more representative. We could usefully find space for a geneticist, a developmental paediatrician, representatives from the Home Office and Department of Health, from the voluntary sector (who do so much to cope with these "hard to like" individuals) and, who knows, in this more progressive day and age, a consumer of the service and a victim? A more recent and near parallel to such an hypothetical group can perhaps be seen in the large conference called by the Secretaries of State for Social Services and the Home Department in July 1999, to receive and comment on their joint proposals for dealing with the management of those persons exhibiting dangerous severe personality disorder (DSPD) (Home Office and Department of Health 1999). As one who was asked to comment on the proposals at this conference, I was painfully aware of the continuing complexities surrounding the phenomenon we label psychopathic disorder. (See Prins 1999 for a shortened version of my paper.) It is of particular interest to note that the government (perhaps very wisely) provided only a loose definition of what it understood dangerous severe personality disorder to be and expressed the firm intention to fund major research into the problem – an intention currently being put into practice. Personality disorder is referred to in the document as "an inclusive term referring to a disorder of the development of personality" and "is not a category of mental illness" (p. 5 footnote 1). At page 9, the document states that the phrase: "Dangerous severely personality disordered (DSPD) is used in this paper to describe people who have an identifiable personality disorder to a severe degree, who pose a high risk to other people because of serious anti-social behaviour resulting from their disorder." These definitions can reasonably be regarded as "loose". For useful commentary on some current concerns see also Laing (1999).

## Development of the concept

There are numerous accounts of the development of the concept of psychopathic disorder and, at the risk of being accused of a degree of invidious selection, I shall only refer to one or two specifically. For those wishing to pursue this aspect in more depth the following authors have provided useful accounts: Cleckley 1976; Hare 1993; Lewis 1974; McCord and McCord 1956; Millon et al. 2003. French "alienists" (psychiatrists) are usually given recognition for the first to describe those we might describe today as psychopathic. Pinel is usually credited with one of the very first descriptions of clinical cases of psychopathic disorder in 1806 and a further descriptive account was provided by Esquirol in 1838. (For an account of Esquirol's description see Finley-Jones 1991.) However, we would be ignoring what history has to tell us if we did not go back in time for further evidence of such behaviour. One could cite the French aristocrat Gilles de Rais, the sexual sadistic murderer of children, Vlad the Impaler and many many others.

An example from biblical times is said to be that of Samson, described (no doubt with tongue in cheek) by Dr Eric Altschuler of the University of California. According to him, Samson had a number of psychopathic characteristics; moreover, as a child Samson had severe personality disorder, "setting things on fire, torturing animals and bullying other children". Altschuler also cites Samson's mother as a possible pathogenic element in his development. Apparently, in the Book of Judges "she is warned not to drink while she is pregnant". Altschuler concludes: "Recklessness and a disregard for others may have run in the family" (reported in *The Independent*, 15 February 2002, citing a paper in *The New Scientist*). To return to Pinel and Esquirol. In Pinel's descriptions it seems likely that he included a number of cases that we would not consider today as falling within modern classifications.

It was in the 1830s that the English alienist and anthropologist, Prichard, formulated his well-known concept of "moral insanity". He described it thus:

> [A] madness, consisting of a morbid perversion of the natural feelings, affections, inclinations, temper, habits, moral dispositions and natural impulses, without any remarkable disorder or defect of the intellect or knowing or reasoning faculties, and particularly *without any insane illusion or hallucination.*
>
> (1835: 135; emphasis added)

In the context of this quotation we should note that "moral" meant emotional and psychological and was not intended to denote the opposite of "immoral" as used in modern parlance. This view of "moral insanity" rested on the, then fairly widely held, controversial belief that there could be a separate moral sense that could, as it were, be diseased. This early notion finds resonance in Cleckley's later postulation that psychopathy was a particular form of "illness". Prichard's views need to be seen against the background of the very rudimentary state of psychiatric and psychological knowledge during his lifetime. In 1891, Koch formulated the concept of *constitutional psychopathy*, implying that there was a considerable innate predisposition; a line of thinking much in keeping with the then contemporary interest in hereditary factors in the causation of delinquency. It is interesting to note a comparable reawakening in more recent times in the study of neuro-physio-psychological processes in the causation of persistent deviancy (see, for example, Blair and Frith 2000; Dolan 1994). In the early 1900s the terms "moral defective" and "moral imbecile" found their way into the Mental Deficiency Act of 1913 (subsequently changed to somewhat less pejorative descriptions in an amending Act of 1927). Certain trends in the 1930s were of importance. Findings from the disciplines of neurology and physiology were being applied to behaviour disorders – prompted no doubt by the sequelae of the widespread epidemics of disorders such as epidemic encephalitis. Freudian perspectives were also being applied increasingly to deviant behaviour in the work of psychoanalytically orientated medical and non-medical professionals such as Melitta Schmideberg, Kate Friedlander, Anna Freud and August Aichorn; they were all interested in the possible childhood roots of serious anti-social behaviour.

In 1939, Sir David Henderson, a distinguished British psychiatrist, published his famous work *Psychopathic States*. He considered that the psychopath's "failure to adjust to ordinary social life is not a mere wilfulness or badness which can be threatened or thrashed out . . . but constitutes a true illness" (p. 19). (For an interesting compilation of 1930s' and 1940s' accounts of work in this field see Eisler 1949.) The later work of Lee Robins is also seminal in this area (see, for example, Robins 1966). The work of

Manie sans délire (madness without delirium or delusion) ——▶ moral insanity ——▶
moral imbecility (defectiveness) (Mental Deficiency Act 1913) ——▶ (constitutional)
psychopathic inferiority ——▶ "neurotic character" ——▶ psychopathy ——▶
sociopathy (USA) ——▶ antisocial personality disorder (DSMIV) ——▶ dissocial
personality disorder (ICD10) ——▶ dangerous severe personality disorder

*Figure 4.1*   From Pinel (1806) to Home Office and Department of Health (1999)

Bowlby on attachment theory has been of profound importance (see, for example, Bowlby 1979); and the work of Sir Michael Rutter has also been of great significance (see Rutter 1999). Since the 1960s attention has been focused on the management of adult psychopathically disordered individuals within institutional settings, notably those adopting a therapeutic community or "social milieu" approach. Figures eminent in this field include psychiatrists such as Jones (1963) and Whiteley (1994).

Summarizing the foregoing, it is possible to trace three important themes in the development of the concept. The first, as Coid (1993) has suggested, was the concept of abnormal personality as defined by social maladjustment – developed in France and later in the UK – leading to the current legal definition of psychopathic disorder (of which more later). The second was the concept of mental degeneracy, also originating in France. The third was the German notion of defining abnormal psychopathic personality types, as illustrated in the work of Schneider (1958). In addition, the concept has not been without attention from central government over the years. It was considered by the Butler Committee as long ago as the early 1970s (HO and DHSS 1975), subsequently in a joint DHSS and Home Office Consultation Document on the topic (DHSS and HO 1986); by the Reed Committee (D of H and HO 1994) and most recently in the joint Home Office and Department of Health policy development document to which I have already referred. The whole topic was also considered further in considerable depth by the Fallon Committee in its inquiry into the personality disorder unit at Ashworth Hospital. See Volume II of the report, which contains very extensive expert evidence on the nature of personality disorder (Fallon et al. 1999). I have provided representation of the stages through which the concept has passed in Figure 4.1.

## Causes and characteristics

There is vast literature concerning the postulated origins of psychopathic disorder and an equally vast literature on its characteristic features. No attempt is made here to review this literature at great length, merely to address certain aspects of it as a prelude to some discussion of problems of management. Postulated origins have included genetic and hereditary factors, cortical immaturity and close familial and environmental influences.[1]

Professor Coid, a respected authority in the field, advocates caution in espousing the notion of psychopathic disorder as a *single* entity. He suggests that:

> The sheer complexity and range of psychopathology in psychopathic disorder has previously led to the suggestion that these individuals could be considered to suffer from a series of conditions that would best be subsumed under a broad generic term "psychopathic disorders" rather than a single entity.
>
>                           (1989: 756) (see also Tyrer 1990; Tyrer et al. 1991)

In recent times, interest has been revived concerning possible "organic" causes, including both major and minor cerebral "insults" in infancy and in the consequences of obstetric complications. If such developments subsequently prove to have unequivocally firm foundations, one could envisage a situation where issues of responsibility (and notably diminished responsibility) may well have to be addressed. This is an arena already fraught with problems concerning the relationship between medicine (notably neurology and psychiatry) and the law. The environment has also been held to play a powerful part in the aetiology of the disorder. It may well be, that as with similar mental disorders, such as the schizophrenias, it is the interplay of social forces and pressures acting on an already vulnerable personality (for whatever reason) that may tend to produce the condition. Some of the highly complicated and sophisticated neuro-physio-chemical research undertaken in recent years fosters speculation that *some* of the answers to the problem of aetiology may eventually be found in the area of brain biochemistry.

Other possibilities are of equal interest. For example, one cannot ignore the evidence, admittedly laboratory based, of such factors as low anxiety thresholds, cortical immaturity (childlike patterns of brainwaves in adults), frontal lobe damage and, perhaps most relevant of all, the *true* (as distinct from the wrongly labelled) psychopath's need for excitement – the achievement of a "high". Such a need is described very graphically in Wambaugh's account of the case of Colin Pitchfork (1989). Pitchfork was convicted of the rape and murder of two teenage girls in Leicestershire during the period 1983–6. In interviews with the police, it is alleged he stated that he obtained a "high" when he exposed himself to women (he had previous convictions for indecent exposure prior to his two major offences); he also obtained a "high" from the knowledge that his victims or likely victims were *virgo intacta*. He is said to have also described an additional aspect of his excitement, namely obtaining sex outside marriage. As with others assessed as psychopathic, he also demonstrated a great degree of charm; for example, he was able to get his wife to forgive him for a number of instances of admitted unfaithfulness. (Pitchfork's case is also of interest in that it involved the earliest attempt to use DNA profiling – a practice that now seems fairly routine.)

### Some key characteristics

Some of these have already been alluded to above. Sir Martin Roth (1990), a doyen of British psychiatry, has suggested (in summary form) that the key features are egotism, immaturity in various manifestations, aggressiveness, low frustration tolerance and the inability to learn from experience so that social demands and expectations are never met. Roth's brief listing encapsulates many of the 16 detailed characteristics suggested by Cleckley in the various editions of his seminal work *The Mask of Sanity* (1976). To these items I would add the following three elements. First, the curious *super-ego lacunae*, rather than the *total* lack of conscience suggested by some authorities. Second, the greater than usual need for excitement and arousal to which I have already referred. Third, a capacity to create chaos among family, friends and those involved in trying to manage or contain them. I would suggest that this last characteristic is one of the most accurate indicators of the *true*, as distinct from the pejoratively labelled, psychopath and is often attested to by those who have extensive clinical experience in dealing with the psychopathically disordered.

The lack of true feeling content (empathy) exhibited by the psychopath was stated graphically some 40 years ago by Johns and Quay (1962) in their comment that psychopaths "know the words but not the music". Rieber and Green (1988) add four salient characteristics in support of the foregoing. These are thrill seeking, pathological glibness, anti-social pursuit of power and absence of guilt. They also give great prominence to the element of thrill seeking. They describe the psychopath as "performing a Mephisto Waltz on the tightrope of danger" (p. 82). It is as though this phenomenon of thrill seeking is necessary to fill the emotional void so often encountered in the psychopathically disordered. This internal "emptiness" has also been stressed by Whiteley (1994). He quotes a former patient writing to him from prison:

> I thought everything I said, did and thought was not real, that I was not real, almost as though I did not exist, so I could never affect anyone because I was not real, no-one could possibly take me seriously because I was not real.

> (p. 16)

If we see psychopathic disorder as a developmental process then we need not rely exclusively on clinical depictions. Its nature, early onset and manifestations are depicted clearly in the aged Duchess of York's reviling of her son Richard III in Act 4 Sc. 4 of Shakespeare's play:

Thou camest on earth to make the earth my hell.
A grievous burden was thy birth to me;
Tetchy and wayward was thy infancy;
Thy school-days frightful, desp'rate, wild and furious;
Thy prime of manhood daring, bold and venturous;
Thy age confirm'd, proud, subtle, sly and bloody,
More mild, but yet more harmful kind in hatred.
What comfortable hour canst thou name
That ever graced me with thy company?

Here, we have the aged Duchess describing graphically some of the characteristics we regard as important in terms of both aetiology and presentation. For example, an apparently difficult birth, long-standing anti-sociality (a requirement of the DSM-IV(R)), the ICD 10 and current mental health legislation in England and Wales, becoming more marked in adulthood; all this accompanied by a veneer of charm and sophistication that only serves to act as a mask for the underlying themes of chaos and potential for destructiveness. It should be emphasized again at this point that neither the DSM nor the ICD 10 refers to psychopathic disorder; the former refers to anti-social personality disorder and the latter to dissocial personality disorder. As previously stated, neither description equates exactly with the current legal description – psychopathic disorder – a word that numerous committees have suggested abandoning, preferring personality disorder – which would not be defined further. However, we should perhaps be mindful of the reference to "naming" in *Romeo and Juliet*: "What's in a name? that which we call a rose / by any other name would smell as sweet" (Act 2 Sc. 2). Changing the name will not necessarily do away with our dislike for such patients/clients/offenders. However, describing and trying to delineate a disorder has the advantage of hopefully setting some boundaries to it and creating typologies that may assist in management, even if the latter is highly problematic (as we shall shortly see). We should also note that a number of clinical and legal authorities consider that the current espousal of the term "psychopathic", and all that this entails in practice, is unhelpful (see, for example, Blackburn 1988; Cavadino 1998; Lewis and Appleby 1988; Maden 1999; Solomka 1996).

## Some problems of management

This section deals predominantly, first, with legal aspects and, second, with clinical matters. To a great extent the two elements should be seen as a whole, but in an attempt to achieve clarity, I have chosen to split them. Readers should note that this is a largely artificial (and somewhat pedantic) distinction.

## Legal aspects

The nature of psychopathic disorder and the problems it has presented to courts and counsel, are likely to bring to the fore powerful views as to the nature of the attitudes towards the disorder. As noted previously, in England and Wales, a legal definition of psychopathic disorder was first introduced in the Mental Health Act 1959. (In Scotland and Northern Ireland the term is not used directly. See Crichton et al. 2001; Darjee and Crichton 2003.) In the 1959 Act, treatability was linked to the definition of the disorder: "and requires, or is susceptible to treatment" (Section 1(4)). The definition of the disorder was left substantially unchanged in the 1983 Act, with the important exception of the removal of the sentence relating to treatability; the latter finds expression in Sections 3, 37 and 45A of the Act, where it must be demonstrated that "such treatment is *likely to alleviate or prevent a deterioration of his condition*" (emphasis added). Section 45A of the 1983 Act (inserted by Section 46 of the Crime (Sentences) Act 1997) makes provision for the so-called "hybrid order". This enables a Crown Court to impose a sentence of imprisonment on an offender (but only in cases where the sentence is not fixed by law, e.g. in convictions for murder). The patient must be diagnosed as suffering from psychopathic disorder and the court may direct that such an individual shall be admitted to a specified hospital. The provision is known as a "hospital and limitation direction".

Should the offender/patient no longer need, or be responsive to, treatment before his or her release date, the responsible medical officer may seek the offender/patient's transfer to prison. The "limitation" element has the effect of a restriction order under Section 41 of the 1983 Act. At the time of writing, it appears that courts have been slow to utilize this new provision. The change occurred due to a growing and understandable reluctance on the part of psychiatrists to manage such people. In the late 1950s there was a degree of optimism that psychiatry and psychiatrists had the answers not only to treatable *mental illness*, such as the major psychoses (e.g. the schizophrenias and affective psychoses) but that this optimism (which was not wholly justified or eventually sustainable even for the psychoses) could be extended to forms of mental *disorder* such as psychopathy. As to whether personality disorder (psychopathy) is an *illness* or *disorder*, Kendall (1999) suggests that: "The historical reasons for regarding personality disorders as fundamentally different from mental illnesses are being undermined by both clinical and genetic evidence. Effective treatments for personality disorders would probably have a decisive influence on psychiatrists' attitudes." Gunn (1999) has suggested an additional reason for the change of emphasis regarding treatability. This lies in the parlous state of general psychiatric provision, more particularly in large conurbations such as London. The legal connotations of treatment have resulted in a number of court rulings, both in England and Wales and in Scotland. In the case of *R. v. Canons Park Mental Health Review Tribunal* (ex parte A. (1995) QB 60), the Court of Appeal held that a mere refusal of a patient to participate in group psychotherapy did not, of itself, indicate untreatability. A case in Scotland *Reid v. Secretary of State for Scotland* (1999) reopened the whole issue (2 WLR 28). In brief, this case concerned an offender–patient detained without limit of time under the provisions of the Scottish Mental Health Act 1984. In a ruling, the Law Lords held that under Section 145(1) of that Act, medical treatment was to be given a broad meaning and that supervised care which endeavoured to prevent deterioration of the *symptoms*, but not the *disorder itself*, might *in a particular case* justify liability to continued detention (emphases added). In hearing this case, the Law Lords decided *inter alia* that the Canons Park case had been wrongly decided. Eldergill (1997) has summarized the degree of latitude that appears to be allowed currently:

> It can be seen that the treatability condition is satisfied if medical treatment in its broadest statutory sense – which includes nursing care – is *eventually* likely to bring some symptomatic relief to prevent the patient's mental health from deteriorating. *There are few (if any) conditions which are not treatable in this sense.*
>
> (p. 225)

However, the saga does not end with the decision in that case. There have been continuing concerns about possible loopholes in the law that would allow dangerous psychopaths to obtain their freedom. Again, in Scotland, the case of Ruddle (*Ruddle v. Secretary of State for Scotland* (1999) GWD 29 1395) led the Scottish Parliament to pass, as a matter of urgency, the Mental Health (Public Safety and Appeals) (Scotland) Act 1999, which has added public safety to the grounds for not discharging patients under Scottish mental health legislation. The main effect of this legislation was to change the definition of mental disorder "to mental illness (including personality disorder) or mental handicap however caused or manifested" and to require continued detention of a restricted patient "if the patient is suffering from a mental disorder the effect of which is such that it is necessary in order to protect the public from serious harm, that the patient continues to be detained in a hospital whether for medical treatment or not" (see Crichton et al. 2001). "One of the 'incidental' effects of this enactment has been to clarify the fact that personality disorder [had] always been included (but by implication only) within the meaning of mental disorder in Scottish mental health legislation" (op. cit.). Crichton et al. suggest that the Act of 1999 merely plugged "a loophole" and that further developments should wait on any action that may be taken as a result of the two major reviews of Scottish mental health legislation and practice by the Millan (1999) and Maclean Committees (2000) (see also Darjee and Crichton 2002).

### Clinical matters

From what we have discussed thus far, it should, I hope, be obvious that those labelled as psychopathic present enormous psychosocio-legal problems and that their day-to-day management causes the professionals involved both headache and heartache. Indeed, the heading for this subsection of the chapter might well have been "Encounters of an uncomfortable kind". Some aspects of mental health and criminal justice professionals' engagement in these "encounters" have already been touched on and the intention in this section is merely to highlight some of them further. My late friend and colleague, Doctor Peter Scott, addressed some of these issues over 25 years ago in a very thought-provoking and under-utilized paper entitled *Has Psychiatry Failed in the Treatment of Offenders?* (1975). Scott suggested that we most frequently fail those who need us most. Such individuals frequently fall into two (perhaps overlapping) categories: the "dangerous offender" and the "unrewarding", "degenerate" and "not nice" offender. Of the "embarrassing" patient Scott maintained that he/she is the patient who is "essentially the one who does not pay for treatment, the coin in which patients pay is "(i) dependence – i.e. being manifestly unable to care for themselves, and thus appealing to the maternal part of our nature; (ii) getting better (responding to our 'life-giving' measures); (iii) in either of these processes, showing gratitude, if possible cheerfully" (p. 8). In other words, those patients/clients/offenders whom Scott had in mind are just the ones who reject our "best efforts", are manipulative and delight in giving us a pretext for rejecting them, so that they can continue on their "unloved" and "unloving" way. In Scott's terms, the "not nice" patients are the ones who "habitually *appear* to be well able to look after themselves but don't and, [as stated earlier] reject attempts to help them, break the institutional rules, get drunk, upset other patients, or even quietly go to the devil in their own way quite heedless of nurse and doctor". Scott went on to suggest other factors that are highly relevant to any consideration of the management of *so-called* psychopaths. I emphasize the word *so-called* here because Scott did not feel there was much merit in distinguishing psychopaths from hardened chronic (recidivist) criminals – a minority view (see Scott 1960). He stated that:

> There is a natural philanthropic tendency to extend help to the defence-less – probably an extension of parental caring . . . if this fails so that embarrassing people or patients are seen to accumulate, then anxiety is aroused and some form of institution is set up to absorb the problem . . . Not all embarrassing patients like being tidied up and these tend to be compulsorily detained . . . Within the detaining institution two opposing aims begin to appear – the therapeutic endeavour to cure

and liberate on the one hand, and the controlling custodial function on the other.

(p. 9)

Scott went on to suggest that although these functions should be complementary "there is a tendency for them to polarise and ultimately, to split, like a dividing cell, into two separate institutions". However, he suggests that "neither of the two new institutions can quite eliminate the tendency from which it fled, so that the therapeutic institution now begins to miss the custodial function and tries hard to send some of its patients back to custody, and the custodial institution is unable to tolerate being unkind to people all the time and begins to set up a new nucleus of therapy" (p. 10). It seems to me that Scott's perceptive "management" observations should be considered carefully by those involved in devising the future institutional care for DSPD individuals envisaged in the policy development paper. So, these are the unlikeable clients/patients/offenders. Often the dislike will operate at an unconscious level. Three quotations from psychiatrists are useful in illustrating this problem and their words are applicable to all professionals working in the field of criminal justice and forensic psychiatry. Maier (1990) suggests:

> Could it be after all these Freudian years, that psychiatrists have denied the hatred they feel for psychopaths and criminals, and thus have been unable to treat psychopaths adequately because their conceptual basis for treatment has been distorted by unconscious, denied feelings from the start?
>
> (p. 766)

A somewhat similar view was proffered some years earlier by Treves-Brown (1977):

> As long as a doctor believes that psychopaths are mostly "bad", his successful treatment rate will be dismal. Since it takes two to form a relationship, an outside observer could be forgiven for suspecting that a doctor who describes a patient as unable to form a relationship, is simply trying to justify his own hostility to his patient.
>
> (p. 63)

And the late Doctor Donald Winnicott (1949), doyen of child psychiatry, writing over 50 years ago about the "anti-social tendency", gave further support for such views, as follows:

> However much he loves his . . . [hard to like] . . . patients he cannot help hating them and fearing them, and the better he knows this the less

will hate and fear be the motives determining what he does for his patients.

(1949: 71)

These three quotations indicate that the mechanism of "denial" is not merely the prerogative of patients and offenders. For a very useful account of denial more generally, see Cohen (2001).

Despite the unattractiveness of such patients and the sometimes unconscious reactions of therapists, a number of forensic psychiatric and criminal justice professionals have expressed a degree of optimism about treatment. Some years ago Tennent et al. sought the opinions of psychiatrists, psychologists and probation officers about treatability. The survey was admittedly small, as was the response rate. However, there was reasonable evidence to suggest that although there were few clear-cut views as to the best treatment modalities, there were clear indications as to those felt to be helpful. For example, there were higher expectations of treatment efficacy with symptoms such as "chronically anti-social", "abnormally aggressive" and "lacking control over impulses" and much lower expectations for symptoms such as "inability to experience guilt", "lack of remorse or shame" and "pathological egocentricity" (Tennent et al. 1993). Some support for the findings of this modest survey can be found in a more extensive survey by Cope on behalf of the Forensic Section of the Royal College of Psychiatrists. Cope surveyed all forensic psychiatrists working in secure hospitals, units and similar settings in England and Wales. The majority of her respondents (response rate 91 per cent) were in favour of offering treatment to severely personality disordered (psychopathic) patients (Cope 1993). Some explanation for this optimism derives from another source. In a fairly recent attempt to ascertain the motivations of consultant forensic psychiatrists for working in forensic psychiatric settings, I discovered that one of the attractions of the work was the challenge presented by psychopaths (Prins 1998). Another fact that emerged from my survey was the need for forensic psychiatrists to work with and encourage their colleagues in general psychiatry to deal with such patients. This is a point emphasized very cogently by Gunn in a recent paper for, as he implies, someone has to deal with such individuals and psychiatry should play its full part (Gunn 1999). For a recent study of work specifically with DSPD patients from the psychiatrists' point of view, see Haddock et al. (2001) and from a nursing perspective, see Bowers (2002).

Some other statements made by my respondents were very illuminating. One of them enjoyed the challenge presented by the severity and complexity of the cases that produced "a kind of appalled fascination". Another attraction was the chance to work with a wide range of agencies and disciplines and to pursue a more eclectic approach to patient care. Stimulation was another important factor (a factor shared with the psychopathic – see earlier discussion). Perhaps it takes one to recognize one! One stated "I

could not envisage 20 years of listening to the neurotic and worried well";
"After forensic psychiatry, other specialities seemed very tame and had
much less variety and challenge."

Whatever form of professional training is eventually formulated in order
to deal more effectively with psychopathically disordered individuals, understanding and management will only be successful through the adoption of a
truly multidisciplinary approach (as suggested in the "imaginary" seminar
quoted at the beginning of this chapter). Such an approach would serve
not only to take the broadest possible view of the topic but, at a narrower
clinical level, should help to obviate potential missed diagnoses (for example,
the importance of organic factors such as brain damage). The late doctor,
Peter Scott, had some interesting observations to make on this aspect over
40 years ago. He stated that:

> This may be the point at which to acknowledge that, with psychopaths,
> highly refined psychotherapeutic procedures applied by medical men,
> are often no more successful, sometimes less successful, than the
> simpler and less esoteric approaches of certain social workers, proba-
> tion officers, [and others] . . . some workers intuitively obtain good
> results with certain psychopaths; it should be possible to find out how
> they do it.
>
> (Scott 1960: 1645)

Sadly, little research information is available to answer Scott's implied
question about treatment success. However, what we do know is that
severely dangerous and deviant behaviour requires calm and well-informed
confrontation. In the words of the late George Lyward – a highly gifted
worker with severely personality disordered boys – "Patience is love that
can wait." Coupled to this is the need to tolerate, without loss of temper,
the hate, hostility, manipulation and "splitting" shown by such individuals
and an ability not to take such incidents as personal attacks. The psychiatrist and psychotherapist, Penelope Campling (1996), has provided an
excellent account of the management of such behaviours. For a very recent
research-based exposition of the potential value of psychosocial therapy for
severe personality disorders see Chiesa and Fonagy (2003). It is also
essential for professionals to have more than an "intellectual" understanding of what the patient has done. Sometimes, this can be "stomach turning"
and offers many opportunities for denial on the part of the professional.
Such understanding requires a degree of what has been described in another
context as "intestinal fortitude", an expression used by Michael Davies,
leader of the BBC Symphony Orchestra, in relation to the playing of certain
problematic orchestral works. (BBC2 broadcast, 10 July 1999.)

It is worth emphasizing once again the importance of the phenomenon
of denial. As stated, it is not the sole prerogative of our clients/patients/

offenders. For, as Pericles says in Shakespeare's play of that name: "Few love to hear the sins they love to act" (Act 1 Sc. 1). The more troublesome and anxiety making the relationship, the more the need *not* to go it alone. This is not an area of work that should be characterized by "prima donna" activities by professionals of either sex, for there are dangerous workers as well as dangerous clients/patients/offenders. In my view there are three qualities that are of paramount importance in dealing with the severely personality (psychopathically) disordered individual. These are *consistence* (the capacity to take a firm line in the face of deflecting activities on the part of the client); *persistence* (efforts may need to be expended over very considerable periods of time, maybe years – a view that is supported by the belief in the occurrence of cortical maturation in some cases, aided by therapeutic interventions) (the longer term benefits of team therapy in institutions such as Grendon Prison are described by Taylor (2000) and see also Coughlin 2003); *insistence* (the capacity to give clear indications that requirements of supervision are to be met in spite of resistance on the part of the client). Such insistence must take priority of place when expectations of what supervision requires of the client are initially set out in the professional/client relationship.

## Future trends

We need to acknowledge that, in strictly scientific terms, we have few hard facts concerning the genesis of severe personality (psychopathic) disorder. What we *do* know is that those suffering from (or, to be more precise, making others suffer from) it are extremely difficult to work with and manage. Mann and Moran (2000) put the matter into perspective rather well when they state:

> Sadly, when looking for evidence to inform decision-making about the placement of personality disordered patients, our knowledge is lacking. Psychiatry has an unfortunate history of being characterized by opinions rather than facts, and in this regard, both the government and psychiatrists need to stand back from firm decisions until more is known . . . [They continue] . . . the whole diagnostic group of per-sonality disordered patients is being judged by the difficulties and anxieties caused by one-sub-group (the so-called "severely personality disordered"). A sense of proportion is required.
>    (p. 11) (see also Maden et al. 2004 and Carroll et al. 2004)

These sensible observations provide a useful introduction to some brief comments on the government's proposals for dealing with "dangerous severely personality disordered" individuals. However, these have to be seen within the context of the broader based proposals for reforming mental health legislation in England and Wales.

In June 2002 the government produced its long-awaited Bill on the reform of mental health legislation. Interestingly, and unusually, the Bill came as a draft, and was accompanied by two documents – one containing detailed explanatory notes on the Bill, and the other is a consultation document. It would seem that the government wished to anticipate likely choruses of criticism and to defuse them as much as possible (DOH 2002a, 2002b, 2002c). It is of interest to note that this highly complicated proposed piece of legislation runs to some 180 sections and nine schedules; these compare with only 149 sections and six schedules in the 1983 Act. Implementation of the new legislation is likely to have enormous financial and human resource implications. The consultation document refers to matters that are not in the draft Bill, but which will also be brought before parliament when a Bill is eventually introduced. Notably, these matters concern a specialist division of a new Health Care Inspectorate, which will replace the Mental Health Act Commission; this new body will have wider powers and sharper teeth. There are also proposals for revised legislation in respect of children and for the protection of healthcare workers and numerous other matters. The following is a brief comment on the general proposals for dealing with persons demonstrating severe personality (psychopathic) disorder and, in particular, DSPD (see Prins 2001 for background material concerning the new proposals).

The government accepted the definition of mental disorder suggested in the review chaired by Professor Richardson (D of H 1999); it is presented as "any disability or disorder of mind or brain which results in an impairment or disturbance of mental functioning". This new composite definition removes "psychopathic disorder" and, as a result, the "treatability test". The latter, of course, had the effect of excluding a number of people considered to have a potential for dangerous behaviour towards others. The consultation document states that: "People with severe personality disorders will have access to services in the same way as people with other forms of mental disorder" (p. 1). In respect of DSPD, the document has this to say:

> There is no separate legislation for "DSPD". The term, which refers to the small group of people with a severe personality disorder *who also represent a high degree of risk to the public*, does not appear in the new Bill. People with personality disorders will be treated in exactly the same way as patients with other mental disorders and will come under compulsory powers if they meet the same conditions for compulsion.
>
> (p. 23; emphasis added)

It goes on to indicate that service developments (for those considered to be dangerous) are not part of legislative proposals but "are part of the wider agenda to provide better mental health services for everyone" (p. 23). However, the document goes on to indicate that services will be provided by specialist units (such as those now being developed at Rampton and Broadmoor Hospitals and HM Prisons Frankland and Whitemoor) (for accounts of the Whitemoor Unit see Bennett 2002; Bowers and Carr-Walker 2002; Storey 2002; for brief details of a prison research study see Erikson 2002). The consultation document posed a number of questions to which responses would be welcomed. One significant question in relation to this chapter is: Will the proposed legislation allow the indeterminate detention of severe personality disordered offenders?

> The new legislation will allow for the detention of someone with mental disorder for as long as they pose a significant risk of serious harm to others as a result of their mental disorder, thereby meeting the conditions for compulsion. In some cases where the mental disorder, and the behaviours arising from it, are complex and difficult to manage, *an individual may be detained in hospital for a long time*. However, to safeguard people from detention where it may not be justified, the new Mental Health Tribunal will regularly review the patient's compulsory treatment order to consider whether the conditions for compulsion continue to be met.
>
> (p. 23; emphasis added)

For a lot of people, a further question arises. What happens if staff in one of the new specialist units consider that such a person is "untreatable" at any stage?

## A cautionary tale

The problems of trying to legislate for persons suffering from severe personality disorder which may, from time to time, make them a danger to themselves and to others, are exemplified in the extraordinary Australian case of Gary David as told by Deirdre Greig in her disturbing book, *Neither Bad nor Mad* (Greig 2002). Her account demonstrates the inability of both the criminal justice and mental healthcare systems to deal with such individuals. His story may be told here very briefly. Gary was born in November 1954 and had a disturbed family history. He died of severe complications arising from grievous self-inflicted injuries in June 1992. Gary's severe personality disorder gave rise to many years of dramatic and highly persistent disruptive and manipulative behaviours. These included serious and highly bizarre episodes of both self-harm and harm to others. The inability of both systems to deal with him effectively led to numerous political manoeuvres to effect his indeterminate detention on the basis of his "dangerousness". This included the passing of one specific piece of legislation to deal solely with his case. Over the years, numerous psychiatric professionals who had had dealings with him could not agree on the nature and extent of his mental disorder or, in fact, agree whether or not he was mentally disordered at all.

Limitations of space preclude detailed discussion of the sad saga of the various commissions of inquiry, court hearings and appeals that dealt with his case. However, what they *do* signify is the highly complex nature of the fluctuating relationships between healthcare and penal institutions already referred to in this chapter. One of the more important (but unsurprising) findings in Greig's account, is suggested by one of her commission sources:

> One lesson to be learned from legal history is that hard cases make bad law and that there is a risk that a hasty and ill-conceived response to one particular case . . . can seriously disturb a larger and well thought structure.
>
> (p. 151)

This chapter has dealt with some very complex material and, for the sake of brevity, some degree of oversimplification has been inevitable. The following is a summary of some of the key points to be borne in mind which readers may find helpful. (For very useful accounts of personality disorders more generally see Livesley 2001; Tyrer and Stein 1993.)

## Summary

### Nomenclature

The name given to the "condition" has changed at various times – ever since Pinel is said to have first described the nature of the disorder at the beginning of the nineteenth century. The changes reflect changing views about crime, heredity etc. It is important to note that the term "psychopathic" disorder as in current English and Welsh legislation does not necessarily equate with the clinical descriptions in the DSMIV or ICD 10. Numerous attempts have been made to remove the term from our legislation since it is regarded as pejorative and unhelpful. Currently, the preferred term is severe personality disorder. However, even if we change the term, professionals will still find "psychopaths" a very problematic group. (See following notes under *treatment*.)

### A spectrum of disorder

Psychopathic disorder is best seen as being on a spectrum of personality disorders, both in terms of classification and severity.

### Aetiology

The debate continues as to whether "psychopaths" are born or made. Evidence seems to be accumulating that neurological "faults" (either inborn or acquired) may have an important role to play, particularly if these "faults" are located within the limbic system. It appears that individuals with such possible faulty development lack the capacity to empathize with others and "gear" into society's requirements. However, it needs to be emphasized that environmental factors have an important part to play, notably in respect of the psychopath's capacity for "role taking" (Gough 1956). Other explanations have involved cortical under-arousal, immature cortical development (as measured on the EEG) and thrill seeking.

### Characteristics

These are well described in the literature and Cleckley's list of points is still used by many clinicians as a "benchmark". Cleckley's listing provided the building blocks for Hare's subsequent checklist. To Cleckley's list I would add the capacity to create chaos for all who surround the psychopath and a notable lack of time sense. In summary, the most important elements would seem to be an absence (not necessarily total) of guilt, an imperviousness to intervention, a distinct lack of empathy towards others; in many a capacity for gratuitous violence and a need to fill an "emptiness" in their lives by arousal.

### Treatability

There is much debate as to the extent to which "psychopaths" are treatable. It is important to recall the difference between the 1959 Mental Health Act, which linked treatability to the definition of the condition, and the 1983 Act, which deleted it from the latter and placed it elsewhere; and, moreover, defines "treatment" in much more circumspect terms. Clinically, professionals (particularly psychiatrists) are divided as to treatability and, in the light of current bed shortages for more "responsive" cases (i.e. mentally ill), are less likely to welcome or be optimistic towards these "hard to like" folk. In addition, once in hospital as a patient, they may be hard to discharge for fear of future harmful behaviour being perpetrated. Having an understanding of the possible causes of the condition will help to decide on the best line of approach. For the impulsive, over-reactive individual, carefully monitored medication may help. (This is *not*, however, to suggest "chemical coshing".) *Much* will depend on the "eye of the beholder" and professionals have to be aware of their own prejudices about these "unlikeable", "unrewarding" and sometimes "scary" people. Some workers do very well with the psychopathically disordered, notably probation officers, and especially those who are in the job long enough to follow these people through the course of their criminal careers and not reject them because of their manipulative, unpleasant and unrewarding behaviour. The key words here are *insistence*, *persistence* and *consistence*.

### The future

The government is much concerned about "managing dangerous people with severe personality disorder". They set out various possibilities, the most disquieting being the apparent possibility of detaining someone on the basis of what it is felt *they might do*. Other weaknesses include the expectation that criminal justice and mental health professionals have foolproof skills in predicting future behaviour and its risks (see Chapter 8). At present, we are trying to treat/manage a very problematic group of people with vast gaps in our knowledge base coupled with a significant lack of capacity for self-examination when trying to engage with such people. Psychopathic disorder is not going to go away whatever we call the condition in future; and it has rightly been called the *Achilles Heel* of criminal justice and psychiatry.

### Concluding comment

Some observations by Gunn provide a fitting conclusion to this chapter:

> In England and Wales we now have an uphill struggle on our hands. We need to persuade our Home Office not to drop its interest and particularly its resource allocation for a needy, hitherto neglected group of patients, but at the same time to back away from new types of prison and new preventive detention laws and focus instead on the well-tried arrangements we already have. It is true that our prisons can do with more psychiatric resources. We have secure hospitals that also need more resources . . . we certainly do not need new and restrictive laws. The United Kingdom has many laws that can be used imaginatively and effectively if we have sufficient and appropriate staff. Politicians, many of whom are lawyers, rush to legislate; we need to provide them with resources.
>
> (Gunn 2000: 75–6) (see also Snowden and Kane 2003)

One can only say "Amen" to that. In the following chapters I shall examine some of the behaviours of those who often gather unto themselves the label "psychopathic". I begin with a consideration of those who commit serious violence and homicide.

# Notes

1  A brief expansion of possible causal explanations of severe personality disorder (Psychopathy)

### Studies of the cerebral cortex

Studies using the EEG (electro-encephalogram) have tended to show that the "slow wave" activity found in the brainwaves of some aggressive psychopaths bears some degree of resemblance to the EEG tracings found in children. Such findings have led to the formulation of a hypothesis of cortical immaturity. Such findings may explain why the aggressive behaviour of some aggressive psychopaths seems to become less violent with advancing years because, as is the case with children, the brain matures. Two further conclusions derived from work in this field should be noted. First, psychopathy may be linked with a defect or malfunction of certain brain mechanisms concerned with emotional activity and the regulation of behaviour. Second, it has been suggested that psychopathy may be related to a lowered state of cortical excitability and to the attenuation of sensory input, particularly input that would, in ordinary circumstances, have disturbing consequences. This may partially explain the apparent callous and cold indifference to the pain and suffering of others that is demonstrated by some seriously psychopathically disordered individuals.

### Importance of the autonomic nervous system

Clinical and other experience has always tended to show the psychopath's general apparent lack of anxiety, guilt and emotional tension. In recent years, experiments carried out (admittedly under laboratory conditions) have tended to give some confirmation to these clinical impressions. For example, it has been shown that during periods of relative quiescence psychopathic subjects tend to be hypoactive on several indices of autonomic activity, including resting level of skin conductance and cardiac activity. Such activity can be measured comparatively easily by galvanometric and similar devices. However, such findings are not without criticism. Too many conclusions should not be drawn from the artificial setting of laboratory testing and few studies have been undertaken of control populations drawn from non-penal and non-specialist hospital sources. Also, we should note that lack of anxiety, guilt and emotional tension are not characteristics peculiar to the psychopathically disordered. Rather, they seem to show this lack in more extreme form than the general population. The various works of Professor Robert Hare in this field provide a balanced appraisal of the "state of the art", especially in relation to the use of rating scales to diagnose and manage psychopathic disorder (see, for example, Hare 1993).

### Psychopathic disorder and the concept of arousal

There is some laboratory-based evidence to suggest that psychopathy is related to cortical under-arousal. Because of this, psychopaths (particularly the seriously aggressive) may seek stimulation with arousing or exciting qualities. It is certainly true that even non-psychopathically disordered offenders, when asked about their motivation for their offences, often report that they derived a "high" or that they did it for "kicks". McCord, an early writer on psychopathic disorder, states that "most psychopaths do not seek security as a goal in itself; rather they crave constant change, whirlwind variety, and new stimuli" (1982: 28). McCord went on to suggest that Ian Brady and the late Myra Hindley illustrated the psychopath's craving for excitement. He says they "explained their actions as simply ways to attain new levels of excitement, a new 'consciousness' and a temporary escape from boredom" (p. 28). This craving for excitement commented on by McCord and others may render the psychopath unaware or inattentive to many of the more subtle cues required for the maintenance of socially acceptable behaviour and for adequate socialization. Such lack of socialization may, of course, be exacerbated by an adverse social environment such as a dysfunctional family background.

### Psychopathy and learning

It is also possible to conclude, albeit very tentatively, that psychopaths do not develop conditioned fear responses readily. Because of this they find it difficult to learn responses that are motivated by fear and reinforced by fear reduction. There is also experimental evidence to suggest (again confirmed in clinical practice) that psychopaths are less influenced than are normal persons by their capacity to make connections between past events and the consequences of their present behaviour. It should be noted that females figure much less frequently than males within the diagnosis of psychopathy. However, some recent research tends to indicate a greater commonality of characteristics between the sexes than supposed hitherto (see Warren et al. 2003).

## References

American Psychiatric Association (1994) *Diagnostic and Statistical Manual of Mental Disorders*, 4th ed., Washington, DC: APA.

Bennett, J. (2002) "The role of prison officers on the dangerous and severe personality disorder unit at HMP Whitemoor", *Prison Service Journal* 143: 9–14.

Blackburn, R. (1988) "On moral judgements and personality disorder: The myth of psychopathic personality revisited", *British Journal of Psychiatry* 153: 505–12.

Blair, J. and Frith, U. (2000) "Neurocognitive explanations of the anti-social personality disorders", *Criminal Behaviour and Mental Health* 10: S66–S81 (special supplement).

Bowers, L. (2002) *Dangerous and Severe Personality Disorders: Response and Role of the Psychiatric Team*, London: Routledge.

Bowers, L. and Carr-Walker, C. (2000) "Working positively and productively in a DSP unit", *Prison Service Journal* 143: 21–3.

Bowlby, J. (1979) *The Making and Breaking of Affectional Bonds*, London: Tavistock.

Campling, P. (1996) "Maintaining the therapeutic alliance with personality disordered patients", *Journal of Forensic Psychiatry* 7: 535–50.

Carroll, A., Lyall, M. and Forrester, A. (2004) "Clinical hopes and public fears in forensic mental health", *Journal of Forensic Psychiatry and Psychology* 15: 407–25.

Cavadino, M. (1998) "Death to the psychopath", *Journal of Forensic Psychiatry* 9: 5–8.

Chiesa, M. and Fonagy, P. (2003) "Psychosocial treatment of severe personality disorder: A 36-month follow-up", *British Journal of Psychiatry* 183: 356–62.

Cleckley, H. (1976) *The Mask of Sanity*, 5th ed., St Louis, CV: Mosby.

Cohen, S. (2001) *States of Denial: Knowing About Atrocities and Suffering*, Oxford: Polity Press (in association with Blackwells).

Coid, J. (1989) "Psychopathic disorders" *Current Opinion in Psychiatry* 2: 750–6.

—— (1993) "Current concepts and classification in psychopathic disorder", in P. Tyrer and G. Stein (eds), *Personality Disorder Reviewed*, London: Gaskell.

Cope, R. (1993) "A survey of forensic psychiatrists' views on psychopathic disorder", *Journal of Forensic Psychiatry* 4: 214–35.

Coughlin, L. (2003) "The effects of relocation of staff changes on individuals with a personality disorder", *British Journal of Forensic Practice* 5: 12–17.

Crichton, J. H. M., Darjee, R., McCall-Smith, A. and Chiswick, D. (2001) "Mental Health (Public Safety and Appeals) (Scotland) Act, 1999: Detention of untreatable patients with psychopathic disorder", *Journal of Forensic Psychiatry* 12: 647–61.

Darjee, R. and Crichton, J. H. M. (2002) "The Maclean Committee: Scotland's answer to the 'dangerous people with severe personality disorder' proposals?", *Psychiatric Bulletin* 26: 6–8.

Darjee, R. and Crichton, J. (2003) "Personality disorder and the law in Scotland: A historical perspective", *Journal of Forensic Psychiatry and Psychology* 14: 394–425.

Department of Health (1999) *Review of the Mental Health Act, 1983: Report of the Expert Committee* (Chairman, Professor Genevra Richardson), CM 4480, London: TSO.

—— (2002a) *Draft Mental Health Bill*, CM 5538-I, London: TSO.

—— (2002b) *Explanatory Notes*, CM 5538-II, London: TSO.

—— (2002c) *Consultation Document*, CM 5538-III, Department of Health: London: TSO.

Department of Health and Home Office (1994) *Report of the Department of Health and Home Office Working Group on Psychopathic Disorder* (Chairman, Dr John Reed, CB), London: Department of Health and Home Office.

Department of Health and Social Security (DHSS) (1986) *Consultation Document: Offenders Suffering From Psychopathic Disorder*, London: DHSS and Home Office.

Dolan, M. (1994) "Psychopathy: A neuro-biological perspective", *British Journal of Psychiatry* 165: 151–9.

Eisler, K. R. (ed.) (1949) *Searchlights on Delinquency: New Psychoanalytic Studies*, London: Imago.

Eldergill, A. (1997) *Mental Health Review Tribunals: Law and Practice*, London: Sweet & Maxwell.

Erikson, M. (2002) "The Prison Cohort Study", *Prison Service Journal* 143: 15–16.

Fallon, P., QC, Bluglass, R., Edwards, B. and Daniels, G. (1999) *Report of the Committee of Inquiry into the Personality Disorder Unit, Ashworth Special Hospital*, Vol. 2, CM 4195, London: TSO.

Finley-Jones, R. (1991) "Psychopathic disorder", *Current Opinion in Psychiatry* 4: 850–5.

Gayford, J. J. and Jungalwalla, H. N. K. (1986) "Personality disorder according to the ICD 9 and DSM III and their value in court reporting", *Medicine, Science and the Law* 26: 113–24.

Gough, H. (1956) "A sociological study of psychopathy". in A. M. Rose (ed.), *Mental Health and Mental Disorder*, London: Routledge & Kegan Paul.

Greig, D. (2002) *Neither Bad Nor Mad: The Competing Discourses of Psychiatry, Law and Politics*, London: Jessica Kingsley.

Gunn, J. (1999) "The Ashenputtel principle", *Criminal Behaviour and Mental Health* 10: 73–6.

—— (2000) "A millennium monster is born", *Criminal Behaviour and Mental Health* 10: 73–6.

Haddock, A., Snowden, P., Dolan, M., Parker, J. and Rees, H. (2001) "Managing dangerous people with severe personality disorder: A survey of forensic psychiatrists' opinions", *Psychiatric Bulletin* 25: 293–6.

Hare, R. D. (1993) *Without Conscience: The Disturbing World of the Psychopaths Among Us*, London: Pocket Books.

Henderson, Sir D. (1939) *Psychopathic States*, New York: Norton.

Home Office and Department of Health (1999) *Managing Dangerous People With Severe Personality Disorder: Proposals For Policy Development*, London: Home Office.

Home Office and Department of Health and Social Security (1975) *Report of the Committee on Mentally Disordered Offenders* (Chairman, Lord Butler of Saffron Walden), Cmnd 6344, London: HMSO.

Johns, J. H. and Quay, H. C. (1962) "The effect of social reward on verbal conditioning in psychopathic and neurotic military offenders", *Journal of Consulting Psychology* 26: 217–20.

Jones, M. (1963) "The treatment of character disorders", *British Journal of Criminology* 3: 276–82.

Kendall, R. E. (1999) "The distinction between personality disorder and mental illness", *British Journal of Psychiatry* 180: 110–15.

Koch, J. W. (1891) *Die Psychopthischen Minderwertigkeiten*, Ravensburg: Maier.

Laing, J. (1999) "An end to the lottery – the Fallon Report on personality disordered offenders", *Journal of Mental Health Law* 2: 87–104.

Lewis, Sir A. (1974) "Psychopathic personality: A most elusive category", *Psychological Medicine* 4: 133–40.

Lewis, G. and Appleby, L. (1988) "Personality disorders: The patients psychiatrists dislike", *British Journal of Psychiatry* 153: 44–9.

Livesley, W. J. (ed.) (2001) *Handbook of Personality Disorders: Theory, Research and Treatment*, New York and London: Guilford Press.

MacLean, Lord (Chairman) (2002) *Report of the Committee on Serious Violent and Sexual Offenders*, Edinburgh: Scottish Executive.

Maden, T. (1999) "Treating offenders with personality disorder", *Psychiatric Bulletin* 23: 707–10.

Maden, A., Williams, J., Wong, S. C. P. and Leis, T. A. (2004) "Treating dangerous and severe personality disorder in high security: Lessons from the regional psychiatric centre, Saskatoon, Canada", *Journal of Forensic Psychiatry and Psychology* 15: 357–90.

Maier, G. J. (1990) "Psychopathic disorders: Beyond counter-transference", *Current Opinion in Psychiatry* 3: 766–9.

Mann, A. and Moran, P. (2000) "Personality disorder as a reason for action", *Journal of Forensic Psychiatry* 11: 11–16.

McCord, W. (1982) *The Psychopath and Milieu Therapy: A Longitudinal Study*, New York: Academic Press.

McCord, W. and McCord, J. (1956) *Psychopathy and Delinquency*, New York and London: Grune and Stratton.

Millan, D. (Chairman) (1999) *Review of the Mental Health (Scotland) Act, 1984 First Consultation*, Edinburgh: Scottish Executive.

Millon, T., Simonsen, E. and Birket-Smith, M. (2003) "Historical conceptions of psychopathy in the USA and Europe", in T. Millon, E. Simonsen, N. Birket-Smith and R. D. Davis (eds), *Psychopathy: Antisocial, Criminal and Violent Behaviour*, New York and London: Guilford Press.

National Institute for Mental Health for England (NIMHE) (2003) *Personality Disorder: No Longer a Diagnosis of Exclusion*, Leeds: Department of Health.

Pinel, P. H. (1806) *A Treatise on Insanity*, New York: Hafner.

Prichard, J. C. (1835) *Treatise on Insanity*, London: Gilbert and Piper.

Prins, H. (1977) "I think they call them psychopaths", *Prison Service Journal* 28: 8–12.

—— (1998) "Characteristics of consultant forensic psychiatrists: A modest survey", *Journal of Forensic Psychiatry* 9: 139–49.

—— (1999) "Dangerous severe personality disorder: An independent view", *Prison Service Journal* 126: 8–10.

—— (2001) "Whither mental health legislation? Locking up the disturbed and the deviant", *Medicine, Science and the Law* 41: 241–9.

Rieber, R. W. and Green, M. R. (1988) "The psychopathy of everyday life" (unpublished manuscript), quoted in Egger, S. Q. (1990) *Serial Murder: An Elusive Phenomenon*, New York: Praeger. p. 82.

Robins, L. N. (1966) *Deviant Children Grown Up: A Sociological and Psychiatric Study of Sociopathic Personality*, Baltimore: Williams and Wilkins.

Roth, Sir M. (1990) "Psychopathic (sociopathic) personality", in R. Bluglass and P. Bowden (eds), *Principles and Practice of Forensic Psychiatry*, London: Churchill Livingstone.

Rutter, Sir M. (1999) "Psychosocial adversity and child psychopathology", *British Journal of Psychiatry* 174: 480–93.

Schneider, K. (1958) *Psychopathic Personalities* (trans. M. W. Hamilton), London: Cassell.

Scott, P. D. (1960) "The treatment of psychopaths", *British Medical Journal* 2: 1641–6.

—— (1975) *Has Psychiatry Failed in the Treatment of Offenders?*, London: Institute for the Study and Treatment of Offenders (ISTD).

Snowden, P. and Kane, E. (2003) "Personality disorder: No longer a diagnosis of exclusion", *Psychiatric Bulletin* 27: 401–3.

Solomka, B. (1996) "The role of psychiatric evidence in passing longer than normal sentences", *Journal of Forensic Psychiatry* 7: 239–55.

Storey, L. (2002) "Staff development in personality disorder services", *Prison Service Journal* 143: 23–6.

Taylor, R. (2000) *A Seven Year Reconviction Study of HMP Grendon Therapeutic*

*Community*, Home Office, Research Development and Statistics Directorate, Research Findings No. 115, London: Home Office.

Tennent, G., Tennent, D., Prins, H. and Bedford, A. (1993) "Is psychopathic disorder a treatable condition?", *Medicine, Science and the Law* 33: 63–6.

Trethowan, Sir W. and Sims, A. C. P. (1983) *Psychiatry*, 5th ed., London: Baillière Tindall.

Treves-Brown, C. (1977) "Who is the psychopath? *Medicine, Science and The Law* 17: 56–63.

Tyrer, P. (1990) "Diagnosing personality disorders", *Current Opinion in Psychiatry* 3: 182–7.

Tyrer, P. and Stein, G. (eds) (1993) *Personality Disorder Reviewed*, London: Gaskell.

Tyrer, P., Casey, P. and Ferguson, B. (1991) "Personality disorder in perspective", *British Journal of Psychiatry* 159: 463–71.

Tyrer, P., Duggan, C. and Coid, J. (eds) (2003) "Ramifications of personality disorder in clinical practice", *British Journal of Psychiatry* 182: 44.

Wambaugh, J. (1989) *The Blooding*, London: Bantam.

Warren, J. I., Burnette, M. I., South, S. C., Chauhan, P., Bale, R., Friend, R. and Patten, I. V. (2003) "Psychopathy in women: Structural modeling and comorbidity", *International Journal of Law and Psychiatry* 223–42.

Whiteley, J. S. (1994) "In pursuit of the elusive category", *British Journal of Psychiatry Review of Books* 7: 7–14.

Winnicott, D. W. (1949) "Hate in the counter-transference", *International Journal of Psychoanalysis* 30: 14–17.

World Health Organization (WHO) (1992) *The ICD 10 Classification of Mental and Behavioural – Clinical Descriptions and Diagnostic Guidelines*, Geneva: WHO.

## Further reading

The following works provide good coverage of aetiology, classification and management:

Cooke, D. J., Forth, A. E., Newman, J. and Hare, R. (eds) (1996) *International Perspectives on Psychopathy*, Leicester: British Psychological Society (compilations of abstracts of papers presented at an international conference in Portugal in 1995).

*Criminal Behaviour and Mental Health* (2002) special supplement on personality disorders, 12: 2.

Dolan, B. and Coid, J. (1993) *Psychopathic and Anti-Social Personality Disorders*, London: Gaskell.

Dowson, J. H. and Grounds, A. T. (1995) *Personality Disorders: Recognition and Clinical Management*, Cambridge: Cambridge University Press.

Livesley, W. J. (ed.) (2001) *Handbook of Personality Disorders: Theory, Research and Treatment*, New York and London: Guilford Press.

Moran, P. (1999) *Anti-Social Personality Disorder: An Epidemiological Perspective*, London: Gaskell.

Millon, T., Simonsen, E., Birket-Smith, N. and Davis, R. D. (eds) (2003) *Psychopathy: Anti-Social, Criminal and Violent Behaviour*, New York and London: Guilford Press.

Special Hospitals Service Authority (1996) *Understanding the Enigma* (summary of an Anglo-Dutch Conference on Personality Disorder and Offending), London: SHSA.

Tyrer, P. and Stein, G. (eds) (1993) *Personality Disorder Reviewed*, London: Gaskell.

In addition to these volumes, the following journals have, in the past decade or so, published numerous papers on severe anti-social personality disorder and psychopathy:

*Criminal Behaviour and Mental Health*
*Criminological and Legal Psychology*
*International Journal of Forensic Mental Health*
*International Journal of Law and Psychiatry*
*Journal of Forensic Psychiatry* (*note*: as from Vol. 14 (2003) this journal is
retitled *Journal of Forensic Psychiatry and Psychology*)
*Journal of Mental Health Law*
*Psychology, Crime and Law*

# Chapter 5

# Bloody deeds*

*Horatio*: So shall you hear of carnal, bloody and unnatural acts.
(*Hamlet* Act 5 Sc. 2)

This chapter and the two that follow should, ideally, be read as a whole, for they each deal with various aspects of violence towards others. In this chapter, the emphasis is predominantly on those offences legally described as offences against persons. Chapter 6 deals with sexually assaultive behaviours of one kind or another and, as such, these can reasonably be described as violent offences (for example, cases of rape and other forms of non-consensual sex). Chapter 7 deals with violence against property in the form of fire raising (arson). Such behaviour will not infrequently also endanger the lives of both intended and unintended victims. Overall then, we have violence as an overarching theme in all three chapters.

This chapter is divided into two main sections. First, a short general discussion of violence as a phenomenon set in a short historical context, followed by some epidemiological material. Second, a discussion of homicide, which in turn is divided into a number of subsections dealing with such matters as manslaughter, infanticide, other forms of child killing, children as killers, and so-called "serial" killing, with special reference to the case of Harold Shipman. Shipman was found dead in his cell at Wakefield Prison on 13 January 2004. He had apparently hanged himself. I also use recent government concerns about violence in the NHS as an example of possible overreaction to social problems. The subject matter of this chapter is vast (particularly with regard to aetiology) and can only be dealt with briefly. The references and the suggestions for further reading will enable the interested reader to pursue his or her knowledge in further depth.

---

* Parts of this chapter appeared in my paper "Cui bono? Withholding treatment from violent and abusive patients in NHS trusts: 'We don't have to take this'" (2002), which appeared in the *Journal of Forensic Psychiatry* 13: 391–406 and is reproduced here by permission.

## Note on terms

The terms *aggression* and *violence* are often used synonymously. This is not strictly correct, since we can behave aggressively without necessarily being violent. Aggression is perhaps best regarded as denoting *assertive* behaviour, which may express itself physically or verbally. Aggression can be further divided into *manifest* aggression (physical aggression, verbal aggression) and *latent* aggression (aggressive fantasies, moods etc.). The following three further distinctions can be made: (1) aggression as evidenced in loss of control (as is some forms of crime and some psychiatric disorders); (2) planned aggression (sometimes known as instrumental aggression) or as goal seeking; (3) structural or institutionalized aggression (as a means of imposing control and/or sanctions). Violence is frequently regarded as destructive aggression – that is, aggression harnessed for harmful purposes. Archer and Browne describe it as "the exercise of physical force so as to injure or damage persons or property; otherwise to treat or use persons or property in a way that causes bodily injury and forcibly interferes with personal freedom" (Archer and Browne 1989: 3) (see also Blackburn 1993: Chapter 9; Hollin 1992: 147 et seq.).

In this chapter I am concerned mainly with those behaviours that are *marked by force, threats and, in most instances, a degree of premeditation.* The event or incident will usually have occurred over a short timespan, but not necessarily so. The debate as to whether aggression and a propensity for violence are all pervasive, innate, or acquired, has continued over the centuries and is documented extensively. In the first edition of his book *Human Aggression* (1975), the late Doctor Anthony Storr stated:

> [T]hat man is an aggressive creature will hardly be disputed. With the exception of certain rodents, no other vertebrate *habitually destroys members of his own species. No other animal takes positive pleasure in the exercise of cruelty upon another of his own kind* . . . there is no parallel in nature to our savage treatment of each other.
>
> (Storr 1975: 9; emphasis added)

In a revised and updated edition of this work he added to this somewhat sombre comment on violence, as follows:

> I think that *Homo Sapiens* has not altered very much in fundamental, physical or psychological characteristics since he first appeared upon the scene; and that the best we can hope for is some slight modification of his nastier traits of personality in the light of increased understanding. We cannot abolish man's potential for cruelty and destructiveness, but we may be partially able to control the circumstances which can lead to their overt expression.
>
> (Storr 1991: 141–2)

In view of the acknowledged universality of the capacity to behave violently, it is of interest to observe that its overt *expression* appears to be determined quite markedly by cultural conditions. In their studies of so-called primitive societies, early anthropologists (such as Mead, Benedict, Murdock and others) demonstrated the great variety that can be shown to exist in the display of aggressive and violent behaviour. Some quarter of a century ago, the psychologist and psychoanalyst Fromm attempted to synthesize some of their early work and to apply it to more developed societies. He found that three different and clearly delineated forms of society could be discerned: *Life-affirmative societies*; *non-destructive-aggressive societies*; *destructive societies*. In *life-affirmative societies*, the main emphasis was on the preservation and growth of life in all forms. "There is a minimum of hostility, violence or cruelty among people, no harsh punishments, hardly any crime, and the institution of war is absent or plays an exceedingly small role" (Fromm 1977: 229). In *non-destructive-aggressive societies*, "aggressiveness and war, although not central, are normal occurrences, and . . . competition, hierarchy and individualism are present" (p. 230). *Destructive societies* are "characterised by much inter-personal violence, destructiveness, aggression and cruelty . . . pleasure in war, maliciousness and treachery" (p. 231). Fromm's view is admittedly very sweeping and some might consider it to be an oversimplification. Nevertheless, it may help us to understand the apparent overt differences in the phenomenon of violence in various societies. It may also help us to understand what appears to be the ubiquitous phenomenon of violence in our own society, whether it be expressed in the home, the school or in some of those institutions established for the avowed purpose of the protection of the vulnerable (for example, establishments for the elderly and hospitals of one kind or another) and in acts of terrorism and other international atrocities – both past and current.

Whatever view we may take about the causes of violence in society, the following points would find a fairly general degree of acceptance:

1  Violence, when shown by non-human animals, is usually purposive, self-protective, and conforms to certain ritualized patterns (Lorenz 1966).

2  In the human species, violence may be sanctioned by a community (Fromm 1977).

3  It appears to take little to disinhibit violence in human societies. As Storr suggests, it seems likely that men and women have always had the potential for the commission of a great deal of violence, but that this is normally kept in check by society's sanctions. These sanctions can, however, change over time – witness the enormity of the atrocities against millions of people during the Nazi regime in the 1930s and 1940s and currently in various parts of the world.

An explanation for such behaviour has been provided by the psychologist Zimbardo in an interview with McDermott (1993). Zimbardo (1973) was the originator of the famous (or infamous, depending on your ethical standpoint) Stanford Prison experiment, in which quite ordinary students were able to inflict suffering and deprivation on their fellows – to such an extent that the experiment had to be stopped prematurely because of its effect on the detainees. Zimbardo suggests three key factors that may be at work in bringing about the capacity for quite normal human beings to behave inhumanely towards others. These consist of (a) de-individualization (loss of personal identifiability and uniqueness); (b) dehumanization (loss of a sense of personal value); and (c) present-time orientation (engaging in current actions without concern for future consequences or past commitments). As with Fromm's views, Zimbardo's also have a broad sweep to them, but they have a certain credibility in the light of a great deal of theorizing about the aetiology and manifestation of violent behaviour.

In this and the following chapters we are most concerned with the situations in which *individual internal* mechanisms of control have broken down (although the broader canvas should not be dismissed). Internal control appears to be mediated by various psychological defence mechanisms – such as denial, repression and projection. Some early psychoanalysts (notably Melanie Klein 1963) claimed, on the basis of not inconsiderable clinical data, that even small infants possess highly destructive and violent urges. These may come to the fore in the face of hunger and frustration. Such urges normally find appeasement but, in the event of failure, serious distortions of personality may occur, as in the case of some of the psychopathically disordered persons described in Chapter 4.[1]

## Rhetoric of violence

A topic frequently (and not always helpfully) debated, is the extent to which the level and frequency of violence are greater in contemporary society than in the past. Anthropological and historical perspectives tend to support the contention that we have a violent past and that although current scenarios may be fuelled by the more frequent ingestion of alcohol and other drugs, we have not, as Storr suggested, altered much in our capacity for violence since we emerged from the caves. From early times playwrights, philosophers and historians attested to this. Shakespeare, that shrewd observer of human nature, attests to the waywardness of youth, for does not the Shepherd say in *The Winter's Tale*:

> I would there were no age between sixteen and three-and-twenty, or that youth would sleep out the rest; for there is nothing in the between but getting wenches with child, wronging the ancientry, stealing, fighting.

(Act 3 Sc. 3)

And the great seventeenth-century philosopher Thomas Hobbes wrote of mankind:

> No arts; no letters, no society; and which is worst of all, continual fear and danger of violent death. And the life of man, solitary, poor, nasty, brutish and short.
>
> (*Leviathan*, Part 1, Chapter 4: 13)

(Interestingly, I find that when I use this quote with my clinical criminology and forensic psychology students, most recognize the last part of the quotation but are not so familiar with the first.) The historian Gibbon wrote of sixth-century Constantinople: "It becomes dangerous to wear any gold buttons or girdles or to appear at a late hour in the streets of a peaceful capital" (quoted in Hankoff 1993: 1–3). Pearson (1983) has demonstrated very clearly that so-called modern "hooliganism" has its origins in pre-Victorian England and that serious crowd misbehaviour at, for example, football matches, is as old as the game itself. Sharpe, a University of York historian, suggested that "mugging" was as prevalent in London in the middle of the nineteenth century (in the very nasty guise of "garrotting") as is alleged today (Sharpe 1992).

Finally, in this brief excursion into the prevalence of violence, my friend and colleague, Sir Michael Day, sometime Chairman of the Commission for Racial Equality, wrote the following in an attempt to give a sense of perspective.

> The world is steeped in the rhetoric of violence. The horror of international terrorism and the menacing of aggression acted out between factions and adherents of religious and political ideologies feed the media and in time may dull our senses. Perhaps it is no worse now than at any other period in man's history, but only seems so, because modern communication has shrunk the world and the modern armoury has enormously increased the consequences of violence. Even if somehow, we manage to distance ourselves from these, however, they still provide a frightening backcloth to the violence and danger represented by some individuals in our society and expose the potential for devastating aggression in all of us.
>
> (Day 1986: xii)[2]

In the light of events of September 2001, Day's observation was prophetic.

It was, I think, Alvin Toffler who, in his book *Future Shock* (1970), coined the phrase "disposable society" to indicate the short-term life of many of our consumable and other items. Maybe, in today's world, we need a new phrase to provide a shorthand description for the possible mainspring of the violent phenomena that we deal with; perhaps "over-reactive society" would be an appropriate term. Why do I say this? As indicated in earlier chapters, we seem to use impulsive and not terribly well thought-out reactions to "untoward" and "unwanted" events. Politicians seem to be the worst culprits (but one can perhaps understand their motives) in their ever increasing use of legislation to deal with "private and personal" ills (see for example Prins 1996). This is very evident in the manner in which criminal justice and mental health legislation has placed what appears to be undue emphasis on public protection and has made for so much difficulty for sentencers and others (see also Chapter 8 and Rex and Tonry 2002). In education, we seem to swing from one extreme to another in our searches for educational "philosophers' stones"; and the manner in which all forms of disaster are met by responses calling for the often vengeful allocation of, and compensation for, blame are yet further examples.[3] One of the best (and tragic) examples of this trend is the "hounding" of paedophiles (and, in the event, non-paedophiles, in some cases). Nearly every major social problem these days seems to arouse the media to call for a "public enquiry"; one must wonder just how many trees have been consumed in the mountains of paper that both public and private inquiries have taken place. Patience and thought do not seem to be the "order of the day" these days. Just as King Richard II in Shakespeare's play of that name declares that "Patience is stale and I am weary of it" (Act 5 Sc. 4), before turning to his gaoler and beating him as his killers arrive to despatch him, so does impatience and lack of careful thought seem to bedevil so much of our legislative and parliamentary processes.[4]

### Current volume of criminal violence

It is important to bear in mind the aphorism attributed to Mark Twain, that "There are lies, damned lies and there are statistics." Although crimes of violence understandably receive the most media coverage and cause the most concern, it is important to emphasize that, taken as a whole, they represent less than 5 per cent of offences recorded by the police; and the more serious of these, for example those that endanger life and armed robbery, constitute only about one-third of 1 per cent of all recorded offences. However, a more comprehensive measure of the *real* extent of violent crime is that provided by the British Crime Survey. The figures given in the Survey (BCS) are more comprehensive than those given in the criminal statistics, since they include accounts by victims not reported to the police. In their survey for the year 1997, Mirlees-Black et al. (1998) define violence for their purposes as "offences of wounding, common assault, robbery and snatch theft". Robbery and snatch theft are counted together as "mugging". There were 3,381,000 such incidents comprising:

- "wounding – assaults with more than trivial injury – there were 714,000 in 1997"

*Table 5.1*  Selection of number of offenders found guilty at all courts or cautioned for offences of violence against the person for the period 1997–2001

|  | 1997 | 1998 | 1999 | 2000 | 2001 |
|---|---|---|---|---|---|
| **Indictable offences** | | | | | |
| Murder | 275 | 256 | 252 | 261 | 285 |
| Attempted murder | 70 | 68 | 76 | 66 | 48 |
| Manslaughter | 244 | 266 | 234 | 238 | 263 |
| Manslaughter (diminished responsibility) | 27 | 15 | 22 | 19 | 20 |
| Infanticide | 3 | 2 | 8 | 2 | 5 |
| Causing death by careless driving while under the influence of drink or drugs | 62 | 63 | 46 | 53 | 51 |
| Wounding or other act endangering life | 2,034 | 1,986 | 1,857 | 1,759 | 1,815 |
| Other woundings | 53,955 | 56,155 | 52,603 | 50,966 | 50,625 |
| **Summary offences** | | | | | |
| Common assault | 28,012 | 35,361 | 41,741 | 41,980 | 43,200 |

*Source*: Extracted from Home Office 2002, Table 5.11.

*Note*: The fluctuations in the figures are fairly minor for the years I have selected. Inflation in the rates for crime such as murder will be accounted for by convictions for large numbers of multiple killings – either in the form of so-called serial killing (see later discussion under homicide) or mass murders as a result of terrorist activity. Salib (2003) provided homicide figures for the period 1979–2001. Averaging his figures produces approximately 300 homicides per year. Convictions for manslaughter *may* show marginal increases in future years if prosecutions for corporate manslaughter become more widespread.

- "common assault – physical assault or attempted assault with, at most, slight bruising – 2,276,000"
- "mugging – actual or attempted theft using force or threat of force and snatch thefts (e.g. bag snatches) – 390,000."

(p. 5)

It has been estimated that "there are four times as many crimes according to the BCS than the police record" (p. ii) and, further, that "not all reported crimes are recorded by the police. In 1997, the BCS estimate[d] that about 54% were" (p. ii). Some indication of the numbers of convictions for serious violence against the person may be found in Table 5.1.

### Risk of experiencing violent crime

The media tend to overemphasize the element of risk of experiencing violent crime. However, the truth seems to be rather different. "The average chance of experiencing *violence* (in 1977) was 4.7% . . .Young men aged 16–

24 were most at risk – 20.9% had been the victim of a violent crime in 1997. Other high risk groups were single parents, the unemployed, private renters and women aged 16–24" (Flood-Page and Taylor 2003: iii). Contrary to widespread general belief, the elderly were least at risk; the sensationalist reporting of the handful of tragic cases of serious harm being caused to the elderly encourages the belief that they are the most at risk. Concerning the use of weapons in violent assaults, Flood-Page and Taylor also report that:

> Three quarters of violent incidents did not involve the use of a weapon. Incidents of mugging were most likely to involve a weapon and domestic violence least likely . . . the most common weapons were knives and hitting implements, followed by glasses or bottles. Domestic incidents had the highest use of hitting implements, and a knife was used in 15 per cent of mugging incidents.
>
> (Flood-Page and Taylor 2003: 59)

It is also worth emphasizing one or two recent additional phenomena in relation to the commission of violent crime. At one time, violent crime seemed almost entirely to be a phenomenon of large urban areas. It now seems to have spread to rural communities and smaller conurbations. Currently, concerns are being expressed concerning the increase in the use of guns in the commission of crime and the association of alcohol and other drugs in the commission of act of violence. In the second edition of this book I reported that "there ha(d) been a serious under-reporting of various forms of violence and harassment in the workplace" (Prins 1995: 148–9). Since that time increasing concern has been expressed about this problem and a small-scale survey I undertook recently provides evidence of this and also further exemplifies current concerns about violence. In 2001 the Department of Health issued a resource guide somewhat provocatively titled *Withholding Treatment from Violent and Abusive Patients in NHS Trusts: "We Don't Have to Take This"* (Department of Health 2001, emphasis added). The Editor of the *Journal of Forensic Psychiatry* asked me to write a commentary on this document (Prins 2002a). In the course of my investigation I reviewed numerous papers that had appeared in a number of forensic psychiatric and psychological journals for the period 1995–2002. Some of my findings are summarized in the following.

### Psychiatric patient violence

The problem of predicting which patients would manifest violent behaviour was demonstrated in a small study by Eaton and colleagues. They found prediction very difficult, but suggested (as others have done) that most violent and assaultive incidents are carried out by a small number of patients (Eaton et al. 2000). Crowding and density of patient populations have often been held to be important factors in the aetiology of patient violence. However, Hardie (1999), for example, did not find that patient density seemed to be associated with incidents of violence and self-harm in a medium secure unit. The complex nature of interactions in understanding assaultive behaviour is to be found in an interesting paper by Gudjonsson et al. (2000). They analyzed some 2,180 violent incident forms and found that nursing staff, followed by fellow patients, were the most likely victims of assault. They comment that "gender, ethnic background, diagnosis and legal section were significantly related to the targets of assault . . . the findings show the importance of studying the interactions between different types of factors with regard to the characteristics and management of incidents" (p. 105) (see also Watts et al. 2003; Wynn 2003). Other papers reviewed also attested to the complex nature of the interactions between patients and staff. However, little attention seemed to have been devoted to the need for staff to examine their own reactions and the extent to which they *may* have unwittingly contributed to a violent incident. One is mindful here of the seminal work of Hans Toch (1992) in his USA study of violent incidents involving the police. He discovered that in some areas, a small but identifiable number of police officers seemed to be involved, on a number of occasions, in violent incidents. What we do know is that assaults by patients on staff can have serious effects on the health of such professionals (see for example Shepherd 1994; Wildgoose et al. 2003; Wykes 1994).

This being the case, we could usefully ask what attempts are being made to help staff to understand such incidents and to promote their own awareness of the importance of their *possible* responsibility for them. Crichton and Calgie stress the importance of the "moral" position taken by nurses. They suggest that "a moral judgment about how blameworthy a patient is perceived to be following an untoward incident, influences how staff respond" (Crichton and Calgie 2002: 32). And O'Keefe, in reviewing the guidelines on the management of imminent violence issued by the Royal College of Psychiatrists concluded that "these guidelines . . . make an excellent attempt to give an overall current view of the management of imminent violence in the health service" (O'Keefe 1999: 398). (For comment on the possible legal liabilities of staff in respect of episodes involving assault, see Andoh 2002 and Miers 1996. A less well-researched area is that concerning the extent to which psychiatric and allied professionals suffer harassment and intimidation by dissatisfied parties involved in litigation. The topic has been usefully reviewed recently by Norris and Gutheil (2003).

### A multidisciplinary "public health" approach

Perhaps, understandably, less seems to have been written about violence and abuse in non-psychiatric health facilities. Schneiden et al. (1995), in commenting on what they regard as an increase of violence in the general practice of clinical forensic medicine, stress the need for more training in this area for forensic medical examiners (formerly known as police surgeons). Crichton (1995) quotes a study by Walker and Caplan (1993) in which they compared psychiatric unit assault rates with violent crime rates in two health districts; they found that the level of in-patient violence reflected the district's level of violence at large. One has to ask to what extent there are "cross-over" points between assaults and abuse committed by those attending accident and emergency departments and those who have criminal records. In an interesting study by Shepherd and Farrington (1996) on the prevention of delinquency with particular reference to violent crime, the authors noted the number of *victims* of violence attending A & E departments appeared to have increased threefold over the period 1974–91. They pointed out that young male delinquents are "as much at risk of injury and other victimization as they are of committing offences" (p. 331). They concluded that "the need for doctors to join forces with social scientists . . . becomes obvious". In support of this contention, they also make the interesting observation that "independently of socio-economic variables, injury in violent crime is associated with a spectrum of disease in young adults comprising drug abuse, assault, elective surgery and trauma which can be explained by underlying impulsivity. Preventing crime and violence should be a central issue in health care" (p. 334). In an earlier paper dealing with the need for an integrated approach, Shepherd suggests that: "Further work is necessary to look for differing illness experience between offenders and the injured and to correlate offending, illness and injury with psychological, behavioural and developmental variables." He uses the term *DATES* syndrome to describe these phenomena: "It comprises drug abuse, assault, trauma and elective surgery" (1995: 351). Support for Shepherd's views also comes from a study by Junger and Wiegersma (1995) in that they found that "social services in general (such as health services and correctional services) do, to a certain extent deal with the same [type of] individuals" (p. 144). And a study by Raine and Liu (1998) also makes a plea for a new generation of biosocial health research. In a Norwegian study, which set out to examine the true level of violence rather than relying solely on criminal *statistics*, Steen and Hunskaar (2001) found that "most victims of violence who are taken care of by the health care system are treated in accident and emergency departments . . . and that [their] findings support the recommendation that combined police and accident and emergency department registrations should be used to monitor violence in a community" (p. 341).

The inference that one can draw from these studies is that violence, both personal, national and global, can be viewed very much as a "public health" problem, a view given compelling impact by the publication of a recent groundbreaking document by the World Health Organization entitled *World Report on Violence and Health* (WHO 2002). In her preface to the Report, the Director-General of the World Health Organization, Gro Harlem Brundtland, has this to say:

> One theme that is echoed throughout this report is the importance of primary prevention. Even small investments here can have large and long-lasting benefits, but not without resolve of leaders and support for prevention efforts from a broad array of partners in both the public and private spheres, and from both industrialized and developing countries . . . Public health has made some remarkable achievements in recent decades, particularly in reducing rates of many childhood diseases. However, saving our children from these diseases only to let them fall victim to violence or lose them later to acts of violence between intimate partners, to the savagery of war and conflict, or to self-inflicted injuries or suicide, would be a failure of public health.
>
> (WHO: xiii)

The complexity of the issues involved is further attested to in a commentary on the report by Soothill (2003). He concludes that:

> Although the [Report] . . . provides an invaluable and welcome service in trying to strip away some of the myths about violence and to expose the facts about violence, this is – as the authors recognise – only a beginning . . . there are massive moral and political issues to confront in shaping our response to violence. Assuming that consensus is easily achieved – or even achievable – may be a way of burying our head in the sand and turning a blind eye to some very real issues.
>
> (p. 14)

It was, perhaps, the kind of thinking outlined in the WHO Report that prompted the Department of Health to produce its resource guide. In doing so it included, as an appendix, a model policy and procedure adopted by Barts and The Royal London Trust – briefly summarized in the following:

### *"A model policy"*

The policy document states that "this policy will only apply to violent/ abusive visitors and patients *who are aged 18 or over*" (emphasis in the original). Steps in the execution of the policy and procedures are set out in detail; these cover "expected standards of behaviour"; "sanctions", which include informal warning, formal written warning (a "yellow card") and, finally, a "red card", which will result in exclusion from the Trust. If we adopt the "soccer" terminology used in the document, the "refereeing" will be undertaken by the clinical director, or nominated deputy. The policy section of the guidance ends with a stern warning, as follows:

Any patient behaving unlawfully will be reported to the police and the Trust will seek the application of the maximum penalties available in law. The Trust will prosecute all perpetrators of crime on or against Trust property, assets and staff.

(p. 10)

One can envisage a situation arising where lawyers representing a defendant in such prosecutions would wish to argue points of interpretation of the law concerning such matters as definitions of trust property, assets and even possibly definitions of the word "staff".

Overall, the policy (which won a Health and Social Care Award) seems to be a genuine and, for the most part, thoughtful attempt to get to grips with a troubling and troublesome area of healthcare and criminal justice practice. It occurred to me that it would be of interest to ascertain to what extent trusts in my own region had produced similar statements. To this end I circulated a letter of inquiry to the three main Leicestershire general hospitals, to the two similar hospitals in Nottingham and Derby, and to four secure – semi and low – establishments in the region. By definition the last type of establishment would deal with potentially violent or violent patients and I thought it might be of interest to compare their procedures with those in general healthcare establishments, such as district general hospitals. What follows is a brief analysis of their responses. A copy of my letter of inquiry may be found as an appendix to the original paper (Prins 2002a).

*Responses*

Following one or two reminders, I obtained replies to my letters of enquiry from five trusts in the region; these being responsible for six "general" hospitals and four secure establishments (one high security, two medium security and one low security). At the time of writing no trust appeared to have formulated a final policy on violent and abusive patients/relatives, but all were working on producing them – and stated they were likely to implement them in the ensuing months. The population served by the secure, semi- and low-secure "estate" is, by definition, likely to be a problematic one. As one of my "forensic" respondents pointed out, "I suppose in some ways our service is geared to understand that the environment we work within is likely to be of high risk and go prepared for this." The same respondent noted the important constraints facing staff in their out-patient work. "The potential risk for violence for those services undertaking triage and out-patient work on new patients without any known history is the more difficult area to assess and to manage. While we do undertake out-patient appointments for assessment, these are always managed within environments in which there are appropriate health and safety and back-up facilities if an incident was to take place." It was also noted by the same respondent that it was a very rare event indeed for their service to withhold treatment on the grounds of violence and/or abuse towards staff. Such a decision would only be made after the most careful consideration (and largely on the grounds of "no further therapeutic treatment viability"). My respondent noted that on only one occasion had this occurred in the three-year existence of their particular service. Most respondents also reported that there had, in fact, been little observed increase in violence or abuse by patients or relatives. However, one trust covering three large general hospitals reported a "gradual increase", but as with all my respondents *had no figures immediately available.*[5] One of my forensic service respondents commented that "we occasionally, but very rarely have a problem with visitors – verbal aggression – but we deal with this in a common sense way". One or two of my respondents remarked on the possible causes of alleged increases in hospital-based violence and abuse. For example, one thought there seemed to be less respect shown towards professionals in general these days. Purely anecdotally, there does seem to be something in this belief, for one can discern a general public lessening of confidence in professionals in a variety of spheres of activity, be they medicine, science, education or the civil service.

It would be unwise to extrapolate too widely from a small sample of responses drawn from one health region (albeit a very large one). It seems likely that firmer evidence of disruptive and violent behaviour may exist in large conurbations such as London. This is exemplified by the following sobering account in *The Independent* of 23 February 2002. Apparently, drug-related violence is regarded as sufficiently serious to constitute "Murder Mile" in the Hackney–Homerton area of London. "Day in, day out, the hospital's medical team deals with more gunshot and knife-inflicted wounds than any other in Britain." "It is reported that the A and E department . . . treats an average of five gunshot cases a month and 50 stabbings" (p. 11). It was suggested that the situation had become so serious in this part of the capital that a senior A & E consultant was actually travelling to Baragwanath Hospital in Soweto, South Africa, to further his expertise. Sadly, at this hospital, they have vast experience in dealing with the results of gang-related violence in their A & E department.

Since a number of my more informal "soundings" stressed the problem created by serious alcohol ingestion, it is interesting to note a contribution by one of our more responsible journalists – Fergal Keane. Writing in *The Independent's Review Section* on 2 March 2002, he identified the cost to the NHS of alcohol-induced illnesses, both in terms of violence and in terms of the long-term disastrous effects of alcohol abuse in individuals. He argues that, as a nation, we are in a state of "denial" about the problem and what to do about it. As he says: "Many find their way into the criminal justice system. Not just the street drunks banged away for being drunk and disorderly, but also the businessmen and women hauled off to the cells because they've trashed the house or committed an assault, [or] the man who kills in the middle of a blackout" (p. 3). Like others quoted earlier in this chapter he calls for a coordinated healthcare/criminal justice approach to the problem.

### Comment

As already suggested, it is difficult to ascertain the actual extent of violence in our society or the extent to which it may have increased in volume in recent times. What we can be somewhat uncomfortably aware of, is an increasing public and political concern about it and an ethos of "something must be done", what that "something" may be, and whether that "something" will provide an effective remedy. I have taken the view, rightly or wrongly, that such a trend is symptomatic of an "overreactive" society. The foregoing example is intended merely as one aspect of the problem of violence, but is an example capable of extrapolation to the problem more generally. Perhaps, more importantly, it will have helped to delineate possible "cross-over" points between those who create serious problems, for example in A & E departments, and those who are "delinquent" in other respects. *Impressionistically*, it does not seem that those forensic psychiatric patients who have records for serious personal violence (such as homicide, arson and rape) will figure largely in populations of violent and abusive hospital patients as seen in A & E departments.

### Some clinical examples – mixtures of motives and crimes

In introducing this chapter, I emphasized the somewhat arbitrary distinction being made between this one and the two that follow. The following case illustrations will hopefully support the contention.

### Case illustration 5.1

A young single man of 24 was convicted by the Crown Court of a series of indecent assaults on women. The facts were that, over a period of several weeks, he had gone out on his cycle at dusk and followed a number of young women along a lonely country lane. Coming up behind them, he attempted to pull them off their cycles, made various obscene suggestions to them and attempted to put his hands up their skirts. He was of previous good character, but had suffered much deprivation in childhood and was of low intelligence. Because of these facts, the court placed him under supervision. However, the seriousness of his premeditated assaultative attacks could have well earned him a prison sentence for what were, in effect, offences of violence.

### Case illustration 5.2

A man in his late forties was charged with the attempted murder of his wife by cutting her throat while she lay asleep. He was normally an extremely docile and placid individual, a carpenter by trade and a very good workman. At his trial it transpired that for some years his wife had carried on "business" as a prostitute. Despite all her husband's entreaties, she refused to give up her lifestyle; in a fit of despair and anger he attacked her. In view of the circumstances of the case the judge sentenced him to five years' imprisonment. The case might, of course, have ended more tragically; his wife might have died from her injuries. In other cases, only the fact that the assailant has been interrupted during his or her assault may limit the harm caused. In some, the intention might not be to kill or seriously injure, but factors, unknown to the assailant, may render the course of events tragic – such as the victim being infirm or having a thin skull, or delay in obtaining the medical emergency services.

Occasionally, the offence as charged may present, in disguised fashion, an underlying desire to perpetrate violence of a more personal kind. Charges of criminal damage (vandalism) sometimes fall into this category.

### Case illustration 5.3

Three adolescent boys were charged with what amounted to an "orgy" of criminal damage to a number of railway carriages parked in a siding. They had systematically broken a large number of carriage windows by hurling fire extinguishers through them, removed dozens of electric light bulbs, threw them around the railway track and urinated over the seats. Several thousands of pounds worth of damage had been caused. The history of each of these boys was revealing. The first lived with his elderly grandparents who, although concerned, were not particularly affectionate. His parents were separated and he rarely saw them. He was a boy with a "chip on his shoulder". The second boy was illegitimate and came from a disordered home background where his mother and sisters engaged in prostitution. He felt himself to be the "odd one out". The third boy, a cousin of the second, was spending a holiday with the family. He was the orphaned child of a distant relative and spent much of his time in a large children's home. It is not unrealistic to speculate that, unconsciously at least, the offences they committed may have been a symbolic manifestation of the aggression they felt towards their families and the wider community.

In other cases, the offender appears to have directed his or her violence from its original source to a more "neutral" one. Scott (1977) cites the legendary Medea as an example who, wishing to get back at her husband, killed her baby saying "that will stab thy heart". He also quotes a clinical case that makes the point graphically (Case illustration 5.4):

### Case illustration 5.4

"A man of 47 asked a female storekeeper at his place of work for an item; she failed to produce it and treated him with scant respect. He picked up a hammer and beat her about the head in a manner which nearly killed her . . . [he was charged with inflicting grievous bodily harm] . . . When examined, he was not mentally ill, not depressed, not paranoid, and was distressed and perplexed by his behaviour. There was no previous crime of any sort. He was an excellent worker, employed beneath his capacity, but had never pressed for advancement. His wife was a somewhat dominant woman who nagged him and frequently expressed her dissatisfaction with his wages. He had not had a holiday away from home for 20 years. In the last few weeks he had had bronchitis, which kept him awake. He was tired and not feeling well, and he was taking a prescribed medication containing codeine. The store-keeper, he had hoped, would treat him with respect. She was an attractive and popular middle-aged woman whom he liked, but had never tried to make a relationship with. When she behaved like his wife he reacted in a way which *could* be interpreted as venting all his suppressed resentment of his wife upon her."

(Scott 1977; emphasis added)

Two further media reported examples of such displaced homicidal violence follow. The first is that of Frederic Blanc – the killer of the English schoolteacher, Fiona Jones in France in 1990. Having quarrelled with his one-time girlfriend who, he alleged, had been seeing other men, he became enraged at seeing Fiona, looking so happy as she cycled through the French countryside. Having apparently failed in his first attempt to kill her, he returned to her body and finished her off with a knife. He claimed that his rage towards his girlfriend just welled up and overcame his hapless and innocent victim. In May 1993 some three years after the event, he was sentenced by a French court to 15 years' imprisonment; the lightness of the sentence surprised many people (information derived from a "True Crimes" drama-documentary on British television on 9 January 1994).

The second case concerns a father who appears to have killed his two small sons aged 7 and 8 as a means of getting back at his recently estranged wife. Some six days after having been given two life sentences he hanged himself in his prison cell. In sentencing him, the judge had said "You took those boys' lives to revenge yourself on your wife" (*The Independent*, 31 March 2003: 11).

The following case comes from my own experience and is also illustrative of displaced aggression.

### Case illustration 5.5

A youth of 16 was charged with causing grievous bodily harm to his elderly employer. Apparently he had attacked him from behind, struck him violently over the head and stolen a sum of money that he had subsequently abandoned. Of previous good character and background, he was remanded for psychiatric examination. He was found to be a youth who experienced great difficulty in countenancing any degree of frustration. There was evidence that on the morning of the offence he had been "got at" by various people in authority and his offence was seen, in part, as a result of poor tolerance of frustration. His mother, who was also interviewed as part of the psychiatric assessment, was felt to have a certain cold detachment about her and she too seemed to have problems in coping with frustration. He was committed to local authority care, given intensive therapy and subsequently did quite well.

## Homicide

Homicide is at the extreme end of the spectrum of violent crime. Its primacy is attested to in biblical and other religious texts and in works of classical literature. Cain is punished by God for his fratricide;[6] the works of Shakespeare and his contemporaries depict its horror (as for example in Shakespeare's *Titus Andronicus* with its bizarre killings, the multiple murders in *Richard III* and the murder in *King Lear*). Webster gives it primacy in his play *The Duchess of Malfi*: "Other sins only speak, murder shrieks out" (Act 4 Sc. 2) and, in the same play, the horror of what the killers have done to their sister (the Duchess) is contained in the chilling line, "Cover her face, mine eyes dazzle." Not only does classical literature attest to the public's interest in murder; there is a virtual stream of contemporary fiction dealing with murder and its detection and an outpouring of television dramas and documentaries. This interest would incline one to the view that murder is commonplace, but the figures given in Table 5.1 should encourage a sense of proportion.

### Legal aspects

Some aspects of the law in relation to homicide were referred to in Chapter 2. The following is a brief recapitulation and further explanation. *Murder* can be briefly described as the unlawful killing of another with malice aforethought. Bowden (1990) provides a definition based on a precis of "Archbold" (a standard legal text) as follows:

> Subject to three exceptions, the crime of murder is committed when a person of sound mind and discretion unlawfully kills any reasonable creature in being and under the Queen's peace with intent to kill or cause grievous bodily harm.

(Bowden 1990: 508)

The definition requires some explanation. Killing the enemy in times of war is not murder; "reasonable creature" means a life in being; it is not murder to kill a child in the womb; this is known as child destruction.

The "three exceptions" referred to by Bowden are:

*Murder is reduced to manslaughter if the accused*:
was provoked
was acting in pursuance of a suicide pact
was suffered from diminished responsibility.

These elements were dealt with in Chapter 2.

*Manslaughter* is defined as unlawfully causing the death of another without malice aforethought. It includes voluntary manslaughter (which includes provocation, diminished responsibility, and killing in pursuance of a suicide pact) (Bowden 1990: 508).

*Involuntary manslaughter* covers cases where the killing was not intended, but where there was an intention to commit an unlawful or dangerous act, gross negligence, or disregard for the lives and safety of others.

*Child destruction* implies the offence of destroying the life of an unborn child; that is to say unless the provisions of the abortion legislation are complied with.

*Causing death by dangerous driving* has gone through a number of classificatory revisions as an offence and has replaced the prosecution of motorists for manslaughter.

*Infanticide* was briefly referred to in Chapter 2. Although there had been a number of statutes dealing with the killing of infant children by mothers from early times, current practice derives from twentieth-century statutes. (For a review of infanticide in England and Wales, see Marks and Kumar 1993.) The specific offence of *infanticide* was introduced because of an increasing reluctance on the part of the judges to pass the death sentence in cases where mothers killed their infant children and the fact that, when they had, the Home Secretary reprieved all mothers so convicted. The Infanticide Act of 1922 referred to the killing of a "newly born child". The current legislation, the Infanticide Act 1938, changed this to specify a child less than 12 months old. It also added a clause indicating that the effect of lactation consequent on the birth could be considered. The relevant section of the Act (Section 1(1)) reads as follows:

Where a woman by any wilful act or omission causes the death of her child being a child under the age of twelve months, but at the time of the act or omission the balance of her mind was disturbed by reason of her not having fully recovered from giving birth to the child or by reason of lactation consequent upon the birth of the child . . . she shall

be guilty of the offence . . . of infanticide . . . and may for such offence
be dealt with as if she had been guilty of the offence of manslaughter of
the child.

Reference to Table 5.1 shows that the number of prosecutions for
infanticide is very small. Although some comfort may be derived from the
comparatively small number of homicide cases, it is possible that reliance
on the criminal statistics provides an underestimate of the true incidence.
Numbers of people disappear from home each year or die in suspicious
circumstances and their fates remain unaccounted for. Recent work by
Biehal et al. (2003) has attempted to examine the problem of persons who
go missing, their backgrounds, the reasons for their "disappearance" and,
where known, their fates. Occasionally, their fates do come to light –
sometimes many years after their disappearance. Notorious examples are
those of the victims of Fred and Rosemary West, Dennis Nilsen and a
number of Shipman's alleged victims.

## Clinical aspects

This heading will be interpreted broadly in order to offer some classification
of homicidal behaviour in behavioural and clinical terms.

### Normal and abnormal homicide

To some people, any form of homicide must indicate a degree of
abnormality. To the extent that life is held to be sacred, any activity that
takes it away by unlawful and forceful acts departs from those norms laid
down by society. This is not to say that such acts may sometimes seem
"understandable" – which is, of course, not quite the same thing. For this
reason, the law recognizes gradations of responsibility for such crimes, as I
demonstrated in Chapter 2. It is a truism that homicide is largely a domestic
affair and that the family is certainly not the "safe haven" that some people
have considered it to be. This is evidenced not only by its primacy as a site
for homicidal acts, but by the wealth of evidence now accumulating of
violence within the family – both spousal, between partners, against children
and against the elderly. As already indicated in Chapter 3, certain forms of
mental disorder and disturbance are not uncommonly associated with
homicidal acts. There have been some large-scale and in-depth studies of
abnormal homicides and one or two of these deserve special mention. The
first was that carried out by West in some 150 cases of murder followed by
suicide in London for the years 1946–62. Not altogether surprisingly, one of
West's main conclusions was that depression in various forms was a very
common precipitating factor (West 1965). Another study was made by
Mowat (1966). He examined a highly selected group of abnormal homicides,

which included 40 male and 6 female patients detained in Broadmoor Hospital. He found a high proportion of them suffered from delusional jealousy (see Chapter 3). Mowat's findings are still of interest today because at the time they concentrated attention on the distribution of delusions from a variety of causes and which have subsequently been investigated more comprehensively by workers such as Mullen (1996).

Gillies (1976) carried out a comprehensive study in the west of Scotland. His findings contradict some of those contained in earlier studies from "south of the border". He based his work on his psychiatric examination of 400 murder cases undertaken for the prosecution between the years 1953 and 1974 (367 males and 33 females); they had been accused of the murder of 307 victims. The salient features he found were maleness, youthfulness, the importance of alcohol, rarity of suicide and a high percentage of psychiatrically "normal" persons. Furthermore, 47 per cent had histories of previous violence. Of the weapons used by the male accused, 56 per cent were sharp instruments, 37 per cent blunt; other methods used by both sexes included shooting and strangulation. Gillies found that most of the crimes in his sample appeared to be *unpremeditated*, apparently unintended and impulsive (for example, precipitated over trifles, often when the parties were "in their cups"; emphasis added).

Mention must also be made of a larger-scale study carried out by Häfner and Böker (1982) in the former Federal Republic of Germany of mentally abnormal violent offenders in the years 1955–64. They found many of the offences occurred within a family setting, but some 9 per cent were strangers. Half of the attacks were planned in advance (compare this finding with those of Gillies); in only about one-quarter of the cases was the crime impulsive. In about half of the cases, a delusional relationship existed, but in about one-fifth there was no recognizable motive. In Häfner and Böker's group, revenge constituted about one-third of the motives in the males; in some 40 per cent of the females the desire was to release the victim from feared distress or illness. Häfner and Böker's study of violence and homicide among mentally abnormal offenders is regarded as a very thorough and method-ologically sophisticated one.

### An attempt to refine the classification of unlawful killing*

During the prosecution and conviction of the late general practitioner, Harold Shipman, he was described in the media as a "serial killer". Such a description seemed to me to be erroneous in the light of what we knew about the behavioural and other characteristics of so-called serial killers. In

---

* Some of the following material and Table 5.2 first appeared in my paper "A proposed socio-legal classification of unlawful killing with special reference to 'serial killing'" in *The British Journal of Forensic Practice* (2000), 2(2): 9–11. It is reproduced here by permission.

*Table 5.2* Unlawful killing: A proposed socio-legal classification

1   Killing as a result of an unlawful or dangerous act, gross negligence or disregard for the lives and safety of others

2   Killing as a result of dangerous (reckless) driving

3   "Political" and associated killing. For example, acts of genocide (Hitler, Stalin, Amin, Hussain), sequential sacrificial killing (as in the Aztec civilization), "cult" killings, killing in the course of warfare, terrorist activity. Some of the perpetrators in this category will show signs of severe personality (psychopathic) disorder and there will be inevitable overlap with some other categories

4   Killing for clear motives of gain or to punish adversaries or competitors. For example, "gang" warfare, Mafia-type activity

5   Killing associated with severe mental disorders. For example, schizophrenic and allied illnesses (such as the presence of "dangerous obsessions"), manic-depressive illness, organic states, mental impairment. Some apparently motiveless killings and the stalking and killing of "celebrity" individuals might be included in this category

6   "Domestic" killings. These are usually, but not always, one-off events, driven by stress and/or provocation, but excluding killing driven by identifiable mental illness (as in 5). This category could include the "mercy killing" of adult children, spouses or partners. It should also be noted that this category may involve several family members, as in the case of Bamber, who is alleged to have killed several of his family on the same occasion

7   Killing facilitated by the ingestion of substances of abuse such as alcohol, other drugs, solvents etc. (this category will overlap with categories 5 and 6)

8   "Carer" killings; these are sometimes committed by those with severe personality disorders such as the former nurse Beverley Allitt and would include the activities of individuals such as Harold Shipman

9   "Mass" killings. These consist of large groups of individuals killed at the same location and at the same time. Examples are, in the UK, Michael Ryan at Hungerford and Thomas Hamilton at Dunblane. In the USA, Charles Whitman in Texas, Richard Speck in Chicago and James Huberty in California

10  Parental or familial child killings. These may be subdivided in the following fashion:
    • child destruction (killing of a child in the womb)
    • neonaticide (killing of the newborn)
    • killing of a child of more than one day old but less than 12 months (including the crime of infanticide)
    • child killing as a result of non-accidental injury (previously known as "battered child syndrome") (see Wilczynski 1997 for discussion of these four subdivisions

11  Killing of parents and/or siblings – overlaps with category 6

12  Children as killers. These are rare, tragic and highly emotional events, as seen for example in the cases of Mary Bell and the two child killers of toddler James Bulger (see later)

13  So-called "serial killing":
    • for gain, but not as in category 4. For example, Madame de Brinvilliers, in 17th-century France, killed various family members over a period of time for material gain
    • for gain, but involving *strangers*. For example, the infamous Sawney Bean who, in 15th-century Scotland, is said to have killed passers-by for their possessions; he then cannibalized some of them. A slightly different example may be found in Paul Hindsmith's opera *Cadillac* based on a story by A. F. T. Hoffman. In the opera, a French goldsmith embarks on a series of serial killings of his customers in order to retrieve gold items he sold to them

*Table 5.2    (Continued)*

- Sexually motivated or control motivated serial killing. In my view this is best categorized as *sequential stranger killing*. Such killing is usually defined as needing at least 3–4 victims, not usually known to the perpetrator; the killings being committed in different locations, usually over a considerable period of time. The emphasis is on repetition, the acts are not committed for gain, but seem to be compulsive in nature and are highly likely to rely on fantasy for their acting out
- (a) *Visionary*. Motivated by delusional beliefs and sometimes by hallucinatory experiences (see category 5). (For detailed discussions see Gresswell and Hollin 1994; Holmes and de Burger 1988: 55–8; Holmes et al. 1998)
  (b) *Missionary*. Motivated by a need to exterminate a particular group of people – for example prostitutes, as in Sutcliffe's case. This sub-classification overlaps with the *visionary*; for example, Sutcliffe could be said to fall into both categories
  (c) *Hedonistic*. This group will include so-called "lust" killings, thrill seeking (for kicks), and for psychological and physical security – derived perhaps from the victim's property (but excluding those in the first category in 13)
  (d) *Power and control*. These killers wish to exercise control over their victim's life and death. Although the motivation is not predominantly sexual, sexually deviant activity may form part of the scenario

*Note*: The killing of large numbers of people over time may justify the label "serial" killing, but as the table shows, it is too broad a term to have much diagnostic, prognostic and management significance. Serial killing as first described and defined by the FBI in the USA is, in my view, best described as "sequential stranger killing" to distinguish it from other forms. However, it has to be acknowledged that my own proposed classification is inevitably arbitrary; as will be seen, there are inevitable overlaps between the various categories and the motivation of individual offenders may change over time.

Gresswell and Hollin (1994) rightly emphasize that many classifications do not "pick up the more subtle interactions between the killer, the victims and the environment. Nor do some of them appear flexible enough to accommodate a killer who may have different motives for different victims and changing motives over time" (Gresswell and Hollin 1994: 5). A recently described further category is that known as Muti murder – murder committed for gathering body parts for purposes of healing (see Labuschagne 2004).

reviewing the literature on unlawful killing, I decided to offer a socio-legal classification that might encompass all types of unlawful killings (homicides) (Prins 2002b). The unlawful killing of single individuals over prolonged periods of time has a long history; examples may be found in Egger (1990), Gresswell and Hollin (1994) and Holmes et al. (1998). Attempts at explaining the phenomenon have included studies into the background and personal pathology of some so-called serial killers (see, for example, Holmes et al. 1998). Claims have also been made for more socio-cultural explanations, see for example Leyton (1989) and more recently Seltzer (1998). The latter locates serial killing within what he describes as the "wound culture" in the USA – a "public fascination with torn and open bodies and torn and opened persons, a collective gathering around shock, trauma and the wound" (Seltzer 1998: 1). I would suggest that much of this theorizing would be more helpful if we were clearer about the different phenomena we are trying to describe, hence my proposed formulation in Table 5.2.

Opinions also vary as to whether or not there has been an increase in recent times in those killings described as "serial". There appears to be no consensus. The public's understanding (or, indeed, *mis*understanding) of the phenomenon has no doubt been fed by various media presentations (literary and audio-visual) such as Harris's *Silence of the Lambs*, the works of Patricia Cornwell, Kathy Reichs and, more recently, by Mo Hayder's somewhat gruesome novel *Birdman*. The UK television series "Prime Suspect", "Waking the Dead", and "Silent Witness" have also had their place in the current scenario. In addition, the names of certain notorious "serial" killers have attained household provenance – for example, Sutcliffe and Nilsen in the UK, Chikatilo and Onoprienko in Ukraine, Dahmer, Bundy, Berkovitz, de Salvo, Kemper and Susan Atkins in the USA. All the foregoing tends to feed public assumptions and fears concerning what is regarded as an all-pervasive menace.

## Some further clinical observations

### Parents who kill their children

Such killings have been classified in a variety of ways. Scott (1973) discerned five types of behaviour:

1  killing of an unwanted child by parents (most frequently the mother)
2  as a result of aggression due to serious mental abnormality
3  behaviour due to the displacement of anger as identified earlier in this chapter (described by some as the "Medea syndrome")
4  cases in which the stimulus seems to arise from the victim (as is sometimes found in the "battered child" syndrome)
5  for altruistic reasons – "mercy killings".

In a more recent empirical study, Wilczynski elaborated on the classifications by Scott and others; she suggested some 10 subdivisions (see Wilczynski 1997: 44–62). The late doctor Patrick McGrath, sometime Medical Director of Broadmoor Hospital, examined a 50-year (1919–69) cohort of 280 female filicide admissions to that hospital from England and Wales (1992). He concluded from his survey:

[T]hat the modal maternal filicide committed to Broadmoor was a white Anglo-Saxon Protestant, aged 31–5, married, suffering from an affective psychosis, altruistically motivated (there is only one "baby-batterer" in the cohort) and not influenced by drink or drugs. She has a previous history of psychiatric referral. The modal victim was the youngest child, of either sex, healthy, the sole victim. The age of the victim was 2–5 years, ranging from 1–29 years. The offence was carried out by readily available domestic means (suffocation, strangulation, gassing, drowning).

(p. 271)

Finally, in a more recent study of various child homicide cases, Dolan et al. describe the histories of 64 men singly accused of killing a single child victim:

> They were characterised by relatively young age and a lack of a long-term stable relationships. Previous psychiatric contact and/or history was noted in one-third of cases. Over half the group had a criminal record and previous violence to children was noted in 28% of cases. Fathers, or surrogate fathers, accounted for nearly two thirds of the accused. In terms of the victims, children under six months were at greatest risk . . . sexually motivated homicide accounted for approximately 18.7% of deaths. Victim behaviours and domestic disharmony acted as precipitants in 64% of the cases, with 54.7% of the victims dying as a result of physical beatings. Alcohol consumption at the material time was more common than noted in previous studies of child homicide.
>
> (Dolan et al. 2003: 153)

On the basis of their research, Dolan et al. suggest that: "There is clearly a need for ongoing research into child homicide, both to monitor trends and evaluate motives and precipitants, particularly in view of the higher than expected frequency of sexually motivated homicides in [our] series" (p. 167). Romain et al. (2003) also conducted a retrospective study in Switzerland of 41 cases of childhood homicide for the years 1990–2000. They discerned two "common profiles". "In the first, one of the parents shot all the children and committed suicide afterwards. The second profile they defined as "fatal child abuse" and concerned younger victims whose cause of death was the result of cranio-cerebral trauma from battering or shaken baby syndrome" (p. 203). These two recent studies demonstrate the range of behaviours leading to the homicides.

### Children who kill

In Chapter 2, I made reference to the legal implications and consequences of the trial of the children Thompson and Venables for the killing of the toddler James Bulger. The trial of these boys reawakened interest in the fairly rare phenomenon of young children as killers.[7] Gunn and Taylor commented in 1993 that "there are only two or three cases each year in Britain" (p. 517). I take this to imply that there are some cases not reported in the press that may be committed by children under the age of criminal responsibility and thus not identified as criminal homicide. Gunn and Taylor quote Wilson (1973) – a journalist – who identified and described some 57 incidents of homicide involving children under the age of 16 between the years 1743 and 1972. Of the 75 children involved (12 girls and 63 boys), 48 were British. Although Wilson described 15 of the children as mentally abnormal, and several were of low intelligence, no cases of frank severe mental illness were recorded. Wilson's series of cases included older children (adolescents) and a more recent report by another journalist – Richard Grant – describes the alleged torturing and killing of a 12-year-old girl by four teenage girls in the USA (*The Independent Saturday Review*, 22 August 1992: 20–24). Two more recent "journalistic" but very well-informed commentaries concerning children who kill are worth mentioning here. The first is Gita Seregny's book *Cries Unheard*, which charts the history and subsequent care and management of Mary Bell (Seregny 1998), and that by Blake Morrison, who covered the trial of Thompson and Venables (Morrison 1997). Both books provide sensitive depictions of the social and family circumstances of these three child killers. Some 35 years ago the distinguished American child psychiatrist, Lauretta Bender, made an important statement concerning the important distinction between pre-pubertal and adolescent killers:

> The psychodynamics of a prepuberty child who has caused a death is that he experiments in fantasy and by acting out to determine if irreparable death is possible. An adolescent makes an effort to deny both guilt for his part in the act that caused the death and to claim amnesia or other repressive defence. Both are usually misunderstood and dangerous.
>
> (Bender 1960: 41)

She found a considerable degree of social deprivation and family pathology. Follow-up revealed continuing deterioration and, for some, the need for mental hospital placement. In studying homicides committed by *older* children, she found that "a constellation of factors was required for a boy or girl to cause a death. There needed to be a disturbed, poorly controlled impulsive child, a victim who acted as an irritant, an available lethal weapon, and *always* a lack of protective supervision by some person who could stop the fatal consequences" (p. 41).

Bender's findings of social deprivation and personal pathology are echoed by Bailey in a recent contribution comparing and contrasting juvenile homicides in the USA and UK: "It may be inferred tentatively that in the UK killings by children or adolescents may be . . . likely to reflect serious personal pathology, although rarely illness such as schizophrenia, than is the case with most other serious crime committed by young people" (Bailey 2000: 151; see also Dolan and Smith 2001; McNally 1995).

Bender's comments are important in connection with the interest aroused by the Bulger tragedy. I have stated elsewhere (Prins 1994) that, as adults, we find it very difficult to comprehend that during the age of "innocence" very young children can engage in homicidal acts. As indicated earlier in this chapter, even very small infants seem capable of murderous rage when frustrated (Klein 1963). Experienced primary school teachers are aware of the vigilance required to prevent mayhem in school playgrounds. And a study of contemporary non-specialist literature reveals the capacity of children to act murderously, as witnessed in Golding's book *Lord of the Flies*. Perhaps, in view of the preceding, we shall have to learn to confront the uncomfortable notion that the killing of children by children may be more frequent than the easily available records show and that only vigilance and active intervention prevent its more frequent occurrence.

## Offender profiling

With the apparent rise in the number of "serial killers", notably in the United States, there has developed an interest in building "profiles" of such persons. Such profiles can sometimes assist police investigators in building up a picture of common psychological, social and environmental characteristics in cases where the killers may manage to elude detection over a prolonged period. Interest in profiling in this country developed sharply in the wake of the Sutcliffe case and involved setting up sophisticated computer-based retrieval systems (see, for example, Doney in Egger 1990 for a description; see also Bilton 2003). Attempts to build profiles in both homicide and non-homicide cases are not new and every good detective operates through his own "computer base" (his brain) a means of forming pictures based on his or her stored experience. Modern technology merely makes this more sophisticated and more readily available to others. In an interesting paper Boon and Davies (1992) trace the history of profiling techniques in the USA. They credit its first major use to the work of a psychiatrist (Brussel) who accurately pinpointed the characteristics of a hard-to-catch bomber. In this country, work on profiling has been taken ahead very much by the activities of Canter and his co-workers at Liverpool University (Canter 1989, 1994). Boon and Davies, from Leicester University, also a noted centre in this field, report that Canter and his colleagues:

> [H]ave found five aspects of the criminal and his or her behaviour to be of help to investigators; residential location, criminal biography, personal characteristics, domestic and social characteristics, and occupational and educational history. Not all of these have been found to be

of equal utility, with the researchers reporting that most help is derived from analysis of details relating to residential location and criminal offence history.

(Boon and Davies 1994: 4; see also Canter 2004;
Copson 1996; Oleson 1996)

A crime writer, who also has professional experience of criminal and forensic investigative techniques, makes a poignant suggestion of what needs to be in the profiler's mind, whatever system he or she uses:

> If violent, aggressive behaviour, dominates your thinking, your imagi-
> nation, you're going to start acting out in ways that move you closer to
> the actual expression of these emotions. Violence fuels more violent
> thoughts and more violent thoughts fuel more violence. After a while,
> violence and killing are a natural part of your adult life and you see
> nothing wrong in it.

(Cornwell 1992: 327)

In recent times, there has been a vast proliferation in the literature on profiling: some can be found under further reading at the end of this chapter.

## Concluding comments

I have covered a great deal of material in this chapter, but there are a number of significant omissions. For example, I have not dealt in any detail with the physical abuse of children or with the apparent increase in cases of serious physical abuse of the elderly. Violent death by assassination, geno-cide and terrorism are, again, only touched on *en passant*. These, and other matters are covered in the further reading section at the end of the chapter. Although my presentation has, for the most part, emphasized clinical aspects, it is of vital importance to try to understand all forms of violent behaviour within a context that includes race, culture, gender and political climate.

## Notes

1  The aetiology of violence is complex. Serious acts of personal violence as
   considered in this chapter would *seem* usually to have their origins in early
   childhood experiences, whether physiological, psychological or close environmental (see comments in Chapter 4). For recent reviews and commentaries on the
   topic see, for example, Alsop (2003), Browne and Pennell (1999), Christoffersen
   et al. (2003) and Fonagy (2003).

2 As I draft this chapter there is much preoccupation with the apparent increase in so-called "gun crime" and the "arms trade". The front page of *The Independent* of 11 October 2003 has a "banner" headline: "A very British way of life and death" and goes on to state that in the week ending 11 October, 109 incidents were uncovered. It reports that: "Anti-gun crime tactics deployed by Scotland Yard are to be deployed throughout the country in an attempt to curb the burgeoning menace of firearms and gang warfare." Whether this is an entirely new phenomenon or whether we are now more conscious of it following one or two distressing and dramatic incidents like the shooting to death of a woman shopkeeper in Nottingham the week previously and a subsequent possible "road rage" gun killing, is a moot point. To what extent "road rage" is an entirely new phenomenon is also uncertain. In line with our current tendency to overreaction, it may be that when our personal space is felt to be threatened on our ever busier highways in an era lacking a coherent transport policy, the phenomenon of "road rage" *may* be more frequent.

3 For example, it has recently been reported that some of the relatives of the Bali bombing are planning to take action against the government for failing to warn travellers of the dangers of a terrorist attack. This litigious preoccupation with risk and compensation is referred to further in Chapter 8.

4 While acknowledging that exchanges in the House of Commons have always had a degree of "ritual" intemperateness, recent exchanges seem to have gone beyond this, to the extent that they have become increasingly vitriolic and personally insulting in nature. The recent party political annual conferences have also witnessed a sad degree of personal "muck raking"; and the dishonourable and illegal activities of some of our politicians do not provide good examples of conduct, particularly for the impressionable young. The media have a large part to play in these scenarios. *The Independent* (not in any sense an overdramatic newspaper) had some trenchant comments to make in its leader of 11 October 2003: "Not for the first time, a cursory reading of the press this week would suggest the country is going to hell in a hand-cart. This time, the rattling carriage contains a raucous payload of young people behaving badly. The case of characters includes professional footballers allegedly engaged in exploitative sex, professional footballers threatening to take their ball home because one of their number failed to take a drug test and professional hooligans trying to follow the hand-cart to Istanbul." This somewhat scary and inflammatory seeming commentary is followed by the following sensible paragraph: "Welcome to the latest moral panic to grip the nation. This one is as specious as most of those that have gone before since medieval witch-hunts, the waves of hysteria often amplified by irresponsible reporting of asylum-seekers, predatory paedophiles, ecstasy, video nasties and many other modern ills" (p. 20).

5 In a report quoted by Jeremy Laurance in *The Independent* of 27 March 2003, the National Audit Office "says that 95,000 incidents of violence and aggression in hospitals were recorded in 2001–02, up from 84,000 in 1999–2000. The rise is believed to be due, in part, to better reporting, but the NAO adds: 'Many trusts consider that increased hospital activity and higher patient expectations particularly in relation to waiting times have also contributed to an increase in the actual level of violence' . . . the NAO estimates that two out of five incidents are not reported, especially by doctors and in mental health units" (p. 13). In the course of my survey, and on a purely "anecdotal" basis, I asked a practising neurologist, two retired physicians (a former paediatrician and a geriatrician) and my wife, an experienced former nursing sister, what their recollections were of A & E departments. All agreed that verbal abuse was not

uncommon and there were incidents of occasional violence (loosely defined). There was some feeling that recourse to alcohol and other drugs might contribute to today's problematic behaviour in A & E departments. My own experience of a number of visits to our local A & E department confirmed a picture of too many "walking wounded", too many minor injuries that I consider could have been dealt with in GP practices and a general abuse of NHS facilities. The resulting overcrowding and serious understaffing in some departments contributes to an atmosphere of tension that, in turn, *probably* increases the possibility of disruptive, abusive and occasionally violent behaviour. A recent BMA survey of some 400 doctors suggests that one in 12 doctors has been assaulted in the year of the survey (2002) (*The Independent*, 16 October 2003: 7).

6   *Homicide*, as indicated in Chapter 2, is the legal and clinical term to cover all forms of unlawful killing; *genocide* is the term used to refer to the deliberate extermination of a people or nation; *parricide* is the term used for killing a near relative or parent; *matricide* for killing of one's mother; *patricide* for the killing of one's father; *uxoricide* for the killing of one's wife and *filicide* for the killing of a child by a parent. Parricidal behaviour has often been viewed and explained in what might best be described as a psychoanalytic framework. However, in a recent paper, Shon and Targonski (2003) suggest "parricides, like general types of homicide, are disproportionately committed by males in late adolescence. Furthermore, fathers are also likely to bear the brunt of lethal violence from sons and daughters alike". They continue: "More significantly, and contrary to the assertions of psychiatrists, clinical psychologists and psychoanalysts, we have found that parricides have declined between the years 1976 and 1998" (p. 399). See also a paper by Marleau et al. (2003) on the differences between completed parricides and attempted parricides suffering from psychosis. Subjects in the attempted parricide group "are more likely to have made threats of harm before the offence, to have a family history of violence, and to have fewer suicidal thoughts after the offense" (p. 277).

7   In an interesting and thought-provoking paper Rowbotham et al. (2003) compare public reactions to the Bulger case with those that occurred in respect of two 8-year-old child killers, Barratt and Bradley, in 1861. The authors discovered that, somewhat contrary to expectation, the reactions of the Victorian public were more temperate than expected and that in both instances the media were less influential in actually shaping public opinion than one would have supposed.

# References

Alsop, M. (2003) "Attention deficit hyper-activity disorder (ADHD) and crime", *Prison Service Journal* 149: 21–4.

Andoh, B. (2002) "Legal aspects of mental hospital regimes", *Medicine, Science and the Law* 42: 14–26.

Archer, J. and Browne, K. D. (1989) "Concepts and approaches to the study of aggression", in J. Archer and K. D. Browne (eds), *Human Aggression: Naturalistic Approaches*, London: Routledge.

Bailey, S. (2000) "Juvenile homicide", *Criminal Behaviour and Mental Health* 10: 149–54.

Bender, L. (1960) "Children and adolescents who have killed", *American Journal of Psychiatry* 116: 510–13.

Biehal, N., Mitchell, F. and Wade, J. (2003) *Lost From View: Missing Persons in the UK*, Bristol: Policy Press.

Bilton, M. (2003) *Beyond Belief: The Hunt for the Yorkshire Ripper*, London: HarperCollins.

Blackburn, R. (1993) *The Psychology of Criminal Conduct: Theory, Research and Practice*, Chichester: John Wiley & Sons.

Boon, J. and Davies, G. (1992) "Fact and fiction in offender profiling", *Newsletter of the Division of Legal and Criminological Psychology* 32: 3–9, Leicester, British Psychological Society.

Bowden, P. (1990) "Homicide", in R. Bluglass and P. Bowden (eds), *Principles and Practice of Forensic Psychiatry*, London: Churchill Livingstone.

Browne, K. and Pennell, A. E. (1998) *The Effects of Video Violence on Young Offenders*. Home Office Research and Statistics Directorate: Research Findings No. 65, London: Home Office.

Canter, D. (1989) "Offender profiles", *The Psychologist* 2: 12–16.

—— (1994) *Criminal Shadows: Inside the Mind of the Serial Killer*, London: HarperCollins.

—— (2004) "Offender profiling and investigative psychology", *Journal of Investigative Psychology and Offender Profiling* 1: 1–15.

Copson, G. (1996) "At last some facts about offender profiling in Britain", *Forensic Up-Date* 46: 4–9.

Cornwell, P. (1992) *All That Remains*, London: Little, Brown & Co.

Crichton, J. H. M. (ed.) (1995) *Psychiatric Patient Violence: Risk and Relapse*. London: Duckworth.

Crichton, J. H. M. and Calgie, T. (2002) "Responding to in-patient violence in a psychiatric hospital of special security: A pilot project", *Medicine, Science and the Law* 42: 30–3.

Christoffersen, M. N., Francis, B. and Soothill, K. (2003) "An upbringing to violence? Identifying the likelihood of violent crime among the 1966 birth cohort in Denmark", *Journal of Forensic Psychiatry and Psychology* 14: 367–81.

Day, Sir M. (1986) Foreword in H. Prins, *Dangerous Behaviour, The Law and Mental Disorder*, London: Tavistock.

Department of Health (2001) *"Cui Bono": Withholding Treatment From Violent and Abusive Patients in NHS Trusts: "We Don't Have to Take This"*, London: Department of Health.

Dolan, M. and Smith, C. (2001) "Juvenile homicide offenders: 10 years' experience of an adolescent forensic psychiatry service", *Journal of Forensic Psychiatry* 12: 313–29.

Dolan, M., Guly, O., Woods, P. and Fullam, R. (2003) "Child homicide", *Medicine, Science and the Law* 43: 153–69.

Doney, R. H. (1990) "The aftermath of the Yorkshire Ripper: The response of the United Kingdom Police", in S. A. Egger (ed.), *Serial Murder: An Elusive Phenomenon*, London: Praeger.

Eaton, S., Ghannan, M. and Hunt, N. (2000) "Prediction of violence on a psychiatric intensive care unit", *Medicine, Science and the Law* 40: 143–6.

Egger, S. A. (ed.) (1990) *Serial Murder – An Elusive Phenomenon*, London: Praeger.

Flood-Page, C. and Taylor, J. (eds) (2003) *Home Office Statistical Bulletin: Crime in England and Wales. 2001/2002, Supplementary Volume*, London: Home Office.

Fonagy, P. (2003) "Towards a developmental understanding of violence", *British Journal of Psychiatry* 183: 190–2.

Fromm, E. (1977) *The Anatomy of Human Destructiveness*, Harmondsworth: Penguin.

Gillies, H. (1976) "Murder in the west of Scotland", *British Journal of Psychiatry* 128: 105–27.

Gresswell, D. M. and Hollin, C. R. (1994) "Multiple murders: A review", *British Journal of Criminology* 34: 1–14.

Gudjonsson, G., Rabe-Hesketh, S. and Wilson, C. (2000) "Violent incidents on a medium secure unit: The target and the management of incidents", *Journal of Forensic Psychiatry* 11: 105–18.

Gunn, J. and Taylor, P. J. (eds) (1993) *Forensic Psychiatry: Clinical, Legal and Ethical Issues*, London: Butterworth.

Häfner, H. and Böker, W. (1982) *Crimes of Violence by Mentally Abnormal Offenders*, Cambridge: Cambridge University Press.

Hankoff, L. D. (1993) "Urban violence in historical perspective", *International Journal of Offender Therapy and Comparative Criminology* 37: 1–3.

Hardie, T. (1999) "Influence of patient density on violence and self-harming behaviour in a medium secure unit", *Medicine, Science and the Law* 39: 161–6.

Hollin, C. R. (1992) *Criminal Behaviour: A Psychological Approach to Explanation and Behaviour*, London: Falmer Press.

Holmes, R. M. and De Burger, J. (1988) *Serial Murder*, London: Sage.

Holmes, R. M., De Burger, J. and Holmes, S. T. (1998) "Inside the mind of the serial murderer", in R. M. Holmes and S. T. Holmes (eds), *Contemporary Perspectives on Serial Murder*, London: Sage.

Home Office (2002) *Criminal Statistics: England and Wales, 2001*, Cm 5696, London: TSO.

Junger, M. and Wiegersma, A. (1995) "The relations between accidents, deviants and leisure time", *Criminal Behaviour and Mental Health* 5: 144–74.

Klein, M. (1963) *Our Adult World and Other Essays*, London: Heinemann.

Labuschagne, G. (2004) "Features and investigative implications of Muti murder in South Africa", *Journal of Investigative Psychology and Offender Profiling* 1: 191–206.

Leyton, E. (1989) *Hunting Humans: The Rise of the Modern Multiple Murderer*, Harmondsworth: Penguin.

Lorenz, K. (1966) *On Aggression*, London: Methuen.

Marks, M. N. and Kumar, R. (1993) "Infanticide in England and Wales", *Medicine, Science and the Law* 33: 329–39.

Marleau, J. D., Millaud, F. and Auclair, N. (2003) "A comparison of parricide and attempted parricide: A study of 39 psychotic adults", *International Journal of Law and Psychiatry* 26: 269–79.

McDermott, M. (1993) "On cruelty, ethics and experimentation: Profile of Philip G. Zimbardo", *The Psychologist* 6: 456–9.

McGrath, P. G. (1992) "Maternal filicide in Broadmoor Hospital – 1919–1969", *Journal of Forensic Psychiatry* 3: 271–97.

McNally, R. (1995) "Homicidal youth in England and Wales: 1982–1992: Profile and policy", *Psychology Crime and Law* 1: 333–42.

Miers, D. (1996) "Liabilities for injuries caused by violent patients", *Medicine, Science and the Law* 36: 15–24.

Mirlees-Black, C., Budd, T., Partridge, S. and Mayhew, P. (1998) *Home Office Statistical Bulletin: Issue 12/98*. London: Home Office.

Mowatt, R. R. (1966) *Morbid Jealousy and Murder*, London: Tavistock.

Morrison, B. (1997) *As If*, London: Granta Publications.

Mullen, P. (1996) "Jealousy and the emergence of violent and intimidatory behaviours", *Criminal Behaviour and Mental Health* 6: 194–205.

Norris, D. M. and Gutheil, J. G. (2003) "Harassment and intimidation of forensic psychiatrists: An update", *International Journal of Law and Psychiatry* 26: 437–45.

O'Keefe, G. (1999) "Review of management of imminent violence: Guidelines issued by the Research Unit of the Royal College of Psychiatrists", *Journal of Forensic Psychiatry* 10: 391–8.

Oleson, J. C. (1996) "Psychological profiling: Does it actually work?", *Forensic Update* 46: 11–14.

Pearson, G. (1983) *Hooligan: A History of Respectable Fears*, London: Macmillan.

Prins, H. (1994) "Psychiatry and the concept of evil: Sick in heart or sick in mind?", *British Journal of Psychiatry* 165: 297–302.

—— (1995) *Offenders, Deviants or Patients?*, 2nd ed., London: Routledge.

—— (1996) "Can the law serve as the solution to social ills? The Mental Health (Patients in the Community) Act, 1995", *Medicine, Science and the Law* 36: 217–20.

—— (2002a) "Cui bono? Withholding treatment from violent and abusive patients in NHS trusts: 'We don't have to take this'", *Journal of Forensic Psychiatry* 13: 391–406.

—— (2002b) "A proposed socio-legal classification of unlawful killing – with special reference to 'serial killing'", *British Journal of Forensic Practice* 2: 9–11.

Raine, A. and Liu, J. H. (1998) "Biological predispositions to violence and their implications for biosocial treatment and prevention", *Psychology, Crime and Law* 4: 107–25.

Rex, S. and Tonry, M. (eds) (2002) *Reform and Punishment: The Future of Sentencing*. Cullompton, Devon: Willam Publishing.

Romain, N., Michaud, K., Horisberger, R., Brandt-Casadevall, C., Krompecher, T. and Mangin, P. (2003) "Childhood homicide: A 1990–2000 retrospective study at the Institute of Legal Medicine in Lausanne, Switzerland", *Medicine, Science and the Law* 43: 203–6.

Rowbotham, J., Stevenson, K. and Pegg, S. (2003) "Children of misfortune: Parallels in the cases of child murderers Thompson and Venables, Barrett and Brady", *Howard Journal of Criminal Justice* 42: 107–22.

Salib, E. (2003) "Effect of 11 September 2001 on suicide and homicide in England and Wales", *British Journal of Psychiatry* 183: 207–12.

Schneiden, V., Stark, M. and Payne-Jones, J. (1995) "Violence and clinical forensic medicine", *Medicine, Science and the Law* 35: 333–5.

Scott, P. D. (1973) "Parents who kill their children", *Medicine, Science and the Law* 13: 120–5.

Scott, P. D. (1977) "Assessing dangerousness in criminals", *British Journal of Psychiatry* 131: 127–42.

Seltzer, M. (1998) *Serial Killers: Death and Life in America's Wound Culture*, London: Routledge.

Seregny, G. (1998) *Cries Unheard: The Story of Mary Bell*, London: Macmillan.

Sharpe, J. (1992) "Hard times revive law and order panic", *The Independent*, 12 April: 2.

Shepherd, J. P. (1994) *Violence in Health Care*, Oxford: Oxford University Press.

—— (1995) "Injury and illness experience in victims of violence with particular reference to DATES syndrome", *Criminal Behaviour and Mental Health* 5: 351–66.

Shepherd, J. P. and Farrington, D. P. (1996) "The prevention of delinquency with particular reference to violent crime", *Medicine, Science and the Law* 36: 331–6.

Shon, P. C. H. and Targonski, J. R. (2003) "Declining trends in US parricides, 1976–1998: Testing the Freudian assumptions" *International Journal of Law and Psychiatry* 26: 387–402.

Soothill, K. (2003) "A new report on violence – a welcome and a warning", *British Journal of Psychiatry* 182: 3–4.

Steen, V. and Hunskaar, S. (2001) "Violence: A prospective study of police and health care registrations in an urban community in Norway", *Medicine, Science and the Law*, 41: 337–41.

Storr, A. (1975) *Human Aggression*, Harmondsworth: Penguin.

—— (1991) *Human Destructiveness: The Roots of Genocide and Human Cruelty*, 2nd ed., London: Routledge.

Toch, H. (1992) *Violent Men: An Inquiry into the Psychology of Violence*, rev. ed., Washington, DC: American Psychological Association.

Toffler, A. (1970) *Future Shock*, New York: Random House.

Walker, W. D. and Caplan, R. P. (1993) "Assaultive behaviour in acute psychiatric wards and its relationship to violence in the community: A comparison of two health districts", *Medicine, Science and the Law* 33: 300–4.

Watts, D., Leese, M., Thomas, S., Atakan, C. and Wykes, T. (2003) "The prediction of violence in acute psychiatric units", *International Journal of Forensic Mental Health* 2: 173–80.

West, D. J. (1965) *Murder Followed by Suicide*, London: Macmillan.

Wildgoose, J., Briscoe, M. and Lloyd, K. (2003) "Psychological and emotional problems in staff following assaults by patients", *Psychiatric Bulletin* 27: 295–7.

Wilson, P. (1973) *Children Who Kill*, London: Michael Joseph.

Wilczynski, A. (1997) *Child Homicide*, London: Greenwich Medical Media Ltd.

World Health Organization (2002) (1) *World Report on Violence and Health.* (2) *World Report on Violence and Health. Summary* (edited by E. G. Krug, L. L. Dahlberg, J. A. Mercy, A. B. Zwi and R. Lozano), Geneva: WHO.

Wykes, T. (1994) *Violence and Health Care Professionals*, London: Chapman & Hall.

Wynn, R. (2003) "Staff's choice of formal and informal coercive interventions in psychiatric emergencies", *International Journal of Forensic Mental Health* 2: 157–64.

Zimbardo, P. G. (1973) "On the ethics of intervention in human psychological research with special reference to the Stanford Prison experiment", *Cognition* 2: 243–56.

## Further reading

### *Violence – general*

Cartwright, D. (2002) *Psychoanalysis, Violence and Rage Type Murder. Murdering Minds*, London: Brunner-Routledge (a psychoanalytic approach to the topic).

Cox, M. (ed.) (1999) *Remorse and Reparation*, London: Jessica Kingsley.

Cullen, E. and Newell, T. (1999) *Murderers and Life Imprisonment. Containment, Treatment, Safety and Risk*, Winchester: Waterside Press.

Howells, K. and Hollin, C. R. (eds) (1989) *Clinical Approaches to Violence*, Chichester: John Wiley & Sons.

Hyatt-Williams, A. (1998) *Cruelty, Violence and Murder: Understanding the Criminal Mind*, London: Jason Aronson (a psychoanalytic approach).

Jones, D. (ed.) (2004) *Working With Dangerous People: The Psychotherapy of Violence*, Oxford: Radcliffe Medical Press (provides a group-analytic approach).

Thompson, C. and Cowen, O. (1993) *Violence: Basic and Clinical Science*, London: Butterworth-Heinemann (for the Mental Health Foundation).

### *Family violence*

Family violence has been comprehensively reviewed by:

Greenland, C. (1990) "Family violence: A review of the literature", in R. Bluglass and P. Bowden (eds), *Principles and Practice of Forensic Psychiatry*, London: Churchill Livingstone.

Clinical aspects have been extensively covered in:

Bentovim, A. (1990) "Family violence: Clinical aspects", in R. Bluglass and P. Bowden (eds), *Principles and Practice of Forensic Psychiatry*, London: Churchill Livingstone.

### *Selected aspects*

Birch, H. (ed.) (1993) *Moving Targets: Women, Murder and Representation*, London: Virago.

Brogden, M. (2001) *Geronticide: Killing the Elderly*, London: Jessica Kingsley.

Brogden, M. and Nijhar, P. (2000) *Crime, Abuse and the Elderly*, Cullompton, Devon: Willan Publishing.

Cavadino, P. (ed.) (1996) *Children Who Kill*, Winchester, Waterside Press.

Martingdale, M. (1993) *Cannibal Killers: The Impossible Monsters*, London: Robert Hale.

Radford, J. and Russell, D. E. H. (1992) *Femicide: The Politics of Woman Killing*, Milton Keynes: Open University Press (good account of gender issues).

Ressler, R. K., Burgess, R. W. and Douglas, J. E. (1988) *Sexual Homicide: Patterns and Motives*, Oxford: Lexington/Macmillan.


### Serial killing

Holmes, R. M. and Holmes, S. T. (eds) (1998) *Contemporary Perspectives on Serial Murder*, London: Sage.
Leyton, E. (ed.) (2000) *Serial Murder: Modern Scientific Perspectives*, Dartmouth: Ashgate Press (comprehensive collection of wide-ranging papers).
Masters, B. (1997) *The Evil That Men Do: From Saints to Serial Killers*, London: Black Swan.


### Profiling

Ainsworth, P. B. (2001) *Offender Profiling and Crime Analysis*, Cullompton, Devon: Willan Publishing.
Britton, P. (1997) *The Jigsaw Man*, London: Corgi Books.
—— (2000) *Picking Up The Pieces*, London: Corgi Books.

(Both the Britton books offer personal accounts by a forensic psychologist.)

Canter, D. (ed.) (2000 and onwards) Series of books on various aspects of offender profiling. Dartmouth: Ashgate Press.
Holmes, R. M. and Holmes, S. T. (1996) *Profiling Violent Crimes: An Investigative Tool*, London: Sage.
Jackson, J. C. and Bekerian, D. A. (1997) *Offender Profiling: Theory, Research and Practice*, Chichester: John Wiley & Sons.


### Biographical accounts

Burn, G. (1984) *Somebody's Husband, Somebody's Son: The Story of Peter Sutcliffe*, London: Heinemann.
—— (1998) *Happy Like Murderers*, London: Faber & Faber.
Masters, B. (1985) *Killing For Company*, London: Cape.
—— (1993) *The Shrine of Jeffrey Dahmer*, London: Hodder & Stoughton.
—— (1996) *She Must Have Known: The Trial of Rosemary West*, London: Transworld Publications.
Wansell, G. (1996) *An Evil Love: The Life of Frederick West*, London: Headline Books.

### Journals

In addition to the journals listed at the end of Chapter 4 the following two contain useful material:

*Homicide Studies*
*Journal of Interpersonal Violence*

A very new publication devoted to investigative psychology and offender profiling has also recently appeared *Journal of Investigative Psychology and Offender Profiling*.

See also special (2003) issue of the *International Journal of Law and Psychiatry*, "Locating women in law and psychiatry" 26, 5. Special (2003) issue "Alcohol and crime", *Criminal Behaviour and Mental Health* 13, 1.

The April 2004 issue of *Medicine, Science and the Law* contains a useful paper by White on homicide and affective disorder and by Mohanty et al. on circumstances of crime in homicidal deaths (44, 2).

The possible motivations driving terrorist suicide bombers are usefully outlined by Soibelman, M. (2004) "Palestinian suicide bombers", *Journal of Investigative Psychology and Offender Profiling* 1: 175–90.

# Chapter 6

# Unlawful sex

Literature is mostly about having sex and not much
about having children. Life is the other way round.
> (David Lodge, *The British Museum is Falling Down* (1965), Ch. 4)

The soft, unhappy sex.
> (Aphra Behn, early "feminist" writer, *The Wandering Beauty* (1698), para 1)

While we think of it, and talk of it
Let us leave it alone, physically keep apart.
For while we have sex in the mind, we truly have
none in the body.
> (D. H. Lawrence, *Leave Sex Alone* (1929))

## Introduction

The chapter epigraphs will, I hope, give some inkling of the conflict and ambivalence that pervade attitudes towards sexuality and, in particular, so-called deviant sexuality. These attitudes have lengthy historical roots and fierce injunctions against the practice of deviant sex can be found in religious works such as the English Bible. For example, homosexuality is described in the Book of Leviticus as an "abomination" and intercourse with animals as "a violation of nature" (Chapter 18, v. 23 and 24). These ancient and pervasive attitudes have found recent vehement expression in the opposition demonstrated against the appointment of the openly gay American clergyman, Gene Robinson, to the office of Bishop, and the withdrawal from appointment to a bishopric by Canon Jeffrey John in the UK. A little thought concerning the numbers of homosexuals in the community and, by implication, within the church would tend to support the view that being "gay" is OK as long as you don't go "public" about it if you are a clergyman. This chapter is being drafted at a time when many of the laws pertaining to unlawful sex have been brought up to date (Sex Offences Act 2003) and the relevance of these important changes will be referred to in relation to the offences I discuss in the following pages. The chapter is divided into *four* sections. First, a brief context-setting background, second, a classification of sexual offences (clinical and legal), third, brief comment on the size of the problem and fourth, the major section, a discussion of some of the more common sexual offences and some briefer references to a selection of rarer sexual misbehaviours that come within the purview of the criminal law.

## Background and context

Sexual conduct depends for its expression on a number of factors, biological (for example hormonal influences), social and familial. In the human species, although hormonal and allied influences have always been considered to be of some importance, there is some evidence that this influence may be increasing as, for example, in the recently somewhat controversial view that there may be a genetic factor in the development of male homosexuality. A wide-ranging overview of the "totality" of sexual behaviour and misbehaviour may be found in the third volume of the *Encyclopaedia of Criminology and Deviant Behaviour* (Davis and Geis 2001). The divergent patterns of sexual behaviour have been described by Kaul in the following terms:

> Sexual behaviour in humans does not necessarily conform to any single pattern. People differ in the type as well as the frequency of preferred activity. The attitudes that different cultures have towards types of sexual behaviour differ as to the attitudes of the same society over a period of time . . . Sexual preference is varied, not only with regard to the physical or other attributes of the partner one chooses, but also the type of sexual activity engaged in.
>
> (Kaul 1993: 207)

These variations are reflected in the criminal law and the manner in which it penalizes some behaviours and not others (as, for example, in the gradual extension of the decriminalization of consenting adult male homosexual behaviour). Five further points can usefully be made by way of introduction. First, sexual behaviour and, in particular, sexual misbehaviour are emotive topics; it will be seen how emotive when I come to discuss paedophilia. Attitudes towards the physical expression of sexuality – even among professionals – are still sometimes based on a degree of ignorance and anxiety. Although there is a great deal more talk about, and open portrayal of, sexual activity of all kinds than in the past, it is by no means certain that such public portrayal has done very much to remove anxieties and inhibitions. Concerns about HIV infection and AIDS have revived fears and taboos about sexual activity; they are reminiscent of those that used to be prevalent in discussions about other sexually transmitted diseases such as syphilis and gonorrhoea. Such taboos and proscriptions may also have their origins in the fact that the sexual and procreative organs (particularly in the female) are closely associated anatomically with the elimination of bodily wastes – hence the importance attached to this conjunction by the early practitioners of psychoanalysis.

Second, we should note that sexual *attractiveness* is often at the heart (either implicitly or explicitly) of much media advertising. The promotion of sexual prowess and attractiveness as highly desirable attributes may, in fact, only serve to make people more anxious about their sexual *performance* than about sexual expression as part of caring adult relationships – be they hetero- or homosexual.

Third, changes in our attitudes towards women in what is still a highly male-dominated society are of great importance. With a continuing degree of ignorance and prejudice we continue to place women in a very ambiguous position, which leads to much confusion concerning our expectations of them. Fourth, we should note some changes in our references to sexual behaviour and misbehaviours. For the most part, we no longer use euphemisms for certain forms of sexual activity. In my youth (some 60 plus years ago!) buggery (anal sex) was never referred to as such, but a well-known Sunday newspaper, which always carried quite detailed accounts of sex offence trials, always referred to such activities as "serious or unnatural offences". In similar terms, oral sexual practices (such as fellatio, cunnilingus, anilingus) were never referred to publicly; now it is commonplace, both in court reporting, publicity about sexually transmitted diseases and in the visual media. Although such practices are now much more openly acknowledged in the light of more liberated views about the legitimacy of a variety of forms of sexual activity, the law still seems somewhat capricious in this respect. This was evidenced when a group of adult sado-masochists were prosecuted and sentenced to imprisonment for engaging in mutually consenting private activity in which various injuries were inflicted on their genitalia. Appeals to the High Court in this country and to the European Court of Human Rights failed; the courts held that in certain circumstances people should be protected even from their own consensual activities. The question of consent is vitally important in the area of sexual activity – as we shall see when we come to consider sexual assaultative behaviour such as rape.

Fifth, any discussion of sexual deviation (and particularly that also adjudged to be criminal) must take into account the idea that sexual feelings and expression are not as dichotomous as some people imagine, for we all have physical and emotional elements of the opposite sex within us – some more than others. In this respect, it is important to be sure that when we discuss overt sexuality we endeavour to be clear about physically endowed sex, on the one hand, and what might be called gender sex (what we feel about our sexuality), on the other. Bancroft puts the matter well:

> We tend to take our gender for granted: "Of course you are male if you have a penis". Usually we can afford to do so, but the processes leading to the ascription of gender identity are so complex it is little wonder they occasionally go wrong.
>
> (Bancroft 1989: 153; see also Bancroft 1991)

The complex web of factors that go to determine sexual *offending* behaviour has been usefully reviewed by Lanyon (1991). Having made these certain few points, can we determine to what extent we can make any helpful distinctions between so-called "normality" and "deviation" in relation to sexual behaviour? I think that the answer has to be a carefully qualified "yes". The qualification is important because, as we have seen, any distinctions will have to be culture bound; they may change over time and can therefore only be seen as broad generalizations. They will also be heavily dependent on different aesthetic preferences. The qualified "yes" can therefore be best expressed as follows. Sexual behaviour encompasses those forms of sexual activity between two adults (and the age of adulthood may vary over historical time) that are acceptable to both parties, do not involve coercion, exploitation or degradation and do not affront the notions of public decency prevailing at the time. Finally, in this general introduction, it is very important to avoid the all too common stereotyping of the sex offender; the "dirty mac" image still holds much sway and, as we shall see when we consider paedophilia, is very prevalent in this particular connection.

In the presentation of these clinical and legal classifications that follows I must emphasize that they will often overlap and should not therefore be considered as discrete entities. The clinical classification is partly derived from Scott (1964) and Prins (1995). (See also Briggs 1994; Gayford 1997; Grubin and Kennedy 1991.)

The areas under consideration in this chapter are as follows:

- Sexual activity not requiring a human partner – for example, the use of animals (bestiality, zoophilia, zooerasty) or objects (fetishism).
- Sexual activity not involving a *willing* partner – for example, rape (hetero- and homosexual), voyeurism ("Peeping Tom" activities), exhibitionism (indecent exposure), necrophilia. These categories link very closely with those in the following one.
- Sexual activity under *unusual* conditions – and here, matters of consent may be all important and continue to occupy a grey area. Some examples are, sexual activity with the elderly (gerontophilia) (see Brogden and Nijhar 2000; Kaul and Duffy 1991; Jeary 2004), with children of

both sexes (paedophilia), consanguineous sexual activity (incest), sexual activity requiring excessive punishment or suffering (sado-masochistic activities), non-self-induced sexual asphyxia (eroticized repetitive hanging), which sometimes results in death. (See Knight 1979; Prins 1991: 90–3.)

● Certain other sexually motivated activities that may present in *masked* form. For example, some types of stealing (underclothes or similar garments from clotheslines), some rare types of fire raising (see Chapter 7), sexual gratification from the sight of, or contact with, human bodily secretions (vampirism), excrement (coprophilia) or urine (*urolagnia* – "golden shower").

It will be obvious that many of these activities will overlap and that the *paraphilias* (to give them their generic title) cover a very wide range of behaviours. Perkins (1991), in a review of classification, suggests the following: (1) *Compensatory* – as a result of social/sexual relationship problems; (2) *displaced aggression* – motivated by anger or hatred; here the concentration is on degrading or defiling the victim and the use of more force than is necessary to overpower the victim; particular victims may be sought out – for example, prostitutes; (3) *sadistic* – more violence than is necessary – as in (2) but it is also cold and deliberate; sexual gratification is derived from the infliction of pain and from the fear shown by the victim; (4) *impulsive/opportunistic* – such offenders have histories of various forms of anti-social behaviour; obtaining sex by force is just another aspect of this lifestyle.

## Legal classification

There are some areas of overlap and the choice of offences to be included is, to some extent, idiosyncratic: Rape and attempts (on males and females); indecent assault (on females and males); buggery and attempts (on males and females); unlawful sexual intercourse with females under age; procuration for sexual purposes; abduction; indecency with children; gross indecency; indecent exposure; bestiality; soliciting for prostitution; importuning; trading in, or possession of, obscene publications; use of children for pornographic purposes (e.g. in order to make films, videos, or to take still or computerized images); making obscene phone calls; sexual interference with a cadaver (corpse); homicide committed for purposes of sexual gratification; conspiracy to corrupt public morals. To this list, we would add some less obvious "sexual" crimes where an apparently non-sexual offence may be sexually motivated. Examples would be some forms of larceny (stealing women's underclothing from clotheslines); "proving" offences, such as taking motorcycles without the owners' consent; certain forms of burglarious activity (where the goods stolen may have sexual connotations, for example, shoes belonging to the female occupier of the premises) or where the behaviour of the burglar appears unusual (for example, slashing bedsheets with a knife). In the first edition of this book I included the offence of bigamy, but on reflection, this is best regarded as an offence against family life. However, it is still categorized as a sexual offence in the criminal statistics.

*It is worth noting that, contrary to general assumption, the more serious sexual offences are almost always punished by immediate imprisonment.* This is particularly noticeable in rape cases. Where sentences for sexual offences have been regarded as too lenient, the Court of Appeal has not been reluctant to increase them, as a number of recent cases have demonstrated (see Stone 2003a: 182–3).

Finally, it is important to observe that the legal classification of sexual offences does not necessarily adequately describe the severity or importance of the offence to the victim. For example, an indecent assault may be as severe to the victim as an attempted rape; and the decision to charge for one or other offence may be fairly arbitrary. As we shall see shortly, the offence of indecent exposure (often regarded quite lightly by some males) can have a marked and traumatic effect on some victims.

## Size of the problem

Contrary to much public opinion, sexual offences constitute a very small proportion of all recorded crimes, something in the order of 2 per cent of all offences and about 1.75 per cent of all persons found guilty of indictable (the more serious) offences. This is not to deny that this small proportion will contain a number of very serious incidents causing much physical and psychological harm to victims. One also needs to be aware of the considerable discrepancy between the numbers of actual sexual offences *known to the police* and the number actually *dealt with or prosecuted*. Reasons for this discrepancy are not hard to find. Victims and witnesses may be reluctant to come forward; corroboration may thus prove problematic. This is a particular concern in cases of alleged child sexual abuse that may come to light (or in some cases *appear* to come to light) long after the events complained of. In a small number of recent institutional sex abuse cases such allegations have proved to be unfounded. There is also much debate concerning the truth of allegations made by adults who claim to have been abused by family members in childhood (for example false, or recovered, memory syndrome) (see Brandon et al. 1998; Brewin 1996; Gudjonsson 1997). Consenting parties may be reluctant to admit to having engaged in unlawful sexual activity and it may therefore prove difficult to show that an offence has occurred. It is also well known that many more sexual offences are committed than are ever reported to the police. For example, the 1998 and 2000 *British Crime Surveys* attempted to provide the "most accurate ever estimates of the extent and nature of sexual victimisation in England and Wales . . . questions were asked

*Table 6.1* Selection of offenders found guilty at all courts for sexual offences for the period 1997–2001[a]

|  | 1997 | 1998 | 1999 | 2000 | 2001 |
|---|---|---|---|---|---|
| Abduction | 4 | 8 | 4 | 6 | 5 |
| Bigamy[b] | 30 | 38 | 47 | 31 | 31 |
| Buggery | 137 | 163 | 122 | 119 | 96 |
| Gross indecency with a child | 231 | 264 | 272 | 240 | 303 |
| Incest | 64 | 72 | 42 | 50 | 45 |
| Indecent assault on a female | 3,401 | 3,246 | 3,189 | 2,924 | 2,847 |
| Indecent assault on a male | 608 | 565 | 606 | 510 | 459 |
| Indecent exposure[c] | 807 | 743 | 649 | 553 | 488 |
| Procuration | 109 | 94 | 66 | 58 | 56 |
| Rape of a female | 599 | 656 | 631 | 594 | 559 |
| Rape of a male | 45 | 46 | 61 | 45 | 53 |
| Unlawful sexual intercourse with girl under 13 | 60 | 78 | 76 | 73 | 67 |
| Unlawful sexual intercourse with girl under 16 | 472 | 511 | 436 | 449 | 437 |

*Source*: Home Office 2001, Tables 5.12 and 5.20

*Notes*: (a) The figures quoted support the contention in the text that the number of offences dealt with are far fewer than the number of offences that actually take place. (b) Bigamy is included here to fill out the picture, but see my earlier comment about its inclusion. (c) Indecent exposure has, until recently, been a summary offence. Under the provisions of the Sex Offences Act 2003 it can now be dealt with summarily and on indictment. This new provision is to be welcomed since it reflects current professional opinion that the offence should be viewed seriously. Evidence suggests that some victims can be considerably traumatized by it; and some exposers go on to commit more serious sexual crimes.

of both men and women aged 16–59" (Myhill and Allen 2002: 1). In relation to female victims, in the year preceding the survey, it was estimated 61,000 victims reported they had been raped and 0.9 per cent of women said they "had been subject to some form of sexual victimisation" (including rape) in this period. In some cases (rape for example) victims may not wish to suffer the trauma of medical and police enquiries, followed by a public court appearance, in which, despite more recent safeguards, both fact and reputation may be challenged and impugned. Parents and other guardians of sexually assaulted children may wish to spare them a similar experience. Males who have been the subject of serious sexual assault are often very reluctant to report the alleged offence because of the humiliation they may feel and, like their female counterparts, exposure to public scrutiny. All these factors described should be borne in mind when considering the figures provided for the years 1997–2001 in Table 6.1.

Although the majority of sexual offences are committed by males, there would appear to have been an increasing trend for women to be involved in sexual crimes in recent years. In a small-scale study of the criminal statistics for a 10-year period ending in 1984, O'Connor (1987) indicated that 0.95 per cent of all sexual offences were committed by women.

He made a detailed study of 19 women convicted of indecency and 62 convicted of other sexual offences. Within the group he found a high incidence of psychopathology. A sizeable proportion were convicted of gross indecency and sexual assaults on children or (in the company of male assailants) aiding and abetting such assaults. An increase in the numbers of women sentenced to terms of imprisonment – for a variety of offences – has been noted in recent years (see Deakin and Spencer 2003). The psychosocial and legal implications of a general rise in female offending is the subject of an interesting special issue of the *International Journal of Law and Psychiatry* (Volume 26: 5, September/October 2003).

## Sexual offences

Having briefly considered the size of the problem, I now go on to examine certain sexual offences in detail. There are obvious problems in singling out specific categories. For example, an offender not infrequently commits more than one type of sexual offence (or a non-sexual offence for that matter); some of the offence categories will therefore inevitably overlap. For example, a rape may end in homicide, either because the killing was planned as part of, or a sequel to, the rape, or the victim may have died as a result of the attack. Death may also have resulted in the assailant's wish to silence the victim to avoid subsequent identification. As we saw in the last chapter, the borderline between sexual and violent offences is a debatable one. It is therefore very important to emphasize that *every case is different* and great care needs to be taken before reaching any generalized conclusions. Despite this caveat, it seems helpful to divide the categories of sexual offences in a fairly crude way. I deal first of all with *indecent exposure*; second, with *sexual offences against children* (paedophilia) and *consanguineous sex* (incest). I include incest with more general sexual offences against children because incestuous behaviour (particularly with young victims) may be regarded as a highly specific form of serious sexual assault. Third, I deal with *rape*, and fourth, with certain aspects of *sexual homicide* and other more rare sexual offences such as *bestiality* and *necrophilia*.

### Indecent exposure

Indecent exposure would appear to be the commonest of all sexual offences, although the actual number of prosecutions is but a minute proportion of its actual incidence. This is because many offences are never reported and even when prosecutions take place the number of other offences of exposure that a defendant may ask to be taken into consideration (TIC) is unlikely to be a true record of the actual number of acts of exposure committed. It is almost exclusively a male offence, although a few women will indulge in such behaviour. Recent changes in the law will, in future, make the offence non-gender specific. Throughout history, the display and emphatic presentation of the male genitalia have been commonly recorded and demonstrated – the use of the "codpiece" being a useful example. Chaucer, in his bawdy *Miller's Tale* has one of the characters putting his "ers" (backside) out of the window; and the practices of "mooning" (exposing the male buttocks out of cars) and "streaking" by both sexes have become fairly commonplace. Until relatively recently, the male form of the offence was dealt with under the somewhat antiquated provisions of the Vagrancy Act of 1834 (as amended by the Criminal Justice Act 1925, Section 42). The offence was dealt with summarily, but repeated offenders could be remitted to the Quarter Sessions (now the Crown Court) for greater punishment as incorrigible rogues. Section 66 of the Sexual Act 2003 now provides that:

(1) A person commits an offence if –
  (a) he intentionally exposes his genitals, and
  (b) he intends that someone will see them and be caused alarm or distress.
(2) A person found guilty of an offence under this section is liable –
  (a) on summary conviction, to a term of imprisonment not exceeding six months or a fine not exceeding the statutory maximum or both
  (b) on conviction on indictment, to imprisonment for a term not exceeding two years.

It is of interest to note here that Section 67 of the Act also creates the new offence of voyeurism ("Peeping Tom"), as follows. A person commits an offence if:

(a) for the purpose of obtaining sexual gratification, he observed another person doing a private act, and
(b) he knows that the other person does not consent to being observed for his sexual gratification. A person also commits an offence if he installs or operates equipment (such as a camera for example) or constructs or adapts a structure or part of a structure with the intention of enabling himself or another person to commit an offence under Section 1 of Section 67 of the Act.[1]

The penalties that can be imposed are the same as for indecent exposure.

## Clinical aspects

Indecent exposure can be regarded as an illegal form of exhibitionism. This latter term is, as Gayford reminds us, somewhat ambiguous since clinically it covers many aspects of exhibitionistic behaviour. Various other clinical terms have been suggested such as sexual exhibitionism, or male genital exhibitionism, thus emphasizing the genital element involved (Gayford 1981). It is unwise to treat the offence behaviour lightly; some exposers are likely to go on to commit more serious sexual contact offences; in the case of the latter exposers, the behaviour may be aggressive, exposing to the victims where there is little chance of "escape", making angry gestures and masturbating in front of them. (For further discussion see MacPherson 2003; Sugarman et al. 1994.) Most victims tend to be adult females and children of either sex and the perpetrators youngish males. Gittleson et al. surveyed 100 nurses: of their sample, 44 of the subjects had been the female victims of exposure, one-third of these on two or more occasions. One-third of all incidents had not been reported to anyone. Interestingly, in over one-fifth of the episodes "the reaction of family and friends in whom the victim confided had been more distressing to the victim than the episode itself" (Gittleson et al. 1978: 61) (see later discussion of paedophilia). A slightly later study in the USA of a group of female college students largely confirmed the findings of the Gittleson study (Cox and McMahon 1978). In a recent study carried out by a former post-graduate student of mine, 72 women were surveyed. The incidence of exposure was fairly similar to the two earlier studies already quoted. However, the survey revealed that the victims found the experience a traumatic one and it had greatly increased their more general fear of sexual crime. They also considered that the police and men in general tended to "trivialise" the offence (Riordan 1999; see also Bennetto 1995). In his book about Jeffrey Dahmer, Masters comments on the former's repeated acts of indecent exposure and suggests that had these activities been acted on at an earlier stage Dahmer's career as a serial killer *might* have been halted. He also suggested that, for Dahmer, indecent exposure represented "wish for sensuality without involvement" (Masters 1993: 71).

Various attempt have been made to classify the behaviour and personality types of indecent exposers (see, for example, Gayford 1981, 1997; MacDonald 1973; Rooth 1975; Yap et al. 2002). The following classification, which readers may find helpful, is my own synthesis of some of those just quoted. It makes no claims to originality:

1   The *inhibited* (and in some cases *latently homosexual*) *young man* who struggles against his impulses to expose himself. He usually exposes with a flaccid (unerect) penis and feels anxious about his behaviour. When such behaviour occurs in adolescence against a family background of prudery or reticence in discussing sexual matters, sex education and simple supportive counselling may be helpful.

2   *Situational exposure.* Here the exposure may take place against a background of marital or other stress (such as the wife or partner's unavailability or due to pregnancy). Simple counselling may also be helpful in such cases.

3    The less inhibited type described earlier who exposes with an erect penis and who may accompany his exposure with masturbation and aggressive and sexually explicit language. Intervention in such cases *may* help to prevent a progression to more serious sex offending. For this reason, it is very important for professional workers to ascertain the circumstances of the exposure *in as much detail as possible* (see, for example, MacPherson 2003; Sugarman et al. 1994).

4    Exposure occurring in a setting of clear mental illness, such as depression, hypomania, schizophrenia or dementia. In such cases, medical intervention aimed at alleviating the illness may bring about a subsequent cessation of the behaviour.

5    Exposure committed by those with moderate to severe learning difficulties. In such cases, the exposure is most likely to be due to lack of social skills and against a background of mounting need for sexual expression. Counselling in such cases can also be helpful. (It is a mistake to assume that even quite severely mentally impaired people cannot be helped by counselling, provided it is tailored to their particular levels of need and understanding.)

6    Cases in which the exposure is facilitated by substance abuse (such as alcohol) reactive depression or simple loneliness.

7    A group of exposers who may be regarded as true "exhibitionists"; these individuals practice exposure as the sole means of obtaining sexual release.

This classification will, it is hoped, provide some clues to aetiology. Additional explanations include a need to assert a wavering or undeveloped masculinity. In some cases (as in point 3) there may be a need to assert power over, to insult or to shock women. The exposure may be a suppressed desire to commit a seriously violent sexual contact offence such as rape. Treatment (best seen as management) has already been briefly touched on. Counselling of various types and intensity may be helpful, although some cases are of such long-standing severity that they have an "addictive" quality and are very resistant to treatment in the sense of "cure". As with all sexual offenders, the communication of genuine interest and warm concern on the part of the counsellor and a degree of "unshockability" are more important than the school of thought or mode of practice espoused. Treatment by whatever mode should have as its aim the facilitation of the offender in managing his life in such a way that temptation and possible relapse are avoided.

### Sexual assaults on children (child molestation, paedophilia)

In the following discussion I am concerned predominantly with sexual assaults on children outside the family (other than incest, which I deal with separately). Child sexual abuse within the family is a topic in its own right and space constraints preclude its treatment here. However, it is important to emphasize that a number of the characteristics shown by those who sexually abuse children outside the family are very similar to those who do so within it. For example, some men who commit incestuous acts with their offspring have a number of characteristics and convictions for sexually assaulting children outside the family.

Sexual offences against children have been widely prevalent throughout history and it also seems to be the case that sexual assaults on children both within and outside the family have been, and are, much more common than is often supposed. It appears that Freud had to revise his original theory of the neuroses. This was based on his view that some neurotic conditions in his female patients had their origins in sexual abuse within their families. Fear of the opprobrium that such a view might fall on him for stating this openly, it has been suggested that he then revised his theory to suggest that the events unearthed during psychoanalysis were of "hysterical" and not factual origin (Masson 1985).

Sexual molesters of children span the social spectrum; for example from the notorious Marshal of France, Gilles de Rais (colleague of Joan of Arc), to the most lowly itinerant. Contrary to public opinion, most paedophilic activity is carried out by those placed in positions of trust towards children – for example parents, friends, teachers, clergy, social workers, doctors and nurses. In clinical terms, the *Diagnostic and Statistical Manual of Mental Disorders* (APA 1994) gives the following criteria for paedophilia:

A.  Over a period of at least six months, recurrent, intense sexually arous-ing fantasies, sexual urges, or behaviours involving sexual activity with a prepubescent child *or* children (*generally* age 13 years or younger).
B.  The fantasies, sexual urges or behaviour cause clinically significant distress or impairment in social, occupational, or other important areas of functioning.
C.  The person is at least age 16 years and at least 5 years older than the child or children in Criterion A.

(p. 528; emphasis added)

Assessors are also asked to specify if the person is:

sexually attracted to males
sexually attracted to females
sexually attracted to both.

Furthermore, if limited to incest and attracted *only* to children (exclusive type).

In a very thoughtful paper, West (1992) places the problem in perspective. He indicates that media activity has "hyped up" fears about sexual abuse of children and although there is a very small number of highly dangerous predatory paedophiles, these constitute a very small proportion of the total picture. He sums up the position in the following fashion:

> A punitive socio-legal policy towards sexual offenders against minors has been driven by public demand. The perception of an appallingly high incidence of serious abuse by incorrigible men has been encouraged by press sensationalism, but criminal statistics and recidivist studies fail to confirm either an escalation of sex crimes against minors or the inevitability of recidivism.

(See also Soothill et al. 2002; Soothill et al. 2004.)
West goes on to make the very important point that:

> Exaggerated perception of risk produces undue restrictions on children's freedom and on their interactions with teachers and other adults. Assumptions of incorrigibility impede the rehabilitation of offenders through vigilantism, stigmatization and barriers to employment. This amplifies deviance and does not protect children.
>                 (West 2000: 51; see also Silverman and Wilson 2002;
>                                             notably Chapter 2)[2]

West's remarks bring a sense of balance to our consideration of the problem. Bearing these in mind, we can now refer to the possible effect of such abuse in *individual* cases. There is evidence to suggest that the physical and emotional trauma that is caused as a result of sudden, unexpected or coercive sexual relationships with children may be considerable. (Dare 1993; Lincoln 2001; Mullen 1990; Spataro et al. 2004.) The following would seem to be the most significant determinants of trauma:

(a)  the victim's previous and current social and psychological environment
(b)  the anxiety engendered by being forced to keep a "guilty secret" (particularly in incest cases)
(c)  the opportunities, or lack of them, for offloading this guilt
(d)  the nature of the pre-existing or current relationship with the assailant or the avenues of escape from it, if any
(e)  the reactions of those having care of the victim; these reactions are arguably more important in determining later guilt or trauma than any of the foregoing factors.

(See also West 2000: 522–5.)

It is important to take a cautious approach to the classification of paedophiles since "pigeon-holing" individuals is seldom a very satisfactory aid to understanding. However, it is recognized that there may be some distinctions to be made between *homosexual* and *heterosexual* paedophiles, although such individuals may assault victims of both sexes. Bluglass (1982) suggests that *homosexual paedophiles* are more likely to have had past involvement with children, to prefer them as sexual partners and to show deviant patterns of sexual arousal. *Heterosexual* paedophiles are somewhat more likely to be situationally motivated, normally to prefer adult women, and to seek out a child only at times of social and environmental stress. A somewhat crude (and perhaps oversimplified) form of classification is to divide paedophiles into (a) *youthful* and (b) *adult* offenders. Youthful offenders may be further divided into two rough sub-categories:

1   inadequate adolescents who may bribe young children into engaging in deviant sexual practices
2   rather more dangerous adolescent offenders who have a history of being sexually abused themselves and who have shown sexually inappropriate behaviour from an early age (see Bagley 1992). They may progress to becoming highly sexually deviant adults (see Pithers et al. 2002).

Adult paedophiles may be divided roughly into:

1   Middle-aged heterosexual paedophiles, socially isolated and incompetent; they may seek the company of children for comfort.
2   Predominantly homosexual paedophiles, whose sexual preferences are by no means dulled by age, even though their sexual capacity may be. *It is very unwise to think that as such individuals become older that they necessarily become less dangerous.* In fact, they may become more easily frustrated and feel less in command (powerful). Any feeling that their young victims (or would-be victims) find them no longer attractive and who rebuff their overtures, may serve to remind them of their waning "powers". In aggressive frustration, they may resort to violent means to achieve their ends. However, it is true to say that not all older paedophiles behave in this fashion. Clark and Mezey (1997) describe a group of 13 child sex abusers *over the age of 65*. They found them to be similar in most respects to sex offenders against children in other age groups, but that they differed in being of higher socio-economic status and more stable backgrounds. They suggest, in respect of offenders of this age and background, that the courts tended to seek non-custodial disposals, viewing them as *less risky*. The authors also suggest that courts were hesitant to use imprisonment because of the physical frailty of some offenders in this age group.
3   Paedophiles of impaired intellect. Social ineptitude and a lack of "moral" sense may contribute to their offending.

4   A group that can be described as multi-anti-social. These men are lacking in general social conformity and may have convictions for non-sexual offences.

5   Paedophiles who are exclusively homosexual and who exert a powerful and coercive influence over their victims. They sometimes see themselves as the "protectors" of disadvantaged youths and are highly resistant to treatment measures.

Finally, it is important to attempt to distinguish between those who use force as a means of gaining cooperation in the act and those offenders for whom the infliction of pain and terror is an end in itself (see also later discussion of rapists). It is also very important to note that recidivism may occur over very long periods of time; the longer the timescale the greater the rise of further offending (see Cann et al. 2004).

*Management*

Although it is a recurring truism that every case will be different, it is possible to make some observations about management that have a general applicability. In my view, the first and perhaps most important point to make is that one should not talk of "curing" sexual offenders. This is because most available evidence supports the view that sexual preferences are usually laid down very early in life and are resistant to change. The problem is exacerbated because we have, as yet, only a hazy picture of the respective contributions made by biological, genetic and wider familial and environmental influences to sexual conduct. It is more realistic to talk about "management" or attitude change and prevention of relapse. This may be facilitated by intensive individual or group psychotherapy of different schools, by powerful behavioural techniques of one kind or another that aim to produce gradual change in sexual orientation or by limited and carefully controlled use of chemotherapeutic methods. Whatever technique is used, it is best to avoid thinking of "cure" and to concentrate on helping sex offenders make more satisfactory adjustments to their behaviour and its consequences. No *single* method of management is likely to be successful; it is best to espouse a multi-method approach (for example, judicious use of chemotherapy is more successful when allied to counselling). It is best not to think globally about sexual offence behaviour, but to try to break the behaviour down into manageable segments and typologies. But perhaps of most importance is the need to remember that all persistent sex offenders (and some less persistent ones) are *highly reluctant to admit to their role in sexual offending and will persistently use evasion and denial.*[3]

This phenomenon of denial is vital in dealing with sex offenders. In an important paper, Mezey et al. (1991) suggest that there are six aspects of denial: (1) denial of the act itself; (2) denial of the child as a person; (3) denial of the child as a victim; (4) denial of adult responsibility; (5) denial of consequences for the child; and (6) denial of consequences for the offender. Denial will, of course, hold a very prominent place in the mind of the sexual offender sentenced to imprisonment; fear of reprisal from fellow inmates may be uppermost in mind. Attempts have been made to introduce special "treatment" programmes in some prisons and limited success has been reported (see Beech et al. 1998; Friendship et al. 2002; West 2002). Community treatment programmes implemented by the probation service have met with a small but encouraging degree of success. See, for example, Hedderman and Sugg (1996). For additional information on the use of and accreditation of prison/probation management programmes, see Rex and Bottoms (2003). One method that has been used to supplement an offender's own account of his sexual preferences and practices is that of *phallometric assessment*. This involves the measurement of erectile tumescence by a gauge attached to the penis. The offender is then shown a variety of arousing situations by means of videos or audiotapes and the degree to which he continues to be aroused when aversive stimuli are introduced or suggested can thus be measured. Such testing is by no means foolproof, since it has been shown that offenders can "fake" their responses. However, such measures may prove useful as adjuncts to reliance on self-reports and the observations of penal and mental health professionals. (For a review of the "state of the art", see Launay 1994, 1999; for the use of polygraphy ("lie detection") in the management of sex offenders, see Grubin 2002.)

### Incest

Incest (consanguineous sexual relationships) is the sexual crime that provokes probably the most emotive reactions. Taboos and injunctions against it have existed since time immemorial and the Book of Leviticus contains the injunction that "no man shall approach a blood relation for intercourse" (Chapter 18, v. 6). However, history reveals that there have been notable exceptions; for example, in the cultures of ancient Egypt and Greece. Mythology and literature are replete with allusions to incestuous conduct and to incestuous themes, for example, in *Hamlet*, *The Duchess of Malfi*, *Wuthering Heights* and Poe's *Fall of the House of Usher*; and, more recently, in Iris Murdoch's *A Severed Head* and *The Cement Garden* by Ian McEwan.

There are a number of reasons for the strict injunctions against consanguineous conduct. First, there are the religious injunctions already referred to. Second, there appears to be a deeply held and primitive horror of consanguineous relationships between parents and their offspring. Third, Freud's view in his work *Totem and Taboo* (1960), in which he suggested that in primitive societies the incest taboo was erected to preserve the power of the paternal tyrant in order that he might prevent the younger males from banding together to deprive him of his sexual rights over the females. Fourth, taboos are said to be powerful because of the serious role confusion that can occur when close kin have sexual relationship. Fifth, there is the view that incestuous relationships may produce a higher incidence of genetic weakness than those found in non-incestuous unions.

It should be noted that it is probably the combination of poor ante-natal and post-natal care, poor nurturing, adverse social environment *and* the incestuous relationships that occur in socially dysfunctional families that produce these results and not the effects of genetic transmission alone. It may surprise readers to learn that incest did not become a criminal offence until 1908 and then only after two failed attempts in parliament (Bluglass 1979). Hitherto, it had been dealt with by the ecclesiastical courts. The Act of 1908 (repealed and re-enacted in the Sexual Offences Act 1956) has now been superseded by the Sexual Offences Act 2003. Under Section 27 of the Act consanguineous relationships are now described as being that of parent, step-parent, grandparent, brother, sister, half-brother, half-sister, aunt, cousin or uncle and foster parent. Thus the new Act broadens the relationships that were contained in earlier legislation and specifically includes step-relationships and foster relationships. The maximum penalty on indictment is 14 years' imprisonment; on summary conviction a sentence of 6 months' imprisonment or a fine not exceeding the statutory maximum, or both. Reference to Table 6.1 indicates that cases of incest are not prosecuted frequently. Generally, a veil of secrecy is preserved within the family. Sometimes the case may only come to light due to pregnancy, because of an attempt at blackmail, through the investigation of some non-related alleged criminal conduct or as a result of a confession by one of the parties. The most outstanding characteristics in the backgrounds in a large proportion of incestuous families are those of social and emotional dysfunction. The following is a somewhat simplified classification of the conditions that obtain in incestuous families. My previous cautionary comments concerning category overlap are also relevant in incest cases:

1   Incest occurring in large, overcrowded families, where the participants almost slip into an incestuous pattern of behaviour. Sibling incest may be a feature of such cases (see, for example, Batten 1983; Gibbens et al. 1978).
2   Very rarely, incestuous relationships develop because of mental impairment or psychotic illness in either or both parties.
3   Cases where the wife (or partner) is absent through death or separation and where the daughter(s) may take over the wife's or partner's role. It may also occur in cases where she is still physically present but where she has abrogated her sexual role. In a few cases, she is not only aware of what is occurring, but is prepared to collude in the practice.

4    Cases in which the father is a dominating and coercive individual who uses threats and/or violence to get his way in the full knowledge that such behaviour is wrong. Such men may have histories of serious alcohol abuse and have convictions for non-sexual offences.

5    Rare instances of the parties not knowing that they are in a consanguineous relationship. For example, a brother and sister who have been separated from each other very early in life, may meet much later and *unknowingly* enter into a sexual relationship. Prior to the 2003 Act, the position seemed somewhat ambiguous. However, Section 28 appears to preclude any criminal proceedings in such instances.

The emotive nature of incestuous behaviour means that professionals have to come to terms with their own incest anxieties and fears. On the whole, the courts take a serious view of incest committed by adult males with their female children; the abhorrence felt for the offence may, to some extent, be vitiated by removing its name from statute since the behaviour is now subsumed under the title of *familial child sex offences*. This *may* have the helpful effect of enabling all concerned to see the offence for what it is – an offence connected with adverse family attitudes and living conditions, calling for social and other intervention rather than punitive wrath borne of irrational feelings. In addition, the use of the term incest meant that we linked together all its variants and treated all cases alike (see Studer et al. 2000). Courts are now being encouraged to take a more flexible approach to sentencing and to make distinctions between cases of severity and those of a less serious nature. In the latter cases, the use of immediate custody may serve to make matters worse. The family will not be helped by further breakdown and the victim may harbour feelings of guilt for having informed the authorities (for, contrary to common belief, some daughters remain fond of their abusive parent). Supervision of the offender with a prohibition placed on immediate contact may be more effective than immediate removal from the family home. However, in some cases of long-term coercive and sometimes violent forms of incestuous abuse of several children, imprisonment may be the only option. A dispassionate view of the problem is still needed. Over 20 years ago Batten wrote: "The incestuous child is readily placed in the role of victim and all the pressures from society and the legal system reinforce this. However, the child is still left with the break-up of the family and a distrust of adults. What is really needed is care and support" (Batten 1983: 252).

### Rape on females

In *Jonathan Wild* (1743, Book III, Chapter 7), Henry Fielding says this: "He, in a few minutes ravished this fair creature, or at least would have ravished her, if she had not, by a timely compliance, prevented him."

Sadly, some women do not manage to avoid the seriously assaultative and predatory attention of males as described by Fielding. The quotation also demonstrates some of the difficulties and ambiguities surrounding consent and compliance that have made convictions for rape problematic. However, recent court decisions have, belatedly, tended to support the view that when a woman says "no" she means it; this has not always been the case. Prosecutions for rape and other sexual assault cases have also been difficult because of the very small number of cases in which false accusations have been proved.

Reference to Table 6.1 indicates that rape cases constitute a fairly sizeable proportion of serious sexual assaults. In recent times there has also been evidence to suggest that the circumstances in which rape has been carried out have been becoming more violent. Lloyd and Walmsley described three main trends. First, a slight increase in the number of offences involving the use of excessive violence; second, an increase in sexual acts in addition to the rape (for example, anal and/or oral sex); third, an increase in the length of time that victims were under the coercion of the offenders (Lloyd and Walmsley 1989; see also Lloyd 1991). The official (statistical) classification of a sexual offence may not give an accurate indication of its severity. For example, there are many gradations of rape and indecent assault, from fairly minor (but perhaps no less traumatic) attempts at rape to serious indecent assaults that may just fall short of it. The belief on the part of certain males that some women may enjoy the experience of being sexually subdued fails entirely to recognize the terror and distress endured by women in such an experience. In recent years, women have been somewhat more willing to report rape to the authorities, but progress in this area is still slow. The reasons are not hard to discern. A woman may be understandably reluctant to go through the ordeal of a searching medical examination; some women have described a degree of clumsiness and lack of sensitivity by inexperienced examiners in the past. Some may be reluctant to report the behaviour to their partners, other family members or friends; this may result in their carrying a quite unnecessary burden of guilt and added torment. The physical consequences of rape, apart from any vaginal, anal, or other injury that may have been caused, are very important. The victims may have become pregnant, have contracted a sexually transmitted disease such as syphilis or gonorrhoea, HIV infection or AIDS. These added traumas will serve to compound their distress. Many women feel so defiled by the experience that they may go to extreme lengths to "cleanse" themselves, for example repeatedly scrubbing their genitalia with powerful disinfectants. In recent years we have begun to recognize the real trauma involved for rape victims and the need for rape counselling, sometimes over prolonged periods. Much of the good work in this area has been promoted by the women's movement and the introduction of rape crisis centres countrywide. However, much more needs to be done, since there are still those who take a less than sensitive view of females' experience of rape (for example, making comments such as "she must have asked for it" or "given out the wrong signals").

## Legal aspects

It is only in fairly recent times that the ingredients of the offence of rape have been afforded full definition, the first *statutory* reference to these ingredients being in the Sexual Offences Act of 1956. Increasing concerns about consent were reflected in the Sexual Offences (Amendment) Act of 1976 and the current legal position is now contained in the Sexual Offences Act of 2003. Section 1 of the Act now defines rape in the following terms: "(1) A person (A) commits an offence if – (a) he intentionally penetrates the vagina, anus or mouth of another person (B) with his penis, (b) B does not consent to the penetrations, and (c) A does not reasonably believe that B consents." Subsection (2) of the Act leaves it to the courts to determine the issues of reasonable belief as follows: "Whether a belief is reasonable is to be determined having regard to all the circumstances, including any steps A has taken to ascertain whether B consents." Sections 74–77 provide more details concerning the determination of consent. Despite these specific provisions there will doubtless be continuing debates in court as to whether consent was, or was not, freely given. It should also be noted here that the sections of the Act are not gender specific, so that male rape is included within the definition, having first been defined as a specific offence in the Criminal Justice and Public Order Act of 1994 (see later discussion of male rape). In a guideline judgement given on 9 December 2002 the Court of Appeal provided revised guidelines for sentencing in rape cases (see Stone 2003c). The maximum sentence for rape remains life imprisonment.

## Classification

There have been a number of studies of what might loosely be described as the epidemiology of rape, an early study carried out by Amir (1971) being one of the most comprehensive. Amir found that, contrary to common belief, about one-third of the victims had been in previous contact with their assailants. Much of Amir's early work has been confirmed by more recent studies, such as those by Muir and Macleod (2003) and Myhill and Allen (2002). In many cases, the rape had been planned and some half of the victims had failed to resist their attackers (a hardly surprising finding given the terror that such attacks will induce). Recent findings also indicate that over fairly long periods of time (in one study six years) rapists and other serious sexual offenders were relatively infrequently reconvicted, in the region of less than 10 per cent; however those who *were* reconvicted, committed very serious crimes (Hood et al. 2002).

The arbitrary nature of *classification* must again be acknowledged. In particular, in attempting any form of classification, problems arise because we are sometimes describing the offence by the nature of the behaviour displayed (for example, aggressive or over-inhibited), sometimes by the choice of victim (for example, children), and sometimes by the presence of other features such as mental disorder (disturbance) (see for example, Fisher and Mair 1998; Grubin and Kennedy 1991). If, for a moment, we disregard those rapes that arise out of allegedly mistaken consent, we find that key features underlying, or associated with most rapes, are anger, a desire to control and aggression. As suggested in Chapter 5, in most cases female rape seems best regarded as a crime of extreme personal violence rather than as an offence aimed at achieving sexual satisfaction per se (see Löbmann et al. 2003). For this reason, a classification proposed some 20 odd years ago by Groth and Hobson (1983) seems a useful starting point. Their typology suggests three clear-cut but overlapping classes of rape:

1  *Anger rape* – motivated by feeling "put down" or by retribution for perceived wrongs.
2  *Power rape* – engaged in as a means of denying deep feelings of inadequacy and insecurity.
3  *Sadistic rape* – victims are usually complete strangers; they may be subjected to torture, bondage and other deviant sexual practices.

Taking Groth and Hobson's classification a little further, the following slightly more detailed typology is proposed:

1  The sexually virile young man, out for what he can get, whose exploitative hedonism is not counterbalanced by finer scruples or concern – the opportunistic rapist. Perhaps we should include here the husband who rapes his wife, although its inclusion here is not altogether satisfactory.
2  The more inhibited, shy young man, who is trying to overcome his feelings of sexual inferiority. He may misinterpret the responses of his victim and not register that "no" means "no". Some such rapists may be latently homosexual and their behaviour could be seen as a defence against their homosexuality. (See also my classification of indecent exposers.)
3  The sexually violent and aggressive. Such offenders have records of other forms of violence, alcohol often plays a large part in narcoticizing inhibition and they may hold the mistaken belief that it may improve their performance; the reverse is, of course, the case, as the porter in *Macbeth* demonstrated so graphically.
4  A group who are potentially highly dangerous, in that they need to gain reassurance by a show of force. West et al. studied a group of

incarcerated rapists who were undergoing group psychotherapy. One of the main features that emerged was that these men suffered severe feelings of inferiority concerning their masculinity (West et al. 1978). Confirmation for this finding may be found in later work by Perkins (1991). This group includes those who set out to defile and denigrate their victims, forcing them to participate in acts of vaginal, anal and oral sex. Many of these men appear to be women haters and one or two may eventually commit sadistic sexual murder (see later).

5   A subgroup of category (4). These men, also potentially highly dangerous, have psychopathic tendencies, seem to have insatiable sexual appetites and may need the resistance of their victims to arouse their potency. Such offenders may obtain sexual pleasure from their sadistic activities (true sadists).

6   Rapists who are found to be suffering from a definable form of mental disorder such as psychosis or mental impairment. Such cases are comparatively rare. Smith and Taylor (1999) suggest that "when a man with schizophrenia commits a serious sex offence the illness is, more commonly than not, relevant to the offence even though a direct symptom relationship may be relatively unusual" (p. 233).

7   A predominantly young group, who rape in groups or packs ("gang bangs"). They are likely to have previous convictions for violence and other offences. They may engage in deviant sexual practices with their victims and subject them to forms of defilement, such as urinating on them. Unlike some of the other typologies presented, they are not, in the main, characterized by gross personal psychopathology.

*Management*

Much of what has been said earlier about other forms of sexual offending can be applied to cases of female rape. The formulation of some kind of typology based on an in-depth assessment will afford clues as to the most appropriate form of management. Brief counselling and training in sexual and social skills may be of help with the first two groups. Those in group (3) may respond to measures aimed at improving their lifestyles and in helping them with their drinking problems. Those in groups (4) and (5) are much harder to manage and may need long-term incarceration in order that psychotherapeutic treatment programmes may take effect. Some success with programmes designed to develop social competence and to modify deviant sexual preferences by various means has been reported in custodial settings (Beech et al. 1998; Friendship et al. 2002; Hedderman and Sugg 1996). The use of anti-androgen medication linked with counselling has already been referred to in the discussion of paedophilia. Those in group (7) may outgrow their unpleasant proclivities, but they need to be removed from circulation for a time, for the protection of society, for purposes of retribution and deterrence and to allow their consciences to develop. No *single* form of management is likely to be effective. It is highly dangerous to espouse with Messianic enthusiasm any one theory or treatment model. A multidisciplinary approach, based on a full assessment of the personal and situational factors in the rapist's life is essential.

Having said this, it is important to emphasize that almost without exception, rape offenders will be sentenced to immediate imprisonment, sometimes for long periods. During such time they may be afforded the opportunity to participate in sexual offending treatment programmes of one kind or another. Such approaches seem to have met with a moderate degree of success, but long-term follow-up and supervision are essential in these cases. This is because recent research tends to show that in the *long term*, re-offending is more common than was once thought to be the case.

## Male rape

As already indicated, male rape is now designated as a specific offence, having parity with female rape. As with female victims, males may be very reluctant to disclose the attack to family, friend or professional helpers. The trauma, both physical and mental, is no less severe than those suffered by their female counterparts. (For accounts see, for example, Huckle 1995; King et al. 2002.) For a recent comprehensive review of male rape in prisons see Knowles (1999) and Banbury 2004.

## Bestiality (zoophilia)

In early modern England, those committing bestiality were liable to the death penalty, as Gayford indicates "often for the animal as well as the human" (1997: 313). Until very recently, the offence of bestiality was dealt with under the Sexual Offences Act 1956, and those convicted could be awarded a life sentence. It is now dealt with under Section 69 of the Sexual Offences Act 2003 as "intercourse with an animal": "A person commits an offence if – (a) he intentionally performs an act of penetration with his penis, (b) what is penetrated is the vagina or anus of a living animal, and (c) he knows that, or is reckless as to whether, that is what is penetrated." On summary conviction, an offender can be sentenced to a term of imprisonment not exceeding 6 months or a fine not exceeding the statutory maximum or both. On conviction on indictment, to a term of imprisonment not exceeding 2 years. Fudge (2000), in a study of bestiality in the sixteenth century, suggests that it was only then that it became a heavily proscribed and punished form of behaviour. She surmises that this was due to concerns about the pollution of the human species and what might best be described as cross-mating between animals and humans. Having studied early records of the behaviour she provides descriptions of sex with a variety of farm and other animals.

The clinical literature on the topic is somewhat sparse and prosecutions rare. However, it is reasonable to assume that its occurrence is probably more common than is generally believed. Duffield et al. (1998) describe and discuss the cases of seven young patients referred to an adolescent psychiatric service dealing with sex abusers. On the basis of their own study and the work of others, they concluded that bestiality was frequently accompanied by other paraphilias (disorders of sexual preference). In summary, the behaviour is most likely to occur mainly in males who may be mentally disturbed or impaired, be socially isolated, have difficulties in making relationships and showing other forms of sexually deviant behaviour. Although the behaviour is now dealt with under the 2003 Act, many people maintain that it could more appropriately have been dealt with under the legislation covering cruelty to animals. However, such a view was not favoured by the Criminal Law Revision Committee. They considered that abolishing the offence would not meet with public approval and legally proscribing it would enable offenders to be afforded treatment under mental health legislation. Against this, one could put forward the view that if the behaviour was dealt with under the cruelty to animals legislation, offenders could still be afforded mental health treatment if this were to be deemed appropriate.

### Necrophilia

Necrophilia, sexual excitement aroused by the dead, or performed with cadavers (corpses) has a long history. Examples may be found in ancient Egyptian records where it is recorded that embalmers were sometimes prone to interfere sexually with the corpses they were preserving. In order to prevent this, an edict was handed down ordering that the bodies should be in a state of putrefaction before embalming activities started. Gayford (1997) suggests that necrophilia can be clinically subdivided in three ways. *Pseudonecrophilia* derives from a psychoanalytic notion of fascination with, or fantasy involving, the dead. *Necrophilous character* consists of "a passionate attraction to all that is dead or decaying" (p. 312). Necrophilia has also been associated with vampiristic and cannibalistic activity in the form of necrophagy (see Hucker 1990; Prins 1990). In *symbolic necrophilia*, specially designated brothels cater for those who wish to indulge their predilections for substitute necrophilic activity. Here, a prostitute plays the part of a corpse, "complete with shroud and coffin". It will be recalled that Nilsen (see Chapter 1) indulged in necrophilic activity. For obvious reasons, prosecutions are rare and the true incidence of necrophilic activity is not known. Certain occupations may facilitate indulgence in the practice, for example, those who work in mortuaries and in undertaking. Until the passing of the Sexual Offences Act 2003, there was no statutory basis for prosecutions for interference (sexual or otherwise) with corpses. In rare instances, prosecutions might be brought for criminal damage (to graves, coffins etc.) or "outrages on public decency". The new Act now makes specific provision, as follows.

Section 70 provides for *sexual penetration of a corpse*. (1) A person commits an offence if – (a) he intentionally performs an act of penetration with part of his body or anything else, (b) what is penetrated is a part of the body of a dead person, (c) knows that, or is reckless as to whether, that which is penetrated, and (d) the penetration is sexual. A person found guilty of the offence is liable (a) on summary conviction to imprisonment for a term not exceeding 6 months, or a fine not exceeding the statutory maximum, or both, (b) on conviction on indictment, to a term of imprisonment not exceeding 2 years.[4]

### Sexual murder

If we exclude the *crime passionelle* and murder committed as a result of sexual jealousy, sexual murder is, fortunately, a rare event. As noted elsewhere, it is sometimes difficult to determine whether a killing has occurred as a result of the pursuit of sadistic pleasure, as a means of keeping the victim quiet (unable to give evidence) or as a result of an unintentional act of violence that has become lethal during some form of sexual activity; for example, the occurrence of manual strangulation during some forms of anal intercourse; and incidents have been described in which death has occurred in the course of fellatio due to aspiration of ejaculate or from impaction of the penis in the hypopharynx (Rupp 1970).

Other possible victims include indiscriminate and "cruising" homosexuals who may be at risk from "queer bashers"; and sometimes a homosexual "overture" towards the wrong person may result in a murder. Those engaged in both male and female prostitution may also be at considerable risk from those seeking deviant practices (see West 1992). Grubin, in a paper on *sexual murder*, suggests that the incidence of sexual murder of women is unknown and quotes criminal statistics which indicate that about one-third of female homicide victims are killed by their spouses (Grubin 1994: 624). He makes the important point that statistics of the true incidence of sexual murder are difficult to obtain, both in the UK and North America. This is because the offence is classified as homicide and not as a sexual offence. The motivation for sexual murder may be very complex. MacCulloch et al. (1983) pointed out in their study of 13 sadistic offenders in a British high-security hospital (not all of them killers) that fantasy played a very important part in the motivation and the preparation leading up to the eventual offence (see also Grubin 1997). In an often quoted paper Brittain (1970) (who was qualified as a forensic pathologist and psychiatrist) provided a clinical composite picture of the sadistic sexual killer. It is important to emphasize that Brittain suggested a *composite* picture and that we should not expect to find all the many features he described in any *single* case (see also Grubin 1994). I have merely selected a few of them for purposes of demonstrating the diversity of psychopathological factors. (For a useful critique of Brittain's views, see MacCulloch et al. 2000.)

Brittain suggests that such killers are often withdrawn, introverted, over-controlled, timid and prudish; for example, taking offence at "dirty jokes". The killer is likely to be over 30 and come from any occupational status, but an unusual number seem to have been employed as butchers or as workers in abattoirs. They often seem to be remarkably ambivalent towards their mothers and their personality profiles appear to show a mass of contradictions with many unresolved psychological conflicts. Their mothers tend to be gentle, overindulgent, but not particularly maternal. Fathers are notably either absent or, if present, rigidly strict. Such offenders tend to have a keen interest in depictions of torture, atrocities, Nazi activities and regalia, the occult and the more bizarre type of horror film. They frequently keep such materials locked away in a room or a shed. They show an irrational preoccupation with the size of their genitalia, which they unrealistically regard as excessively small. Their sex lives are poor or non-existent. In the course of the offence, the offender may insert articles such as a torch, milk bottle or poker with great force into the victim's vagina or rectum. Their murders, usually carefully planned, are ferocious and bizarre in their execution. Sexual intercourse may not necessarily accompany the murder but they may masturbate beside the corpse. It has been suggested that "the brutal and murderous assaults actually are a substitute for the sexual act" (Schlesinger and Revitch 1983: 214). The prognosis for such offenders is not good and some of them seem to welcome the control afforded by incarceration because they are troubled by their sadistic impulses and activities. However, those in charge of them and who share the responsibility for making recommendations about future dangerousness have to guard against being misled by *appearances* of good behaviour and apparently sincere protestations of reform (see Chapter 8 of this volume).

## Cautionary concluding comments

The range of behaviours that constitute sexual offending is vast and complex. It is necessary to reiterate the need for professionals to try to overcome their misconceptions and prejudices so that we may "hear" what such offenders are saying as non-judgementally as possible. This is very important because the behaviour of some sex offenders is not only bizarre but may well fill us with revulsion. However, demonstrations of dispassionate compassion should not blind us to the manner in which such offenders or offender–patients may engage in various forms of denial of their behaviour. On the credit side, some sex offenders (and sometimes those convicted of the more serious crimes) are distressed and disturbed by their behaviour, its effects on others and have a desire to change. Although there is an undoubted need for the development of sensible typologies, there is also a need to avoid stereotyping and to maintain an open mind. To achieve this, a multi-method, multidisciplinary approach is likely to be the most effective. Sexual offending appears in many guises and sometimes the most disguised forms may be the most ominous prognostically. In my view, it is premature to talk about "cure"; in the "management" of the offender, the work must be towards helping him deal with his impulses in a more acceptable way; the provision of viable alternative forms of behaviour is perhaps the most we can hope to achieve. Despite the recently established complex system of registration and the collection of data concerning prior convictions and allegations of serious sexual misconduct, things continue to go seriously wrong, as the case of Ian Huntley has recently demonstrated.

Following his conviction for the murder of the 10-year olds Jessica Chapman and Holly Wells, it became clear that Ian Huntley's previous history rendered him highly unsuitable for work that would bring him into contact with children. His history contained several allegations of unlawful sexual intercourse with under-age girls, an accusation of indecent assault on a 12-year-old girl and four allegations of rape. It was stated that lack of evidence prevented prosecution in nearly all these cases. However, in one of the rape cases, a prosecution had been brought but the charges had subsequently been withdrawn. It emerged that the lines of communication between the Humberside and Cambridgeshire police forces were unsatisfactory, data that should have been retained were prematurely discarded and the provisions of the data protection legislation misinterpreted. As I write this (December 2003) independent and internal inquiries have been set up and their findings awaited. It is apparent that even when systems are set up to prevent such eventualities, communication problems and inadequacies in recording (including a certain degree of dilatoriness in initiating adequate records) and inconsistent recording procedures between police forces may vitiate best intentions. The decision about when to keep information on record and at what stage to destroy it is not always easy, but wisdom (and maybe hindsight) would seem to dictate that allegations such as those in the Huntley case would have been singled out for indefinite retention. (See *The Independent*, 18, 19 and 20 December 2003 for detailed discussion of these issues.)

## Notes

1   Detailed explanations and interpretations of the sections relating to indecent exposure and voyeurism may be found in the draft explanatory notes that accompany the Act.

2   Unfortunately, there have been a number of instances of vigilantism; the most notable probably being the demonstration in 2001 at Paulsgrove, a suburb of Portsmouth, following the sexual abuse and killing of Sarah Payne. Moves to introduce a form of "Megan's law", based on the practice in some states in the USA, have fortunately not been successful. This form of "outing" was promoted largely by the *News of the World*. In a short but powerful commentary on the long-standing harassment and subsequent alleged murder of a 73-year-old paedophile in the north of England, Paul Vallely emphasizes the importance of "scapegoating". He reminds us that in Leviticus (Chapter 16 v. 10) the "scape-goat was an animal which was symbolically laden with the sins of the community and then driven out into the wilderness". He continues, "Societies also do this with people; we make them the Other; offer them up and send them out. The process of demonisation is about denying the full humanity of an individual and reducing him to his offence" (*The Independent*, 12 December 2003: 24). The Sex Offenders Registration Scheme introduced by the Sex Offenders Act 1997 does not allow public access to those required to be registered within its terms. However, such access is permitted in the USA. In a thoughtful contribution Thomas (2003) gives cogent reasons why the adoption of "open access" in the UK would raise a number of problematic issues (see also Winick 2002). The sex offender registration scheme was supplemented by the Crime and Disorder Act 1998. This allows magistrates to impose certain restrictions on a sex offender (such as control of their movements) whose behaviour indicates they might do serious harm. There is also provision under the Police Act 1997 for the issue, in certain circumstances, of certificates indicating a person's previous convictions (or lack of them). One of the aims of such certification is to prevent sex offenders from securing employment that would bring them into contact with children (see West 2000 for further details).

3   Advances in communication technology have many benefits, but they have also produced hazards, some of which could not perhaps have been readily foreseen. In the last few years there have been a number of cases where paedophiles have been able to "groom" children and young people via the internet. In September 2003 one internet provider, Microsoft, announced that it was closing its "chat-rooms" to "curb [the] paedophile threat" (*The Independent*, 24 September 2003: 1). More general concerns regarding grooming have now been reflected in the provisions of the Sexual Offences Act 2003. The associated problem of making indecent images of children is dealt with under Sections 45 and 46 of the Act and the Court of Appeal has recently issued detailed guidelines on sentencing in such cases (see Stone 2003b).

4   Interpretation of the section may be found in the draft explanatory notes that accompany the Act. (See also Stevenson et al. 2004.)

# References

American Psychiatric Association (APA) (1994) *Diagnostic and Statistical Manual of Mental Disorders*, 4th ed., Washington, DC: APA.

Amir, M. (1971) *Patterns of Forcible Rape*, Chicago: Chicago University Press.

Bagley, C. (1992) "Characteristics of 60 children and adolescents with a history of sexual assault against others: Evidence from a comparative study", *Journal of Forensic Psychiatry* 31, 299–309.

Banbury, S. (2004) "Coercive sexual behaviour in British prisons as reported by adult ex-prisoners", *Howard Journal of Criminal Justice* 43, 113–30.

Bancroft, J. (1989) *Human Sexuality and its Problems*, 2nd ed., London: Churchill Livingstone.

—— (1991) "The sexuality of offending: The social dimension", *Criminal Behaviour and Mental Health* 1, 181–92.

Batten, D. A. (1983) "Incest: A review of the literature", *Medicine, Science and the Law* 23, 245–53.

Beech, A., Fisher, D., Beckett, R. and Scott-Fordham, A. (1998) *An Evaluation of the Prison Sex Offender Treatment Programme. Research Findings No. 79*, Research, Development and Statistics Directorate, London: Home Office.

Bennetto, J. (1995) "Victims of 'flashing': Perceived threat of rape or murder", *The Independent* 24 July: 6 (quoting from an unpublished study by R. Beck, "Rape from afar: Men exposing to women and children", Cardiff: University College of Wales).

Bluglass, R. (1979) "Incest", *British Journal of Hospital Medicine*, August, 152–7.

—— (1982) "Assessing dangerousness in sex offenders", in J. R. Hamilton and H. Freeman (eds), *Dangerousness: Psychiatric Assessment and Management*, London: Gaskell.

Brandon, S., Boakes, J. and Glaser, D. (1998) "Recovered memories of childhood sexual abuse: Implications from clinical practice", *British Journal of Psychiatry* 172, 296–307.

Brewin, C. R. (1996) "Scientific status of recovered memories", *British Journal of Psychiatry* 169, 131–4.

Briggs, D. (1994) "Assessment of sexual offenders", in M. McMurran and J. Hodge (eds), *The Assessment of Criminal Behaviour in Clients in Secure Settings*, London: Jessica Kingsley.

Brittain, R. P. (1970) "The sadistic murderer", *Medicine, Science and the Law* 10: 198–208.

Brogden, M. and Nijhar, P. (2000) *Crime, Abuse and the Elderly*, Cullompton, Devon: Willan Publishing.

Cann, J., Falshaw, L. and Friendship, C. (2004) "Sexual offenders discharged from prison in England and Wales: A 21-year reconviction study", *Legal and Criminological Psychology* 9: 1–10.

Clark, C. and Mezey, G. (1997) "Elderly sex offenders against children: A descriptive study of child sex abusers over the age of 65", *Journal of Forensic Psychiatry* 8: 357–69.

Cox, D. J. and McMahon, B. (1978) "Incidents of male exhibitionism in the United States of America as reported by victimized female college students", *International Journal of Law and Psychiatry* 1: 453–7.

Dare, C. (1993) "Denial and childhood sexual abuse", *Journal of Forensic Psychiatry* 4: 1–4.

Davis, N. and Geis, G. (eds) (2001) *Sexual Deviance*, Vol. 3 of *Encyclopaedia of Criminology and Deviant Behaviour*, Hove, Sussex: Brunner-Routledge.

Deakin, J. and Spencer, J. (2003) "Women behind bars: Explanations and implications", *Howard Journal of Criminal Justice* 42: 123–36.

Duffield, G., Hassiotis, A. and Vizzard, E. (1998) "Zoophilia in young sex abusers", *Journal of Forensic Psychiatry* 9: 294–304.

Fisher, D. and Mair, G. (1998) *A Review of Classification Systems for Sex Offenders.*

*Research Findings No. 78*, Research Development and Statistics Directorate, London: Home Office.

Freud, S. (1960) *Totem and Taboo*, London: Routledge & Kegan Paul.

Friendship, C., Blud, L., Erikson, M. and Travers, R. (2002) *An Evaluation of Cognitive Behavioural Treatment for Prisoners. Research Findings No. 161*, London: Home Office.

Fudge, E. (2000) "Monstrous acts: Bestiality in early modern England", *History Today* 50: 20–5.

Gayford, J. J. (1981) "Indecent exposure – a review of the literature", *Medicine, Science and the Law* 21: 233–42.

—— (1997) "Disorders of sexual preference: A review of the literature", *Medicine, Science and the Law* 37: 303–15.

Gibbens, T. C. N., Way, C. and Soothill, K. L. (1978) "Siblings and parent-child incest offenders", *British Journal of Criminology* 18: 40–52.

Gittleson, N. L., Eacott, S. E. and Mehta, B. M. (1978) "Victims of indecent exposure", *British Journal of Psychiatry* 132: 61–6.

Groth, A. N. and Hobson, W. F. (1983) "The dynamics of sexual assault", in L. B. Schlesinger and E. Revitch (eds), *Sexual Dynamics of Anti-Social Behaviour*, Springfield, IL: Charles C. Thomas.

Grubin, D. (1994) "Sexual murder", *British Journal of Psychiatry* 165: 624–9.

—— (1997) "Predictors of risk in serious sex offenders", in C. Duggan (ed.), *Assessing Risk in the Mentally Disordered. British Journal of Psychiatry*, 170: Supplement No. 32.

—— (2002) "The potential use of polygraphy in forensic psychiatry", *Criminal Behaviour and Mental Health: Special Supplement* 12: S45–53.

Grubin, D. and Kennedy, H. G. (1991) "The classification of sexual offenders", *Criminal Behaviour and Mental Health* 1: 123–39.

Gudjonnson, G. (1997) "Members of the British False Memory Society: The legal consequences of the accusations for the families", *Journal of Forensic Psychiatry* 8: 348–56.

Hedderman, C. and Sugg, D. (1996) *Does Treating Sex Offenders Reduce Offending? Research Findings No. 45*, Research, Development and Statistics Directorate, London: Home Office.

Home Office (2001) *Criminal Statistics For England and Wales, 2001*. Cm 5696, London: TSO.

Hood, R., Shute, S., Feilzer, M. and Wilcox, A. (2002) *Reconviction Rates of Serious Sex Offenders and Assessments of Their Risk. Research Findings No. 164*, Research Development and Statistics Directorate, London: Home Office.

Hucker, S. (1990) "Necrophilia and other unusual philias", in R. Bluglass and P. Bowden (eds), *Principles and Practice of Forensic Psychiatry*, London: Churchill Livingstone.

Huckle, P. L. (1995) "Male rape victims referred to a forensic-psychiatric service", *Medicine, Science and the Law* 35: 187–92.

Jeary, K. (2004) "Sexual abuse of elderly people: Would we rather not know the details?", *Journal of Adult Protection* 6: 21–30.

Kaul, A. (1993) "Sex offenders – cure or management?", *Medicine, Science and the Law* 33: 207–12.

Kaul A. and Duffy, S. (1991) "Gerontophilia – a case report", *Medicine, Science and the Law* 31: 110–14.

King, M., Coxell, A. and Mezey, G. (2002) "Sexual molestation of males: Associations with psychological disturbance", *British Journal of Psychiatry* 181: 153–7.

Knight, B. (1979) "Fatal masochism – accident or suicide?", *Medicine, Science and the Law* 19: 118–20.

Knowles, G. J. (1999) "Male prison rape: A search for causation and prevention", *Howard Journal of Criminal Justice* 38: 267–82.

Lanyon, R. I. (1991) "Theories of sex offending", in C. R. Hollin and C. Howells (eds), *Clinical Approaches to Sex Offenders and Their Victims*, Chichester: John Wiley & Sons.

Launay, G. (1994) "The phallometric measurement of sex offenders: Some professional and research issues", *Criminal Behaviour and Mental Health* 4: 48–70.

—— (1999) "The phallometric assessment of sex offenders – an up-date", *Criminal Behaviour and Mental Health* 9: 254–74.

Lincoln, C. (2001) "Genital injury: Is it significant? A review of the literature", *Medicine, Science and the Law* 41: 206–16.

Lloyd, C. (1991) "Changes in the pattern and nature of sex offences", *Criminal Behaviour and Mental Health* 1: 115–22.

Lloyd, C. and Walmsley, R. (1989) *Changes in Rape Offences and Sentencing*, Home Office Research and Planning Unit, London: Home Office.

Löbmann, R., Greve, W., Wetzels, P. and Bosold, C. (2003) "Violence against women, consequences and coping", *Psychology, Crime and Law* 9: 309–31.

MacCulloch, M., Gray, N. and Watt, A. (2000) "Brittain's sadistic murderer syndrome revisited: An associative account of the aetiology of sadistic sexual fantasy", *Journal of Forensic Psychiatry* 11: 401–18.

MacCulloch, M. J., Snowden, P. R. and Wood, P. J. W. (1983) "Sadistic fantasy, sadistic behaviour and offending", *British Journal of Psychiatry* 143: 20–9.

MacDonald, J. M. (1973) *Indecent Exposure*, Springfield, IL: Charles C. Thomas.

MacPherson, G. J. D. (2003) "Predicting escalation in sexually violent recidivism: Use of the SYR-20 and PCL:54 to predict outcome with non-contact recidivists and contact recidivists", *Journal of Forensic Psychiatry and Psychology* 14: 615–27.

Masson, J. (1985) *The Assault on Truth: Freud's Suppression of the Seduction Theory*, Harmonsworth: Penguin.

Masters, B. (1993) *The Shrine of Jeffrey Dahmer*, London: Hodder & Stoughton.

Mezey, G., King, M., Vizzard, E., Hawkes, C. and Austin, E. (1991) "A community treatment programme for convicted child sex offenders: A preliminary report", *Journal of Forensic Psychiatry* 2: 11–25.

Muir, G. and Macleod, M. D. (2003) "The demographic and spatial patterns of recorded rape in a large UK metropolitan area", *Psychology Crime and Law* 9: 345–55.

Mullen, P. (1990) "The long-term influence of sexual assault on the mental health of victims", *Journal of Forensic Psychiatry* 1: 14–34.

Myhill, A. and Allen, J. (2002) *Rape and Sexual Assault of Women: Findings From the British Crime Survey. Research Findings No. 159*, Research, Development and Statistics Directorate, London: Home Office.

O'Connor, M. (1987) "Female sex offenders", *British Journal of Psychiatry* 150: 615–20.

Perkins, D. (1991) "Clinical work with sex offenders in secure settings", in C. R. Hollin and K. Howells (eds), *Clinical Approaches to Sex Offenders and Their Victims*, Chichester: John Wiley & Sons.

Pithers, W. D., Gray, A. and Davis, M. E. (2002) "Investing in the future of children: Building programs for children or prisons for adult offenders", in B. J. Winick and J. La Fond (eds), *Protecting Society from Sexually Dangerous Offenders: Law Justice and Therapy*, Washington, DC: American Psychological Association.

Prins, H. (1990) *Bizarre Behaviours: Boundaries of Psychiatric Disorder*, London: Tavistock/Routledge.

—— (1995) *Offenders, Deviants or Patients?*, 2nd ed., London: Routledge.

Revitch, E. and Schlesinger, L. B. (1981) *Psychopathology of Homicide*, Springfield IL: Charles C. Thomas.

Rex, S. and Bottoms, A. (2003) "Evaluating the evaluators: Researching the accreditation of offender programmes", *Probation Journal: The Journal of Community and Criminal Justice* 50: 359–68.

Riordan, S. (1999) "Indecent exposure: The impact upon the victim's fear of sexual crime", *Journal of Forensic Psychiatry* 10: 309–16.

Rooth, F. G. (1975) "Indecent exposure and exhibitionism", in T. Silverstone and B. Barraclough (eds), *Contemporary Psychiatry*, Ashford: Headley Brothers.

Rupp, J. C. (1970) "Sudden death in the gay world", *Medicine, Science and the Law* 10: 189–91.

Schlesinger, L. B. and Revitch, E. (eds) (1983) *Sexual Dynamics of Anti-Social Human Behaviour (especially Chapter 11)*, Springfield IL: Charles C. Thomas.

Scott, P. D. (1964) "Definition, classification, prognosis and treatment", in I. Rosen (ed.), *The Pathology and Treatment of Sexual Deviation*, London: Oxford University Press.

Silverman, J. and Wilson, D. (2002) *Innocence Betrayed, Paedophilia, The Media and Society*, Cambridge: Polity Press.

Smith, A. and Taylor, P. J. (1999) "Serious sex offending against women by men with schizophrenia: Relationship of illness and psychotic symptoms to offending", *British Journal of Psychiatry* 174: 233–7.

Soothill, K., Francis, B., Ackerley, E. and Fligelstone, R. (2002) *Murder and Serious Sexual Assault: What Criminal Histories Can Reveal About Future Serious Offending. Police Research Series Paper 144*, Research, Development and Statistics Directorate, London: Home Office.

Soothill, K., Peelo, M., Pearson, J. and Francis, B. (2004) "The reporting trajectories of top homicide cases in the media: A case study of *The Times*", *Howard Journal of Criminal Justice* 43: 1–14.

Spataro, J., Mullen, P. E., Burgess, P. M., Wells, D. L. and Moss, S. A. (2004) "Impact of child sexual abuse on mental health. Prospective study in males and females", *British Journal of Psychiatry* 184: 416–21.

Stevenson, K., Davies, A. and Gunn, M. (eds) (2004) *The Sexual Offences Act 2003*, Oxford: Oxford University Press.

Stone, N. (2003a) "In court: Rape: New guidelines", *Probation Journal: The Journal of Community and Criminal Justice* 50: 182–3.

Stone, N. (2003b) "In court: Indecent images of children", *Probation Journal: The Journal of Community and Criminal Justice* 50: 315–19.

—— (2003c) "In court: Generic application of rape guidelines", *Probation Journal: The Journal of Community and Criminal Justice* 50: 413–14.

Studer, L. H., Clelland, S. R., Aylwin, A. S., Reddon, J. R. and Monro, A. (2000) "Rethinking risk assessment for incest offenders", *International Journal of Law and Psychiatry* 23: 15–22.

Sugarman, P., Dumughn, C., Saad, K., Hinder, S. and Bluglass, R. (1994) "Dangerousness in exhibitionists", *Journal of Forensic Psychiatry* 5: 287–96.

Thomas, T. (2003) "Sex offender community notification: Experiences from America", *Howard Journal of Criminal Justice* 42: 217–28.

West, D. J. (1992) *Male Prostitution: Gay Sex Services in London*, London: Duckworth.

—— (2000) "Paedophilia: Plague or panic", *Journal of Forensic Psychiatry* 11: 511–31.

West, D. J., Roy, C. and Nichols, F. L. (1978) *Understanding Sexual Attacks*, London: Heinemann.

Winick, B. (2002) "A therapeutic jurisprudence analysis of sex offender registration and community notification laws", in B. J. Winick and J. La Fond (eds), *Protecting Society From Sexually Dangerous Offenders: Law, Justice and Therapy*, Washington, DC: American Psychological Association.

Yap, A. K., Lim, L. E., Ong, S. H., Chan, K. L. and Chan, A. O. M. (2002) "Personality of males charged with outrages of modesty", *Medicine, Science and the Law* 42: 167–71.

## Further reading

### General background

Bancroft, J. (1989) *Human Sexuality and its Problems*, 2nd ed., London: Churchill Livingstone.

Davenport-Hines, R. (1991) *Sex, Death and Punishment*, London: Fontana.

Holmes, R. M. (1991) *Sex Crime*, Sage: London (useful broad introduction).

Home Office (2002) *Protecting the Public: Strengthening Protection Against Sex Offenders and Reforming the Law on Sexual Offences*, Cm 5668, London: TSO.

Marshall, W. L., Anderson, D. and Fernandez, U. (1999) *Cognitive Behavioural Treatment of Sex Offenders*, Chichester: John Wiley & Sons.

Matravers, A. (ed.) (2003) *Sex Offenders in the Community: Managing and Reducing the Risks*, Cullompton, Devon: Willan Publishing.

Scully, D. (1991) *Understanding Sexual Violence*, London: HarperCollins (useful "feminist" perspective).

Soothill, K., Francis, B., Ackerley, E. and Fligelstone, R. (2002) *Murder and Serious Sexual Assault: What Criminal Histories Can Reveal About Future Serious Offending*, Home Office, Research, Development and Statistics Directorate, *Police Research Series, Paper 144*. London: Home Office.

Teague, M. (1994) *Rapists Talking About Rape: An Exploration of Masculine Culture in Criminal Justice*, Norwich: University of East Anglia.

Winick, B. J. and La Fond, J. Q. (eds) (2003) *Protecting Society from Sexually Dangerous Offenders: Law, Justice and Therapy*, Washington, DC: American Psychological Association (excellent compilation of contributions).

## Offences against children

Howitt, D. (1996) *Paedophiles and Sexual Offences Against Children*, Chichester: John Wiley & Sons (broad social perspective).

La Fontaine, J. S. (1998) *Speak of the Devil. Tales of Satanic Abuse in Contemporary England*, Cambridge. Cambridge University Press (excellent review of a "moral panic").

Morrison, T., Erooga, M. and Beckett, R. C. (1994) *Sexual Offending Against Children*, London: Routledge (good, practical discussion of the subject).

Renvoize, J. (1982) *Incest: A Family Pattern*, London: Routledge & Kegan Paul.

Silverman, J. and Wilson, D. (2002) *Innocence Betrayed: Paedophilia, The Media and Society*, Cambridge: Polity Press (excellent recent survey of the problem of sexual abuse of children).

# Chapter 7

# "Up in smoke"

I hear the alarm at dead of night,
I hear the bells – shouts!
I pass the crowd – I run!
The sight of flames maddens me with pleasure.
(Walt Whitman, *Poems of Joy*, 1860)

This chapter deals with four main issues. First, a brief historical background to the topic, second, a short exposition of the law in the UK, third, an outline of the size of the problem, and fourth, a discussion of some issues of classification and management. In England and Wales, arson is the legal term used to describe acts of unlawful fire raising. In other jurisdictions (notably the North Americas) the preferred terms are fire raising, fire setting, incendiarism and, in certain cases, pyromania and pathological fire setting. (For a review of the last, see Barnett and Spitzer 1994.) Whatever term we use to describe the unlawful use of fire, we should acknowledge at the outset that it constitutes a very serious form of crime. Not only is it regarded as a very serious form of offending behaviour because the harm caused to persons and property may be very considerable, but it is also an offence that can be committed at "one remove" and may involve many victims, some of them unintended. It is also a very difficult crime to detect, although recent advances in forensic science have greatly improved methods of detection (see Arson Prevention Bureau 2003; Home Office n.d.).[1] As we shall see, the motivations of arsonists are complex and courts are inclined to call for psychiatric reports in all but the most *apparently* straightforward cases. I emphasize the word *apparently* because even what appear to be the clearest of motives (such as setting a fire in order to claim insurance compensation for a failing business) may be associated with an underlying psychiatric problem (see Prins 2000, 2001). However, Soothill has wisely suggested caution in seeking psychiatric explanations in cases where the behaviour is merely baffling, since this tends to "medicalize" socially problematic behaviour – a matter that was referred to in Chapter 3 of this book (see Soothill 1991).

As is well known, fire may be both used and abused. The phenomenon has played a prominent part in the myths of humankind. Some examples are the legend of the Phoenix, which lived for hundreds of years, burned itself to death and then rose again from its ashes; of Prometheus, who stole fire from the gods and who became the origin of much later psychoanalytic theorizing about fire raising; the neophyte youth Phaethon who, having lost control of his father's chariot, was killed by Zeus with a thunderbolt before he could cause further harm. In the more factual pages of history, we can find many references to incendiary mixtures and devices; these include interesting sketches of mortars made by Leonardo da Vinci. In more recent times (and notably in the mid-nineteenth century) it appears that the medical profession began to turn its attention to explanations of fire-raising behaviour and, at a later date, psychoanalysts put forward various complex if somewhat controversial explanations linking fire-raising behaviour to sexual dysfunction of one kind or another. Although classical psychoanalytic explanations of fire-raising behaviour (based largely on Freudian interpretation of the myth of Prometheus) do not find much favour today, it is fair to say that sexual dysfunction is found not infrequently in the backgrounds of some persistent fire raisers (see Barker 1994; Hurly and Monahan 1969; MacDonald 1977; Prins 1994). It is of more than ephemeral interest to note the extent to which the phenomenon of fire is often linguistically linked to aggression and sexuality. For example, we speak or write of "white hot" rage, "heated arguments", "enflamed passions", to have the "hots" for someone of the opposite (or same) sex, "to burn with desire", and so on. Language represents cultural values and can be very influential in our modes of thinking about the existence of fire in its many powerful forms.

## The law in the UK

### Arson

The law relating to arson would appear to have a lengthy history. Geller states that:

> Ancient Roman legal texts recognized arson and defined penalties for this offence. In France, prior to the French Revolution, deliberate arson was punished by death – hanging for commoners and decapitation for nobles. Under some circumstances, arsonists were burned alive . . . In Britain, during the reign of George II convicted arsonists . . . were banished from the country.
>
> (Geller 1992: 283)

The legal definition of arson varies from one country to the next; no attempt is made to define it internationally. Other jurisdictions have comparable statutes and penalties. The word itself is derived from Anglo and old French and from mediaeval Latin – *ardere* – *ars* to burn (*Concise Oxford English Dictionary*). In England and Wales, prior to 1971, the offence of arson was dealt with under common law. Currently, it is dealt with under the provisions of the Criminal Damage Act 1971. Similar provisions apply in Northern Ireland. In Scotland, it is dealt with under a number of common law offences such as "wilful fire raising" and "culpable and reckless fire raising". Section 1 of the Criminal Damage Act 1971 states as follows:

1(1) A person who without lawful excuse destroys or damages any property belonging to another intending to destroy or damage any such property or being reckless as to whether any such property would be destroyed or damaged shall be guilty of an offence.

(2) A person who without lawful excuse destroys or damages any property, whether belonging to himself or another –

(a) intending to destroy or damage any property or being reckless as to whether any such property would be destroyed or damaged; and

(b) intending by the destruction or damage to endanger the life of another or being reckless as to whether the life of another would be thereby endangered;

shall be guilty of an offence.

(3) An offence committed under this section by destroying or damaging property by fire *shall be charged as arson*.

(emphasis added)[2]

Under Section 4 of the Act, the offences of both arson and endangering life are punishable with maximum penalties of life imprisonment, the latter being used most frequently in cases of persistent fire-raising behaviour where severe personality disorder associated with vengeful feelings may be in evidence. In addition, similar cases, and those in which clearly definable mental illness or mental impairment may be involved, are sometimes dealt with in England and Wales by way of the mental health legislation (Mental Health Act 1983, Hospital Order with Restrictions Sections 37/41).

## Size of the problem

In recent years, concern about the increase in arson has been noted on a worldwide basis. In the UK, Home Office figures indicate that in 1998 "malicious fires rose by 2% to 88,300 and arson is currently causing damage costing £4 million every day" (Arson Prevention Bureau 1999: 1). Home Office figures for *convictions and cautions* for arson show a somewhat fluctuating picture year on year (Home Office 2001a, 2001b). In 2001 some

2,700 offenders were found guilty of arson and some 1,144 were cautioned. There were 115 convictions for criminal damage endangering life showing an overall steady increase from 1999 onwards. There was a marked decline in the numbers cautioned for the offence – some 23 compared with a peak of 128 in 1997 (source: *Criminal Statistics: England and Wales 2001*, Table 5.16).[3] "Arson is now the largest single cause of major fires in the UK and it is on the increase" (Arson Control Forum 2002). "In 1999 arson cost England and Wales £2.1 billion" (Home Office 2001a). "In an average week, arson results in: 3,600 deliberately started fires, 60 injuries, 2 deaths and a cost to society of at least £40 million" (Arson Control Forum 2002). "False alarms for the year ending September, 2002 showed a one per cent rise, some 292,9000, with 68,700 of those incidents described as malicious" (*The Independent*, 6 August 2003: 6). Of particular concern to authorities is the very large number of arson attacks on schools. For example, during 1998 there were 1,014 attacks causing more than £35 million pounds' worth of damage. In percentage terms, schools are more likely to suffer a malicious fire than any other type of building. About 65 per cent of all school fires are classified as malicious. The Arson Prevention Bureau launched a national initiative in 1998 with a view to reducing the "unacceptable level of arson attacks on schools" (APB 2000: 4). There has also been a marked increase in malicious car fires: in 1998 there were some 50,000; these resulted in 20 deaths and 80 injuries (APB 2000: 1). One can only speculate on causes for these two worrying phenomena. Sadly, there seem to be sufficiently large numbers of disaffected young people in our society to account for a large proportion of these attacks. Not all arson attacks on cars can be laid at the door of vandalistic youth. Insurance companies are aware of cases where a motor vehicle may be "fired" in order to claim on an insurance policy or used as a means of ending a hire-purchase liability. Similar concerns have been expressed in the rest of Europe and also particularly in the USA. Figures from the US Department of Justice indicate that the juvenile arrest rate for arson increased by more than 50 per cent between 1987 and 1994 (Snyder 1998). (For a detailed breakdown of arson statistics for arson and "fires of doubtful origin", see Arson Prevention Bureau 1999.)

## Classification

Numerous attempts have been made to provide typologies of arsonists: the first large-scale attempt being the well-known early study by Lewis and Yarnell (1951). (For an account of this study, and of some later attempts to provide typologies during recent years, see Prins 1994: 99.) Two broad, useful groupings have been proposed by Faulk (1994). *Group I* consists of those cases in which the fire serves as a means to an end (for example, revenge, fraud or a plea for help); *Group II* consists of those cases where the

*Table 7.1*  Suggested classification of arsonists

Arson committed for financial reward (insurance, fraud, etc.)
Arson committed to cover up another crime (for example, burglary or homicide)
Arson committed for political purposes (terrorist and associated activities)
Self-immolation as a political gesture. (Strictly speaking, not arson as such, but included
    here for completeness, see Prins 1994)
Arson committed for mixed motives (for example, during a phase of minor depression,
    as a cry for help, or under the influence of alcohol or other drugs)
Arson due to the presence of formal mental disorder (for example, severe affective
    disorder, schizophrenic illness, organic mental disorder, mental impairment)
Arson due to motives of revenge – against (i) an individual or individuals; (ii) society, or
    others, more generally
Arson committed as an attention-seeking act (but excluding the motives set out under
    mixed motives) and arson committed as a means of deriving sexual satisfaction and/or
    excitement (for example, pyromania); described by some authorities as "pathological"
Fire raising by young adults ("vandalistic")
Arson by children

Notes: In a retrospective study of 153 adult arsonists who had been referred to him for psychiatric
examination, Rix (1994) broadened our original classification to include: desire for re-housing;
carelessness; anti-depressant (to relieve feelings of depression); and proxy in which the offender had
acted on behalf of another who had borne a grudge.
    A number of areas have initiated experimental treatment programmes for young arsonists. These
are the result of collaboration between social services departments, the educational psychology
service and fire services. Two examples are to be found in the schemes mounted in Nottingham and
Newcastle (see APB 2000 and *Nottingham Evening Post* 9 March 2000: 6, 12).

*fire itself* is the phenomenon of interest. In 1985 two psychiatrist colleagues
and I examined the files of 113 imprisoned arsonists eligible for parole
(Prins et al. 1985). From this small-scale and highly selected sample, we
derived the classification shown in Table 7.1.

Although this rudimentary classification has been adopted over the years
by a number of workers, it has certain weaknesses. For example, it
"collates" the *behavioural* characteristics of fire raisers, various *types* of fire
raiser *and* their *motives*. In a very comprehensive and critical review of the
psychiatric literature on arson, Barker underlines some of the weaknesses of
our classification. For example, where we categorized in fire raising due to
formal mental disorder, she suggests that this relies heavily on "a description of mental states, which may merely affect motivation, rather than
being in themselves motives" (Barker 1994: 16–17). Barker favours future
classifications being "elaborated in terms of multi-axial systems of
description, analogous to that found in DSMIII(R)" (Barker 1994: 20).
She goes on to suggest that "such a system emphasises the notion of arson
merely as a symptom to be viewed in the context of the whole person, not
only to delineate different syndromes of arsonists, but also to identify
individual points of therapeutic intervention and future dangerousness" (p.
20). In a more recent and important contribution, Canter and Fritzon have
suggested that more will be gained from concentrating on the *settings* (my

emphasis) in which arson takes place as a means of sharpening typologies. They suggest four "themes to arson".

> *Two* relate to expressive acts (a) those that are realised within the arsonist's own feelings, being analogous to suicide, and (b) those that are acted on objects, like the burning of symbolic buildings. The other two relate to instrumental acts (c) those that are for personal indulgence, similar to personal revenge, and (d) those that have an object focus, such as hiding evidence from a crime.
> (Canter and Fritzon 1998: 73; see also Häkkänen et al. 2004)

Recent research, such as that just quoted (and which seems to derive to some extent from recent work on offender profiling), would seem to have considerable potential for future developments in classification.

### Characteristics and motivation

Arsonists appear to be *mostly* young adult males and many of them have considerable relationship difficulties. A large proportion have problems with alcohol and some of them are of below average intelligence (see Murphy and Clare 1996). When women commit repeated acts of fire raising and have some accompanying degree of mental disorder, however slight, they are more likely than their male counterparts to be given a psychiatric disposal (see Coid et al. 1999; Noblett and Nelson 2001).

Studies of arsonists indicate considerable evidence of abuse and unstable childhoods and serious psychological disturbance, particularly among females. However, despite media presentations to the contrary, and as already indicated, a direct sexual motivation for arson is rare, although many arsonists have problems in making satisfactory sexual relationships. Those who engage in arson for purposes of revenge are likely to be potentially the most dangerous. Such persons are like the monster in Mary Shelley's *Frankenstein*, who says: "I am malicious because I am miserable." These are the arsonists who have problems in dealing with their feelings of anger and frustration at real or imagined wrongs. There now follows a short account of some of the main motivational aspects. (A more detailed presentation with accompanying case illustrations may be found in Prins 1994.)

### Arson committed for financial or other reward

In these cases the aim of the arsonist is to gain some financial or similar reward. The apparent increase in the burning of vehicles referred to earlier would fall into this category. However, the motives may not be so clear cut, as some individuals who set fire for apparent gain in this fashion may, for example, also be suffering from a degree of depression due to overwhelming financial or other difficulties.

### Case illustration 7.1

A woman set fire to her one-bedroomed flat causing not only the destruction of her own home but two neighbouring flats as well. As a result of the fires, an elderly neighbour, who lived two flats away, sustained injuries from which he died. In court it was alleged that the defendant had doubled her insurance on her home contents and set the fire in order to deal with increasing debts. It was also alleged that, on the night before the fire, she had removed some of her own property to a relative's home. The judge told the defendant that although she did not intend to cause injury she knew there were elderly residents nearby and that the risk of injury would be high. She was sentenced to seven years' imprisonment.

(*Independent*, 16 June 1992: 5; 30 June 1992: 5)

### Arson to conceal other crimes

Sometimes acts of arson will be committed in order to conceal a variety of offences. These may range from theft to murder. Sometimes such activities may be engaged in order to remove the means of DNA identification. Such fires may cause enormous damage, particularly if they are set to cover offences such as burglarious activities in large and well-stocked warehouses. Woodward (1987) cites an instance of this kind of fire setting. A warehouse of a shipping company was destroyed by fire. The goods stored there included TV sets, car tyres and other goods that would catch fire quickly. From the forensic examination at the scene of the fire, it was apparent that burglarious activity had taken place before the fire had been set.

### Arson committed for political purposes

There are two main motives for arson committed by political activists. The first concerns the desire to destroy the property of those they are against; the second is the publicity gained for the activists' cause. The one-time alleged destruction of "second homes" by Welsh activists would be illustrative of the first and the former activities of the work of the IRA and other paramilitary and fascist organizations would be illustrative of the second. A disturbing trend is the number of outbreaks of arson and similar attacks on so-called "foreigners". Although the main motives are often seen to be political, there are also sometimes psychopathological elements, such as the feeling of power such activities may provide. To this extent, the motivation may be mixed as, for example, in the case of other offences such as serious sexual assault.

### Self-immolation

These cannot really be regarded as cases of arson, but an act of self-immolation may have serious consequences for the lives of others as the following example shows.

### Case illustration 7.2

A young woman in the north of England tried to kill herself in her bedroom by dousing her body in petrol and then attempting to ignite it. This having failed, she subsequently tried to blow herself up (and the other residents of the house) by turning on the gas taps and striking matches. Fortunately, this attempt also failed. However, the legal ingredients of a charge of endangering life through arson were sustainable and the defendant was admitted compulsorily to a psychiatric hospital under the Mental Health Act 1983. At the time she was found to have been suffering from a serious depressive illness, but subsequently made a reasonably good recovery. This example also illustrates the problem of trying to "pigeon-hole" people since the young woman's problem could have been classified under the heading of mental disorder.

Ritualized self-destruction – mainly for political reasons – sometimes occurs. A report in *The Independent* of 21 May 1991 (p. 2) describes the ritual suicide of Kim Ki Sol who wrote, "There are many meanings to my act today" before "setting himself alight and jumping in flames from the roof of a seven story building at Seoul's Sogang University". Culture-based self-immolation is not, of course, a new phenomenon as, for example, we see in the instance of a woman who becomes a "suttee". Barker describes a number of young members of a group known as Ananda Marga, "who immolated themselves" as a protest "against the imprisonment in India of their leader". Two of them said that their "self-immolation is done after personal and independent decision. It is out of love for all human beings, for the poor, for the exploited, the suffering" (Barker 1989: 54–5). Some years ago Topp (1973) drew attention to the extent to which self-destruction by fire seemed to have shown a slow but steady increase in penal establishments. He suggested that such individuals who choose an obviously very painful method of death are likely to be those who have some capacity for splitting off feelings from consciousness. Some may be epileptics in a disturbed state of consciousness. However, in all such cases of self-immolation, we should remember that people probably vary enormously in their pain thresholds. Some would succumb very quickly to such an agonizing method of self-destruction. One imagines that shock and asphyxiation would probably occur within a very short space of time so that the severe pain caused by the burning of vital tissues would not have to be endured for too long. Such may have been the fates of some of the early martyrs who chose to suffer death at the stake. Occasionally, such sufferers were "granted the merciful privilege . . . of having a small bag of gunpowder hung around [the] neck in order to speed their demise and so reduce [their] suffering" (Abbot 1991: 167).

### Arson committed for mixed and unclear reasons

These are cases in which it is difficult to ascribe a *single specific* motive. Such cases may include the presence of a degree of mild (reactive) depression which may lead the fire raiser to direct anger at a spouse or partner, thus revenge may also play a part. This group will also include cases in which the fire raising may be a disguised plea for help or a reaction to sudden separation or bereavement; in some of these cases alcohol appears to be relevant and may lead to "befuddled" activity on the part of the individual, who may unwittingly cause a conflagration.

### Arson due to serious mental disorder

Functional psychoses may play a part in some acts of fire raising, notably the schizophrenias. Such cases will most likely be accommodated in secure or semi-secure hospitals of one kind or another. Manic-depressive psychosis features occasionally, the classic case being that of Jonathan Martin, the early nineteenth-century arsonist who set fire to York Minster (see Prins 1994 for case examples).

### Arson associated with "organic" disorders

Occasionally, brain tumour, injury, epilepsy, dementia or metabolic disturbance may play a part. For example, although epilepsy is not commonly associated with fire raising, one should always be on the lookout for the case in which such a crime has been committed, when the person appeared not to be in a state of clear consciousness or when onlookers were present. (For examples of brain damage and other organic states and their relationship to fire raising, see Hurly and Monahan 1969. For the possible relationship between learning disability and arson, see Murphy and Clare 1996; Prins 1994.)

### Arson motivated by revenge

Those incidents motivated by revenge are potentially the most dangerous. However, in considering the link between motives of revenge and arson, it is important to stress that it is hazardous to try to place motivations for fire-raising behaviour in discrete categories; the vengeful fire raiser may show clear signs of identifiable mental illness, may be mentally and/or physically impaired, or may not be "ill" in any formal psychiatric sense. However, their dangerous potential is considerable, as the following case illustration demonstrates.

### Case illustration 7.3

A man aged about 30 had developed a passionate and quite unshakeable belief that a young woman was in love with him. His passions were not reciprocated; in fact they were actively resisted on several occasions. So obsessive were this man's amorous desires that they had a delusional quality. As a means of gaining attention to his plight and of getting back at the young woman concerned he placed an incendiary device in her home with the avowed intention of killing her and her family. Fortunately, a family member spotted it and dealt with it before the fire took too great a hold. Many years after this event, the offender (detained in hospital on a hospital order without limit of time) still harboured vengeful feelings and seemed quite without insight into what he had done or compassion for his intended victim.

Thus, is it important to stress here that the vengeful arsonist is likely to harbour his destructive desires over a very long period.

### Pyromania

Pyromaniacs are arsonists who do not appear to be suffering to any significant extent from formal mental disorder or to be operating from motives of gain or revenge. They appear to derive a pathological excitement from, and involvement in, setting the fire, attending the scene, busying themselves at it or having called out the fire brigade in the first instance. The DSMIV (APA 1994) lists six differential criteria for the diagnosis of the condition:

1   Deliberate and purposeful fire setting on more than one occasion.
2   Affective arousal and tension prior to the act.
3   Fascination with, and attraction to, fire and its situational context.
4   Pleasure, gratification or relief when setting fires or witnessing or involvement in their aftermath.
5   The exclusion of other causes.
6   The fire setting is not "better accounted for" by conduct disorder or anti-social personality disorder.

(paraphrased from DSMIV, APA 1994: 616)

### Sexually motivated arson

Fras (1983) has summarized much of the history of the relationship between sexual satisfaction/excitement and arson (see also Prins 2001). The infrequency of the relationship in practice should not blind professionals to the possibility of its existence in certain cases or its similarity to sex offending. As Fras states: "In its comparative, stereotyped sequence of mounting pressure . . . it resembles the sexual perversions, as it may parallel them in its imperviousness to treatment" (p. 199). It is noteworthy that Hurly and Monahan found 54 per cent of the arsonists they studied in Grendon had clear psychosexual difficulties and marital problems and that 60 per cent reported difficulties in social relationships with women (see also Prins 2001).

### Young adult vandalism and arson

The backgrounds and motivations of adolescent and young adult arsonists appear to be rather different from those characterizing children who set fires. The adolescents and younger adults we looked at in our prison sample seemed to have been motivated more specifically by boredom and to have engaged in the behaviour for "kicks". It is not unknown for bored and disaffected young employees to set fire to their places of work. Cases have been reported in the hotel and catering industry. As with school and vehicle arson, there was often an accompanying element of getting back at a society that did not appear to care about them. Unlike child fire raisers, their backgrounds seemed less socially and psychologically disturbed. It is also important to note that the arson offences committed by this age group are often closely associated with the ingestion of alcohol. The following case illustration shows how some of these elements may be combined.

### Case illustration 7.4

A group of five unemployed older teenagers (ages ranging from 16–19) had been to a disco where they had imbibed a fair amount of alcohol, although they were not drunk. They had waited for a considerable time for the last bus home only to find they had missed it. They had been whiling away their time at the bus stop indulging in a fair amount of horseplay. As they became more impatient, their horseplay escalated into more aggressive activity. They smashed the windows of a large outfitter's shop nearby, entered it and began damaging the contents. In the course of this activity, one of them lit some waste paper while others looked on encouraging him. A fire soon took hold engulfing the premises and rapidly destroying the shop and its contents.

### Child arsonists

The literature on children as arsonists suggests that they come, predominantly, from disturbed and dysfunctional family backgrounds and exhibit a range of conduct disordered behaviours from an early age. Some of the earlier studies lack control group populations, thus making the results somewhat inconclusive. However, a fairly large-scale study of fire raising in a "normal" population was conducted by Kafry (1980). She studied the fire behaviour and knowledge in a random sample of 99 boys of approximately 8 years of age. Kafry found that interest in fire was almost universal, that "fire-play" was carried out by 45 per cent of the boys studied and that interest in fire began at a very early age. An ominous finding was that although the children's parents seemed aware of the risks of fires, a large percentage did not provide any adequate instruction and warning to their children. Those children who played with matches and raised fires seemed to be more mischievous, aggressive, exhibitionistic and impulsive than those who expressed no such interest. The findings are of interest because these characteristics seem to be similar to those demonstrated in a number of adult arsonists, particularly those of aggression and impulsiveness. Later studies seem to be consonant with Kafry's findings (see for example Jacobson 1985a, 1985b; Santtila et al. 2003; Stewart and Culver 1982; Strachan 1981; Vandersall and Weiner 1970; Wallqvist and Norlander 2003). For further accounts of child fire-setting behaviour see Wooden and Berkey (1984). Two quotations make a fitting conclusion to this section. The first is from Dryden's *The Hind and the Panther* (III: 389): "And thus the child imposes on the man"; and the second "Tall oaks from little acorns grow" (David Everett, 1769–1813).

## Management

It should be obvious from the foregoing and Table 7.1 that no *single* form of management is likely to be effective. Because fire-raising behaviour is so diverse and, as Barker suggests, best treated as a "symptom", every case deserves painstaking analysis, however "obvious" the motivation may seem. The classifications already outlined, even with their acknowledged deficiencies, will hopefully facilitate the process of management. The latter can be highlighted in the following fashion:

1   Distinguish the *fraudulent* arsonist.
2   Distinguish the *politically motivated*. However, it is wise to remember that some politically motivated arsonists will also have mental health problems.
3   Distinguish the *vandalistically motivated*.
4   Distinguish those who are driven to arson by clear evidence of *mental disorder*, notably functional psychosis, organic disorder and learning disability.
5   Distinguish those who appear to be *pyromaniacs* as defined in DSMIV.
6   Distinguish those comparatively rare cases in which *sexual disorder* of one kind or another seems to play a significant role.

7 Distinguish those driven by motives of *revenge*. This group may include a number of arsonists currently classifiable under the mental health legislation in England and Wales as suffering from psychopathic disorder. This category may of course overlap with some of the foregoing.

Successful management must rest on a multifaceted approach and the ability of all members of psychiatric or criminal justice teams to cooperate in the interests of the arsonist and the community. The management of arsonists has no place for "prima donna" activity. A very helpful example of a multidisciplinary approach may be found in a paper by Clare et al. (1992). The authors describe in detail their management of a case that required an understanding of both physical and learning disabilities and a capacity to work intensively using eclectic behavioural techniques over a prolonged period of time. Despite minor setbacks, the patient, who had been subject at one time to containment in a high-security hospital, remained free of his long-standing fire-raising behaviour at 4-year follow-up. It would be mistaken to believe that formal psychoanalytically based psychotherapy had no place in the management of psychotic and seriously personality disordered arsonists. The late Doctor Murray Cox described some very useful group work with such patients in Broadmoor. In doing so, he made the very important point that "the almost limitless range of clinical presentations means there is no neat unitary hypothesis which can underlie the behaviour of all patients convicted of arson" (Cox 1979: 344). Interesting exploratory work is currently being undertaken in our high-security (special) hospitals, although the long-term benefits of such work have yet to be assessed. Vengeful arsonists may do so because they feel wronged or misunderstood. Any attempts that can be made to help them find ways in which they may achieve more satisfaction from their life experiences are to be welcomed. Many of them are socially inept; they set fires as a means of communication and to draw attention to themselves, so that techniques aimed at improving their self-regard, self-image and social competence should help to minimize the risk of future offending. Social skills training has an important part to play with this group of arsonists.

## Summary

Not only is arson a very worrying offence, but also it has shown a steady increase in recent years. Its causes are complex and various attempts at classification have not been entirely successful. The recidivistic nature of fire raising is emphasized in a recent and important contribution by Soothill et al. (2004). Their paper replicates an earlier study of the criminal careers of arsonists (Soothill and Pope 1973). They compared their original small sample of arsonists with three new series convicted in all courts in 1963, 1980 and 2000–2001. In this later study they found an increasing number of females and a rise in the average age of both sexes. In their later series previous convictions for violence and criminal damage (including arson) are also much more in evidence. Within what is a 20-year follow-up period the proportion reconvicted for arson has *more than doubled* (emphasis added). They conclude that "the situation in relation to arson has deteriorated significantly over the past forty years" (Soothill et al. 2004: 27) (see also Barnett et al. 1999). Recent attempts to view arson as a "symptom" appear to offer the hope of more successful modes of management. This chapter has only outlined the problems. The references cited and the suggestions for further reading should enable those who wish to pursue the topic in greater depth to do so.

## Notes

1   For those readers wishing to inform themselves about fire scene investigation see Prins (1994: Chapter 4). Also Kathy Reichs, a crime novelist with extensive forensic pathology experience, describes such activities in some detail in her novel *Death du Jour* (Chapters 2–4) (Reichs 1999).

2   The House of Lords, in allowing the appeals of two boys aged 11 and 12 against their convictions for arson, clarified the definition to be used where recklessness was invoked by the prosecution. As follows: "A person acts recklessly within the meaning of Section 1 of the 1971 Act with respect to (i) a circumstance where he was aware of a risk that it exists or will exist; (ii) a result when he is aware of a risk that will occur; and it is, in the circumstances known to him, unreasonable to take the risk" (*R. v G. and another* (2003) UKHL 50) (reported in *The Independent Law Report* by Kate O'Hanlon, *The Independent* 22 October 2003: 18) (judgment delivered 22 October).

3   The criminal statistics do not give a complete picture. More accurate figures of the number of possible offences can be found in the biennial *Home Office Fire Statistics*, which include details of fires of "doubtful" or "malicious" origin (see, for example, Home Office 1996).

## References

Abbot, G. (1991) *Lords of the Scaffold: A History of the Executioner*, London: Robert Hale.

American Psychiatric Association (APA) (1994) *Diagnostic and Statistical Manual of Mental Disorders*, DSMIV(R), Washington, DC: APA.

Arson Control Forum (2002) *First Annual Report*, for Department For Transport, Local Government and the Regions, London: Arson Control Forum.

Arson Prevention Bureau (1999) *Annual Report*. London: Arson Prevention Bureau.

—— (2000) *Arson Intelligence Newsletter* No. 31, March: 4.

—— (2003) *Ten Years of Fighting Arson*, London: Arson Prevention Bureau.

Barker, A. F. (1994) *Arson: A Review of the Psychiatric Literature*, Maudsley Monograph No. 35. Oxford: Oxford University Press.

Barker, E. (1989) *New Religious Movements: A Practical Introduction*, London: HMSO.

Barnett, W. and Spitzer, M. (1994) "Pathological fire-setting 1951–1991: A review", *Medicine, Science and the Law* 34: 4–20.

Barnett, W., Richter, P. and Renneberg, B. (1999) "Repeated arson: Data from criminal records", *Forensic Science International* 101: 49–54.

Canter, D. and Fritzon, K. (1998) "Differentiating arsonists: A model of fire-setting actions and characteristics", *Legal and Criminological Psychology* 3: 73–96.

Clare, I. C. H., Murphy, D., Cox, D. and Chaplin, E. H. (1992) "Assessment and treatment of fire-setting: A single case investigation using a cognitive-behavioural model", *Criminal Behaviour and Mental Health* 2: 253–68.

Coid, J., Wilkins, J. and Coid, B. (1999) "Fire setting, pyromania and self-mutilation in female remanded prisoners", *Journal of Forensic Psychiatry* 10: 119–30.

Cox, M. (1979) "Dynamic psychotherapy with sex offenders", in I. Rosen (ed.), *Sexual Deviation*, 2nd ed., Oxford: Oxford University Press.

Faulk, M. (1994) *Basic Forensic Psychiatry*, 2nd ed., Oxford: Blackwell Scientific Publications.

Fras, I. (1983) "Fire-setting (pyromania) and its relationship to sexuality", in L. B. Schlesinger and E. Revich (eds), *Sexual Dynamics of Anti-Social Behaviour*, Springfield, IL: Charles C. Thomas.

Geller, J. L. (1992) "Pathological fire-setting in adults", *International Journal of Law and Psychiatry* 15: 283–302.

Häkkänen, H., Pvolakka, P. and Santilla, P. (2004) "Crime scene actions and offender characteristics in arsonists", *Legal and Criminological Psychology* 9: 197–214.

Home Office (1996) *Summary Fire Statistics*, London: Home Office (Fire Department).

—— (2001a) *Cost of Fire in England and Wales in 1999*, London: Home Office.

—— (2001b) *Criminal Statistics. England and Wales*, Cm 5696, London: TSO.

—— (n.d.) *Safer Communities: Towards Effective Arson Control: The Report of the Arson Scoping Study*, London: Home Office.

Hurley, W. and Monahan, T. M. (1969) "Arson, the criminal and the crime", *British Journal of Criminology* 9: 4–21.

Jacobson. R. (1985a) "Child fire-setters: A clinical investigation", *Journal of Child Psychology and Psychiatry* 26: 759–68.

—— (1985b) "The sub-classification of child fire-setters", *Journal of Child Psychology and Psychiatry* 26: 769–75.

Kafry, D. (1980) "Playing with matches: Children and fire", in D. Canter (ed.), *Fires and Human Behaviour*, Chichester: John Wiley & Sons.

Lewis, N. D. C. and Yarnell, H. (1951) *Pathological Fire-Setting (Pyromania)*, Nervous and Mental Disease Monographs, No. 82, New York: Coolidge Foundation.

Macdonald, J. M. (1977) *Bombers and Firesetters*, Springfield, IL: Charles C. Thomas.

Murphy, G. H. and Clare, I. C. H. (1996) "Analysis of motivation in people with mild learning disabilities (mental handicap) who set fires", *Psychology, Crime and Law* 2: 153–64.

Noblett, S. and Nelson, B. (2001) "A psychosocial approach to arson: A case-controlled study of female offenders", *Medicine, Science and the Law* 41: 325–30.

Prins, H. (1994) *Fire-Raising: Its Motivation and Management*, London: Routledge.
—— (2000) "The special problem of arson (fire-raising)", in M. G. Gelder, J. J. Lopez-Ibor and N. Andreasen (eds), *New Oxford Textbook of Psychiatry*, Vol. 2, Oxford: Oxford University Press.
—— (2001) "Arson and sexuality", in C. D. Bryant, N. Davis and G. Geis (eds), *Encyclopedia of Criminology and Deviant Behaviour*, Vol. III, Philadelphia and Hove, Sussex: Brunner-Routledge (Taylor & Francis).
Prins, H., Tennent, G. and Trick, K. (1985) "Motives for arson (fire-setting)", *Medicine, Science and the Law* 25: 275–8.
Reichs, K. (1999) *Death du Jour*, London: Heinemann.
Rix, K. B. (1994) "A psychiatric study of adult arsonists", *Medicine, Science and the Law* 34: 21–34.
Santtila, P., Häkkänen, H., Alison, L. and Whyte, C. (2003) "Juvenile fire-setters: Crime scene actions and offender characteristics", *Legal and Criminological Psychology* 8: 1–20.
Snyder, H. N. (1998) *Juvenile Arsonists 1997*, Washington, DC: US Department of Justice, Office of Justice Programs, Office of Juvenile Justice and Delinquency Prevention.
Soothill, K. (1991) "Arson", in R. Bluglass and P. Bowden (eds), *Principles and Practice of Forensic Psychiatry*, London: Churchill Livingstone.
Soothill, K. L. and Pope. P. J. (1973) "Arson: A twenty-year cohort study", *Medicine, Science and the Law* 13: 127–38.
Soothill, K., Ackerley, E. and Francis, B. (2004) "The criminal careers of arsonists", *Medicine, Science and the Law* 44: 25–40.
Stewart, M. A. and Culver, K. W. (1982) "Children who set fires: The clinical picture and a follow-up", *British Journal of Psychiatry* 140: 357–63.
Strachan, J. G. (1981) "Conspicuous fire-setting in children", *British Journal of Psychiatry* 138: 26–9.
Topp, D. O. (1973) "Fire as a symbol and as a weapon of death", *Medicine, Science and the Law* 13: 79–86.
Vandersall, T. A., and Weiner, J. M. (1970) "Children who set fires", *Archives of General Psychiatry* 22: 63–71.
Wallqvist, R. P. and Norlander, T. (2003) "Fire-setting and playing with fire during childhood and adolescence: Interview studies of 18-year-old male draftees and 18–19-year-old female pupils", *Legal and Criminological Psychology* 8: 151–8.
Wooden, W. S. and Berkey, M. L. (1984) *Children and arson: America's middle class nightmare*, London: Plenum Press.
Woodward, C. D. (1987) "Arson: The major fire problem of the 1980s", *Journal of the Society of Fellows, The Chartered Insurance Institute*, Pt. I., 2: 55–86.

## Further reading

Arson Prevention Bureau. This organization publishes regular bulletins and other publications relating to arson. The address is: 51 Gresham Street, London EC2V 7HQ.
Arson Prevention Bureau (1998) *Accommodating Arsonists in the Community: Guidance For Hostel Managers*, London: Arson Prevention Bureau.

Arson Prevention Bureau (2000) *Prevention and Control of Arson in Industrial and Commercial Premises*, London: Arson Prevention Bureau.

Barker, A. F. (1994) *Arson: A Review of the Psychiatric Literature*, Maudsley Monograph No. 35, Oxford: Oxford University Press.

Home Office (Fire Department) biennial fire statistics.

Prins, H. (1994) *Fire-Raising: Its Motivation and Management*, London: Routledge.

# Chapter 8

# The "crystal ball" of risk assessment*

Clinical assessment is not primarily about making an accurate prediction but about making *defensible* decisions about dangerous behaviour.

(Grounds 1995)

The best decision in a single case cannot, under uncertainty, guarantee the best (or good) outcome. *To assume that a bad outcome implies a bad decision is the most fundamental and wide-spread of all fallacies!*

(Dowie 1990)

Never predict anything, particularly the future.

(statement attributed to Samuel Goldwyn, film producer)

Many of the individuals described and discussed in earlier chapters in this book have committed very serious offences that may have been dealt with by long periods of detention, either in mental healthcare or penal establishments. At some point in their stay in such establishments considerations will have arisen concerning their eventual release into the community. In other cases (where there is no record of previous offences) individuals may commit a serious crime such as homicide and subsequent inquiry may reveal that some of the "warning signs" that *might* have prevented such an occurrence may have been missed; had they been spotted, a tragedy *might* have been averted. These eventualities have been highlighted in recent years by a large number of mandatory inquiries into homicides committed by patients known to the mental health and allied services (see prologue and

---

* Some of the material in this chapter is from my (2002) article "Incapacitating the dangerous in England and Wales: High expectations – harsh reality", which appeared in the *Journal of Mental Health Law* 6, reproduced with permission from Northumbria Law Press.

Prins 2004). Issues concerning risk assessment and management are complicated and the essential elements can only be touched on in this chapter. I deal with them in detail in my book on risk assessment and management (Prins 1999). The present chapter is divided into the following sections: First, a brief examination of the climate and context in which risk assessment and management currently take place, second, a brief examination of legal and administrative aspects, third, some semantic considerations and fourth, clinical problems.

## The culture of risk and blame

"Risk is ubiquitous and no human society can be considered risk free" (Royal Society 1992). As already indicated in this book, we know that human beings are made anxious about ambiguity and uncertainty and will engage in dubious and sometimes harmful practices to avoid them. Much recent and current concern about so-called "dangerous" people has its roots in these phenomena; unless they are properly understood, many of our efforts aimed at dealing with such people will fail. Beck (1998) puts an eloquent gloss on the matter, as follows:

> Calculating and managing risks which nobody really knows has become one of our main preoccupations. That used to be a specialist job for actuaries, insurers and scientists. Now we all have to engage in it, with whatever rusty tools we can lay our hands on – sometimes the calculator, sometimes the astrology column.
>
> (1998: 12)

It is crucial to understand the uncertainty of risk prediction (see later). This is particularly important at the present time when blame is so quickly apportioned in a variety of hazardous and tragic circumstances, be they homicides, train, air or sea disasters, flood damage or BSE. Much concern about risk is media driven; if mental health, criminal justice and legal professionals are forced into making predictions, there may be an assumption on the part of the public that such professionals are capable of getting it right every time. The latter will then assume (perhaps unwittingly) a mantle of infallibility and will have to count the cost when they get it wrong, as from time to time they assuredly will. It is worthwhile emphasizing that homicide inquiries are a good example of this problem and one that needs placing in perspective. We know factually that the number of homicides committed by persons with mental disorders (particularly mental illness) is very small (and has, in fact, contrary to public opinion, actually declined over the past decade), but the media seem to have vastly influenced the politicians in their somewhat frenetic search for solutions (see, for example, Taylor and Gunn 1999). It is also worth remembering (as a means of gaining historical perspective) that "fashions" in criminal justice and mental health come and go. Soothill (1993) has demonstrated very usefully the manner in which this may occur. He cites as examples our almost 10-year cyclical preoccupations with, for example, homosexuality and prostitution, with rape, with physical child abuse and with so-called "satanic" child sexual abuse etc. As I showed in Chapter 5 recent preoccupation has been with so-called "serial killing" – a much ill-used and abused term, which often serves to obfuscate rather than illuminate. It has recently been pointed out to me that our current "folk devils" (as described by Cohen in 1972) appear to be "stalkers" and "errant doctors" (Dr Edward Petch, *Personal Communication*, 13 June 2001).

Reference has recently been made to the hazards of prediction; it is worthwhile commenting on this aspect in a little more detail. The sometime science correspondent of *The Independent* – William Hartston – once expressed our inadequacies very well, as follows:

> Such are the risks we all run every day that, if you are an adult between 35 and 54, there is roughly a one-in-400 chance you will be dead within a year. *Homo sapiens* is a bit of a twit about assessing risks. We buy lottery tickets in the hope of scooping the jackpot, with a one-in-14 million chance of winning, when there's a one-in-400 chance that we won't even survive the year . . . the evidence suggests that our behaviour is motivated by panic and innumeracy.
>
> (*The Independent*, 19 September 1997: 10–11)

The realities of our being involved in a hazardous event can be seen in Table 8.1.

The perceptions of risk as outlined in Table 8.1 have very important implications for risk assessment and management. Measures to reduce risks may have unseen (and sometimes hazardous) consequences. For example, as Hartston suggested in his article: "Wearing seat belts may make drivers more reckless because they feel safer; and marking a road as an 'accident black spot' may reduce accident figures so successfully that it ceases to be a black spot – it was only dangerous in the first place because people didn't know how dangerous it was." I have sometimes wondered if the introduction of "speed humps" and "speed tables" will, over time, have the intended desired effect. Many drivers become frustrated by them and they may, in fact, demonstrate their frustration by acts of careless or negligent driving immediately *after* traversing them. An example drawn from earlier times tends to lend support to these contentions. Adams (1995) cites the introduction of the Davy Lamp, which was intended to save lives in the mining industry; but, as Adams suggests, it *actually* resulted in an *increase* in explosions and fatalities because the lamp permitted mining activity to be

*Table 8.1*    Likelihood of involvement in a hazardous event

| | |
|---|---|
| Being struck by lightning | one in 10 million |
| Contracting CJD by eating "beef on the bone" | one in 6 million |
| Drowning in the bath | one in 800,000 |
| Death from homicide | one in 100,000 |
| Death playing soccer | one in 25,000 |
| Death in a plane crash | one in 20,000 |
| Death from being involved in a road accident | one in 8,000 |
| Death from 'flu | one in 5,000 |
| Death from smoking 10 cigarettes a day | one in 200 |

*Source: Daily Telegraph* 5 December 1997: 9

*Notes:* Compared with the risk of death from eating beef on the bone, the other risks quoted are far more substantial; as the author of the article from which these figures are extrapolated states, the risk is "so small that it almost tips off the scale" (R. Uhlig, *Daily Telegraph* 5 December 1997).
 Statistical odds may be expressed in the following fashion:

| | |
|---|---|
| Negligible risk is | less than one in 1,000,000 |
| Minimal risk is | one in 100,000 to one in 1,000,000 |
| Very low risk is | one in 10,000 to one in 100,000 |
| Moderate risk is | one in 100 to one in 1,000 |
| High risk is | greater than one in 100 |

*Source:* Sir Kenneth Calman, Former Chief Medical Officer of Health, Department of Health, as quoted in *The Guardian* 3 October 1996: 6

*One death equals:*
500 million staircases climbed
200 million baths taken
200 million roads crossed
75 million trains boarded
15 million car journeys
10 million flights on a jet aeroplane
4 million cycle trips
3 million acts of unprotected sex
2 million cigarettes smoked

carried out at deeper levels where the explosive methane content was much higher (Adams 1995: 211).

## Professional perceptions of risks

There can be little doubt that there has been a massive growth in what can best be called the "risk industry". This is exemplified in concerns about safety in the home, safety at work, the development of casualty services and those associated with childcare.

 Adams (1995) suggests that we may all tend to overdo the risk prevention business. He cites as examples, overestimates of household risks lead to unnecessary expenditure on insurance; the design of buildings that take into account hazards that can be rated as almost zero, such as earthquakes in areas where these are unlikely; overzealous safety measures on the railways leading to increases in passenger costs, which, in turn, may drive people away from the railways on to the roads, thus creating greater driving hazards; abnormal fears of mugging and similar attacks may lead the elderly and other vulnerable people to lead unnecessarily isolated lives. Adams suggests that there are two types of human. The first is zero-risk man *homo prudens*, personifying "prudence, rationality and responsibility" (p. 17). He describes this creature as "a figment of the imagination of the safety profession". The second is a type of being within every one of us, a creature he describes as *homo aleatorius*: "dice man, gambling man, risk-taking man"; his descriptions give further credibility to the importance of *irrationality* in human risk-taking behaviour or abstention from it.

### Definitions of risk

In 1983 the Royal Society produced a report on *risk*. This was subsequently revised in the light of development in knowledge and practice and a further version appeared in 1992 (Royal Society 1992). In their introduction to this later report, the authors concentrated their minds on a range of terms used in the literature on risk, some of which are as follows:

- *Risk* is defined in terms of the probability "that a particular adverse event occurs during a stated period of time, or results from a particular challenge" (p. 2).
- A *hazard* is defined as "the situation that in particular circumstances could lead to harm" (p. 3).
- *Risk assessment* is used to "describe the study of decisions subject to uncertain circumstances" (p. 3). The Royal Society working group divided risk assessment into *risk estimation* and *risk evaluation.*
- *Risk estimation* "includes: (a) the identification of the outcomes; (b) the estimation of the magnitude of the associated consequences of these outcomes; and (c) the estimation of the probabilities of these outcomes" (p. 3).
- *Risk evaluation* is "the complex process of determining the significance or value of the identified hazards and estimated risks to those concerned with or affected by the decision" (p. 3).
- *Risk management* is "the making of decisions concerning risks and their subsequent implementation, and flows from risk estimation and risk evaluation" (p. 3).

The authors of that report cautioned against equating *risk* with *danger*. To put it simply, *risk* may be seen as the probability of an event occurring and *danger* may be seen as the extent of the hazard or harm likely to accrue. The term "acceptable risk" is frequently used by decision takers and policy makers. The authors of the Royal Society Report, supporting the views expressed by Layfield in his report on the Sizewell B nuclear plant inquiry, prefer the term "tolerable". Layfield considered that the use of the term "acceptable" did not reflect the seriousness of the problems involved in risk-taking activities; he suggested the term "tolerable" as being a more accurate description of what was involved. Following Layfield's report, the Health and Safety Executive defined "tolerable risk" in the following fashion:

> "Tolerability" does not mean "acceptability". It refers to the willingness to live with a risk to secure certain benefits and in the confidence that it is being properly controlled. To tolerate a risk means that we do not regard it as negligible or something we might ignore, but rather as something we need to keep under review and reduce still further if and as we can.
>
> (Health and Safety Executive 1988, quoted in Royal Society 1992)

### Risk prediction

There is a vast and ever growing literature on the prediction of risk. See for example, Adams (1995), Monahan and Steadman (1994), Monahan et al. (2001, especially Chapters 1 and 7) and Royal Society (1992). If, by prediction, we mean the capacity to get it right every time, the short answer has to be "no". If we have more modest goals and ask if there are measures that could be taken to attempt a possible reduction in dangerous behaviour, then it is possible to give a qualified "yes". Pollock and Webster have put the matter very succinctly: "From a scientific perspective [the question] is impossible to answer since it is based upon an unscientific assumption about dangerousness, namely that it is a stable and consistent quality existing within the individual" (Pollock and Webster 1991). They suggest that a translation into more appropriate terms would produce the following question:

> What are the psychological, social and biological factors bearing on the defendant's . . . behaviour and what are the implications for future [behaviour] and the potential for change?

Despite the fact that considerable actuarial and computer-facilitated research has been carried out into the prediction of anti-social behaviour generally, this tends to suggest that although actuarial techniques can discriminate between high-risk and low-risk *groups*, there will also be a residual majority in the *middle-risk* groups whose re-offending rates are too near 50–50 to be much use prognostically in *the individual case*. For example, in an evaluation of two risk and need assessment instruments in use by the Probation Service, it was found that although the devices predicted reconviction more successfully than "chance levels" the devices were not "appropriate for use as the main method of assessing dangerousness" (*Home Office, Findings* No. 143, 2001, p. 2). However, actuarial models and rating scales are becoming increasingly popular as witnessed by the use of the psychopathy rating scales referred to in an earlier chapter – the PCL-R and similar instruments. For a critical review of the weaknesses of actuarial predictions in respect of *sexual offenders*, see Craig et al. (2004).

For some years, workers in the criminal justice and mental health fields have taken comfort from the oft-quoted statement by the American psychologist Kvaraceus that "nothing predicts behaviour like behaviour" (1966). However, as recent commentators such as Gunn, have pointed out, such statements may rest on statistical error and reinforce the fallacious view that risk is a static phenomenon and unaffected by changes in social and other circumstances (Gunn 1996). At the end of the day, as MacCulloch et al. state:

> Predicting and preventing violence is a fundamental part of clinical practice . . . forensic psychiatrists, psychologists and clinical criminologists are asked to assess cases to make a prediction of the likelihood of harm to others in the future.
> (1995: 61) (see also Kettles et al. 2003; Krauss and Lee 2003)

## Legal and administrative aspects

A number of legislatures, notably in some of the states on the continent of North America, have made attempts to define dangerousness for the purposes of incarceration of individuals adjudged to be dangerous, be this incarceration in penal or mental healthcare institutions. In the UK, there are currently no statutes that attempt to define dangerous individuals specifically, although the law does recognize for example such offences as reckless (dangerous) driving, endangering the lives of passengers and being in possession of, or distributing, dangerous drugs. However, as we will see, in recent times the notion of dangerousness has been an important consideration in criminal justice and mental health legislation (Baker 1993; Buchanan 2002 (Part I)). It is also of interest to note that in the last few years there has been an increase in the use of the "life" (indeterminate) sentence for cases not involving homicide. This has been justified in various court of appeal decisions on the grounds that by such means offenders considered to be dangerous (but not necessarily mentally abnormal within the meaning of the current mental health legislation) can be incarcerated until such time as the authorities (for example, the Parole Board) consider, on the basis of expert advice, that they may be safely released. However, it should also be noted that decisions based solely on concerns about dangerousness appear to have recently become "contaminated" by considerations based on political expediency. This would appear to have occurred in the case of the late Myra Hindley and some others. So far as those formally judged to be mentally disordered are concerned, current mental health legislation recognizes the concept of potential dangerousness. Thus, Sections 2 and 3 of the 1983 Mental Health Act (England and Wales), make provision, *inter alia*, for the compulsory detention of an individual with a view to the "protection of other persons" and, as we saw in earlier chapters, Section 41 of the Act makes provision (subject to certain criteria being satisfied) for placing an order restricting discharge on a person made the subject of a hospital order to protect the public from "serious harm". More specifically, the proclivities of some offender–patients are recognized in the setting up and maintenance of the three high-security hospitals in England and Wales (Broadmoor, Rampton and Ashworth) for those patients who "exhibit dangerous, violent or criminal propensities" (National Health Service and Community Care Act 1990, Section 4). During the past two decades the law and practice relating to both mentally abnormal and dangerous offenders have been examined by five different groups – *the Butler Committee, the Scottish Council on Crime, the "Floud" Committee, the Reed Committee* and, most recently, in the joint *Home Office and Department of Health* report on *Managing People with Severe Personality Disorder* (see Prins 1999: Chapter 2; Chapter 5 this volume).

## What's in a name?

The words "danger", "dangerousness" and "risk" have little real meaning on their own. It is only when placed in context that they become useful, but any interpretation must, to some extent, be subjective. Walker makes a useful point when he suggests that "dangerousness is not an objective quality, but an *ascribed* quality like trustworthiness. We feel justified in talking about a person as dangerous if he has indicated by word or deed that he is more likely than most people to do serious harm" (Walker 1983; emphasis added). The Butler Committee, in examining the notion of *dangerousness in relation to mentally abnormal offenders*, considered it to be "a propensity to cause serious physical injury or lasting psychological harm. Physical violence is, we think, what the public are most worried about, but the psychological damage which may be suffered by some victims of other crimes is not to be underrated" (HO and DHSS 1975: 59). Practising clinicians and others who have day-to-day contact with those deemed to be dangerous, generally agree with the late doctor Peter Scott's definition that dangerousness is "an unpredictable and untreatable tendency to inflict or risk irreversible injury or destruction, or to induce others to do so" (Scott 1977). Some clinicians, for example, Tidmarsh, have suggested that Scott's inclusion of unpredictability and untreatability can be questioned, since the anticipation and modification of a danger does not necessarily minimize the risk (1982). However, Scott did suggest that a key element in the notion of dangerousness was the risk of repetition in the face of measures to reduce it. He also stressed another very important element, namely that its use as a label might contribute to its own continuance – a point that should be heeded by lawyers, sentencers and criminal justice and mental health professionals.

For our purposes, it is worth noting Floud's statement that "risk is in principle, a matter of fact, but danger is a matter of judgement or opinion" (Floud 1982). Thus, the notion of dangerousness implies a prediction, a concern with future conduct. Most authorities agree that apart from a very small group of individuals who may be intrinsically dangerous because of some inherent physical or other defect (which may make them particularly explosive), the general concern is with the *situation* in which the combination of the *vulnerable* individual with a *provoking incident* may spark off explosive and dangerous behaviour. As noted by the Butler Committee: "The individual who spontaneously 'looks for a fight' or feels a need to inflict pain or who searches for an unknown sexual victim is fortunately rare, although such people undoubtedly exist. Only this last category can be justifiably called: 'unconditionally' dangerous."[1] *Risk* and *danger* may be distinguished in the following somewhat oversimplified fashion.

Risk may be said to be the *likelihood* of an event occurring and danger may be said to be the *degree of damage (harm)* that may occur should the event take place. Grounds makes the important additional point that both of these also need to be distinguished from worry:

> They are not well correlated and judgements and decisions based on worry may not be well founded. The problem is that feelings of worry are expressed by professionals in the vocabulary of risk. The feeling "I am very worried about X" is likely to be translated into "X is a high risk" in written and spoken communications. Worry may, however, be excessive or insufficient in relation to the risk. The test is the same as for risk: how well grounded is it in history?
>
> (Grounds 1995: 54–5)

"Dangerousness" of course means different things to different people. If I asked readers of this book to rank the following people in order of their dangerousness, they would probably find themselves in some difficulty. Of the following who, for example, would be considered the most dangerous? The bank robber, the persistent paedophile, the person who peddles dangerous drugs to children, the person who drives when knowingly unfit to do so, the swimmer who has a contagious disease, but continues to use the public baths, the bigoted patriot, national leader or politician who believes they are always right, the computer hacker, the person who is HIV positive or has AIDS who persists in having unprotected sexual intercourse with a variety of partners,[2] the consortium that disposes of toxic waste products without safeguards, forensic mental health or criminal justice professionals who always act on their own initiative without adequate consultation with colleagues and who believe that their "personality" will "get them by" in dangerous situations? All these people present hazards of one kind or another depending on the situation in which they find themselves.

## Clinical problems

Sentencers (both professional and lay) and mental health and criminal justice professionals have to carry out their work of limiting "mayhem" within the constraints of the complex legislative and administrative frameworks referred to earlier in this book. This legislative framework has become so complex that even experienced sentencers find some of the legal requirements difficult to interpret. It would be worth considering whether a consolidating piece of legislation dealing with serious and high-risk offenders should to be introduced. Professionals not only have to deal with these legal complications, but also have to carry out their work within the current "blame culture" and to endeavour to balance offenders' and offender–patients' needs against the need to protect the public. As has already been stated, the current political climate puts a premium on the latter and has recently been re-enforced in the passing of the Criminal Justice Act 2003. I now point out some of the pitfalls for professionals and suggest ways in which practice might be improved. I begin by providing four case illustrations in order to demonstrate some of the dilemmas involved.

### Case illustration 8.1

"Paul" is in the community on conditional discharge from hospital (Sections 37/41 Mental Health Act 1983). The order had been imposed for killing his wife. He had been detained in hospitals for some 10 years before being conditionally discharged by a Mental Health Review Tribunal (MHRT). The facts of his original offence were that, having killed his wife (by manual strangulation) he had secreted her body and it was some months before it was discovered. At the time of his arrest he had been seeing another woman on a regular basis. A year after being conditionally discharged into the community he informed his supervising probation officer that he had been seeing a woman and hoped to marry her. In this case the probation officer's responsibilities seemed quite clear. In the first instance, the development needs to be reported to the Home Office mental health unit – which has central government responsibility for mentally disordered offenders. Second, the officer needs to ascertain from "Paul" more details of this new relationship. In the course of such discussion "Paul" would need to be advised that he should inform the woman of his past history (given the particular circumstances of his original offence). Should

"Paul" be unwilling to do so his probation officer (having taken advice from his line management, and maybe the Home Office), would need to inform "Paul" that in the light of his refusal to do so, he would have to inform her himself.

To some, perhaps, this might seem like an intrusion into an offender–patient's personal liberty, but the broader issue of the protection of the public, in this case the woman he is seeing and maybe others, necessitates such action. The issues seem clear cut. In other cases there are grey areas that require careful consideration of who else should be involved – as illustrated in Case illustration 8.2.

## Case illustration 8.2

"Tom" is a 60-year-old offender released on life licence for killing a child during a sexual assault. He had been convicted on a previous occasion of indecent assault and had then been made the subject of a hospital order without restrictions (Section 37 Mental Health Act 1983). He had been living in the community on life licence for about two years and had so far not given his probation officer any cause for concern. His probation officer has just received a phone call stating that "Tom" has been seen "loitering" by the bus stop outside a local primary school. What should his probation officer do about this development? There would appear to be several steps that need to be taken. First, further information is required as to the source and reliability of the information received. This is of particular importance at a time when "public" and "political" concerns about paedophilic behaviour are highly visible (see Chapter 6). Did this information come via the school or, for example, from a bystander who knew "Tom's" history and was perhaps out to make trouble for him by deliberately misconstruing a quite innocent piece of behaviour? (After all, he *could* have been waiting for a bus quite legitimately.) The second step in trying to elucidate the problematic behaviour would be to arrange a very urgent appointment to see "Tom". Why, for example, was he at this particular bus stop? His responses would have to be judged in the light of details about his previous offences. It would be very ominous if, for example, the circumstances of the offence for which he received his life sentence were similar to his present behaviour. Third, the probation officer would have to consider the pros and cons of contacting the school and/or the local police to ascertain if any complaints or comments had been received concerning similar conduct by "Tom". Whatever steps the probation officer takes, *the offender is entitled to be told of the action proposed and the reasons for it.* Such information will be likely to be received and accepted more easily had "Tom" been given very clear indications at the start of his life licence (or conditional discharge, if he had been dealt with through the mental healthcare system) concerning his obligations under their terms. "Tom" needs to be made aware of his supervisor's responsibilities to report any apparently untoward conduct. Sadly, there have been occasions in the past when mutual expectations and obligations have not been shared openly. In such cases an offender or offender–patient can feel legitimately surprised when speedy and sometimes apparently condign action is taken. Some other aspects of the "need to tell" are illustrated in the next two case examples.

*Note*: This case situation arose and was dealt with *before* the current sex offender registration procedures were in force.[3]

## Case illustration 8.3

A psychiatrist had been seeing a male patient on a regular informal out-patient basis over a period of several months. In the past, he had had a number of compulsory admissions to hospital for a paranoid psychosis. (Sections 2 and 3 of the Mental Health Act 1983.) During a recent session with his psychiatrist, he revealed a powerful belief that a former girlfriend had been unfaithful to him, that he has been following her and that he feels like killing her. What should the psychiatrist do? In the first instance, he needs to check back over past records to see if similar beliefs have been expressed on other occasions and what the outcomes were. Second, he needs to make a careful appraisal of the quality of the patient's intended actions, discussing the case with other professionals and/or his professional bodies. For example, the circumstances of the self-reported "stalking" require careful and detailed evaluation, as does the quality of his expressed feelings about killing her. *Feeling* like killing someone is not quite the same as expressed threats to kill (which, in law, constitute a criminal offence). If his past history reveals similar threats and his *current* threats have a delusional intensity, then the psychiatrist would be exercising appropriate professional responsibility if he arranged for the patient's former girlfriend to be warned about his feelings.

## Case illustration 8.4

My fourth example concerns a case in which the offender–patient had given clear indication of possible intended harm. This concerned events uncovered during a homicide inquiry that I chaired. The perpetrator of the homicide, who had been known to the mental healthcare and a number of other agencies, had given a clear written warning to his supervising social worker of his possible intentions. He wrote a letter from the prison in which he was then being held – as follows:

> I think that jail is the Best place for me at the moment because it sort's my head out. If I was on the street I would put peples life at risk, so that's over with.
>
> [original spelling]

We commented as follows:

> Although in retrospect, everyone [now] considered that this letter was important and significant, at the time, its content and import were not com-municated [by social services] to the Probation Service . . . With hindsight, it

would appear that the content of this letter might have prompted a referral for further psychiatric assessment.

(Prins et al. 1998)

It is hoped that these short case examples illustrate some of the dilemmas faced by professionals and will serve as an introduction to the concluding section of this chapter, which contains the following elements:

- aspects of communication
- vulnerability
- establishing an effective baseline
- improving practice.

### Aspects of communication

A non-mental health and criminal justice professional has wisely stated that: "All tragedy is the failure of communication" (Wilson 1974). Such a statement embraces four aspects of communication that are relevant to this discussion:

1   The need for good interprofessional communication. For example, case conferences and public protection committees sometimes fail to work as effectively as they could because of the mistaken belief that multi-agency is synonymous with multidisciplinary when, in terms of role perceptions and territorial boundaries, it clearly is not. (For an account of an imaginary case conference, see Prins 1999: 127–9.) *Multi-agency public protection arrangements (MAPPA)* were given a statutory foundation by Sections 67 and 68 of the Criminal Justice and Court Services Act 2000 and implemented in April 2001. Bryan and Doyle outline the legal responsibilities now placed on police and probation services in England and Wales as follows:

> Establish arrangements for assessing and managing the risk of serious harm posed by certain sexual, violent and other dangerous offenders; review these arrangements with a view to monitoring their effectiveness [and] prepare and publish an annual report on the discharge of these arrangements within the area.
> (Bryan and Doyle 2003: 29; see also Kemshall 2003; Tancredi 2004)

Readers interested in pursuing these responsibilities *with particular reference to child protection* should consult two reports issued by HM Inspectorate of Probation and HM Inspectorate of Constabulary (2002, 2002). Issues of confidentiality are prominent in relation to interagency functioning and often impede it. (For a useful account of this problem see Morris 2003.)

2   The need for adequate communication between worker and offender/ offender–patient and an understanding of the impediments to this. These include ambivalence, hostility, fear and denial, not only on the part of the offender–patient, but also that of the worker. Denial is by no means the sole prerogative of offenders and offender–patients. Maybe both offenders, offender–patients and their professional workers should heed Banquo's advice to his fellows:

> And when we have our naked frailties hid,
> That suffer in exposure, let us meet,
> And question this most bloody piece of work,
> To know it further.
>
> (*Macbeth* Act 2 Sc. 3)

3   How well do professionals "hear" the concerns of the carers of their charges? In the Andrew Robinson enquiry, it became clear that Andrew's parents had tried to draw attention repeatedly to their fear of his continued psychotically motivated aggression and violence towards them. Their home had become a place of terror and accounts of their fears appear to have gone unheard (Blom-Cooper et al. 1995). Similar accounts of lack of family involvement may be found in a number of other homicide inquiries (see Prins 1999: Chapter 5).

4   The need for professionals to be "in touch" with the warring and less comfortable parts of themselves. This need may show itself for example in misperceptions of race and gender needs; in our inquiry into the death of Orville Blackwood in Broadmoor, we considered that perceptions of young African-Caribbeans as always being "big, black and dangerous" might seriously have handicapped some of the staff's handling of this group of offender–patients (Prins et al. 1993).

There may also be unresolved and professionally limiting personal conflicts about certain specific forms of conduct, notably those involving extreme sexual deviation. Perhaps professionals working in this field should heed the statement by Pericles in Shakespeare's play of that name that "Few love to hear the sins they love to act" (Act 1 Sc. 1) (see also Chapter 6 this volume).

### Vulnerability

The assessment and management of dangerous behaviour and the risk factors involved are concerned, essentially, with the prevention of vulnerability, namely taking care not to place the offender or offender–patient in a situation in which they may be highly likely to re-enact their previous pattern(s) of dangerous behaviour. The recognition of this reduces the vulnerability of both the public to the commission of "unfinished business" and the vulnerability of the offender/offender–patient (Cox 1979).

### Establishing an effective baseline

All the research and clinical studies in the area of risk assessment and management in criminal justice and mental health attest to the importance of obtaining the basic facts of the situation. It is this kind of evidence that decision-making bodies, such as courts, Mental Health Review Tribunals, the Parole Board and the Home Office require in order to make the most effective decisions. This necessitates having an accurate and full record of, for example, the index offence, or other incident and, in addition, the person's previous history, especially their previous convictions. A bare legal description tells us nothing about seriousness of intention at the time of the offence, or its prognostic significance. This has become of increasing importance today when "plea bargaining" and advocates' attempts to persuade courts to "downgrade" offences have become more frequent. An incident that may well have had the ingredients to justify an original charge of attempted murder may eventually end up, by agreement, as one of unlawful wounding. Neither do the bare details of an offence give any real indication of motivation. For example, burglary may take the form of a conventional break-in or it may have more ominous prognostic implications if, say, the only items stolen were the shoes belonging to the female occupant of the premises. In similar fashion, those males who expose themselves to women in an aggressive fashion associated with erection and masturbatory activity need to be distinguished from those who are more passive and who expose from a distance without erection; the former group are those who are sometimes more likely to go on to commit serious sexually assaultive offences. Scott, in his seminal paper on assessing dangerousness in criminals, stressed the need for a most careful scrutiny of all the facts (Scott 1977). However, as we will see in Chapter 9, 60 years earlier, Freud, and Umberto Eco more recently, made similar observations.

Some useful guidance on the basic requirements for risk assessment may be found in the Department of Health's *Guidance on the Discharge of Mentally Disordered People and their Continuing Care in the Community* (DOH (NHS Executive) 1994). The advice emphasizes the following points, among others, advocated by the panel of inquiry into the case of Kim Kirkman:

[P]ast history of the patient; self reporting by the patient at interview; observation of the behaviour and mental state of the patient; *discrepancies between what is reported and what is observed*; statistics derived from studies of related cases and prediction indicators derived from research.

(West Midlands Health Authority 1991; emphasis added)

Similar points were made by the former Association of Chief Officers of Probation (ACOP) in its *Guidelines on the Management of Risk and Public Protection*. For example, they suggest such questions as:

Who is likely to get hurt? How seriously and in what way? Is it likely to happen right now, next week or when? How often? In what circumstances will it be more rather than less likely to occur? Is the behaviour that led to the offending continuing? What is he/she telling you, not only by words but also by demeanour/actions?

(ACOP 1994)

High hopes have been placed on various procedures for risk *registration*. However, some of the evidence I once gathered from the fields of childcare and probation seems to indicate that risk registration does not *necessarily* ensure good practice (Prins 1995). Some of us might be forgiven for thinking that we live in the age of the "tick" box and the "protocol". "Audit" is the order of the day, but whether its somewhat obsessional hold on administrators and others aids practice is not altogether clear. One consultant psychiatrist has recently gone as far as to coin a new word for this preoccupation – "formarrhoea" (Hardwick 2003). However, some attempts to produce quite impressive screening devices seem useful, as in the Home Office's offender assessment system (OASys) harm-screening document.

### Improving practice

There is no doubt that many professionals carry out very high-quality work in cases requiring risk management. However, there have been instances when the quality of work has shown deficiencies; some of these deficiencies have been highlighted in recent inquiries, such as those into the cases of Andrew Robinson (1995) and Jason Mitchell (1996). I now wish to illustrate why this might be and how such deficiencies might be remedied. Basically, it has to do with asking uncomfortable questions. I have tried to group these questions under seven headings in order to describe them as seven possible sins of omission. But before doing so, one or two preliminary general observations may be helpful. Professionals in this difficult and often highly charged area need two types of supervision and support. The first is the support and supervision that holds them accountable to their organization for what they do. The second, and equally important, is the supervision from line management that enables them to do more effective and empathic work. It is very important for workers to have the chance to share perspectives with their peers. This may assist in the development of knowledge and confidence. The following seven areas of questioning may go some way to providing more effective engagement:

1   Have past precipitants and stresses in the offender/offender–patient's background been removed? If still present, are they amenable to further work and, more importantly, has the worker the courage to deal with them? A period of long-term work with an offender or offender–patient may induce in the worker a form of "familiarity", which may blind them to subtle changes in the individual's social and emotional worlds. If we have worked very hard to induce change through the establishment of a "good" relationship, we may not wish to do any-thing that may challenge that; we may prefer not to know. Genders and Player, in their study of Grendon Prison, state that they were often reminded of the words of the old song "I wish I didn't know now what I didn't know then" (Genders and Player 1995).

2   What is the person's current capacity for dealing with provocation? It is useful to reiterate Scott's advice that aggression may be deflected from a highly provoking source to one that may be scarcely provoking at all (Scott 1977). Some of our most perplexing cases are those in which serious violence has been caused to the "innocent stranger" in the street. Careful scanning of the immediate environment may enable us to sense (and perhaps help the individual to avoid) potentially inflam-matory situations (see Chapter 9). For example, to what extent has the over-flirtatious wife or partner of a jealous husband (partner) courted a potentially dangerous situation by sarcasm, making denigrating remarks about sexual prowess, been otherwise contemptuous or worn provocative clothing? The same is true with the male in the provocative role, as is the case from time to time, in male homosexual relation-ships. Detailed accounts of previous provoking incidents are therefore vital in order to assess future risk and provide effective continuing management.

3   How does this offender–patient continue to view him or herself? The need for a "macho" self-image in a highly deviant male sex offender is often based on unresolved past conflicts with women. This may make him likely to continue to take his revenge by way of serious sexual assaults accompanied by extreme violence and degradation of his victims.

4   To what extent have we been able to assess changes for the better in this person's capacity to feel empathy for others? Does this individual still treat others as objects rather than as persons on whom to indulge their deviant desires and practices? As we saw in Chapter 4 the true, as distinct from the pejoratively labelled psychopath, tends to see all those around him (or her) as malevolently disposed.

5   To what extent does the behaviour seem person specific or as a means of getting back at society in general, as we saw is the case of some arsonists? The person who says with continuing hatred in their voice, "I know that one day I'm going to kill somebody", has to be taken very seriously. To what extent are thoughts of killing or injury still present? Is there a pleasurable feel to their talk about violent acts? Is there continuing interest in such material as violent pornography, horror videos, the occult, atrocities, torture, etc.? Sometimes the "evidence" is less tangible and "hunches" need to be relied on, but always carefully followed up and checked out. Thus, Commander Dalgleish in P. D. James' *Original Sin* described his "instinct" [as something] that he sometimes distrusted, but had learned not to ignore (James 1994).

6   How much continuing regard has been paid to what the offender/ offender–patient actually did at the time of the offence? Was it so horrendous that they blotted it out of consciousness? For example, did they wander off in a semi-amnesic state or, on realizing what they had done, summon help immediately? Or did they, having mutilated the body, go off happily to a meal and a good night's sleep? How much are they still claiming it was a sudden and spontaneous crime, when the evidence shows planning and premeditation? What was the significant role of substance abuse of one kind or another? Prisons and, to a lesser extent, secure hospitals are not ideal places for testing out future proclivities in such people. However, escorted periods of leave with close supervision may enable alcohol intake and its effects to be assessed. The persistent paedophile on an escorted group outing to the seaside may alert observant nursing staff to continuing abnormal sexual interest by having eyes only for the semi-naked children playing on the beach. In similar fashion, staff may report patients' interest (and arousal) when in the presence of the children of visitors to the ward, or to pictures of children on the television. How much is known about what "aids" to sexual fantasy they are storing in their rooms or cells? (For example, newspaper clippings, graphic details from court depositions.) The offender–patient who says he is writing his life history in a series of exercise books could well be asked to show them to us; somewhat surprisingly, they are very often willing to do so. We may find detailed descriptions of continuing violent and/or sadistic fantasies, which are being used as rehearsal for future activity. All these indicators, coupled with psychophysiological measures, may help us to obtain a better, if not conclusive, perception of likely future behaviour. (For some further illustrative material see Prins 1999: 141 et seq.)

7   To what extent can we discern that this individual has begun to come to terms with what they did? It is important for all professionals and decision makers to regard protestations of guilt and remorse with a degree of caution. As Russel and Russel (1961) state:

A person who expresses guilt is to be regarded with vigilance. His next move may be to engineer a situation where he can repeat his activities (about which he expresses guilt), but this time with rationalisation and hence without guilt. He will therefore try to manipulate his victim into giving him a pretext.

(1961: 34)

Sometimes, an offender or offender–patient may be reluctant to acknowledge the truth of what they have done for fear of causing hurt to relatives and others close to them. The late doctor Patrick McGrath, sometime Medical Superintendent at Broadmoor, cited the case of a paedophilic sadistic killer who consistently denied his guilt in order to spare his "gentle devoted parents who could not believe his guilt". When they died, within a fairly short while of each other, he willingly admitted his guilt and in due course was released (McGrath 1989). Neither should we forget that in relation to confession and guilt, offender/offender–patients may, in fact, not be guilty of any crime, as a number of *causes célèbres* have so sadly demonstrated.

## Concluding comments

In this chapter I have endeavoured to place notions of dangerousness and risk within recent contexts. I have provided some helpful examples of ways in which the supervision of potentially dangerous offenders might be made more effective. Although the advent of sophisticated computational techniques has undoubtedly provided a platform for actuarial advances, it is still the worker at the *individual* level who has to make prognostic judgements and undertake the hazards of ongoing supervision (see Maden 2003; Mullen 2002). It is comparatively easy and safe to predict what someone will do two weeks or even a month hence; much more hazardous to predict what they might do in a year's time.

Central to the task of the criminal justice or mental health professional in high-risk cases is a commitment to detail and to tracing connections between behaviour patterns. In a review of Gail Bell's book *The Poison Principle*, Forrester – a forensic psychiatrist – makes the following very apposite comment:

Detail forms the substance of forensic psychiatry in the same way that the investigations of a physician might invoke various . . . [tests], so the investigative forensic-psychiatrist must put together a fully corroborated personal narrative, or be charged with pitiful neglect.

(Forrester 2003: 467)

It also involves a great deal of personal soul searching in order to come to grips with behaviour that is frequently anxiety making and sometimes horrifying. It also calls for operating with a greater degree of surveillance and close monitoring than is customary in some areas of "counselling". It certainly involves a capacity not to attempt to "go it alone" and in this area of work there is no place for "prima donna" activities. Despite the difficulties (or maybe because of them), many workers enjoy the challenge presented by those who have shown, or are adjudged likely to show, dangerous behaviour towards others. Such was the view of a small group of consultant forensic psychiatrists when asked for the reasons why they chose to specialize in forensic psychiatry (see Prins 1998).

Sadly, but perhaps understandably, politicians and the general public have very high expectations that mental health and criminal justice professionals can "get it right" every time. Professionals can only give of their best on the understanding that they are not infallible; and if society has ordained that risks through legislation will be taken, then occasional failures are inevitable. Decision making is often not only complex but emotive (Peay 2003). Maybe if professionals are occasionally found "wanting", it is because, as Rumgay and Munro suggest, they feel powerless to "intervene effectively" (2001). In other instances, it may be that people cannot take on board the notion that killers such as Shipman, for example, could behave as they did since such behaviour defies all expectations (Smith 2003a, 2003b).

It might be considered fitting to end this chapter with some words by Ulysses in Shakespeare's *Troilus and Cressida*:

> no man is the lord of any thing,
> Though in and of him there be much consisting,
> Till he communicate his parts to others.

> (Act 3 Sc. 3)

## Notes

1   In the 1970s and early 1980s the words "danger" and "dangerousness" were more in evidence than today. Gradually, it has become more common (and sensible) to speak and write about "risk". Risk *assessment* and *management* are sometimes viewed as discrete entities. In my view, they should be seen as part of seamless practice, since *management* should entail continuing *reassessment*.

2   A man was recently convicted and sentenced to a substantial term of imprisonment for inflicting "biological" grievous bodily harm by such means. It was said to be the first instance of this kind in England and Wales. However, there had been an earlier conviction for such an offence in Scotland.

3   It should be noted here that the probation service has undergone major changes in both organization and practice in recent times. It became the National Probation Service in 2001 and now consists of 42 probation areas. Probation boards have replaced probation committees and central government now funds

the full costs of the service. There has been a decided shift to law enforcement and public protection as significant aims of the service's work. The service is also increasingly involved in work with victims, but this work has developed with some degree of inconsistency. (For a short account, see Penal Policy File No. 92, *Howard Journal of Criminal Justice*, 42, 5, December 2003: 504–6.) A further interesting development has been the involvement of psychologists in the work of the service; for example, the appointment of trainee psychologists to *both* prison and probation areas; an indication of a planned "joined up" correctional service. In terms of risk assessment the provisions contained in the Criminal Justice Act 2003 will involve the service in the assessment of further "dangerous offenders", notably those sentenced for sexual and violent crimes. A very recent development has been the planned merger between the probation and prison services – which can perhaps now be described as a correctional service. It is known as the *National Offender Management Service* (NOMS). However, some recent accounts indicate that morale in the Probation Service is currently not very high. There would appear to be a lack of satisfaction with the manner in which the service is being managed and concern that older ways of working with offenders are being increasingly denigrated (see, for example, Atkinson (2004) and Farrow (2004)).

## References

Adams, J. (1995) *Risk*, London: University College London Press.

Association of Chief Officers of Probation (ACOP) (1994) *Guidelines on the Management of Risk and Public Protection*, London: ACOP.

Atkinson, D. (2004) "The 'What Works' debate: Keeping a human perspective", *Probation Journal: The Journal of Community and Criminal Justice* 51: 248–52.

Baker, E. (1993) "'Dangerousness' – the neglected gaoler: Disorder and risk under the Mental Health Act, 1983", *Journal of Forensic Psychiatry* 3: 31–52.

Beck, U. (1998) "Politics of risk society", in J. Franklin (ed.), *The Politics of Risk Society*, Cambridge: Polity Press.

Blom-Cooper, Sir L. QC, Hally, H. and Murphy, E. (1995) *The Falling Shadow: One Patient's Mental Health Care, 1978–1993*, London: Duckworth.

Bryan, T. and Doyle, P. (2003) "The 'MAPPA'", *Prison Service Journal* 147: 29–36.

Buchanan, A. (ed.) (2002) *Care of the Mentally Disordered Offender in the Community*, Oxford: Oxford University Press.

Cohen, S. (1972) *Folk Devils and Moral Panics*, London: McGibbon and Kee.

Cox, M. (1979) "Dynamic psychotherapy with sex offenders", in I. Rosen (ed.), *Sexual Deviation*, 2nd ed., Oxford: Oxford University Press.

Craig, L. A., Browne, K. D., Stringer, I. and Beech, A. (2004) "Actuarial risk assessment of sexual offenders: A methodological note", *British Journal of Forensic Practice* 6: 16–32.

Department of Health (NHS Executive) (1994) *Guidance on the Discharge of Mentally Disordered People and Their Continuing Care in the Community*, HSG/94/27, 10 May.

Dowie, J. (1990) "Clinical decision making: Risk is a dangerous word and hubris is a sin", in D. Carson (ed.), *Risk Taking in Mental Disorder: Analyses, Policies and Political Strategies*, Chichester: SLE Publications.

Farrow, K. (2004) "Still committed after all these years? Morale in the modern-day

Probation Service", *Probation Journal: The Journal of Community and Criminal Justice* 51: 206–20.

Floud, J. (1982) "Dangerousness and criminal justice", *British Journal of Criminology* 22: 213–23.

Forrester, A. (2003) "Review of G. Bell, *The Poison Principle: A Memoir of Family Secrets and Literary Poisonings*", *Journal of Forensic Psychiatry* 14: 465–8.

Genders, E. and Player, E. (1995) *Grendon: A Study of a Therapeutic Prison*, Oxford: Clarendon Press.

Grounds, A. (1995) "Risk assessment and management in clinical context", in J. Crichton (ed.), *Psychiatric Patient Violence: Risk and Response*, London: Duckworth.

Gunn, J. (1996) "The management and discharge of violent patients", in N. Walker (ed.), *Dangerous People*, London: Blackstone Press.

Hardwick, P. (2003) "Formarrhoea", *Psychiatric Bulletin* 27: 388–9.

Health and Safety Executive (1988) *The Tolerability of Risks From Nuclear Power Stations*, London: HMSO.

Home Office (Her Majesty's Inspectorate of Constabulary) (2002) *Protecting Children From Potentially Dangerous People: An Inter-Agency Inspection on Children's Safeguards*, London: Home Office.

Home Office (Her Majesty's Inspectorate of Probation) (2002) *Safeguarding Children: The National Probation Service Role in the Assessment and Management of Child Protection Issues*, London: Home Office.

Home Office and Department of Health and Social Security (1975) *Report of the Committee on Mentally Abnormal Offenders* (Chairman, Lord Butler of Saffron Walden), Cmnd 6244, London: HMSO.

James, P. D. (1994) *Original Sin*, London: Faber.

Kemshall, H. (2003) "The community management of high-risk offenders: A consideration of 'best practice' – multi-agency public protection arrangements (MAPPA)", *Prison Service Journal* 46: 2–5.

Kettles, A. M., Robson, D. and Moody, E. (2003) "A review of clinical risk and related assessments in forensic-psychiatric units", *British Journal of Forensic Practice* 5: 3–12.

Krauss, D. A. and Lee, D. H. (2003) "Deliberating on dangerousness and death: Jurors' ability to differentiate between expert actuarial and clinical predictions of dangerousness", *International Journal of Law and Psychiatry* 26: 113–37.

Kvaraceus, W. (1966) *Dangerous Youth*, Ohio: Columbus Press.

MacCulloch, M., Bailey, J. and Robinson, C. (1995) "Mentally disordered attackers and killers: Towards a taxonomy", *Journal of Forensic Psychiatry* 6: 41–61.

Maden, A. (2003) "Standardised risk assessment: Why all the fuss", *Psychiatric Bulletin* 27: 201–4.

McGrath, P. (1989) "Book review", *British Journal of Psychiatry* 154: 154–427.

Monahan, J. and Steadman, H. (1994) *Violence and Mental Disorder: Developments in Risk Assessment*, Chicago: University of Chicago Press.

Monahan, J., Steadman, H. J., Silver, E., Appelbaum, P. S., Robbins, P. C., Mulvey, E. P., Roth, L. H., Grisso, T. and Banks, S. (2001) *Rethinking Risk Assessment: The MacArthur Study of Mental Disorder and Violence*, Oxford: Oxford University Press.

Morris, F. (2003) "Confidentiality and the sharing of information", *Journal of Mental Health Law* 9: 38–50.

Mullen, P. E. (2002) "Response to Professor Tony Maden's training in standardised risk assessment", in *Forum* (June 2002). *Forum: Newsletter of the Forensic Faculty of the Royal College of Psychiatrists* 5: 1 (November).

Peay, J. (2003) *Decisions and Dilemmas: Working With Mental Health Law*, Oxford: Hart Publishing.

Pollock, N. and Webster, C. (1991) "The clinical assessment of dangerousness", in R. Bluglass and P. Bowden (eds), *Principles and Practice of Forensic Psychiatry*, London: Churchill Livingstone.

Prins, H. (1995) " 'I've got a little list' (Koko, Mikado), But is it any use? Comments on the forensic aspects of supervision registers for the mentally ill", *Medicine, Science and the Law* 35: 218–24.

—— (1998) "Characteristics of consultant forensic psychiatrists: A modest survey", *Journal of Forensic Psychiatry* 9: 139–49.

—— (1999) *Will They Do it Again? Risk Assessment and Management in Criminal Justice and Psychiatry*, London: Routledge.

—— (2004) "Mental health inquiries – cui bono", in J. Manthorpe and N. Stanley (eds), *The Age of the Inquiry*, London: Routledge.

Prins, H., Ashman, M., Steele, G. and Swann, M. (1998) *Report of the Independent Panel of Inquiry into the Treatment and Care of Sanjay Kumar Patel*, Leicester: Leicester Health Authority.

Prins, H., Backer-Holst, T., Francis, E. and Keitch, I. (1993) *Report of the Committee of Inquiry into the Death in Broadmoor Hospital of Orville Blackwood and A Review of the Deaths of Two Other Afro-Caribbean Patients. "Big, Black and Dangerous"?*, London: Special Hospitals Service Authority (SHSA).

Royal Society (1992) *Risk: Analysis, Perception, Management*, London: Royal Society.

Rumgay, J. and Munro, E. (2001) "The lion's den: Professional defences in the treatment of dangerous people", *Journal of Forensic Psychiatry* 12: 357–78.

Russel, C. and Russel, W. M. S. (1961) *Human Behaviour*, Boston, MA: Little Brown.

Scott, P. D. (1977) "Assessing dangerousness in criminals", *British Journal of Psychiatry* 131: 127–42.

Smith, Dame Janet (2003a) *The Shipman Inquiry: Second Report: The Police Investigation of March, 1998*, CM 5853, London: TSO.

—— (2003b) *The Shipman Inquiry: Third Report: Death Certification and the Investigation of Deaths by Coroners*, CM 5854, London: TSO.

Soothill, K. (1993) "The serial killer industry", *Journal of Forensic Psychiatry* 4: 341–54.

Tancredi, T. (2004) "Multi-agency protection arrangements", in G. Towl and D. Crighton (eds), *Psychology and Probation Services*, Oxford: Blackwell.

Taylor, P. and Gunn, J. (1999) "Homicides by people with mental illness: Myth and reality", *British Journal of Psychiatry* 174: 9–14.

Tidmarsh, D. (1982) "Implications from research studies", in J. Hamilton and H. Freeman (eds), *Dangerousness: Psychiatric Assessment and Management*, London: Gaskell.

Walker, N. (1983) "Protecting people", in J. Hinton (ed.), *Dangerousness: Problems of Assessment and Prediction*, London: Allen & Unwin.

West Midlands Health Authority (1991) *Report of the Panel of Inquiry Appointed to Investigate the Case of Kim Kirkman*, Birmingham: West Midlands Health Authority.

Wilson, J. (1974) *Language and the Pursuit of Truth*, Cambridge: Cambridge University Press.

# Further reading

## Books – general

Braggins, J. and Martin, C. (eds) (1995) *Managing Risk: Achieving the Possible. Conference Report, University of Nottingham*, April 1995, London: Institute for the Study and Treatment of Delinquency.

Dowie, J. and Lefrere, P. (eds) (1980) *Risk and Chance: Selected Readings*, Milton Keynes: Open University Press.

Duggan, C. (ed.) (1997) *Assessing Risk in the Mentally Disordered. British Journal of Psychiatry* 170, Supplement 32.

Home Office, Department of Health and Welsh Office (1997) *Notes For the Guidance of Social Supervisors: Mental Health Act, 1983. Supervision and After-Care of Conditionally Discharged Restricted Patients*, London.: Home Office

Kemshall, H. (2003) *Understanding Risk in Criminal Justice*, Maidenhead: Open University Press.

Kemshall, H. and Pritchard, J. (1996) *Good Practice in Risk Assessment and Management*, Vol. 1, London: Jessica Kingsley.

—— (1997) *Good Practice in Risk Assessment and Management*, Vol. 2, *Protection, Rights and Responsibilities*, London: Jessica Kingsley.

Moore, B. (1996) *Risk Assessment: A Practitioner's Guide to Predicting Harmful Behaviour*, London: Whiting and Birch.

National Association for the Care and Resettlement of Offenders (NACRO) (1998) *Risks and Rights: Mentally Disturbed Offenders and Public Protection. A Report by NACRO's Mental Health Advisory Committee*, London: NACRO.

## Articles – general

Jamieson, L. and Taylor, P. J. (2002) "Mental disorder and perceived threat to the public: People who do not return to community living", *British Journal of Psychiatry* 181: 399–405.

Tidmarsh, D. (1997) "Psychiatric risk, safety cultures and homicide inquiries", *The Journal of Forensic Psychiatry* 8: 138–51.

See also special issue of Psychology, Crime and Law (2004) 10, 3, especially papers by Blackburn, Ogloff and Davis and Ward and Ecclestone.

## Articles – statistical aspects

Douglas, K. S. and Ogloff, J. R. P. (2003) "Multiple facets of risk for violence: The impact of judgemental specificity on structured decisions about violence risk", *International Journal of Forensic Mental Health* 2: 19–34.

Doyle, M., Dolan, M. and McGovern, J. (2002) "The validity of North American risk assessment tools in predicting in-patient violent behaviour in England", *Legal and Criminological Psychology* 7: 141–54.

Gale, T. M., Hawley, J. and Sivakumaran, T. (2003) "Do mental health professionals really understand probability? Implications for risk assessment and evidence-based practice", *Journal of Mental Health* 12: 417–30.

Holdsworth, N. and Dodgson, G. (2003) "Could a new mental health act distort clinical judgement? A Bayesian justification of naturalistic reasoning about risk", *Journal of Mental Health* 2: 451–62.

Krauss, D. A., Sales, B. D., Becker, J. V. and Figueredo, A. J. (2000) "Beyond prediction to explanation in risk assessment research", *International Journal of Law and Psychiatry* 23: 91–112.

Loza, W., Villeneuve, D. B. and Lozo-Fanous, A. (2002) "Predictive validity of the violence risk appraisal guide: A tool for assessing violent offender's recidivism", *International Journal of Law and Psychiatry* 25: 85–92.

Szmukler, G. (2003) "Risk assessment: 'Numbers and values'", *Psychiatric Bulletin* 27: 205–7.

# Chapter 9

# "The play's the thing"*

The play's the thing
Wherein I'll catch the conscience of the king.

(*Hamlet* Act 2 Sc. 2)

I hope that the preceding chapters will have indicated that those individuals who form the subject matter of this book are often very difficult to understand and to deal with. Their behaviour is often baffling, anxiety provoking and will frequently stretch our capacities for empathic understanding. Obviously the technical literature frequently referred to in this text will bring some aid, as will the views and (hopefully) support of supervisors and colleagues in a variety of disciplines; and of course our own ongoing experiences can be useful "storehouses" of aid. Despite all these sources of assistance, it is important not to overlook additional resources, for example, the insights that may be gained from literary and similar works, as has been demonstrated in some of the preceding chapters. This chapter is intended to provide a more detailed coverage of the topic and hopefully will be found helpful as a "prompter" (an expression used by the late doctor Murray Cox and Alice Theilgaard (Cox and Theilgaard 1994)).

Three short quotations will help set the scene. The first, is a statement by Salman Rushdie from an unpublished lecture (given on his behalf by another during his "wilderness years"). He said: "Literature is the one place in any society where, within the secrecy of our own heads, we can hear voices talking about everything in every possible way."

---

* Some of the material in this chapter first appeared in my (2001) article "And now for something completely different: Forensic practice – a complementary view", *The British Journal of Forensic Practice* 3(2): 11–21. The material concerning Lady Macbeth is taken from my (2001) article "Did Lady Macbeth have a mind diseas'd? (a medico-legal enigma)", which appeared in *Medicine, Science and the Law* 41, 2 reproduced by kind permission of the British Academy of Forensic Sciences.

What he seems to be saying is that literature can sometimes help us to face and deal with difficult bits of reality that we cannot deal with by more "technical" means.

The second, penned some 70 years earlier, is from a letter written in the condemned cell, by the ill-fated Edith Thompson, hanged for a crime she probably did not commit. She said: "We live and die . . . in the books we read" (quoted in Weiss 1988: 7).

And third, McDonagh states that: "Social concerns can be produced in literary works, making literary documents important sources of information regarding the symbolic or ideological function of people" (McDonagh 2000: 49). (See also Beveridge 2003; Hart 2002; Holmes 2002; McGrath 2002; Oyebode 2002 for further allusions to the place of literature in counselling and psychotherapy.)

## Dealing with ambiguity and uncertainty

Those who work with the deviant and the disturbed – particularly those whose behaviour has been adjudged to be unpredictable and potentially dangerous – have to tolerate a considerable degree of uncertainty and ambiguity in their work. As Sacks says, "man is a meaning seeking animal" (Sacks 1991) searching for meaning in all kinds of behaviours, particularly those deemed to be abnormal, baffling, and sometime bizarre (see Prins 1990). Just as nature is said by scientific colleagues to abhor a vacuum, so do men and women seek relief from ambiguity and uncertainty. The problems inherent in this were well depicted by J. B. Priestley in his novel *Over the Long High Wall*. He said:

> Both the fanatical believers and the fixed attitude people are loud in their scorn of what they call "woolly minds" . . . it is the woolly mind that combines scepticism of everything with credulity about everything. Being woolly, it has no hard edges because it bends, it does not break . . . the woolly mind realises that we live in an unimaginable, gigantic, complicated, mysterious universe. To try to stuff the vast bewildering creation into a few neat pigeon-holes is absurd. We don't know enough, and to pretend we do is mere intellectual conceit . . . the best we can do is to keep looking out for clues, for anything that will light us a step or two into the dark . . . the woolly mind can be silly at times, but even so, it finds out more and enjoys more than the rat-trap intelligence. Second rate scientists are never woolly minded, whereas great scientists let their minds go woolly between experiments.
>
> (Priestley 1972: 27)

## Listening and observing

An American educationalist, writing of the contribution that literature can make to criminology, suggested that the great playwrights such as "Shakespeare, Sophocles, or Dostoevsky . . . were as dauntless as Columbus, ranging fearlessly over the geography of interior life. Though often melancholy, the insights of artists are alert to subtleties of thought and emotion and represent the harvests of the candid eye" (Kelly 1991: 45). Those involved in forensic psychiatric practice and criminal justice often pride themselves on being good observers, listeners and harvesters of "the candid eye". However, we know from experience that this is not always the case and golden opportunities for therapeutic intervention are sometimes missed. It takes a bold professional to expose for public gaze his or her missed perceptions and opportunities for therapeutic engagement. Casement, a psychoanalytic psychotherapist (and one-time probation officer), has done this with much courage in two very useful books. In the second of these, entitled *Further Learning from the Patient* (Casement 1990; see also Casement 1985) he provides a very useful illustration of his purpose. In a description of his analysis of a patient's dream-life, he points out to the patient what appears to be the latter's preoccupation with his need to protect his penis from expected hurt or threat. The patient says, "I am afraid of it being broken off". The patient's *own* description and implied interpretation of what psychoanalysts would term "castration anxiety" was, in fact, more compelling and graphic than that of the therapist; for as Casement suggests, with hindsight, the patient was not just describing a penis, but an *excited* penis; "it cannot be broken off unless it is erect" (p. 18; emphasis added). One does not have to be a committed Freudian or a follower of psychoanalytic thinking to see the diagnostic and prognostic importance of such an illustration. It demonstrates the need to engage in encounters with offenders or patients with a degree of what the late doctor Murray Cox (visiting consultant psychotherapist at Broadmoor) illuminatingly described as "hovering attentiveness" (Cox 1990). This need to listen attentively is urged on us by all modern teachers of psychotherapeutic techniques, but its claim for urgent attention is not new. In the Old Testament, Job reminds us of the need to *really* listen when he rebukes his companions for their apparent lack of emotional engagement and succour. For, does he not say "listen to me, but do listen, and let that be the comfort you offer me. Bear with me while I have my say" (Book of Job, 21: 2–3)?

Reference has been made to the need for the "candid eye". One sometimes wonders whether it is always as effective as it should be in observing outward appearances as indicators of inner turmoil and need. St Augustine once said: "My words were uttered in no ordinary manner; my forehead, cheeks, eyes, colour, tone of voice, cried out more clearly than the words I spake" (Cox and Theilgaard 1987: 152). In Shakespeare's *The Winter's Tale* may be found these thought-provoking words: "There was speech in their dumbness, language in their very gesture". (Act 5 Sc. 2). A further helpful example is to be found in *Richard II*. Richard, having imposed lifelong banishment on Henry Bolingbroke, rescinds it in part, imposing it for a finite period instead. For he has recognized the grief it has caused Bolingbroke's father (Richard's uncle, the aged and dying John of Gaunt); he says to Gaunt "Uncle, even in the glasses of thine eyes I see thy grieved heart" (Act 1 Sc. 3). There is a similar and finely observed piece of behaviour in one of Shakespeare's less often performed plays, *Troilus and Cressida*. Ulysses says of Cressida, who is being somewhat intransigent, "There's language in her eye, her cheek, her lip. Nay, her foot speaks: her wanton spirits look out at every joint and motive of her body" (Act 4 Sc. 5). And, in the second part of *Henry IV*, we find the line, "Thou tremblest, and the whiteness in thy cheek is apter than thy tongue to tell thy errand" (Act 1 Sc. 1). Of course, the converse of what has just been suggested may also be true. Ben Jonson, in *Discoveries* has a character say, "Speak that I may *see* thee" (emphasis added); and does not Lear say "Look with thine ears" (Act 4 Sc. 6)?

## Some specific forensic psychiatric illustrations

I now focus on some more specific forensic psychiatric aspects. Workers in the field of forensic psychiatry and clinical criminology are frequently concerned with the prevention of vulnerability – not only in the overriding interests of the public at large, but of the offender or offender–patient. A graphic reminder of the need to reduce this dual vulnerability is to be found in some words spoken by Shakespeare's *King John*. Reflecting on, and perhaps regretting, the blinding he has ordered to be executed by Hubert on the young prince Arthur, the King says, "How oft the sight of means to do ill deeds makes deeds ill done!" (Act 4 Sc. 2). Workers are often faced with having to recognize and deal with such vulnerability and take steps to reduce it. This is often an uncomfortable experience, but they need to be mindful of Northumberland's words in the second part of *Henry IV* when he says, "But I must go and meet with danger there, or it will seek me in another place" (Act 2 Sc. 3); and at a later point in historical time, Edmund Burke in 1792, could make the equally compelling observation that "Dangers by being despised grow great". On a more humorous note, the dangers of not recognizing vulnerability are caricatured cleverly in Chapter III of Evelyn Waugh's *Decline and Fall*; "Here, the 'progressive' prison governor – Sir Wilfrid Lucas-Dockery – provides a psychotic and deluded carpenter, serving a life sentence for decapitation, with a saw with which the deluded man promptly cuts off the prison chaplain's head! Forensic-psychiatric workers are often faced with the problem of having to make statements and predictions based upon what offenders or offender–

patients say about what they have done or not done many years earlier. It is often extremely difficult to get "inside their heads" as it were, in order to try to determine what their *true* feelings may have been at the time of their crime. Denials, perhaps facilitated by the passage of time, may well have tended to obscure what they really felt and believed. A comment by Job is pertinent when he says "When I stop to think I am filled with horror and my whole body is convulsed" (*Book of Job* 21: 6 p. 583). And in *Julius Caesar*, Brutus says "Between the acting of a dreadful thing and the first motion, all the interim is like a phantasma, or a hideous dream" (Act 2 Sc. 1). The need to blot out recollection is cogently expressed in Donna Tartt's novel *The Secret History* (1992). One of her characters says "Some things are too terrible to grasp at once. Other things – naked, sputtering, indelible in their horror – are too terrible to really grasp at all. It is only later in solitude, in memory, that the realisation dawns" (p. 326). The primacy of homicide in the catalogue of crime is well attested to in many sources. As Ben Jonson says in *Bartholomew Fair*, "It is the very womb and bed of enormity" (I: vi); and in his adjuration to Noah, the Lord says: "He that sheds the blood of man, for that man his blood shall be shed, for in the image of God has God made man" (*Genesis*: 9: 6).

Two further quotations remind us of violent death. The first concerns death by strangulation. Here is the Earl of Warwick describing Gloucester's death in *Henry VI Pt II*:

> But see, his face is black and full of blood,
> His eye-balls further out than when he lived,
> Staring full ghastly like a strangled man;
> His hair uprear'd, his nostrils stretch'd with struggling;
> His hands abroad display'd, as one that grasp'd
> And tugg'd for life, and was by strength subdued.
> Look! on the sheets his hair, you see is sticking;
> His well-proportion'd beard made rough and rugged,
> Like to the summer's corn by tempest lodged.
> It cannot be but he was murder'd here;
> The least of all these signs were probable.
>
> (Act 3 Sc. 2)

And what of death by poisoning? In his description, Hamlet's father says that its effect:

> Holds such an enmity with blood of man
> That swift as quicksilver it courses through
> The natural gates and alleys of the body,
> And with a sudden vigour it doth posset

And curd, like eager droppings into milk,
The thin and wholesome blood: so did it mine.

(Act 1 Sc. 5)

Such a description reminds us very powerfully of poisoners like the late Graham Young, who poisoned again shortly after his release from Broadmoor. (For a fascinating, scholarly, yet easy to read account of the history and logistics of poisoning, see Bell 2002.) Such evocations are important in bringing home to forensic psychiatric professionals and others, the full impact of what some of their offender/patients have actually done. As we saw in Chapter 8, it is, therefore, very important to examine the full facts of their situations and offences in considerable detail. This reduces opportunities for denial and evasion, both on the part of the offender *and* the worker. Concerning the immediate environment, P. D. James has a compelling observation to make in her novel *A Taste for Death*. She says, "people's living space, and the personal possessions with which they surround themselves . . . (are) . . . inevitably fascinating . . . an affirmation of identity, intriguing both in themselves and as a betrayal of character, interest . . . (and) . . . obsessions" (James 1987). This need for detail is illustrated further in Peter Ackroyd's novel *Hawksmoor*. The detective says:

You can tell a great deal about the killer from the kind of death he inflicts: an eager person will kill in a hurried manner, a tentative person will do it more slowly . . . you must remember, too, the sequence of actions which follow the murder; most killers are stunned by their action. They sweat; sometimes they become very hungry or thirsty; many of them lose control of their bowels at the moment of death, just as their victims do . . . murderers will try to recall the sequence of events: they will remember exactly what they did just before and just after . . . but they can never remember the actual moment of killing. The murderer always forgets that, and that is why he will always leave a clue.

(Ackroyd 1985: 159)

Another fictional detective also stresses the need to absorb the full details of the offence and the offender's situation. Ruth Rendell's Chief Inspector Wexford in *Kissing the Gunner's Daughter* is depicted as follows: "Wexford sat looking at the scene-of-crime photographs . . . the kind of pictures no-one but himself would ever see, the results of *real* violence, real crime. Those great dark splashes and stains were real blood. Was he privileged to see them or unfortunate?" (Rendell 1992). Freud (1914) put the requirement to consider facts very well when he said: "I learnt to follow the unforgotten advice of my master Charcot: to look at the same things again and again until they themselves began to speak." And in more recent times Umberto Eco makes a similar point in *Foucault's Pendulum*. He says, "No piece of information is superior to any other. Power lies in having them all on file and then finding the connections" (Eco 1989). Failure to engage in this discovery and assessment of facts may have harmful consequences for offenders or offender–patients. Hamlet reminds us of this when he says, "Yet have I something in me dangerous, which let thy wisdom fear" (Act 5 Sc. 1).

One of the most challenging of phenomena in working with the highly deviant and disturbed is the manner in which those who can commit the most sickening of crimes can appear to be so thoroughly ordinary and inoffensive as, for example, in John Christie's murderous conduct. It is brought out with startling clarity in some of those who commit sadistic sexual murder. (See, for example, Brittain 1970 and this volume Chapter 6). Such jarring incompatibilities are brilliantly demonstrated in analogous fashion in Marlowe's historical tragedy *Edward II*. In Act V, Scene v, Edward is in prison, having been reduced to a state of disorientation through being moved from one castle dungeon to the next over a prolonged period. He is in a state of what would today be described as *sensory deprivation*. It has been resolved to murder him; the barely hidden theme behind the murder is the revenge to be taken by those of so-called normal sexual orientation for the King's homosexuality and in particular his favouritism for his beloved Piers de Gaveston. (It is important to remember that Marlowe wrote the play during a time of considerable repressive activity against homosexuals and against a background of recent legislation that gave legal sanction for this.) Lightborn, the hired assassin (who seems, on hindsight, to have qualities of gratuitous cruelty amounting to the psychopathic) tells his assistants: "I shall need your help; see that in the next room I have a fire, and give me a spit, and let it be red hot . . . a table and a feather-bed." Later, he seems to take a sadistic delight in toying with the enfeebled King, "ne'er was there any so finely handled as this king shall be", "O speak no more, my lord; this breaks my heart. Lie on this bed and rest yourself awhile". Edward seems to realize that his time has come and appears to recognize the significance of the instruments assembled to bring about his death. He says, "O spare me or despatch me in a trice." Lightborn says to his assistant, "So lay the table down and stamp on it, but not too hard lest that you bruise his body." There then follows the horrendous anal assault with the red hot spit. A further, and much more recent gloss has been offered on Marlowe's interpretation of this event by the contemporary writer Peter Whelan (1992) in his play *The School of Night* (first performed by the Royal Shakespeare Company at The Swan, Stratford on 4 November 1992). Musing on his own likely fate, Marlowe says of the Queen:

Her only concern is whether I be killed for sodomy [he was an acknowledged homosexual], atheism or treason . . . and which dreadful deaths to devise. Perhaps for sodomy, the one they used on Edward the Second that I was not allowed to put in the play. Held down while a cow's horn was inserted in his anus and a red hot iron pushed through to his bowels. No, that was a secret killing arranged so that when the horn was taken out there was no mark visible on the body. They wouldn't want that! What use is an invisible injury to the State? (II: iv)
(Whelan 1992: 87–8)

Not infrequently, forensic psychiatric professionals and their colleagues have to deal with those whose behaviour is either caused by, or closely allied to, frank mental illness. Delusional jealousy in its various guises is a good illustration. Its essential features of irrationality were outlined in Chapter 3. Depression, often in severe form, features in the lives and activities of many offenders and offender–patients. As I showed in Chapter 3, it may, of course, involve the taking of life, as in the case of severely depressed parents who kill or attempt to kill their children and kill or attempt to kill, themselves. It is not at all easy to enter the psychic world of the severely depressed individual and empathize with the bleak agony that this condition creates. Many writers have tried to capture its quality. Burton, in *The Anatomy of Melancholy*, considered that: "If there is a hell upon earth, it is to be found in a melancholy heart." The poet John Clare (who spent long periods in asylums), in one of his more lucid and productive periods, evoked the condition magnificently: "Yet nothing starts the apathy I feel, my soul is apathy, a ruin vast. Time cannot clear the ruined mass away, the summer looks to me as winter's frost." He also describes in graphic terms the familiar picture of a fading body image. "Wilt thou go with me, when the path has lost its way . . . when stones will turn to flooding streams . . . where life will fade like visioned dreams and mountains darken into caves . . . wilt thou go with me, through this sad non-identity?" (quoted in Hamilton 1953). And again, on the same theme: "Life is to me a dream that never wakes. Night finds me on this lengthening road alone. Love is to me a thought that ever aches, a frost-bound thought that freezes life to stone" (quoted in Reeves 1973). More modern writers have also evoked the mood of clinical depression very ably. Ruth Rendell (writing as Barbara Vine) describes it in *Gallowglass* as follows:

People talk about being depressed when they really mean they're feeling low, pissed off, under the weather. They don't know what depression is. Real depression is something else. It's when you haven't got anything, when everything goes – wants, needs, will, caring, hope, desire . . . It's when you can't make decisions any more, any sort of decision, like, shall I get up out of this bed and go to the bathroom or not? Or, shall I pick up this cup of tea and drink some or shall I just go on staring at it? It's when you don't want anything and can't do anything and don't want the opposite of not wanting anything, whatever that is, and haven't got anger or fear any more or even panic. And that's not the end of it. You get deeper in. You get to the place where you can't see colours or hear people speaking to you and inside your head is something that washes around when you move. It's water in there, a sink of it, dirty water with oil floating on the top in those rainbow rings. That's the only colour that you can see, the rainbow circles of the oil on the dirty water slurping round inside your head.

(Vine 1990: 14)

Severe mental illness, in its various forms, has been depicted by numerous writers; for example Gogol, in *Diary of a Madman*, Sayer, on a catatonic schizophrenic state in *Comforts of Madness* and a drug-induced psychotic episode is described in Waugh's *Ordeal of Gilbert Pinfold*. The contemporary writer, Patrick McGrath, also manages to capture the powerful evocations of both severe and borderline psychosis; for example, in his short stories, *Blood and Water* (1989), and in his novels *Spider* (1992), *Dr Haggard's Disease* (1993), *Asylum* (1996) and *Martha Peake* (2000). He acknowledges that many of these skilful and often haunting depictions owe much to his early up-bringing in Broadmoor Hospital, where his late father was its medical superintendent for 25 years.

Two other recent references to the literature are worth mentioning. The first is by the late Professor Derek Russell Davis, entitled *Scenes of Madness – A Psychiatrist at the Theatre*. In this volume, Davis uses some of the world's great literature, and in particular, Shakespeare and Ibsen, to illustrate clinical psychopathology (Davis 1992). The second, edited by the late Murray Cox, is entitled *Shakespeare Comes to Broadmoor*. This is a moving account of the impact of the performance of some of Shakespeare's tragedies on the acting and directing staff of the Royal Shakespeare Company, the hospital residents, their carers and others (Cox 1992).

As we have already seen, forensic psychiatric professionals and their colleagues also have to deal with that most elusive group of individuals – the psychopathic, or those showing severe anti-social personality disorder or dissocial personality disorder (to use the preferred *clinical* terms). (Some literary illustrations of such disorder were provided in Chapter 4.)

At its best, literature demonstrates the powerful and persuasive function of metaphor – a phenomenon of inestimable value in promoting understanding of baffling and worrying deeds and misdeeds. One of the most compelling examples of its use may be found in one of Shakespeare's greatest plays – *Hamlet*. Murray Cox (in his programme notes for the Adrian Noble production of the play at Stratford on 20 March 1993) suggested that in the play: "It is as we move from mortuary to myth that we find the more firmly woven fabric of context and content through which *Hamlet* envelops us." Cox sees the theme of "defective ceremony" as being central to the play "The theme of the dead not letting go of the living is . . . one of the constant thematic threads in Hamlet." (The powerful presence of dead souls is, of course, also pervasive in a number of Ibsen's plays – notable illustrations being found in *Ghosts*.) In Act 3 Sc. 2 Hamlet, perplexed, ambivalent, hostile, yet indecisive, demonstrates the depth of his confused and turbulent feelings towards his mother and others when he says: "Now could I drink hot blood, and do such bitter business as the day would quake to look on." Bearing in mind his fraught condition, these are powerful words indeed – conjuring up powerful imagery of a potential for future mayhem, especially if we also remember Claudius's later words "How dangerous is it that this man goes loose!" (Act 4 Sc. 3). Hamlet's words are not, of course, intended to convey that he is about to behave like Count Dracula! However, as already indicated, they are important in relation to his *possible* future behaviour, for does he not, in the same scene, make plans to see his mother? "Soft, now to my mother . . . let me be cruel, not unnatural. I will speak daggers to her but use none" (Act 3 Sc. 2). One may think this a poignant statement of ambivalent hostility, but not one *necessarily* pressaging future mayhem, *until* one reviews, with the benefit of hindsight, the events in the very next scene. For in the course of confronting his mother, Hamlet stabs and kills the unfortunate Polonius who is hidden behind the arras. We might well ask whether this was a sad coincidence brought about as a result of Hamlet's psychic turmoil and stress and/or a piece of displaced aggression as described in Chapter 5?

Finally, let us consider the forensic psychiatric and literary aspects of the "case" of Lady Macbeth. Her character has often been presented as evil and semi-demonic; in this presentation an attempt is made to outline some forensic psychiatric aspects that may help us to understand her (and others like her) in a more sympathetic light. In my more detailed consideration of the play (Prins 2001), I acknowledged the helpful comments on a draft by Harriet Walter, CBE and Sir Antony Sher in their respective roles of Lady Macbeth and Macbeth; I do so again here. I am not sure what aspect of the play holds the strongest fascination for me; is it the powerful literary and visual imagery that impels the play along at such a relentless pace? Is it the supernatural element? Is it the political content – of an overwhelming thrust for power, which, as Fergal Keane (1999) says, makes it very much a play for our time? Or, is it a fascination with the personalities of the principal characters – the Macbeths and, in particular, that of Lady Macbeth? This last question was compellingly reawakened for me having seen the Royal Shakespeare Company's production of the play with Antony Sher and Harriet Walter. This production has been rightly hailed by the critics as the best for a long time; and, for me, it focused my thoughts particularly on Lady Macbeth's character and the extent to which so many past productions have tended to "demonize" her – a portrayal studiously and sensitively avoided by Harriet Walter, "at once unsentimentalised . . . and achingly sad" (Taylor 1999). What kind of woman was she? What hidden frailties might have been responsible for her journey from that of dominating procurer of her husband's ambition to subsequent despair and suicide? In what follows, I present some aspects of her character as recorded in the play's text and which seem to me to have relevance to a number of cases in which women who have counselled, procured or actually committed homicide, have tended to be either demonized, on the one hand, or depicted as mentally ill, on the other. This is an illustration of the manner in which male conflicting and ambivalent attitudes towards the opposite sex have been demonstrated throughout the ages.

In the case of Lady Macbeth we might choose to consider the possibility of dual diagnosis – namely personality disorder *and* mental illness. There is an associated matter of forensic psychiatric interest – albeit of a somewhat hypothetical nature – namely the question of criminal responsibility. Had the Macbeths been indicted for their crimes in contemporary times, no doubt Lady Macbeth, had she lived, could have been charged with conspiracy to murder by virtue of her smearing the sleeping grooms with blood and also with being an accessory to the killing of King Duncan. For not only does she smear the sleeping grooms with blood in order to incriminate them but, prior to this, she has drugged them "with wine and wassail [and] so convince/ That memory, the warder of the brain,/ Shall be a fume, and the receipt of reason/ A limbeck only; when in swinish sleep/ their drenched natures lie as in a death" (Act 1 Sc. 7).

For his part, Macbeth could have been charged not only with the killing of the grooms but with procuring the murders of Banquo, the failed murder attempt on Fleance and the killings of Lady Macduff and her children.

There seems to be no likely exculpation for Macbeth on the grounds of mental disturbance (abnormality). However, one writer has speculated (and in so doing, seriously strained credulity) that Macbeth may have suffered from epilepsy. This is based solely on Macbeth's words "Then comes my fit again" (Act 3 Sc. 4) and upon Lady Macbeth's subsequent explanation to their guests in the banquet scene: "My Lord is often thus, and hath been from his youth" (Act 3 Sc. 4) (see Kail 1986: 90). Surely "fit" in this context (the failed killing of Fleance) is much more likely to mean a disturbance of his peace of mind: "I had else been perfect" (Act 3 Sc. 4)? What kind of defence might have been put forward for Lady Macbeth had she lived? Had she actually *committed* a murder, then a defence of diminished responsibility might have been proffered ; it seems likely that some kind of disturbance (abnormality) of mind would have been raised – personality disorder perhaps and/or a depressive illness (see later). In what follows, some of these issues are discussed briefly in the light of speculation about

Lady Macbeth's life as recorded in the text of the play and brought to life so vividly by Sher and Walter's portrayals of their relationship.

## Lady Macbeth

### Age, marriage and progeny

Commentators on the play have conjectured that the Macbeths are probably a couple in their forties and childless (for example, Macduff says "He has no children") (Act 4 Sc. 3). It is, of course, this childlessness that gives the spur to Macbeth's later murderous activities and it is strengthened by the witches' prophecy that no heirs of Macbeth's shall succeed him; that Banquo's progeny will generate a line of kings. But, what does this childlessness mean to Lady Macbeth? It would *appear* that she has had a child or children in the past, but not perhaps, by Macbeth. (Shakespeare does not tell us; had he wanted to, he would have done so.) For, in that famous (or for some, infamous) passage (Act 1 Sc. 7) she says:

> I have given suck, and know
> How tender 't is to love the babe that milks me:
> I would, while it was smiling in my face,
> Have pluck'd my nipple from his boneless gums,
> And dash'd the brains out.

Knights suggests that the "I have given suck" passage not only denotes unnatural feelings, but that "they are also strange – peculiar compounds which cannot be classified by any one of the usual labels: 'fear', 'disgust', etc." (Knights 1984: 195). But it is *just* these latter feelings that forensic psychiatric and criminal justice professionals need to engage with.

Lady Macbeth's case would be no exception. Two further points merit attention. First, does the "I have given suck" refer to a *dead* child by a first or their own marriage? Or, is the child still living? This seems unlikely. One might reasonably speculate that such a child (or children for that matter) may be dead, bearing in mind the high infant mortality rate of those times; the reference by the witches to "birth strangled babe(s)" is also relevant here. Second, if this was perhaps a dead child, it *might* have an important bearing on Lady Macbeth's relationship to her husband, her conflicting emotions and her subsequent decline into mental illness. Walter suggests that in thinking herself into the part of Lady Macbeth she has "imagined a repeated failure to bring any child beyond infancy. This could easily result in a prolonged and severe depression – one of many believable ways in which a woman would react to this tragedy" (personal communication, 11 February 2000) (see also my later discussion of her suicide). We should note, and not just in passing, that the killing of children figures quite largely throughout the play (for example, Fleance, references to dead children by the witches and the killing of Macduff's children). There are some grounds for seeing Lady Macbeth as a vulnerable individual. This is an important surmise in forensic psychiatric terms, because professionals may ignore a person's vulnerability born of *past* traumas because their *current* behaviour horrifies us by its malignity. Murderous intention and activity masking a basic vulnerability are afforded a degree of emphasis by Mangan, who poses the question whether or not Lady Macbeth's character is so drawn as to reduce the feelings of hatred and horror we harbour towards Macbeth? Lady Macbeth is "envisaging killing her own suckling child . . . she is conjuring up the tenderest moment she can imagine in order to bring home the urgency of her appeal to Macbeth . . . Lady Macbeth achieves a level of brutality which is specifically and consciously dependent upon the denial of her own capacity for pity. What she says to Macbeth is so shocking, not simply because it is an image of *'un-natural womanhood'*, but because what she is rejecting and shutting out of life is so vividly and precisely imagined" (Mangan 1991: 199; emphasis added). Surely there are lessons here for those in the forensic psychiatric and criminal justice systems. A further indicator of her possible vulnerability can be seen in her response to her husband's indecision about murdering Duncan. She says: "But screw your courage to the sticking-place and we'll not fail." She is not saying *you* will not fail, it is a conjoint statement, "we'll not fail" (Act 1 Sc. 7). Perhaps the most striking physical affirmation of her vulnerability is her faint (Act 2 Sc. 3) following the discovery of the murder of Duncan and the grooms. Bradley points out that Macbeth takes no notice; it is left to Macduff to call out, "Look to the lady." Commentators differ as to whether the faint was genuine or not. Considering the context in which she faints, I believe the faint to be genuine. As Bradley suggests: "She was no Goneril. She knew she could not kill the King herself: "Had he not resembled my father as he slept, I had done't" (Act 2 Sc. 2), "carry back the daggers, see the bloody corpse, and smear the faces and hands of the grooms" (Bradley 1985: 418). The impression this event made on her is graphically revived much later in the play when she says: "Yet who would have thought the old man to have had so much blood in him?" (Act 5 Sc. 1). Such a statement, hinting at past but undisclosed guilt for homicidal deeds, is worth assimilation by all forensic psychiatric and criminal justice professionals (see Prins 1999, notably Chapter 5). Finally, we should note that she needed wine to embolden her: "That which hath made them drunk hath made me bold" (Act 2 Sc. 2).

### Her death

Notwithstanding the preceding comments, Bradley considered that "the greatness of Lady Macbeth . . . [lay] . . . almost wholly in courage and force of will" and that "she is, up to her light, a perfect wife" (Bradley 1985:

311–16). But it was a "will" that was going to dissolve in mental confusion, decline and suicide. What was to follow at the end of her life seems to find prognostication early on in the play when she says "these deeds must not be thought/ after these ways; so, it will make us mad" (Act 2 Sc. 2); and, following her joint attainment of the throne she seems to be overtaken by a degree of what might perhaps be described as reactive depression:

Nought's had, all's spent,
When our desire is got without content:
'T is safer to be that which we destroy
Than by destruction dwell in doubtful joy.

(Act 3 Sc. 2)

We can conjecture that the knowledge of the murder of Macduff's wife and "babes" might have been the final straw that triggered her descent into mental illness. "The Thane of Fife had a wife: where is she now?" (Act 5 Sc. 1). Her "disease" is given full reign in the so-called sleep-walking scene; so-called, because in most somnambulistic states reasonably lengthy utterances (however bizarre) are somewhat rare. No doubt Shakespeare wished to paint the most dramatic portrait he could of a mind teetering on complete breakdown. (For automatisms, see Chapter 3, this volume.) What are we to make of her behaviour in the last hours of her life? The gentlewoman (nurse) charged with her care says:

I have seen her rise from her bed,
throw her nightgown upon her, unlock
her closet, take forth paper, fold it,
write upon 't, read it, afterwards
seal it, and again return to bed;
yet all this while in a most fast sleep.

(Act 5 Sc. 1)

Salkeld contends that: "In her *insanity*, Lady Macbeth takes to furtive and compulsive writing. She disseminates in script a terrible secret knowledge, yet censors it and conceals her text before returning to sleep" (Salkeld 1993: 112; emphasis added). It may be that in her highly disturbed state she is remembering her husband's own tortured state of mind when he says:

In the affliction of these terrible dreams
That shake us nightly. Better be with the dead,
Whom we, to gain our peace, have sent to peace,
Than on the torture of the mind to lie
In restless ecstasy.

(Act 3 Sc. 2)

Is it too fanciful to suggest that, in clinical terms, Lady Macbeth is clearly hallucinating?

> Yet here's a spot . . . yet who would have
> thought the old man to have had so much
> blood in him? . . . Here's the smell of the blood still;
> all the perfumes of Arabia will not sweeten this
> little hand . . . look not so pale . . . to bed, to bed: there's
> knocking at the gate . . . give me your hand.
>
> (Act 5 Sc. 1)

The distinguished psychiatrist, the late Professor Russell Davis, suggested that Lady Macbeth's final illness might have been precipitated by her husband's absence from her in the field of battle. Because of this, she had lost his support. Davis also quotes Freud's highly speculative suggestion that her transformation in the sleep-walking scene is a reaction to her continuing childlessness (see earlier comments). Davis considered that "the picture she presents in the sleep-walking scene is typical in many respects of an acute reactive psychosis: the obsessive attention to a particular detail, in this case the 'damned spot', preoccupation by fantasy and apparent watchfulness . . . immersion in a world of fearful fantasy is favoured by the dark, which reduces engagement with the real world – hence her comment to have 'light by her continually'" (Davis 1992: 42). The picture he paints would perhaps be supportive of a depressive psychotic reaction in a personality disordered individual.

The physician in this scene displays qualities of good practice that many inexperienced forensic psychiatric and criminal justice professionals could do well to emulate. For example, he is cautious about relying too heavily on the reports of others, preferring to gather data about his patient at first hand:

> I have two nights watched with you, but
> can perceive no truth in your report. When
> was it she last walked?
>
> (Act 5 Sc. 1)

He also shows a good appreciation of the need to make an accurate record of the facts:

> Hark! she speaks. I will set down what comes from
> her, to satisfy my remembrance the more strongly.
>
> (Act 5 Sc. 1)

Despite his acknowledged awareness of his own limitations ("This disease is beyond my practice . . . more needs she the divine than the physician" (Act 5 Sc. 1)), he is sensitive to the need for good risk assessment:

> Look after her;
> Remove from her the means of all annoyance,
> And still keep eyes upon her.

(Act 5 Sc. 1)

Finally, as Davis suggests, the doctor is no doubt aware of the past violence in her life and her own possible desire for death, "'t is safer to be that which we destroy" (Act 3 Sc. 2), and in her depressive utterance concerning past evil deeds: "What's done cannot be undone" (Act 5 Sc. 1).

## Implications for forensic psychiatric and criminal justice practice

The Lady Macbeths of this world puzzle, revolt and frighten us. As already suggested, it is all too easy to "demonize" the female of the species when she indulges in acts we find abhorrent in men and doubly so in women. This can be seen, for example, in the demonization of "serial" killers such as the late Myra Hindley and Rosemary West. The "mad–bad" divide becomes blurred, bewilders us and often confounds our professional practice. Walter considers that, "Lady Macbeth *could* be me or other women in the audience. It is a stretch (and I hope a huge one) but it is a possibility" (Walter, personal communication, 11 February 2000). Preoccupation with the horror invoked by the behaviour may blind us to a more "appreciative" understanding; and indications of malaise (often only hinted at) may be overlooked. (The word "appreciative" is used here in its sociological sense, namely, a sensitive, empathic understanding.) The perception of such indicators and a disengagement from bias and prejudice require that degree of "hovering attentiveness" so ably demonstrated in much of the late Murray Cox's work. Finally, the use of dramatic presentation when performed with a unique blend of force and sensitivity can allow us to view puzzlement and horror from a "safe" distance but, at the same time, encourage us to increase our empathic understanding and professional practice (see Prins 1999). However, we can only do this if we really hearken to the "text" as good actors and actresses do; and in so doing we may "catch" the hidden nuances of meaning so that we may "pluck from the memory a rooted/sorrow, [and] raze out the written troubles of the brain" (Act 5 Sc. 3). Sher suggests that "Shakespeare's psychological studies are so detailed and complex that they make for puzzling reading, but are absolutely thrilling to play. *His characters remain as mysterious and multi-layered as people are in real life*" (Sher, personal communication, January

2000; emphasis added). However, it is of course important to emphasize the dangers "of extrapolating too uncritically from literary 'symptomalogy' to the day-to-day conditions presented by 'real' patients and offender patients". Salkeld makes a similar point in stressing the importance of the socio-political context in which playwrights such as Shakespeare and his contemporaries composed their works (Salkeld 1993; see also Feder 1980 in her discussion of King Lear's madness, pp. 119–46; and Mangan's discussion of Othello's jealousy (Mangan 1991)).

# References

Ackroyd, P. (1985) *Hawksmoor*, London: Sphere Books.

Bell, G. (2002) *The Poison Principle: A Memoir of Family Secrets and Literary Poisonings*, London: Pan.

Beveridge, A. (2003) "Should psychiatrists read fiction? *British Journal of Psychiatry* 182: 385–7.

Bradley, A. C. (1985) (first published in 1904) *Shakespearean Tragedy*, Houndmills, Hants: Macmillan.

Brittain, R. (1970) "The sadistic murderer", *Medicine Science and the Law* 10: 198–207.

Casement, P. (1985) *On Learning From the Patient*, London: Tavistock.

—— (1990) *Further Learning From the Patient: The Analytic Space and Process*, London: Routledge/Tavistock.

Cox, M. (1990) "Psychopathology and treatment of psychotic aggression", in R. Bluglass and P. Bowden (eds), *Principles and Practice of Forensic Psychiatry* (Section VII, Chapter 17, pp. 631–9), London: Churchill Livingstone.

Cox, M. (ed.) (1992) *Shakespeare Comes to Broadmoor: The Performance of Tragedy in a Secure Psychiatric Hospital*, London: Jessica Kingsley.

Cox, M. and Theilgaard, A. (1987) *Mutative Metaphors in Psychotherapy: The Aeolian Mode*, London: Tavistock.

—— (1994) *Shakespeare as Prompter: The Amending Imagination and the Therapeutic Process*, London: Jessica Kingsley.

Davis, D. R. (1992) *Scenes of Madness: A Psychiatrist at the Theatre*, London: Routledge.

Eco, U. (1989) *Foucault's Pendulum*, London: Secker & Warburg.

Feder, L. (1980) *Madness in Literature*, Princeton, NJ: Princeton University Press.

Freud, S. (1914) *On the History of the Psychoanalytic Movement*, London: Hogarth Press.

Hamilton, M. (1953) "The mind in jeopardy", *British Journal of Psychiatric Social Work* 7, 25–9.

Hart, D. (2002) "When language weakens", *Psychiatric Bulletin* 26: 137–8.

Holmes, J. (2002) "Are poetry and psychotherapy too 'wet' for serious psychiatrists?", *Psychiatric Bulletin* 26: 138–40.

James, P. D. (1987) *A Taste For Death*, London: Sphere Books.

Kail, A. (1986) *The Medical Mind of Shakespeare*, Balgowlah, NSW: Williams and Wilkins.

Keane, F. (1999) Programme notes for Royal Shakespeare Company's production of Macbeth.

Kelly, R. J. (1991) "Mapping the domains of crime: The contribution of literary works to criminology", *International Journal of Offender Therapy* 35: 45–61.

Knights, L. C. (1984) (first published in 1963) "Macbeth as a dramatic poem", in L. Lerner (ed.), *Shakespeare's Tragedies: An Anthology of Modern Criticism*, Harmondsworth: Penguin.

Mangan, M. (1991) *A Preface to Shakespeare's Tragedies*, London: Longman.

McDonagh, P. (2000) "Diminished men and dangerous women: Representations of gender and learning disability in mid-nineteenth century Britain", *British Journal of Learning Disabilities* 28: 49–53.

McGrath, P. (1989) *Blood and Water and Other Tales*, London: Penguin.

—— (1992) *Spider*, London: Penguin.

—— (1993) *Dr Haggard's Disease*, London: Viking (Penguin).

—— (1996) *Asylum*, London: Viking (Penguin).

—— (2000) *Martha Peake: A Novel of the Revolution*, London: Viking (Penguin).

—— (2002) "Problems of drawing from psychiatry for a fiction writer", *Psychiatric Bulletin* 26: 140–3.

Oyebode, F. (2002) "Literature and psychiatry", *Psychiatric Bulletin* 19: 362–3.

Priestley, J. B. (1972), *Over the Long High Wall*, London: Heinemann.

Prins, H. (1990), *Bizarre Behaviours: Boundaries of Psychiatric Disorder*, London: Routledge/Tavistock.

—— (1999) *Will They Do it Again: Risk Assessment in Criminal Justice and Psychiatry*, London: Routledge.

—— (2001) "Did Lady Macbeth have a mind diseas'd? (A medico-legal enigma)", *Medicine, Science and the Law* 41: 129–34.

Reeves, J. (1973) *Selected Poems of John Clare*, London: Heinemann.

Rendell, R. (1992) *Kissing the Gunner's Daughter*, London: Arrow Books.

Sacks, J. (1991) *The Persistence of Faith: Religion, Morality and Society in a Secular Age*, London: Weidenfeld & Nicolson.

Salkeld, D. (1993) *Madness and Drama in the Age of Shakespeare*, Manchester: Manchester University Press.

Tartt, D. (1992) *The Secret History*, Harmondsworth: Penguin.

Taylor, P. (1999) "Bloody, bold and resolute at last", *The Independent* 18 December.

Vine, B. (1990) *Gallowglass*, London: Viking.

Weiss, R. (1988) *Criminal Justice: The True Story of Edith Thompson*, Harmondsworth: Penguin.

Whelan, P. (1992) *The School of Night*, London: Warner Chappell Plays.

## Further reading

Wilson, S. (1995) *The Cradle of Violence: Essays on Psychiatry, Psychoanalysis and Literature*, London: Jessica Kingsley (draws on an eclectic range of "case" materials).

The use of film and the novel as an aid to "cultural competence training" is afforded in:

Bhugra, D. (2003) "Using film and literature for cultural competence training", *Psychiatric Bulletin* 27: 427–8.

—— (2003) "Teaching psychiatry through cinema", *Psychiatric Bulletin* 27: 429–30.

Byrne, P. (2003) "Commentary on Bhugra: 'Using film and literature for cultural competence training and teaching psychiatry through cinema'", *Psychiatric Bulletin* 27: 431–2.

Oyebode, F. (2003) "Commentary on Bhugra: 'Using film for cultural competence training'", *Psychiatric Bulletin* 27: 433.

Organizations such as *Geese Theatre* have done much to use dramatic productions in efforts to help prisoners and offender–patients understand their own attitudes and behaviours. For a brief account see:

Gibson, B. (1998) "Lifting the mask", *The Magistrate* February, 1998: 8–9.

For two accounts of how actors endeavour to "empathize" with those they portray see:

Sher, Sir Antony (1985) *Year of the King: An Actor's Diary and Sketchbook*, London: Chatto & Windus/Hogarth Press (on preparing to play the part of Richard III).

Walter, H. (1999) *Other People's Shoes: Thoughts on Acting*, London: Viking.

# Epilogue

Ev'ry motion has some end.
(Byrom, *The Soul's Tendency Towards Its True Centre* (1773))

As with most books, this one has been many months in its gestation. Various matters were raised in the prologue and, in bringing this work to a conclusion, some of them can be returned to, as a number of them will have been overtaken by events. In returning to them I propose to take brief opportunity to share some thoughts on the future management of *Offenders, Deviants or Patients?* The much awaited and criticized draft Mental Health Bill has not yet come before parliament and now seems unlikely to do so before the next election. In November 2003 Dr John Reid, Secretary of State for Health, indicated that further consultations were to take place (*The Independent*, 27 November 2003). However, a second draft Bill is currently before Parliament (see Chapter 2). Looking back on the numerous government documents that preceded the publication of the two Bills (can two Bills ever have had so many wordy antecedents?) one is left wondering (admittedly with a degree of hindsight) whether the "root and branch" review of the 1983 Act, ordered by Paul Boateng, when he was Minister of State in the Health Department, was really as necessary, as a number of individuals thought at the time. Although it had become clear that there were defects in the 1983 Act, many of them could have been put right by amending legislation or by administrative orders. The all-important question of consent really requires separate legislation and its detailed absence in the Bill has engendered considerable disquiet among many mental health workers, both professional and "lay".

The implementation of the Human Rights Act 1998 has enabled some ethical and jurisprudential problems inherent in the 1983 Act to be dealt with. It is worth noting that to date, despite a number of mental health cases that have been dealt with under the terms of the 1998 Act, no major "scandals" appear to have come to light. Many of the criticisms of the Bill have centred around the proposed management of offender–patients, the subjects of this book. Justified alarm has been expressed in relation to the somewhat Draconian proposals to deal with those allegedly showing the political category of dangerous severe personality disorder and I referred to these in Chapter 4.

I would hazard a guess, and it can be no more than a guess, that when the Bill eventually reaches parliament for debate, it will be in a somewhat watered-down form. It may be that wiser counsels will have prevailed and professional and government officials' advice been heeded by the politicians. Perhaps the appropriate advice to the latter should be that of Prudence, the chambermaid in Ben Jonson's play *The New Inn*: "Beware you do not conjure up a spirit you cannot lay" (Act III Sc. ii). Reference has been made in a number of places in this book to the government's preoccupation with issues of public protection. As I write this epilogue the latest Criminal Justice Act (2003) has arrived. It is a massive enactment running to some 339 Sections and 38 Schedules. It will no doubt require careful interpretation and will occupy lawyers and the judiciary for years to come. Some Sections of the Act deal with mentally disordered offenders, for example, inquiries into mental state and the making of community psychiatric rehabilitation orders (formerly known, in common parlance, as "psychiatric probation orders"). It is interesting to note here that a non-medically qualified professional, namely a chartered clinical psychologist, may provide such treatment in addition to, or instead of, a psychiatrist. Of perhaps greater significance (and scope for contention) are the sections of the Act dealing with "dangerous offenders", a term not used specifically in previous legislation. The relevant sections and schedules sanction the use of life and extended sentences of imprisonment for those convicted of specified violent and sexual offences. Since compulsory aftercare will follow such sentences, this will involve additional work for the National Probation Service and the deployment of its skills in risk assessment (see Chapter 8). I would like to re-emphasize comments I made elsewhere in this book that in the last 10 years we have witnessed a virtual "avalanche" of criminal justice legislation. One feels that some of it has not been sufficiently thought through. It seems to indicate that our political leaders too often make visceral responses to serious social problems when a little more reliance on cerebration would not be out of place. It is perhaps fortunate that the judges have not shrunk from using "loopholes" in some of the legislation to exercise a degree of discretion in their sentencing practice. For example, the government's efforts to crack down on "career burglars" and persistent drug dealers by the "three strikes and you're out" provisions appear to have been largely ignored by the judiciary. In 2002 only two 3-year mandatory sentences on repeat burglars were imposed and no mandatory sentences enforced for regular drug trafficking. In the field of youth justice, a similar reluctance is apparent. For example, "child safety orders", which provide for very young unruly children to be placed under supervision, have only resulted in a handful of such orders. And anti-social orders, aimed at teenage anti-sociality, also appear to have had a very poor take-up (as reported in *The Independent*, 29 December 2003: 4). And in early 2004 the Lord Chief Justice (Lord Woolf) was severely critical of political involvement in judicial matters.

A further very recent example of the manner in which government "edginess" may result in premature and ill-thought out responses may be seen in their decision to allow armed "sky marshals" to be on board certain transatlantic passenger jets in the interests of public safety. The decision seems to be based on acquiescence in an American edict aimed at reducing acts of terrorism on aircraft. Critics, including the British Air Line Pilots' Association (BALPA), have described the decision as "dangerous" and "flawed". This is based on the sensible view that allowing armed individuals to be on board is likely to create an additional hazard and could result in serious risk to passengers in the event of an armed confrontation with terrorists (*The Independent*, 30 December 2003: 2).

Professor Nigel Walker, in his scholarly work *Crime and Punishment in Britain* (1968), lists some 13 "aims of a penal system". The 13th he describes as "compulsory benevolence" citing, for example, the enforcement of school attendance (p. 10). It may be that this term could usefully be applied to aspects of our penal and criminal justice policy and practice in the last decade, representing as it does the ethos that the "state knows best".

Many of the aforementioned enactments have been accompanied by a large number of circular instructions and guidance from central government; some of them helpful, some only adding to the deluge of paper overwhelming professionals as they try to carry out their task of reconciling patient/client/offender need with public protection. Alongside this wealth of documentation there has developed a significant increase in the use of rating scales for measuring such phenomena as psychopathic disorders – for example, the Hare psychopathy scales and the various assessment schedules used by the probation and allied services. Their use (or, as some would say, possible misuse) throws into sharp relief the controversial issue of actuarial versus clinical prediction. A sense of proportion is required in this matter. Actuarial forecasting can be helpful in estimating and predicting how a certain *group* of individuals may behave, but tells us little to reassure us about the future behaviour of the *individual* sitting on the other side of the desk. There is a further danger for professionals. Preoccupation with the need to "fill in" the necessary checklist ("put the tick in the right box") may eliminate the need for further conjecture and subsequent clinical work. Allied to these concerns is the issue of "clinical governance" – yet another new term for what is essentially the practice of monitoring. Such clinical oversight has its uses but, increasingly, one suspects that it may be sapping individual initiative and activity. It also tends to lower professional morale and engender a "looking over one's shoulder" attitude that may also stunt enterprise and a degree of informed risk taking. In a perceptive letter to the *British Journal of Psychiatry*, a psychiatrist laments the passing (by editorial edict) of the publication of individual case reports in favour of "original research". He suggests that such reports can contribute greatly to our understanding of individual cases. As he aptly observes: "The nomothetic stating of laws approach takes precedence while the detailed study of an individual patient is marginalised as trivia" (Williams 2004: 84).

One issue that emerges from examining the management of some of the individuals described in this book is the need for multidisciplinary thinking and activity (see for example Chapters 4, 5 and 8). A recently published epidemiological study of mental health patients in criminal justice populations exemplifies this need. By means of a "tracking system", "data were collected over a three-year period for all individuals who had contact with the criminal justice system and mental health services in an English county". In the county population under review of some 800,400 individuals, "some 30,329 were offenders. More than a third had used a health or social care service during the three-year period; 8.0% were mentally disordered". The authors suggest that their research provides "for the first time substantive quantitative evidence of the relationship between crime and mental disorder". They conclude that "the results can be used as the basis for further work to target assessment and risk reduction measures at those most at risk" (Keene et al. 2003: 168). The need for an integrated approach to healthcare for assault victims has also recently been put forward by Shepherd and Bisson (2004).

One of the most striking professional developments in the past decade has been the continuing emergence of the discipline of forensic psychology. It has become recognized increasingly that forensic psychologists have an important part to play as members of clinical teams. In addition, it has been recommended that they should be appointed to decision-making panels such as the Mental Health Review Tribunal and, in the consultation documents accompanying the draft Mental Health Bill, it is suggested that they assume a role equivalent to that of responsible medical office as leaders of clinical teams. Professor Gudjonsson, in his inaugural professorial lecture, "Psychology Brings Justice", suggests that "clinical and forensic psychology has a great deal to offer the courts but expert testimony must be grounded in scientific work . . . we must continue to educate colleagues and the legal profession about the contribution of psychology to judicial proceedings" (Gudjonsson 2003: 166). One of these contributions has been in the area of offender profiling and in the newly designated discipline of investigative psychology, spearheaded by Professor David Canter and his colleagues at Liverpool University (see for example their recently published *Journal of Investigative Psychology and Offender Profiling*; see also Needs and Towl 2004). I am conscious that, having singled out forensic psychology for specific mention, I might be accused of neglecting other disciplines. I should emphasize that forensic psychiatry is now a well-established discipline and is now a separate faculty of the Royal College of Psychiatrists.[1] Nursing has its own Forensic Psychiatric Nursing Association.[2] The probation service has become a national organization and the service's own journal, in its new format, combines academic rigour with well-informed comment on practice. Time alone will tell whether the proposed merger of the probation and prison services will improve the effectiveness of both. Mental health law now has its own specialist UK journal (the *Journal of Mental Health Law*) produced by the Law School at Northumbria University. In its first four years it has published a wide range of papers on mental health legal issues.

By referring to developments in victimology last, I do not wish to be seen as minimizing their importance in the deliberations of both criminal justice and mental health practitioners. Much has been done to give "ear" to their justifiable concerns and this can only be a good thing. There is, however, one caveat I would wish to enter. There is a thin and important dividing line between giving careful heed to the views of victims concerning the disposal of and/or eventual return of serious offenders to the community and their views being given undue weight in the sentencing and post-sentence processes. Although a good deal of attention has been paid to the *victims'* families and their shock and grief, less attention seems to have been paid to the families of the perpetrators. The need for these "secondary victims" to be afforded help and the conflicts that arise have been usefully emphasized by Rock:

> At the forefront is the gap that can yawn between the rational, reasoned, universalistic, precedent-driven and cool talk of the professional and the impassioned, particularistic and hot talk of some survivors' representatives, two kinds of talk that cannot sustain a coherent conversation for very long.
>
> (Rock 1998: 198; see also Rock 1996)

The aim of this book has been to afford a modest and largely clinical contribution to the management of some very difficult and worrying individuals. As such, they defy ready categorization (as I have pointed out at various places in the text). They require a degree of calm reflectiveness and emotional "distancing" (but not coldness); a degree of dispassionate compassion. Overreaction to some admittedly appalling crimes is to be avoided, by politicians, professionals, the media in all its forms, and public alike. It is the individual who should be at the core of our endeavours and perhaps a quote from the essayist Pope would make a fitting conclusion to this book – a book that has probably raised more questions than it has answers: "Know then thyself, presume not God to scan; the proper study of mankind is man" (*An Essay on Man: Epistle 2*).

## Notes

1  The contribution that forensic psychiatry is making to the management of dangerous severe personality disorder (DSPO) would appear to have been recognized in the award of an OBE in the New Year's Honours List (2004) to my former colleague, Doctor Ian Keitch, psychiatrist in charge of the Personality Disorder Unit at Rampton High-Security Hospital. The citation reads "for services to mental health *and public safety*" (emphasis added) (*The Independent*, 31 December 2003).
2  The forensic psychiatric nursing contribution to the management of DSPD is described by Bowers (2002).

## References

Bowers, L. (2002) *Dangerous and Severe Personality Disorder: Response and Role of the Psychiatric Team*, London and New York: Routledge.

Gudjonsson, G. H. (2003) "Psychology brings justice: The science of forensic psychology", *Criminal Behaviour and Mental Health* 13: 159–67.

Keene, J., Janacek, J. and Howell, D. (2003) "Mental health patients in criminal justice populations: Needs, treatment and criminal behaviour", *Criminal Behaviour and Mental Health* 13: 168–78.

Needs, A. and Towl, G. (eds) (2004) *Applying Psychology to Forensic Practice*, Oxford: Blackwell and British Psychological Society (BPS).

Rock, P. (1996) "The inquiry and victims' families", in J. Peay (ed.), *Inquiries After Homicide*, London: Duckworth.

—— (1998) "Murderers, victims and survivors", *British Journal of Criminology* 38: 185–200.

Shepherd, J. P. and Bisson, J. I. (2004) "Towards integrated health care: A model for assault victims", *British Journal of Psychiatry* 184: 3–5.

Walker, N. (1968) *Crime and Punishment in Britain*, rev. ed., Edinburgh: Edinburgh University Press.

Williams, D. R. R. (2004) *Letter*, "In defence of the case report", *British Journal of Psychiatry* 184: 84.

# Author index

# Subject index

Note: page numbers in **bold** refer to diagrams, page numbers in *italics* refer to information contained in tables.